PLC 13th
PLC 15th

HAYNER PUBLIC LIBRARY DISTRICT-ALTON
0 00 30 01639255

155.633   Levinson, Daniel J.,
LEV   d. 1994.

        The seasons of a
        woman's life.

$27.50

DATE			

HAYNER PUBLIC LIBRARY DISTRICT
ALTON, ILLINOIS

OVERDUES .10 PER DAY. MAXIMUM FINE
COST OF BOOKS. LOST OR DAMAGED BOOKS
ADDITIONAL $5.00

D0966349

HAYNER PLD/ALTON SQUARE

Also by Daniel J. Levinson

The Authoritarian Personality (1950)
with Theodor W. Adorno, Else Frenkel-Brunswik, and R. Nevitt Sanford

The Patient and the Mental Hospital (1957)
Co-edited with Milton Greenblatt and Richard H. Williams

Patienthood in the Mental Hospital:
Role, Personality and Social Structure (1964)
with Eugene B. Gallagher

The Executive Role Constellation:
An Analysis of Personality and Role Relations in Management (1965)
with Richard C. Hodgson and Abraham Zaleznik

The Seasons of a Man's Life (1978)
with Charlotte N. Darrow, Edward Klein, Maria H. Levinson, and Braxton McKee

THE SEASONS OF
A WOMAN'S LIFE

THE SEASONS OF A WOMAN'S LIFE

by
Daniel J. Levinson
in collaboration with
Judy D. Levinson

 Alfred A. Knopf   New York   1996

HAYNER PUBLIC LIBRARY DISTRICT
ALTON, ILLINOIS

THIS IS A BORZOI BOOK
PUBLISHED BY ALFRED A. KNOPF, INC.

Copyright © 1996 by Douglas F. Levinson and Mark E. Levinson
All rights reserved under International and Pan-American Copyright
Conventions. Published in the United States by Alfred A. Knopf, Inc.,
New York, and simultaneously in Canada by Random House of
Canada Limited, Toronto. Distributed by Random House, Inc., New York.

Owing to limitations of space, acknowledgments for permission to
reprint previously published material may be found following the Index.

Library of Congress Cataloging-in-Publication Data
Levinson, Daniel J., d. 1994.
The seasons of a woman's life / by Daniel J. Levinson :
in collaboration with Judy D. Levinson. — 1st ed.
p.   cm.
Includes index.
ISBN 0-394-53235-X
1. Middle-aged women—United States—Psychology.   2. Housewives—
United States—Psychology.   3. Women in business—United States—
Psychology.   4. Maturation (Psychology)—United States.
5. Adulthood—United States. I. Levinson, Judy D.   II. Title.
HQ1059.5.U5L48   1996
155.6'33—dc20   95-20893   CIP

Manufactured in the United States of America
First Edition

AUTHOR'S NOTE

If we are to learn about lives in adulthood, people must be willing to
tell their life stories and trust that their privacy and the privacy of
others will be respected. As a researcher I am committed to honoring
this trust. Pseudonyms, "Anonymous," and disguised details have been
used in this book in an effort to protect the privacy of the forty-five
women research participants as well as the privacy of others.

ACS— 0996

*Dedicated to the forty-five women interviewed
in this study, who shared their life stories
in the hope of improving future women's lives*

Contents

Preface

How does it happen that a man like myself at the culmination of his career, wishing to choose wisely the few remaining projects to which he can devote himself, should spend fifteen years attempting to understand the adult development of women? It is partially the legacy of a mother who left her Russian shtetl alone in 1890, at the age of 14, worked in the garment industry sweatshops of London and New York City for many years, became a union organizer and a passionate advocate of women's rights, and, after marrying and becoming a mother at 34, spent the next sixty years as a housewife and private feminist. It comes, too, from a father who admired and shared his wife's feminism while also wanting her traditionalism. Perhaps the most important result is not that I have incorporated both the feminism and the traditionalism—but that I have had a keen awareness of these contradictory themes in myself, in other men and women, and in female-male relationships. That awareness has been intensified and developed further by the current phase of the long-term gender revolution in which I believe our species is now engaged.

My research on adult development began in 1967. Eleven years later I published *The Seasons of a Man's Life*. Exploring the research literature, I concluded that very little was known about the adult life course and that the standard research methods (questionnaires, surveys, tests, structured interviews) would be of limited value in exploring this new field. I chose instead to develop a new method of Intensive Biographical Interviewing through which individual lives could be examined in greater depth. The use of this method limited the sample size to a maximum of forty. It seemed to me that there were significant gender differences in adult life and development. To include twenty men and twenty women would do justice to neither and might result—as it often has in the past—in an allegedly "general" theory based primarily on the evidence from men. My final decision to study men rather than women was based largely on personal considerations: I had an intense desire to understand my own adult development.

The seeds of this book lie in that earlier one. While deciding to focus initially on men, I promised myself to do a second, parallel study of women. The present book fulfills that promise. The study of women is central in my vision of my own work and of the field of adult development in general. As I wrote in *The Seasons of a Man's Life,* "It is essential to study the adult development of both genders if we are to understand either." We cannot adequately understand men by the study of men alone, nor women solely by the study of women. It is also important—perhaps essential until our footing is more secure—that women and men work together in the study of each gender.

I have been keenly aware that I began the study of women with concepts and findings derived chiefly from the study of men. I do not believe that it is possible today for anyone, male or female, to undertake the study of women's development without being heavily influenced by concepts, assumptions, and ways of thinking based primarily upon the experience and writing of men. A strongly male-centered view of adult life has for centuries been prevalent in our scientific and cultural institutions. It will take time, effort, and sharpened awareness of gender issues to achieve a more balanced view.

In *The Seasons of a Man's Life,* it was difficult to say which aspects of the theory and findings were true of human development generally and which held for men only. The present study provided the opportunity (and indeed the necessity) of arriving at a clearer distinction. My primary aim was to tap as directly as possible into the lives of women. I wanted to generate new concepts based on the actualities of women's lives, without losing what was valuable from the study of men. Conversely, I wanted to make appropriate use of what I already knew, without blinding myself to new evidence and insights. Work on this dilemma led me to explore two questions of basic importance in the study of development:

(1) Can we create a gender-free conception of adult human development, a framework that captures what is most essentially human and common to both genders?

(2) Within that general framework, can we create a gender-specific conception of the adult development of women? This is the driving question of the present book.

I have made strenuous efforts to overcome the limitations stemming from my own gender and from my previous study of men. These efforts began in the early 1970s, when I was engaged in the study of men. I encouraged Wendy Stewart to do her doctoral dissertation on the adult life structure development of women, and was an adviser on her study, one of the first to deal solely with women. A few years later, I was similarly involved in a dissertation by Susan Taylor Jackson. I also consulted with Janice Ruffin on her dissertation, which studied the adult development of African-American women. These studies indicated that my theory of adult development held in its broad outlines for women as well as men, while also giving evidence of some important gender differences within the general framework.

In 1979, a year after the publication of *The Seasons of a Man's Life*, I began exploratory work on this project. By one of those curious synchronicities in human life, I was approached just then by the Financial Women's Association of New York (FWA). The members of the Financial Women's Association are women executives and professionals working in the financial district and corporate headquarters and banks of New York City. Their level of achievement and income would make a large part of the population of the United States envious. The FWA was interested in sponsoring and raising funds for a study of the kind that I was planning. After canvassing the field, they came up with a list of researchers on which I was the only male. Other things being equal, they would have chosen a female. However, they were interested in careers and, like me, wanted to place career development in the context of individual life development. They felt, as I did, that an intensive study using in-depth interviewing would be more productive than standard survey research. They supported my interest in comparing businesswomen with other samples. When the FWA proposed to sponsor my work, I felt that I had passed an important test. And, in deciding to accept, I understood that much more than funding was involved. It made historical as well as personal sense to me that this project should involve a cross-gender collaboration in its sponsorship. In the years since then I have come to understand more deeply the importance of cross-gender collaboration in human life generally, and certainly in the study of development.

My thanks to the committee members of the FWA who planned the study with me: Patricia (Tosh) Barron, Susan Fisher, Jo Ann Heffernan Heisen, Madie Ivy, Ilene Leff, Melinda Lloyd, and Candice Straight. Tosh Barron kept the vision of this project alive through several years of fund raising. Contributions from many corporate sources allowed the research to become a reality. My thanks for their generous support to the following corporations: American Can Company, American Standard, Bankers Trust, Colgate-Palmolive, General Electric Foundation, INA, Marsh & McLennan, Mc-Kinsey & Company, Ogilvy & Mather, Reader's Digest Association, Seiden & De Cuevas, Sperry & Hutchinson, Sun Oil, Textron, U.S. Home, Xerox, and John Whitehead Foundation. In addition to contributing funds to this project, Xerox also donated a word processor on which the book manuscript was typed. My thanks to Jim McGuire of Xerox, who kept the Xerox 860 running in good order for over a decade.

Teachers Insurance and Annuity Association entered the project as a co-sponsor in 1981. Their support expanded the scope of the study to include the sample of academic women. I am grateful to Peggy Heim, senior research officer of TIAA, for her support of the project. My gratitude goes to Carol Schreiber, who has been a supportive friend and colleague in this enterprise. She gave generously of her time and helped in the fund raising.

Early in 1980 I had the funds to hire an initial staff and begin the interviewing. The interviewing was done between 1980 and 1982. Cross-gender collaboration was important in every aspect of this project. I formed a staff group of eight women and three men, besides myself. We varied in age, social origins, race, ethnicity, discipline, and point of view. The staff members included Lesley Bottoms, Ann Dahl, Elizabeth Dickey, Kelin Gersick, Winston Gooden, Judy Levinson, Maria Levinson, Judith Meyers, Susan Taylor Jackson, Edwin Wallace, and MaryBeth Whiton.

Our weekly staff meetings were devoted chiefly to the discussion of biographical interviewing, of individual lives, and of theoretical issues. There was often heated controversy about the relevance of various concepts from my own and others' theories. As the work progressed, we found that there were at least as many differences in outlook and insight among the women, and among the men, as between women and men. The intensive study of other lives led each of us to a closer examination of our own lives. We became more aware of the complex meanings of gender in ourselves and in our relationships with women and men. The staff meetings thus furthered not only the research but also our own intellectual and emotional growth. The final product has been crucially influenced by the group effort. Later, the writing of the book was shaped and colored by my collaboration with Judy Levinson. From the beginning to end, then, this has been a bi-gendered effort.

Each staff member on this study made a heroic effort to grasp the life experience of each subject and to avoid the trap of assuming that women's lives and experiences are either totally the same as men's or totally different. I want to thank each staff member for her or his part in this effort and for all contributions to the research. My thanks also to staff member Judith Meyers for her coding and analysis of the questionnaire data.

In the summer of 1982 the interviewing was completed, the funds depleted, and the staff group dispersed. Since then, this project has essentially been a collaboration between myself and my wife, Judy Levinson. Together we analyzed individual lives, compared samples, and wrote this book. She has been my partner in this enterprise from the start. Judy has made a major contribution to this book; she developed the method of biographical reconstruction to analyze the qualitative interviews and wrote all of the vignettes. She also made significant contributions to the theoretical work. She has helped me personally to understand the elemental conflict that exists between women and men, as well as the forces that bring us together and make each gender much more than it could be without the other.

For me personally this project has been a profound developmental experience. I have been living for fifteen years with forty-five women in my head, trying to see life from their perspective and to work out my relationship with them. Through this biographical work, I have come to see more clearly how much women and men have to offer each other. I see, too, how strong are the barriers that separate men from women, and the feminine from the masculine within the self. I believe I have been able to claim more of the feminine in myself without losing what I value of the masculine.

Many individuals and institutions have been of great help over the past fifteen years. My appreciation to the Department of Psychiatry, Yale University. Boris M. Astrachan, then Director of the Connecticut Mental Health Center, has been a valued colleague and friend; this study has benefited in countless ways from his personal interest and administrative support.

The day-to-day operation of this project was managed with great competence by Immaculata Ferrucci and Arlene O'Brien. Bonnie Grawoig made excellent transcriptions of the interviews. These three women helped to make the research run more smoothly, and I thank them.

I wish to thank anonymously the academic institutions who welcomed us and allowed us to conduct questionnaire surveys and the interviewing. Several faculty members and administrators were of essential help to me on this project. Their names must remain anonymous as well, but they have my deepest thanks and appreciation.

My greatest thanks go to the forty-five pioneering women in this study who shared their life stories. They sacrificed much in an attempt to lead fuller lives more on their own terms and to create the basis for more choice for tomorrow's daughters and sons. I cannot thank you by name but I express my gratitude to you anonymously for the gifts of your experiences and insights.

Daniel J. Levinson

Daniel Jacob Levinson died on April 12, 1994. He had completed the manuscript of this book several months before he died, and since then I have worked with the book's editor, Charles A. Elliott, on the final editorial process. Elliott has been a wise and very patient editor.

So many friends and family members have helped me through this painful and important process of completing the book manuscript, and I wish to express my appreciation to them. Florence Ficocelli, Jeannie Hayes, and

Stella Palm have been the best of friends. My love and thanks to Daniel's family, especially to his sons, Mark and Douglas Levinson, and to his grandchildren, Amber, Michael, Matthew, and David. My love and thanks also to my family: Nan, Karen, Jaime, Arthur, Reta, and especially my nephew-son Dan Gawlak, who reminded my heart to laugh again. My love and gratitude go also to my nephew-son Bryan Gawlak, who stayed with me during those initial dark days and weeks after Daniel's death. Bryan helped to keep my spirit alive, and he helped me remain engaged in life. He worked as my assistant in the final editorial process. I could not have done this work without him.

The manuscript received the careful scrutiny of Bryan J. Gawlak, Connie J. G. Gersick, Kelin E. Gersick, Douglas F. Levinson, Dorian S. Newton, Peter M. Newton, Carol T. Schreiber, and Susan Taylor Jackson. I am grateful for their helpful suggestions and emotional support. Each gave generously to the editing of the manuscript, and it is a better book because of their contributions.

Daniel had not made final reference notations in the book manuscript. The help of Peter Newton, Carol Schreiber, and Susan Taylor Jackson were of central importance in my effort to make reference notations. I thank them and apologize for any references that have been omitted.

My eternal love and gratitude go to my husband, Daniel, with whom I had a most remarkable journey. For Daniel and me, love and work were inextricably intertwined. We formed a collaborative partnership in the writing of this book that enriched each of our lives as well as our joint relationship. Daniel was the theoretician/writer, and I was the biographical reconstructor. Working on the completion of this book manuscript without Daniel has been a time of great sorrow and great joy, and it is my final gift to my beloved Daniel.

Daniel was a wise and gentle man who touched the hearts and lives of many. This book represents the final installment of his legacy to the world; his spirit will live on as long as his work has a relevance to other people's work and lives and offers them something of value to help them on their journey through the seasons of life.

Judy D. Levinson

Note: Over the years since the interviews were conducted for this research project, we have lost track of many of the women who were interviewed, as well as some staff members. If you participated in this project, please write to Judy Levinson, in care of the publisher, Alfred A. Knopf, Inc.; I'd like to make sure you receive a copy of this book.

I

A View of Adult Development and a View of Gender

1 The Study of Women's Lives

How do women's lives evolve in adulthood? This question, seemingly so simple and straightforward, has rarely been asked in psychology or the other human sciences. Very little research has been done on the life course of the individual human being, female or male, in psychology, psychiatry, biology, the social sciences, and the humanities. Indeed, "life course" is one of the most important yet least examined terms in these fields. It refers to the evolution of an individual life from beginning to end. The key words are "evolution" and "life."

The word "evolution" indicates sequence, temporal flow, the unfolding of a life—be it an individual, a society, an organization, or any other open system—over the years. The evolution of a life involves stability and change, continuity and discontinuity, orderly progression as well as stasis, regression, chaotic flux. It is not enough to focus solely on a single moment or chapter in the life, nor to study the same individuals at intervals of several years as in standard longitudinal research, assuming simple continuity in the intervening periods. Rather, we must examine "lives in progress" (the felicitous phrase is Robert White's) and follow the temporal sequence closely and continuously over a span of years.

The word "life" is also of crucial importance. A life is, above all, about the engagement of a person in the world. To study an individual life we must include all aspects of living. A life involves significant interpersonal relationships—with friends and lovers, parents and siblings, spouses and children, bosses, colleagues, and mentors. It also involves significant relationships with groups and institutions of all kinds: family, occupational world, religion, community. When we study any of these significant relationships, we must consider the nature of the social context in which it occurs, what goes on in the relationship at a relatively overt, behavioral level, and the subjective wishes and meanings that shape the person's involvement in it. We must include as well the bodily aspects of life—genetic endowment, biological development, health and illness, bodily fitness and impairment. To study the life course it is necessary to look at an individual life in its complexity at a given time and to delineate its evolution over time.

The study of the life course has presented almost insuperable problems to the human sciences. Each discipline has claimed as its own special domain one aspect of life, such as personality, social structure, culture, or biological functioning, and has neglected or minimized the others. The life course itself has been split into unconnected segments, such as childhood or old age, without recognizing the place of each segment in the life cycle as a whole. The result is fragmentation. I believe that a new multidisciplinary field of study will emerge in the next few decades.

Biography, the description of an individual life, offers another approach. For the most part, biographers have focused on their subjects' public work (be it fiction, painting, political leadership, or whatever) without considering sufficiently how the work is in the life and the life in the work. In addition, most biographies are concerned with a single life, not with a comparison of several lives or with broader theoretical issues. Well-done biographies can be of enormous value to the understanding of the life course generally. The present study is strongly biographical in method and spirit. It is part of an effort to form a boundary between the humanities and the sciences. Rather than one book-length biography of a single woman, this book contains briefer biographies of forty-five women. I have sought to capture the uniqueness of each individual life and, at the same time, to define and describe developmental principles that shape women's lives generally.

Major Aims and Questions

My primary aim was to learn about the life course and development of women from the late teens to the mid-forties. This is not a comparative study of women *versus* men. It is, rather, an in-depth exploration of women's lives. Equal attention has been given to common themes that hold for women generally, to differences between various groups of women, and to the unique character of each individual life. I wanted to gain a detailed picture of every life in order to show the diversity of women's lives under various social and psychological conditions. Much of the recent research on gender differences has tended to create an oversimplified image of "woman" in opposition to an equally stereotypical image of "man." My findings support the view that women are similar to men in certain basic respects and different in others, and that the lives of both genders are wonderfully varied.

The method of study was Intensive Biographical Interviewing. I sought to draw out each woman's life story, as she experienced it, from childhood to the present. I explored the major events, relationships, strivings, and imaginings of her life, with attention to both external realities and subjective meanings. This method, which I initially developed during the research for my book *The Seasons of a Man's Life*, has proved to be ideally suited to the exploration of the individual life course, without built-in assumptions about gender and gender differences.

The key questions animating the present study were these:

(1)   Is there a human life cycle—an underlying order in the human life course, a sequence of seasons through which our lives must pass, each in its own unique way? Earlier I found that the male life cycle evolves through an age-linked sequence of *eras*: childhood, early adulthood, middle adulthood, late adulthood, and late late adulthood. Do women have a fundamentally different life cycle? Since the concrete life circumstances and the timing of specific events are different in many ways for women, I could not assume in advance that they would go through the same sequence of eras. (Indeed, I initially decided to study the two genders separately in order to attend fully to the differences.) To my surprise, the findings indicate that *women go through the same sequence of eras as men, and at the same ages.* There is, in short, a single human life cycle through which all our lives evolve, with myriad variations related to gender, class, race, culture, historical epoch, specific circumstances, and genetics. My view of this life cycle is given in Chapter 2.

(2)   Is there a process of adult development analogous to the earlier process of child development? The human sciences have been studying child development for over a century. It is generally recognized that there is a basic developmental pattern in the first twenty years or so of life. All human beings apparently go through a sequence of developmental periods—prenatal, infancy, early childhood, middle childhood, and adolescence—before reaching that final amorphous state called adulthood. The study of child development seeks to determine the universal order and the general developmental principles that operate to produce uniquely individual lives. Research on child development is concerned equally with the universal and the idiosyncratic; it is concerned with the emergence of the unique individual out of the universal human. Of course the idea of developmental order includes the existence of disorder, even chaos. A period of relatively stable structure, we find, is followed by a period of flux in which we move from one structure to another.

What about adult development? Does it make sense to look at adult life from a developmental perspective similar to that used in childhood? Until recently this question was rarely asked. It was assumed that development is in its nature a childhood phenomenon: the process by which we evolve from conception to adulthood. Likewise, it has been assumed that senescence is a process of decline or negative growth that shapes our evolution in old age. In between, it would seem, we are on our own, changing in response to specific events but without any developmental order. The study of adult development is in its infancy and struggling to establish itself in the neglected space between child development and gerontology. Paradoxically, we know a lot about specific features of adult life—marriage, divorce, child-rearing, work, illness, stress—but very little about the meaning of adulthood as a season in the life cycle. We have, as it were, a detailed picture of many trees but no conception of the forest and no map to guide our journeys through it. One of my major aims is to form a conception of the life cycle and a map broad enough to provide guidelines for the infinitely varied pathways by which it may be traversed.

In *The Seasons of a Man's Life* I presented my own initial map of the developmental periods in men's lives over the course of early and middle adulthood, from roughly 17 to 65. These periods are *not* periods in a single aspect of living, such as personality, cognitive, moral, or career development. They are, rather, periods in the development of the adult *life structure*—the underlying pattern or design of a person's life at a given time. The life structure of a man, I found, evolves through a sequence of alternating periods, each lasting some five to seven years. A period of building and maintaining a life structure is followed by a transitional period in which we terminate the existing structure and move toward a new one that will fully emerge in the ensuing structure building-maintaining period.

I did not assume that the periods in life structure development would be the same in their nature and timing for women as for men. As with the eras, however, I made the surprising discovery that women and men go through the same sequence of periods at the same ages. At the same time, there are wide variations between and within the genders, and in concrete ways of traversing each period. My current view of human adult development is given in Chapter 2. This view is still provisional, but it has strong empirical grounding in my own and others' research.

(3)   What is the significance of gender in women's lives? In my opinion, equal attention should be given to the gender differences in concrete life course and to the gender similarities in basic developmental pattern. In seeking to understand the deeper sources of the observed gender differences, I have developed a theoretical perspective on the meanings of gender and the differential place of females and males in our society.

My perspective on gender is presented in Chapter 3. The central concept is *gender splitting*—a sharp division between feminine and masculine that permeates every aspect of human life. Gender splitting takes many forms: the rigid distinction between feminine and masculine in the culture and in the individual psyche; the division between the domestic world and the public occupational world; the Traditional Marriage Enterprise, with its distinction between the male husband/father/provisioner and the female wife/mother/homemaker; the linkage between masculinity and authority, which makes it "natural" that the man be head of household, executive and leader within the occupational domain, and predominant in a patriarchal social structure.

The actual forms of gender splitting vary widely among cultures and historical periods, but the underlying process has operated powerfully in most societies we know about. In the last few centuries the forces of institutional and technological change have tended to modify and blur the traditional gender splitting. This in turn has led to changes in the meanings of gender and the relationships between women and men generally. We are now in the early stages of a vast historical transition. The traditional patterns are eroding but satisfactory new ones have not yet been discovered and legitimized. Evidence of our confusion and conflict is given in the current social-political turmoil regarding reproductive rights, "family values," and the place of women in the occupational world.

(4) How are these conceptions of development and of gender reflected in the lives of individual women? Chapters 4 through 15 follow the women studied through the successive developmental periods to age 45. I will try to show how my concepts emerge out of, and are grounded in, the individual biographies. At the same time, I will show how this theoretical perspective helps to illuminate and make sense of an actual life. My goal throughout is to demonstrate both the underlying order and the manifest diversity, uniqueness, and frequent disorder in the lives of women.

I turn now to a brief consideration of the methods employed to answer the above questions, especially on the methods of interviewing and selecting a sample. My purpose is not to give a highly technical account, but to show how the choice of research methods was shaped by the questions and my way of thinking about them. The questions, substantive ideas, and procedures for gaining relevant evidence were organically connected. Most of the commonly used methods would have prevented me from exploring what I had in mind.

The Biographical Method: Intensive Biographical Interviewing and Biographical Reconstruction

This study is biographical in approach and method. My primary goals were: (1) to elicit the life stories of a number of women; (2) to construct a biography of each one in her own words; and (3) to learn something from this rich material about the nature of women's adult development and about specific life issues relating to friendship, work, love, marriage, motherhood, good times and bad times, the stuff that life is made of. These goals strongly influenced the research methods.

The standard quantitative methods of survey research, testing, and brief structured interviewing are very useful for certain purposes, as I know from my earlier research. They allow us to study the largest sample in the shortest time, using a staff composed mainly of technicians and a computer that makes statistical order out of masses of raw numbers. It is hardly more difficult or costly to study a sample of 500 than of 100. At their best, these methods provide the aura of rigor, quantification, and high technology which gives this mode of research the ring of objectivity and true science, which in turn makes it easier to obtain research grants. Considering the convenience and the appearance of scientific legitimacy such methods offer, they are hard to give up, even when it makes no real sense to use them. Unfortunately, they are poorly suited to exploratory research in a field relatively lacking in theory, in descriptive knowledge, and in measuring instruments of demonstrated validity.

I decided that, despite the difficulties involved, it was essential to use and develop further the method of Intensive Biographical Interviewing initially developed in *The Seasons of a Man's Life*. This is a time-consuming process. In the present study, an interviewer and a research participant typically met weekly for a series of eight to ten sessions over a two- or three-month period. A session lasted one and a half to two hours. For each participant there were fifteen to twenty hours of taped interviews yielding some two hundred to three hundred typed pages. Owing to budget constraints, six of the faculty members were interviewed two to four times, for a total of four to eight hours. The interviews were held when and where the participant preferred, usually in her home or workplace or in the interviewer's office. The interviewing was done by a staff of eight women and four men, including myself (see Preface). The staff met regularly to discuss individual lives, the sample as a whole, and various subsamples, issues in interviewing, our evolving ideas about gender and adult development, specific concepts and controversies, and the work of others.

The primary aim of Intensive Biographical Interviewing is to enable the participant to tell her life story from childhood to the present. The word "story" is of fundamental importance here. It is common in academic settings to say that we are getting a "history"—a clinical case history, developmental history, work history, or family history. Such histories focus selectively on particular events and issues of importance to the history taker. When we want to learn about the life course, however, the term "story" is more appropriate. The person telling her story is identified by the researcher, and experiences herself not as a patient, client, or research subject (that is, object), but as a *participant* in a joint effort. The participant is more freely and fully engaged when she feels invited to tell her story in her own terms, and when she feels that the interviewer is a truly interested listener/participant in the storytelling. The story is the medium in which various messages are delivered—about joys and sorrows, times of abundance and times of depletion, the sense of wasting one's life or of using it well, efforts at building, maintaining, and ending significant relationships.

The task of telling the story is mainly the participant's. The interviewer's task is to facilitate the storytelling: to listen actively and empathically, to affirm the value of what she or he is hearing, to offer questions and comments that help the participant give a fuller, more coherent, and more textured account. The biographical interviewer is different from the survey interviewer, whose task is to obtain specific information on specific topics, and from the psychotherapist, whose task is to help the participant understand and modify her inner problems. The interviewer's interest in the life story and responsiveness to it are crucial factors in the participant's readiness to tell it, especially those parts that are deeply satisfying and/or painful.

My collaborator, Judy D. Levinson, developed the method of Biographical Reconstruction in the analysis of the qualitative interview material, which helped us hear the many subjective voices of the women. As I have said, the primary aim of Intensive Biographical Interviewing is to enable the participant to tell her *life story*—to give a relatively full account of the life course—from childhood to the present. The story is the raw material out of which the biography is reconstructed. The great challenge is to describe the individual life course as richly as possible and to generate concepts that represent its underlying complexity, order and chaos. The method of Biographical Reconstruction enables us to condense and order some two hundred to three hundred pages of interview transcript pages while preserving the life story in the woman's own voice. This method provides a crucially important first step in the construction of the life. It shortens and makes more manageable the many hours of interview material while maintaining its qualitative meanings and themes. Once this step has been taken, we are in a much better position to identify major life themes that hold for all three samples, to develop concepts and hypotheses, and to give rich descriptive findings about the adult development and meanings of gender for women generally.

The biographical method has inherent limitations, especially in the reliance on memory and reconstruction, but it also has major advantages and ought to be recovered from the limbo to which psychology has relegated it. This method has special value for the study of life structure development. It is the only one that enables us to obtain a complex picture of the life structure at a given time and to delineate its evolution over a span of years. It is well suited for gaining a concrete sense of the individual life course, for generating new concepts, and for developing new hypotheses that are rooted in theory and relevant to the lived life.

The Women Studied: Homemakers and Career Women

The choice of research method influenced the size and character of the sample. I decided to study forty-five women in all, fifteen in each of three samples. This number was small enough so that we could obtain relatively full life stories, yet large enough to provide a picture of individual lives under widely varying conditions. In addition, we obtained questionnaire data from several hundred women, the pool from which our interviewees were selected. Since the study dealt with the life course until age 45, there were arguments for selecting a sample currently in their middle to late forties. Instead, I chose to include women ranging in age from 35 to 45. This age distribution has the disadvantage that its younger members have not completed the entire sequence to 45, but it has several compensating advantages. Women of about 45 can describe their lives until that age and give a rich account of the recent years, but their story of the earlier years may not be as full. Women in their late thirties generally describe their twenties and early thirties with more immediacy and vividness. In eliciting and interpreting a life story, we must take into account the vantage point from which it is told. A person of 45 reviewing her life until 30 is telling the story from a different vantage point than she would have at 30 or 40. All research, no matter how rigorous its design and measurement, inevitably presents problems of interpretation. No single study can be conclusive.

On what basis should the sample for this kind of study be formed? There are many possibilities. Some are clearly better than others but no single one is "best." I decided on the following: (1) homemakers; (2) women with careers in the corporate-financial world; (3) women with careers in the academic world.

The Homemakers

The fifteen homemakers were drawn randomly from the city directory of the greater New Haven area (excluding only the small number in careers of the kind represented by the other two samples). They were a good cross section of the general population and varied widely in social class, education, religion, ethnicity, work, and marital history. They lived mainly as traditional homemakers in a family-centered pattern. The nature and extent of their outside work were quite varied: a few had not worked at all outside the home; some had worked off and on at unskilled or semiskilled jobs; still others were in "female" occupations such as nursing and schoolteaching. They differed also in the evolution of their involvement in outside work. For some, a job had always been a burden to be undertaken only out of financial necessity, and not a source of satisfaction or meaning in life. For others, outside work became increasingly important, joining family as a central component of their lives. This sample reveals the durability of the traditional pattern as well as the profound forces that are changing it.

Women with Corporate-Financial Careers

These fifteen career women were at the opposite extreme from the homemakers. They were employed in major corporate-financial organizations in the New York City area. They were part of the first generation in which a sizable number of women (though still a small minority) entered a high-status male occupational system and tried to make occupation a central component of their life structure. Some of them held professional-technical positions such as investment analyst or portfolio manager, with no managerial responsibilities. Others had management staff positions in areas such as human resources, public relations, and corporate planning, which were not on a track leading to the highest levels. Very few women in this sample, or in the corporate world, had positions involving line authority in the corporate structure. Their average annual income in the early 1980s was about $60,000, with a range of roughly $25,000 to over $200,000. It would be considerably higher in 1990s dollars. In the larger pool from which the sample was selected, the great majority were in their thirties; a smaller number were in their early forties and very few over 45; before the 1970s a career path in this field was virtually closed to women. About half were unmarried, slightly more childless. Both the benefits and the costs of this life were substantial.

The Women with Academic Careers

The sample of fifteen faculty members in colleges and universities was intermediate between the first two. Like the businesswomen they were struggling to combine career and family, but the corporate world is even more stressful and sexist than the academic and provides even less support for combining career and family. They all were employed at one of several institutions located in the New York–Boston corridor. Each of these institutions provided rather different career paths for women, and their faculty members varied somewhat in social and educational background. In all of the institutions, however, the female faculty were largely in junior faculty or marginal (non–tenure track) positions and more were in the humanities than the sciences. The women in this sample were highly diverse with regard to academic rank, field of study, and social background, as well as educational, occupational, and marital/family history.

These samples are certainly not an accurate cross section of the national population, but this is not a statistical study. The great majority of American women are still primarily homemakers. Although most of them have jobs, few have a long-term occupational career. Women with corporate or academic careers such as those studied here are still in a small minority. Their numbers are increasing, however. A better understanding of their lives will be of growing importance to individual women and men, to work organizations, and to the direction of our future social policies.

Many significant groups are not represented in our sample. However, there are great differences between the samples and great variation within each. The intensive study of individual lives enabled us to explore the complexity, subtlety, and variety of those lives and to free ourselves from the stereotypical images of "woman" that flourish in this time of gender splitting. In comparing the lives of the homemakers and the career women, it became clear that we have much to learn about the current state of the Traditional Marriage Enterprise and the issues women face when they attempt to modify it.

Chapters 2 and 3 present more fully the perspectives on adult development and on gender, which form the twin vantage points from which I shall then examine women's lives. Chapters 4 through 9 follow the homemakers through the successive developmental periods to age 45. Chapters 10 through 15 do the same for the career women, identifying themes common to both career samples while also noting differences between the faculty members and those in the corporate-financial world.

2 The Human Life Cycle: Eras and Developmental Periods

Is there a fundamental order in the human life course? Most people would say no. After all, each life is unique in its pattern at a given time and in its evolution over time, and many lives are notable for their disorderly, even chaotic quality. Yet two images common to virtually all societies suggest that underlying the manifest variety and disorder there is a basic sequence that all lives go through in their own individual ways.

(1) The *life cycle*: there may be seasons in the life course just as there are seasons in the year and evolving phases in many aspects of nature.

(2) *Development* is now ingrained in our thinking about childhood and can be extended into adulthood. The study of childhood is largely about child development—about the ways in which we develop, biologically, psychologically, and socially, from infancy to adulthood. Does development then stop? May not our adult lives evolve in accordance with developmental principles? These questions have been largely neglected in the human sciences.

My own conception of the life cycle and of developmental periods in adulthood is in part a product of the present study and might have been reserved for a concluding chapter. I discuss it here, however, because it gives the reader a perspective from which to examine and understand the individual lives described in subsequent chapters.

The Life Cycle

The idea of the life cycle goes beyond that of the life course. In its origin this idea is metaphorical, not descriptive or conceptual, but it is useful to retain the primary imagery while moving toward something more precise. The imagery implies an underlying order in the human life course; although each individual life is unique, everyone goes through the same basic sequence. The course of a life is not a simple, continuous process; there are qualitatively different phases or seasons. The metaphor of seasons appears in many contexts. There are seasons of the year. Spring is a time of blossoming, and poets allude to youth as the springtime of the life cycle. Summer is the season of greatest passion and ripeness. An elderly ruler is "the lion in winter." There are seasons within a single day—dawn, noon, twilight, the full dark of night—each having its counterpart in the life cycle. There are seasons in love, war, politics, artistic creation, illness. The imagery suggests that the life course evolves through a sequence of definable seasons or segments. Change goes on within each season, and a transition is required for the shift from one to the next. Every season has its own time, although it is part of and colored by the whole. No season is intrinsically better or more important than any other. Each has its necessary place and contributes its special character to the whole.

What are the major seasons of the life cycle? Neither popular culture nor the human sciences provide a clear answer to this question. The modern world has no established conception—scientific, philosophical, religious, or literary—of the life cycle as a whole and of its component phases. We have no popular language to describe a series of age levels after adolescence. We use words such as youth, maturity, and middle age, but they are ambiguous in their age linkages and meanings. The ambiguity of language stems from the lack of any cultural or scientific definition of adulthood and how people's lives evolve within it.

The predominant view divides the life course into three parts: (1) An initial segment of about twenty years is usually identified as *childhood*, or childhood and adolescence, or the "formative years" prior to adulthood. (2) A final segment starting at around 65 is known as *old age*, which is commonly regarded both as part of "adulthood" and as a sequel to it. Various euphemisms, such as "senior citizen" or "golden years," have been used at times but do little to dispel our deep anxiety about this season of the life cycle. (3) Between these segments lies an amorphous time vaguely known as *adulthood.*

The study of child development seeks to determine the universal order and the process by which our lives become increasingly individualized. Historically, the great psychologists in this field, such as Freud and Piaget, conceived of development as the process by which we become adult—which means that it stops with the cessation of adolescence. Given this view, they had no basis for concerning themselves with the possibilities for adult development or with the nature of the life cycle as a whole.

An impetus to change came in the 1950s when geriatrics and gerontology were established as fields of human service and research. Unfortunately, gerontology has not gone far in generating a conception of the life cycle or of development in adulthood. One reason, perhaps, is that it skipped from childhood to old age without examining the intervening adult years. Our present understanding of old age will be enhanced when more is known about adulthood; the later seasons can then be connected more organically to the earlier ones.

Early in this century, Carl G. Jung was perhaps the first modern voice in psychiatry-psychology to focus on the possibility of adult personality development. He took the position that personality development simply cannot progress very far by the end of adolescence—just far enough to allow us to begin living as adults and assuming the responsibilities required by family, work, and community. The inner struggles of the twenties and thirties, said Jung, deal mainly with the "shadow," the repressed childhood desires and attributes that Freud had brought to light. After 40, we may begin to develop many archetypes—potentials within the self—that remain relatively primitive until mid-life. The archetypes and the self assume increasing importance in middle and late adulthood.

At about the same time, the Dutch anthropologist Arnold van Gennep was examining the life cycle from a more societal perspective. His book *Rites of Passage* (first published in 1908) dealt with major life events such as birth, death, marriage, and divorce. Many societies deal with these events by constructing rites of passage—ceremonial occasions that shape the person's movement from one status or group to another. Persons in passage or transition are a potential threat to society because they are poorly integrated in the groups they are leaving as well as in the groups they are entering. For society, rituals are a form of social control: they help to ensure that individuals properly terminate their membership in a particular generation or social position and become securely ensconced in a new one. For the individual, the rituals provide a collective vehicle for gaining personal control over the anxieties that such transitions generate.

As an anthropologist, van Gennep understandably dealt more with the cultural than the psychological aspects of this phenomenon. Psychologists and psychiatrists tend to go to the other extreme. An adequate understanding ultimately requires joint consideration of both culture and personality. Van Gennep viewed the life cycle as a series of major life events and passages occurring within a cultural framework. This approach must be combined with one that takes account of personality and that examines the entire life course, rather than just the highlighting events.

José Ortega y Gasset, the great Spanish historian-philosopher, presented in *Man and Crisis* (first published in 1933) a remarkable conception of the life cycle and the flow of generations in history. On the basis of both individual and societal considerations he identified five generations, each representing a season of the life cycle: *childhood*, age 0 to 15; *youth*, 15 to 30; *initiation*, 30 to 45; *dominant*, 45 to 60; and *old age*, 60+. Collectively, all five generations coexist at any moment in human society. Life in each generation is shaped by the particular point in history at which it exists. Each of us moves over time from one generation to the next. The generational divisions thus contribute to the shape of the life cycle, and the potentials in the life cycle affect the ways in which generational boundaries are drawn.

Ortega's youth generation (age 15–30) roughly corresponds to what I call the *novice phase* of early adulthood. In this phase, we take our first tentative steps toward working, building a family, and establishing a place in the adult world. His initiation generation (30–45) is, from my perspective, in the *culminating phase* of early adulthood. In our early thirties we are responsible but junior members of a social world. By our early forties we are entering a more senior position and joining the dominant generation. In the initiation generation we receive the wisdom and control of our seniors; we also begin slowly to assert our own authority and to create moderately or radically new ideas and goals. In the dominant generation we join and to some degree modify the establishment that governs every social institution. At any given moment in history, the initiation and dominant generations largely determine the future of society, and the relations between them are of tremendous historical importance. It is ironic that the years from approximately age 30 to 60, about which we know the least, have the most fundamental significance for the collective as well as individual well-being of humanity.

The culminating figure in this brief review is Erik H. Erikson. With the publication of *Childhood and Society* in 1950, he became the most influential developmental theorist of the time. The book might well have been called "Life Cycle and Society." Its distinctive creativity was to place childhood within an articulated framework of the life cycle and to generate the study of adult development. Erikson's developmental concepts deal primarily with the individual life course. He emphasized the process of living, the idea of life history rather than case history, the use of biography rather than therapy or testing as the chief research method. In studying a life, his first step was to examine its course over the years. He then sought to explore the ways in which the life course reflected the engagement of *self* (psyche, personality, inner world) and *external world* (society, culture, institutions, history).

Erikson posited a sequence of eight *ego stages*. Each stage predominates in, and is most appropriate for, a specific *age segment* of the life cycle. The first five stages cover a series of age segments from infancy through adolescence. The last three stages occur in age segments identified by Erikson as young adulthood, adulthood, and old age. Stage six, Intimacy vs. Isolation, clearly begins at the start of "young adulthood" at around 20. Stage eight, Integrity vs. Despair, initiates "old age" in the sixties. Erikson was most elusive about the onset of stage seven, Generativity vs. Stagnation, and has been interpreted variously. My own reading of his texts, especially *Gandhi's Truth*, is that generativity begins at about 40 and remains a primary concern throughout middle adulthood. A key issue in this stage is one's relationship to the generations of younger adults. In Ortega's terms, generativity is a major task of the dominant generation, which has the responsibility for educating the youth generation and fostering the development of the initiation generation so that they will, in time, be ready to succeed (and perhaps exceed) their seniors.

Erikson had a complex view of the childhood years. His view of the adult years from roughly 20 to 60, and of the two ego stages within them, provides a valuable starting point for the study of adult development, but much more is needed. The problem of segments of the life cycle is not Erikson's alone; it is a fundamental issue that has generally been ignored or blurred. Most textbooks on human development devote 60 percent or more of their pages to childhood, 20 percent or less to adulthood, and about 20 percent to old age.

On what basis can we distinguish one season of the life cycle from another? A segment of the life cycle must be characterized by an underlying unity in the overall character of living during those years. It cannot be defined solely in terms of one aspect of living. There is now a well-established life cycle framework for the first twenty years or so. We refer to it broadly as childhood: the season of growth toward adulthood. Within it is a series of smaller segments such as early childhood, middle childhood, and adolescence (which is, in effect, late childhood). There is no corresponding consensus about the adult seasons of the life cycle, even though a good deal has been learned about specific features of adult life—social roles and relationships in family, work, and other contexts, adaptation to major life events, stability and change in personality.

In order to establish adult development as a major field of study, we must address three major tasks: to describe the individual life course as it evolves; to form a conception of the life cycle and the place of adulthood within it; and to determine how development proceeds in adulthood. This will provide a framework within which specific events, roles, relationships, and developmental processes can be studied in a more integrated fashion. I turn now to my own conception of the life cycle and adult development.

Eras: The Macrostructure of the Life Cycle

I conceive of the life cycle as a sequence of eras (see page 18). Each era has its own bio-psycho-social character, and each makes its distinctive contribution to the whole. There are major changes in the nature of our lives from

**DEVELOPMENTAL PERIODS
IN THE ERAS OF EARLY AND
MIDDLE ADULTHOOD**

(adapted from *The Seasons of
a Man's Life*, Knopf, 1978)

LATE ADULT TRANSITION: *Age 60–65*

*Culminating Life
Structure for Middle
Adulthood: 55–60*

**ERA OF LATE
ADULTHOOD: 60–?**

*Age 50 Transition:
50–55*

*Entry Life Structure
for Middle Adulthood:
45–50*

MID-LIFE TRANSITION: *Age 40–45*

*Culminating Life
Structure for Early
Adulthood: 33–40*

**ERA OF MIDDLE
ADULTHOOD: 40–65**

*Age 30 Transition:
28–33*

*Entry Life Structure
for Early Adulthood:
22–28*

EARLY ADULT TRANSITION: *Age 17–22*

**ERA OF EARLY
ADULTHOOD: 17–45**

**ERA OF PRE-
ADULTHOOD: 0–22**

one era to the next, and lesser though still crucially important changes within eras. They are partially overlapping; a new era begins as the previous one approaches its end. A *cross-era transition*, which generally lasts about five years, terminates the outgoing era and initiates the next. The eras and the cross-era transitional periods form the broad structure of the life cycle, providing an underlying order in the flow of all human lives yet permitting myriad variations in the individual life course.

Every era and developmental period begins and ends at a well-defined average age, with a range of about two years above and below this average. The idea of age-linked phases in adult life goes against our conventional wisdom. Nevertheless, research on women as well as men consistently reveals these age linkages.

The first era, *childhood*, extends from birth to roughly age 22. It is the era of most rapid growth. The first few years of life provide a transition from birth into childhood. During this time the newborn becomes biologically and psychologically separate from the mother and establishes an initial distinction between the "me" and the "not-me"—the first step in a continuing process of individuation. Early childhood is followed by middle childhood and adolescence.

The years from about 17 to 22 constitute the *Early Adult Transition*, a developmental period in which the era of childhood draws to a close and early adulthood gets under way. It is part of both eras and not fully within either. We modify our relationships with family and other components of the childhood world, we begin forming an adult identity, and we begin taking our place as adults in the adult world. From a childhood-centered perspective, one can say that development is now largely completed and the child has gained the maturity to be an adult. Textbooks on developmental psychology commonly take this view. Taking the perspective of the life cycle as a whole, however, we recognize that the developmental attainments of one era provide only a starting point from which to begin the next. The Early Adult Transition represents, so to say, both the full maturity of childhood and the infancy of early adulthood. We are at best off to a shaky start, and new kinds of development are required in the new era.

The second era, *early adulthood*, lasts from about 17 to 45. It begins with the Early Adult Transition. It is the adult era of greatest energy and abundance, and of greatest contradiction and stress. Biologically, the twenties and thirties are the peak years of the life cycle. In social and psychological terms, early adulthood is the season for forming and pursuing youthful aspirations, establishing a niche in society, raising a family, and, as the era ends, becoming a "senior member" of the adult world. This can be a time of rich satisfactions in terms of love, sexuality, family life, occupational advancement, creativity, and realization of major life goals. But there can be crushing stresses, too: we undertake the burdens of parenthood and, at the same time, of forming an occupation; we incur heavy financial obligations when our earning power is still relatively low; we have to make crucially important choices regarding spouse, family, work, and lifestyle before we have the maturity or life experience to choose wisely. Early adulthood is the era in which we are most buffeted by our own passions and ambitions from within, and by the demands of family, community, and society from without. Under reasonably favorable conditions, the rewards of living in this era are enormous; but the costs often equal or exceed the benefits.

The *Mid-life Transition*, from roughly 40 to 45, brings about both the termination of early adulthood and the start of middle adulthood. My research indicates that the character of a life is always appreciably different in the middle forties than it was in the late thirties.

This book deals primarily with the lives of women in early adulthood, as they traverse the developmental periods from the Early Adult Transition through the Mid-life Transition.

The third era, *middle adulthood,* starts with the Mid-life Transition and lasts from about 40 to 65. During this era our biological capacities are below those of early adulthood but normally still sufficient for an energetic, personally satisfying, and socially valuable life. Unless our lives are hampered in some special way, most of us during our forties and fifties become "senior members" in our own particular worlds, however grand or modest they may be. We are responsible not only for our own work and perhaps the work of others, but also for the development of the current generation of young adults who will soon enter the senior generation. It is possible in this era to become more maturely creative, more responsible for self and others, more universal in outlook and less tied to narrow tribal values, more dispassionately purposeful, more capable of intimacy and sensual loving than ever before. Unfortunately, middle adulthood is for many persons a time of progressive decline—of growing emptiness and loss of vitality.

The next era, *late adulthood,* starts at about 60. The *Late Adult Transition,* from 60 to 65, is a developmental period linking middle and late adulthood. I have discussed this era in Chapter 2 of *The Seasons of a Man's Life.*

This conception of the life cycle requires us to re-examine the very idea of development. We commonly think of development in childhood as synonymous with growth, with the realization of individual potential. In its basic meaning, however, development is a process of evolution. It is not the same as growing; or, to put it more precisely, it has the twin aspects of positive growth and negative growth — of "growing up" and "growing down." A term for the former is *adolescing*, which literally means "moving toward adulthood" and suggests positive growth toward a potential optimum. A term for the latter is *senescing*, which means moving toward old age and suggests negative growth and dissolution.

Both adolescing and senescing go on during the entire life cycle, but their character and relative balance change appreciably from era to era. Our approach to development in one era cannot provide a literal model for development in other eras. In childhood we are mostly adolescing, although each step in growth may entail some form of loss. The child's growth in understanding the "real" world may be associated with a decline in creative imagination. Theories of child development deal chiefly with positive growth: the successive stages form a progression from lower to higher on a developmental scale. Dramatic advances in body size and function, cognitive complexity, adaptive capability, and character formation support the idea that each stage represents a "higher developmental level" than the previous one. However, the attributes that show such rapid growth up to age 20 or so tend to stabilize in early adulthood and then gradually decline after about 40, when biological senescing begins its inexorable predominance over adolescing. Childhood-centered views of development are thus likely to yield a rather bleak picture of adult development, since they tend to ignore the often rich potentialities and achievements of middle and late adulthood.

In late adulthood we are mostly senescing, but some vitally important adolescing may be done toward the end of the life cycle as we seek to give fuller meaning to our lives, to life and death as ultimate stages, and to the condition of being human. The approach of death itself may be the occasion of our growing to full adulthood.

In early and middle adulthood, adolescing and senescing coexist in an uneasy balance. The study of adult development must take account of both. Our adult lives are a story of interweaving growth and decline. Although the potential for positive growth exists in adulthood, it is less assured than in childhood and takes different forms. There is also some degree of negative growth, but it takes different forms in the successive eras. For some persons, early and middle adulthood is primarily a time of increasing vitality and fulfillment (though not without struggle and pain); for others, it is a time of increasing triviality, stagnation, and inner deadness. Both of these extremes, and the large middle ground between them, can teach us a great deal about human strength and vulnerability. Adult development has its own distinctive character. It has to be studied in its own right, not simply as an extension of childhood or a prelude to old age.

The Life Structure

My approach to adult development grows out of, and is shaped by, the foregoing views regarding the life course and the life cycle. I am primarily interested in apprehending the nature of a person's life at a particular time and the course of that life over the years. Personality attributes, social roles, and biological characteristics are aspects of the life and, from a life course perspective, should be placed within the context of the life.

The key concept to emerge from my research is the life structure: the underlying pattern or design of a person's life at a given time. This book, like *The Seasons of a Man's Life*, is largely about the development of the life structure in adulthood. The developmental periods described here are periods in life structure development. I'll start with the concept of life structure and then go on to its evolution in adulthood.

The meaning of this term can be clarified by comparing life structure and personality structure. A theory of personality structure provides a way of thinking about a concrete question: What kind of person am I? Different theories offer numerous ways of thinking about this question and of characterizing oneself or others in terms of attributes such as wishes, conflicts, defenses, traits, skills, values.

A theory of life structure is a way of thinking about a different question: What is my life like now? As we begin reflecting on this question, many others come to mind: What are the most important parts of my life, and how are they interrelated? Where do I invest most of my time and energy? Are there some relationships—to spouse, lover, family, occupation, religion, leisure, or whatever—that I would like to modify, to make more satisfying, or to eliminate? Are there some things not in my life that I would like to include? Are there interests and relationships, now absent or occupying a minor place, that I would like to make more central? In pondering these questions, we begin to identify those aspects of the external world that have the greatest significance to us. We characterize our relationship with each of them and examine the interweaving of the various relationships. We inevitably find that our relationships are imperfectly integrated within a single pattern or structure.

The primary components of a life structure are the person's *relationships* with various others in the external world. A significant relationship may be with an immediately present Other—a friend, lover, spouse, parent, or offspring. The Other also may be a person from the past, a symbolic or imagined figure, a group or institution, an aspect of nature, a loved (or hated) place, even a painting or a book.

In describing a relationship we must consider: (1) what the Person and the Other *do* with each other; (2) the subjective *meanings* involved; (3) what the Person gives and receives—materially, emotionally, socially; (4) the social context of the relationship; (5) the place of the relationship in the person's life structure and how it connects to other relationships; (6) its evolution over time within the life structure.

The concept of life structure requires us to examine the nature and patterning of an adult's relationships with all significant others, and the evolution of these relationships over the years. Relationships are the stuff our lives are made of. They give shape and substance to the life course. They are the vehicle by which we live out—or bury—various aspects of ourselves; and by which we participate, for better and for worse, in the world around us.

A life structure may have few or many components. The *central components* are those that have the greatest significance for the self and the life. They receive the greatest share of one's time and energy, and they strongly influence the character of the other components. Only one or two components—rarely as many as three—occupy a central place in the structure. The *peripheral components* are easier to change or detach. They involve less investment of self and can be modified with less effect on the fabric of one's life. There may also be important *unfilled components*: a person urgently wants but does not have a meaningful occupation, a marriage, a family; and this absent component plays a major part in the life structure.

Most often, marriage/family and occupation are the central components of a person's life. There are wide variations, however, in their relative weight and in the importance of other components. Seen as a component of the life structure, the *family* is a complex world that involves many persons, activities, and social contexts. It may include the current nuclear family of spouses and children (or the part of it that is intact), previous marriages and families, the family of origin (parents and offspring), the extended family, "the family" as a symbol that includes many generations in the past and implies continuity with future generations. The relationship to family is also interwoven with the relationship to ethnicity, race, occupation, cultural traditions.

Likewise, *occupation* is likely to be a major component of the life structure. Occupation is not simply a matter of specific work activities and rewards; nor is it simply a matter of membership in a particular occupational category. Work engages a person in an elaborate occupational world. To understand what part work plays in a woman's life, we must examine her manifold relationships to various parts of the work world and to the whole, and see how occupation is interwoven with other components of the life structure.

In addition to family and occupation, the life structure often includes other components: love relationships; friendships; relationships to politics, religion, ethnicity, and community; leisure, recreation, and the use of solitude; relationship to the body (including bodily health and illness, vigor and decline); memberships and roles in many social settings. Underlying and permeating all relationships with the external world is the relationship to the self.

The life structure forms a boundary between self and world and mediates the relationship between them. This boundary can be understood only if we see it as a link, as something that connects self and world yet is also partially separate. It is in part the cause, the vehicle, and the effect of that relationship. The life structure grows out of the engagement of self and external world. Its evolution is shaped by factors in the self and in the world. It requires us to think simultaneously about self and world rather than making one primary and the other secondary or derivative. A theory of life structure must draw equally upon psychology and the social sciences (and biology, when it deals with adult biological development).

As we get clearer about the basic structure of a life, we can explore in more detail the *external aspects*—events, social contexts, roles, influences of all kinds—as well as the *internal aspects*—subjective meanings, motives, conflicts, personal qualities. The life structure is the framework within which these aspects are interwoven. To see only the outlines of the structure without its specific content is to have only a schematic view of the life. To focus on details—even a large number of details—without grasping the overall evolving structure is to perceive fragments but to miss the life. To include both in some balance is a major aim of this book.

Periods in Adult Life Structure Development

There is not much order in the sequence of specific events, actions, social roles, and personality changes within an individual life course, and certainly no universal order. When we examine the evolution of the life structure, however, an underlying order (with infinite variations) does emerge: the life structure develops through a standard sequence of periods during the adult years. In this sequence, periods in which we build and maintain a structure alternate with transitional periods in which the structure is transformed.

The primary tasks of a *structure-building* period are to form and maintain a life structure and enhance our life within it: we make certain key choices, form a structure around them, and pursue our values and goals within this structure. Even when we succeed in maintaining a stable structure, life is not necessarily tranquil. The tasks of making major life choices and building a structure are often stressful indeed and may involve many kinds of change. Structure-building periods ordinarily last five to seven years. Then the life structure that has formed the basis for stability comes into question and must be modified.

A *structure-changing or transitional period* terminates the existing life structure and creates the possibility for a new one. The primary tasks of every transitional period are to reappraise the existing structure, to explore the possibilities for change in self and world, and to move toward commitment to the crucial choices that form the basis for a new life structure in the ensuing period. Transitional periods ordinarily last about five years. Almost half our adult lives is spent in developmental transitions. No life structure is permanent—periodic change is a part of the nature of our existence.

The periods of early and middle adulthood are shown on page 18. Each period begins and ends at a well-defined average age, within a variation of two years above and below the average. Our main concern in this book is with early adulthood. A summary of the periods in middle adulthood gives a backdrop for our understanding of early adulthood and of the Mid-life Transition that bridges the two eras. The formulation of the developmental periods from 45 to 65 is based upon exploratory studies of women and men, using interviews and biographies. The pattern shown differs from the corresponding one in *The Seasons of a Man's Life* in two respects: the names of the structure-building periods have been changed in the interest of theoretical preciseness (but the meanings are the same); and the present diagram shows more clearly that every cross-era transition is part of both the eras it links. The developmental periods unfold as follows:

(1)   *Early Adult Transition* (age 17–22) is a cross-era transition in which we terminate childhood and initiate early adulthood. A cross-era transition involves not only a change in life structure but a fundamental turning point in the life cycle. We are on the boundary between eras—concluding one and creating a basis for the next, without a clear idea of what is to come. This period is part of the two eras and not fully in either.

(2)   *Entry Life Structure for Early Adulthood* (age 22–28). The tasks now are to make some key choices (especially regarding love/marriage/family, occupation, separation from family of origin, and lifestyle) and to organize one's life as a young adult. The first life structure built in an era is necessarily provisional; it is an initial attempt to make a place for oneself in a new world and a new generation.

(3)   *Age 30 Transition* (age 28–33) occurs in mid-era. It provides an opportunity to reappraise the Entry Life Structure, to do some further work on individuation (including undone work of earlier transitions), and to ex-

plore new possibilities out of which the next structure can be formed. It is a time of moderate to severe developmental difficulty for most women and men.

(4) *Culminating Life Structure for Early Adulthood* (age 33–40). The primary developmental task here is to form a structure within which we can try to establish a more secure place for ourselves in society and to accomplish our youthful dreams and goals. We are moving from "junior" to "senior" membership in the adult world.

(5) *Mid-life Transition* (age 40–45) is a developmental bridge between early and middle adulthood and is part of both eras. We terminate the life structure of the thirties, come to terms with the end of "youth" as it existed in early adulthood, and try to create a new way of being young-and-old appropriate to middle adulthood. The work of mid-life individuation is an especially important task of this period; it forms the inner matrix out of which a modified self and life evolve over the rest of this era.

(6) *Entry Life Structure for Middle Adulthood* (age 45–50). The primary task of this period is to create an initial structure for the launching of middle adulthood. This structure is often dramatically different from that of the late thirties. Even when it is superficially similar (for example, one is in the same job, marriage, community), there are important differences in the relationships that form the central components of the life structure. We establish an initial place in a new generation and a new season of life.

(7) *Age 50 Transition* (age 50–55) is an opportunity to reappraise the Entry Life Structure, to engage in some further exploration of self and world, and to create a basis for the structure to be formed in the ensuing period. It is a mid-era transition, analogous to the Age 30 Transition. Developmental crises are common in this period, especially for persons who have made few significant life changes, or inappropriate changes, in the previous ten to fifteen years.

(8) *Culminating Life Structure for Middle Adulthood* (age 55–60). This structure, like that of the thirties, provides a vehicle for the realization of the era's major aspirations and goals.

(9) *Late Adult Transition* (age 60–65) concludes middle adulthood and initiates late adulthood. It requires a profound reappraisal of the past and a shift to a new era. We create a basis for building, in the next period, an Entry Life Structure for Late Adulthood.

We thus find the same sequence of developmental periods in early adulthood and middle adulthood:

(1) A *Cross-era Transition* (17–22, 40–45, 60–65) terminates the outgoing era and initiates the new one.

(2) A period of building and maintaining an *Entry Life Structure* (22–28, 45–50) for the era.

(3) A *Mid-era Transition* (28–33, 50–55) permits reappraisal and modification of the Entry Life Structure and exploratory efforts toward the formation of a new one.

(4) A second, *Culminating Life Structure* (33–40, 55–60) for the era.

(5) and (1) A *Cross-era Transition* brings this era to a close and, at the same time, thrusts us into the next era.

The first three periods of early adulthood, from roughly 17 to 33, constitute its *novice phase*. They provide an opportunity to move beyond adolescence, to build a provisional but necessarily flawed Entry Life Structure, and to learn the limitations of that structure. The two final periods, from 33 to 45, form a *concluding phase* which brings to fruition the efforts of this era and launches us into the next.

A similar sequence exists in middle adulthood. It, too, begins with a novice phase of three periods, from 40 to 55. The Mid-life Transition is both an ending and a beginning. In our early forties we are in the full maturity of early adulthood and completing its final chapter; we are also in the infancy of middle adulthood, just beginning to learn about its promise and dangers. We remain novices in every era until we have a chance to try out an Entry Life Structure and then to question and modify it in the Mid-era Transition. In the concluding phase—the periods of the Culminating Life Structure and the Cross-era Transition that follows—we complete an era and begin the shift to the next. During the novice phase we are, to varying degrees, both excited and terrified by the prospects of living in a new era. To varying degrees, likewise, we experience the concluding phase as a time of rich satisfactions and of bitter disappointments, discovering as we so often do that the era ultimately gives us much more and much less than we had envisioned.

This view of a standard, age-linked sequence of eras and developmental periods in adulthood violates the conventional wisdom of our culture, and of the human sciences, in several major respects. It appears to contradict the widespread finding that there is no comparable sequence of periods in the adult development of personality, cognition, occupational careers, families. Why should an age-linked sequence hold for life structure development when it does not hold for the others? I do not know *why* this sequence exists, but that it *does* exist is indicated by the research evidence. As I see it, my theory and the others are different but not contradictory. The sequence of eras and periods provides a framework within which the evolution of more specific aspects of living can better be understood. In time, I believe, we will have the basis for a more inclusive theory within which all aspects of development can be contained.

Finally, I must admit that I am surprised and even somewhat embarrassed by the order and elegant simplicity of this sequence. Between 17 and 65 we go through two eras, early and middle adulthood, which begin and end with a Cross-era Transition. Each era provides the opportunity for an Entry Life Structure and a Culminating Life Structure, which are linked by a Mid-era Transition. I did not initially expect to find much order, and certainly not an order of this kind. I must report, however, that this construction best fits the available evidence for women as for men.

The "Satisfactoriness" of the Life Structure

As noted above, many theories of child development propose a sequence of stages in which each stage is developmentally higher or more advanced than the preceding one. This view may hold for childhood, but it is questionable at best for adulthood. We know too little about the complexities and contradictions of the human life course to make the judgment that one life structure is developmentally higher than another. The Culminating Life Structure of the thirties is not necessarily more advanced developmentally than the Entry Life Structure of the twenties. Likewise, in comparing the Culminating Life Structure of early adulthood with the Entry Life Structure of middle adulthood, we have to take account of the change in eras, which present new possibilities and new burdens. I use the term "period" rather than "stage" in order to evoke the imagery of an evolving historical process rather than a layered series of static entities. When we know more about the kinds of life structures people build at different ages, under different conditions, we may be better able to identify variations in developmental level among life structures.

While deferring the question of developmental level, I have found it useful to develop another concept: the *satisfactoriness* of the life structure. Like all other attributes of the life structure, satisfactoriness has both external and internal aspects. Externally, it refers to the structure's viability in the external world—how well it works, what it provides in the way of advantages and disadvantages, successes and failures, rewards and deprivations. Internally, it refers to the structure's suitability for the self, that is, what aspects of the self can be lived out within this structure? What aspects must be neglected or suppressed? What are the benefits and costs of this structure for the self? In attempting to evaluate the satisfactoriness of a life structure, we must consider both its viability and its suitability, in the light of external circumstances as well as inner resources.

Satisfactoriness of the life structure is not the same as "level of adjustment" or "life satisfaction" as these are usually assessed in survey research. A person's self-rating on a nine-point scale of "life satisfaction" tells us virtually nothing about the satisfactoriness of his or her life structure. Some people feel quite satisfied with lives that are reasonably comfortable and orderly but in which they have minimal engagement or sense of purpose. Their lives have much viability in the world but little suitability for the self. When the self is so little invested in the life, the life in turn can offer little to the self. Likewise, people who are passionately engaged in living, and who invest the self actively in the life structure, may experience more turmoil and suffering than those who are less engaged. They may ask more of life than it can provide. The intense engagement in life yields more abundant fruits but exacts a different and in some ways greater toll. Assessing the satisfactoriness of the life structure is thus a complex matter. It cannot be done by means of a few behavioral criteria or questionnaire items.

It is important to distinguish between the development of the life structure and the development of the self. Many psychologists who have intellectual origins in the study of childhood think of development as growth in various aspects of the self. The study of adult development inevitably goes beyond the focus on the self. It requires us to examine the life course, to study the engagement of the self in the world, and to move beyond the view of the self as an encapsulated entity. As we learn more about the evolution of the life structure, we will have a sounder basis for studying the adult development of the self.

Transitional Periods in Life Structure Development

The idea of transition is central to many theories. A transition is a process of change that forms a bridge between X and Y. X and Y may be two subjects in discourse, two jobs or cities, two themes in a musical composition, two distinctive structures. To be "in transit" is to be in the process of leaving X (without having fully left it) and, at the same time, of entering Y (without being fully a part of it). The transition forms a *boundary region* linking X and Y. This boundary space is part of X and Y yet qualitatively different from both. A transition thus carries the imagery of a turning point, a shift in course, a process of cutting, sifting, separating, an attempt to resolve contradictions, a time of transformation rather than stability. Only by giving up what I now have at X do I create the opportunity to enter Y. A transition is a time of promise, of hope and potential for a better future. It is also a time of separation and loss.

A transitional period in life structure development involves three main developmental tasks: (1) *termination* of the existing life structure; (2) *individuation*; and (3) *initiation* of a new structure. One might suppose that these tasks follow a consecutive order: first, we terminate the past. Third, we initiate a new life; in between, as a basis for change, is the work of individuation. But development does not proceed in so logical a manner. The three tasks may interweave throughout a transitional period; or a person may attempt to initiate a new structure at the start of a transition, before doing much terminating or individuating. I'll discuss each task briefly in turn.

Termination

A termination is, most simply, an ending, a conclusion, a final step. However, the termination of a significant relationship plays an important part in our lives precisely because it represents not only an ending, but also a beginning. It is more realistic to conceive of a termination as a major qualitative change in the character of a relationship; it ends one form of the relationship and starts a new form. This view places the termination in a broader time perspective, regarding it as both an outcome of the past and a starting point for the future.

The "Other" in a significant relationship may, as noted earlier, be a person (living, dead, or imaginary), a group, institution, or social movement, a symbol or place. If the Other has little value or significance for me—if I lose a possession of no importance, if I lose contact with a person or group of only casual interest to me—it passes out of my life with almost no consequences. The situation is very different for relationships which form major components of my life structure and in which I have made a great investment of self. The termination of such relationships is more protracted and has far greater consequences for my future life.

The most dramatic terminations involve total loss of contact with the Other: a loved one dies; a valued group is dissolved; the therapy ends, and I no longer see the therapist; a bitter quarrel leads to permanent parting from a friend or mentor; a geographical move (voluntary or coerced) forces me to leave a world I may never see again. I experience a profound loss and must come to terms with painful feelings of abandonment, helplessness, grief, and rage. Although the Other is no longer externally available, the relationship does not die. Over time the lost Other is more fully internalized and exists as an internal figure. The relationship continues to evolve in my self and my life; certain aspects of it are ended but other aspects survive and new ones are added. Losing the earlier relationship, I gradually create a new one.

In most cases, however, termination does not involve total separation from the Other. We continue to have some contact, but a crucial change occurs in the character of the relationship. An intense mentoring relationship is followed by bitter conflict or by affectionate but distant acquaintanceship. A marriage ends in divorce, and the relationship goes on in new forms.

A termination is thus not an ending but a turning point: the relationship must be transformed. There is sometimes, but not always, a clear-cut terminating event such as a death, divorce, geographical move, graduation. The event dramatizes one point in the termination process, which generally begins long before the identifying event and continues long after. The termination creates anxiety over being left behind, guilt over deserting or betraying the other, fear of having to start out afresh on one's own. It is important for both parties to determine what they will keep in the relationship and what they will give up. They need time to see whether there is a basis for an improved relationship, whether the whole thing must go under, whether they will remain in an essentially oppressive or dead relationship.

The termination of a single relationship is difficult enough. In a life structure transition the problem is compounded: it is necessary to terminate the current structure of one's life and, in a cross-era transition, the outgoing era. The basic question is not simply: What am I going to do about my marriage, or my work, or my lack of leisure? It is, rather: What am I going to do about my life? I may concentrate first on one particular component—the most painful one, or the one that seems most amenable to change—but in time I will have to deal with the others and with the overall structure.

In the Early Adult Transition, for example, we are in the process of separating from parents. The developmental task is *not* to end the relationship altogether. It is important to reject certain aspects (for instance, being the overly submissive or defiant child in relation to all-controlling parents). But it is important also to sustain other, more valued aspects, and to build in new qualities such as mutual respect between distinctive individuals who have separate as well as shared interests. The parents, often in their forties and working on their own developmental tasks, are at least as involved in the effort to transform the relationship. If it cannot be modified in a way appropriate to the life season of both parents and offspring, it will become increasingly stressful and may even wither away. Moreover, the relationship with parents is but one component of the initial adult life structure. This component influences, and is influenced by, relationships to occupation, to friends and lovers, perhaps to the political, religious, and cultural worlds in which the person is becoming a member. In a transitional period many relationships must be weighed, sifted, tested, and selectively incorporated into a fragile structure.

Individuation

Individuation, or the "separation-individuation process," is widely recognized as an important aspect of child development. During the first few years of life we take the first step in individuation, establishing a boundary between the "me" and the "not-me," and forming more stabilized relationships with the external world. In this first cross-era transition, we shift from life in the womb to existence as a person in the world. Individuation advances further in the Early Adult Transition, with the initial consolidation of an adult identity, greater differentiation from parents, and preparation for a future life as an adult. But we still have a long way to go. If we do not become more individuated in middle adulthood than we were at 20, our lives are very limited indeed.

Individuation is often regarded as a process occurring solely within the self. In my view it is broader than this: it involves the person's relationship both to self and to external world. With greater individuation of the self, we have a clearer sense of who we are and what we want. We draw more fully on our inner resources (desires, values, talents, archetypal potentials). We are more autonomous, self-generating, and self-responsible. The self is more integrated and less rent by inner contradictions. Individuation occurs as well in our relation to the external world. With more individuated relationships, we feel more genuinely connected to the human and natural world. We are more able to explore its possibilities and to understand what it demands and offers. We give it greater meaning and take more responsibility for our personal construction of meaning. We are capable of more *mutual* relationships, without being limited to a narrowly "selfish" concern with our own gratification or to an excessively "altruistic" concern with the needs of others. We accept more the ultimate reality of both our aloneness and our membership in the cosmos.

I conceive of individuation in part as a developmental effort toward the resolution of four polarities, which are of fundamental importance in human evolution and in the individual life cycle. They are: *Young/Old, Destruction/Creation, Masculine/Feminine, Engagement/Separateness*. Each of these pairs forms a polarity in the sense that the two terms represent opposing tendencies or conditions. Although they are in some sense antithetical, both sides coexist in every person and every society.

At every age we are both Young and Old. At 40, for example, we feel older than the youth, but not ready to join the "middle aged" generation. We feel alternately young, old, and in-between. If we cling too strongly to the youthfulness of our twenties, we cannot establish our place in the generation of middle adulthood. If we give up on being young and on sustaining our ties to the youth, we become dry, rigid, prematurely old. It is a problem of balance: the developmental task in every transitional period is to become Young/Old in a new way appropriate to that era in the life cycle.

The Destruction/Creation polarity presents similar problems of conflict and reintegration. Every transition activates a person's concerns with death and destruction. In the Mid-life Transition of the early forties, for example, we experience more fully our own mortality and the actual or impending deaths of others. We become more aware of the many ways in which other persons, even our loved ones, have acted destructively toward us (with malice or, often, with good intentions). What is perhaps worse, we realize that we have done irrevocably hurtful things to our parents, lovers, spouse, children, friends, rivals (again, with what may have been the worst or the best of intentions). At the same time, we have a strong desire to become more creative and loving: to create products that have genuine value for self and others, to participate in collective enterprises that advance human welfare, to contribute more fully to the coming generations in society. In middle adulthood a person can come to know, more than ever before, that powerful forces of destructiveness and of creativity coexist in the human soul—in my soul— and can be integrated in many ways, though never entirely.

Likewise, all of us at mid-life must come more fully to terms with the coexistence of masculine and feminine parts of the self. The splitting of masculine and feminine, so strong in childhood, cannot be overcome in early adulthood. It is a continuing task of middle and late adulthood.

Finally, we must integrate the powerful need for engagement in the external world with the antithetical but equally important need for separateness. The integration of these and other polarities is a great vision which many have sought to realize but no one can fully attain.

We can work on these polarities at any time during the life course. During the transitional periods, however, both the opportunity and the need to attain greater integration are strongest. When the life structure is up for reappraisal and change, when we feel to some degree suspended between past and future, it is especially important to heal the deep divisions in the self and in our most significant relationships. (For a fuller discussion of polarities, see *The Seasons of a Man's Life.*)

Initiation

As noted earlier, a transition is both an ending and a beginning. As an ending, it requires us to deal with termination, loss, separation, departure, completion. As a beginning it presents the task of initiation: exploring new possibilities, altering our existing relationships, and searching for aspects of self and world out of which new relationships might evolve. The process of exploring, making and testing provisional choices, and questing in new directions may go on throughout a transitional period.

To initiate is to make a *choice*, and the work of initiation is most clearly reflected in the choices we make. In the simplest case, a choice is a single act, such as selecting a scarf or an item on a menu. The most important life choices are more complex. We do not select a friend, spouse, occupation, religious or political outlook in a momentary, all-or-none way. Instead, we go through a much more extended thinking-feeling-exploring process. The initial choice is to enter into a relationship with an Other (person, group, entity of whatever kind). I start to make some investment of self in the relationship, often without a conscious sense of choosing. I count on some reciprocal response from the Other. The relationship evolves over time. The Other and I make many specific choices along the way: to end the relationship, to continue it as is, to modify it in one direction rather than another. The choice may be based to various degrees on our own preferences and on external opportunities/constraints. The process of choosing often has both conscious and unconscious aspects. I understand it in one way as it happens and in other ways at different times in the future. From a developmental point of view, the process of "getting married" ordinarily goes on for several months or years before and after the wedding. And it is one of many phases in an enduring relationship.

Every significant relationship is thus not a static entity but an evolving process in which both parties make a series of choices. Each choice must be seen within the broader temporal sequence, especially during a transitional period. Even when it is made with great enthusiasm, a choice made in a transitional period necessarily has a provisional quality that stems from the exploratory quality of a transition. Exploration requires tentativeness: if we are highly committed to one option, we are not free to explore others.

As a transition comes to an end, it is time to make more long-term choices, to give these choices meaning and commitment, and to start building a life structure around them. The choices mark the beginning of the next structure-building period. They are, in a sense, the major product of the transition. When all the efforts of the past several years are done—all the struggles to improve work or marriage, to explore alternative possibilities of living, to come more to terms with the self—we must decide, "This I will settle for," and start creating a life structure that will provide a vehicle for the next step in the journey.

Crises in Life Structure Development

Some transitions evolve fairly smoothly: we re-form the existing life structure without much overt disruption or conscious distress. The period is experienced as a time of relative stability or positive change in which the difficulties are readily manageable. A transition may go smoothly because the previous structure was quite satisfactory and needed only minor changes. In some cases, however, the life structure is unsatisfactory but the transition passes without much change because we are not ready (for various internal and external reasons) to acknowledge the flaws and to work at modifying them. The unacknowledged problems often surface in a later period, when they exact a heavier cost.

A *developmental crisis* occurs when a person is having great difficulty in meeting the tasks of the current period. Transitional periods are often times of moderate to severe crisis. The crisis is about being suspended in transit— caught between the ending of one life structure and the beginning of another, not knowing which way to turn. During a severe crisis we feel that we can move neither forward nor backward, that we are in imminent danger of the loss of a future. Crises may also occur in structure building-maintaining periods. A crisis at the start of such a period stems from severe problems in establishing an adequate structure. It occurs late in the period if the established structure becomes extremely difficult to sustain.

In *The Seasons of a Man's Life*, I introduced the concept of the Mid-life Transition and of the developmental crises that often occur within it. Since then, the term "mid-life crisis" has been widely used in the mass media as well as the academic literature, and is often attributed to me. Unfortunately, most writers use this term as a sort of catchall, without explicitly defining it or putting it in context. The most common view of it is that a mid-life crisis is an inappropriate or maladaptive response to a stressful event. These writers have in mind not a developmental crisis but an *adaptive crisis*—a problem in coping with a highly stressful situation such as combat, illness, or abuse. Such adaptive crises may occur anywhere in the "middle years." The age at which a crisis occurs depends primarily on the external event that triggers it. Age is of little import in this point of view, since it has no conception of the life cycle or of age-linked periods in adult development. A mid-life crisis is regarded as entirely negative and to be avoided. A woman is said to be undergoing a mid-life crisis when, for example, she responds to family problems or bodily signs of aging with "out of character" behavior such as getting divorced, having an affair, or "acting like an adolescent." The way to resolve the crisis is to gain some coping skills to reduce the level of stress, or to get treatment for the neurotic problems that interfere with successful adaptation.

A crisis in life structure development is qualitatively different from an adaptive crisis. They may go on concurrently but must be understood and managed differently. We cannot understand either without taking both into account. A stressful situation is more likely to produce an adaptive crisis if it occurs within a developmental period that is problematic in other ways. Likewise, the severity of a developmental crisis will be increased by a highly stressful event.

To determine whether a person is in a developmental crisis, and what it is about, we must look beyond the single stressful event and the emotional-behavioral adaptation to it. We must consider the person's life more broadly, identify the current period in life structure development, and assess the extent of difficulty she is having with the developmental tasks of that period—tasks of building and maintaining a life structure, or transitional tasks of termination, individuation, and initiation.

Developmental crises are influenced by specific external stresses and internal vulnerabilities, but they are not due solely to these factors. They have multiple sources in the difficulties of forming or transforming a life structure. The "causes" of a particular life change are more complex than any current theory recognizes; the outcome of a developmental period (especially a transitional one) cannot be predicted. Finally, a developmental crisis is not solely negative. It may have both benefits and costs. The potential costs involve anguish and pain for oneself, hurt to others, and a less satisfactory life structure. The potential benefits involve the formation of a life structure more suitable for the self and more viable in the world.

Gender Similarities and Differences

This alternating sequence of structure building-maintaining periods and transitional periods holds for both women and men. It thus provides a general framework of human development within which we can study the lives of individuals of all classes, cultures, and genders. Both genders go through the same periods of adult life structure development just as they go through the same periods of infancy and adolescence. These periods are part of human development and have common human characteristics. Nevertheless, they operate somewhat differently in females and males. Within the general framework of human life structure development, the genders differ greatly in life circumstances, in life course, in ways of going through each developmental period. Women form life structures different from those of men.

They work on the developmental tasks of every period with different re-sources and constraints, external as well as internal.

The developmental perspective must thus be combined with a gender perspective—a way of thinking about the meanings of gender and the place of women and men in the current epoch of human history. The gender perspective emerging from this study is presented in the next chapter.

3   The Significance of Gender in Women's Lives

While women's lives are obviously different in basic respects from those of men, I was surprised by the extent and power of the differences revealed by this study. It became essential to develop a theoretical perspective on the meanings of gender and the shaping influence of gender in the lives of women as well as men. My perspective on gender is grounded in the findings of the present research. It draws as well upon many sources: work on the history, anthropology, sociology, and psychology of gender; feminist studies; fiction by women; biographies of women; and the analysis of these from the vantage point of gender.

My central concept is gender splitting. This term refers not simply to gender differences but to a splitting asunder—the creation of a rigid division between male and female, masculine and feminine, in human life. Gender splitting has been pervasive in virtually every society we know about in the history of the human species, although there are wide variations in its patterning. What is regarded as "feminine" in contrast to "masculine" has varied among societies, classes, and historical periods, but the splitting is universal. To a much greater degree than is usually recognized, women and men have lived in different social worlds and have differed remarkably in their social roles, identities, and psychological attributes. The splitting operates at many levels: culture, social institutions, everyday social life, the individual psyche. It creates antithetical divisions between women and men, between social worlds, between the masculine and feminine within the self. It also creates inequalities that limit the adult development of women as well as men. I will focus on four basic forms of gender splitting:

(1)   The splitting of the domestic sphere and the public sphere as social domains for women and for men;

(2)   The Traditional Marriage Enterprise and the split it creates between the female homemaker and the male provisioner;

(3) The splitting of "women's work" and "men's work";

(4) The splitting of feminine and masculine in the individual psyche.

When gender splitting operates most strongly, women are likely to live primarily as homemakers in a Traditional Marriage Enterprise, to center their lives in the domestic sphere, to engage solely in women's work, and to accept and value in themselves and other women only those qualities identified as "feminine." At the same time, women are likely to be subordinated and marginal in the public world, to be limited provisioners and authorities in the family, to have difficulty engaging in "men's" work, and to experience as alien those personal qualities identified as "masculine."

The division between the domestic sphere and the public sphere is of fundamental importance for women's (and men's) development. The public sphere includes the economy, government, and other nonfamilial institutions of every society. Since occupations comprise the bulk of this domain, I shall refer to it also as the occupational sphere. Men's lives have traditionally been centered in the public sphere, which is their territory and under their control. Women have participated in this sphere as well, but largely on marginal, subordinated, segregated terms.

The domestic sphere consists of a household and its surrounding familial-social world. In our society, its primary unit has traditionally been the nuclear family—parents and their offspring. This century has seen an increase in the number of single-parent (mother) headed households. The nuclear family may also be closely connected with its extended family (grandparents, uncles, aunts, cousins, others) as part of a single household or an integrated social network. In virtually all societies, for countless generations, women's lives have been centered in the domestic sphere. It has been the key source of their identity, meaningful activity, and satisfaction, as well as dissatisfaction.

The Traditional Marriage Enterprise

The women in the homemaker sample led predominantly traditional, family-centered lives. The beginnings of their family life were in the marriage and the kind of life the two partners envisaged as they entered the state of matrimony. We usually think that marriage is mainly a matter of the emotional relationship between the partners. In fact, marriage is never simply about being in love. It often takes place when one or both partners are not in love. It often does not take place even when two persons are in love. A marriage is, first of all, about building an enterprise in which the partners can have a good life, according to their lights. The marital relationship can best be understood within the context of this enterprise. The concept of the "marriage enterprise" is one of the major fruits of this research.

Among the homemakers, the primary aim of matrimony was to build and maintain what I call a Traditional Marriage Enterprise. Its goal is to have children, to create a certain kind of family life, and to continue (with some improvements) the basic traditions of the family of origin. There is a well-defined division of labor between the partners. The woman/wife/mother serves primarily as homemaker, caring for the young and centering her life predominantly in the nuclear (and, when possible, extended) family. The man/husband/father, in contrast, serves as provisioner, devoting himself mainly to outside work and bringing back the resources needed to sustain the family. Men generally feel responsible for their families and want to be caring fathers and husbands, but they do so by involving themselves much more strongly in the work world than in the family.

The splitting of homemaker and provisioner stems from, and helps to sustain, the pervasive gender splitting in human life generally. It is essential to bear in mind that homemaking and provisioning are not simply roles within the family. They are, more broadly, ways of living that involve family, occupation, and many other social contexts, as we shall see.

Along with the division of labor goes a division of authority. In the Traditional Marriage Enterprise, the man is "head of the household" and ultimate source of authority within the family. He delegates responsibility for most domestic work to his wife, but she has little authority in her own right and little sense of inner authority, especially in relation to males. Likewise, men occupy the dominant positions and exercise primary authority in the major institutions of the public sphere. Patriarchy—the rule of the father—has been a universal theme (with many variations in pattern and degree) in most human societies.

The Traditional Marriage Enterprise thus involves a certain kind of partnership between female homemaker and male provisioner. They do very different kinds of work, on unequal terms, but between them they manage what is needed to form and sustain a family. The enterprise serves to contain and integrate the gender splitting that it initially helped to produce. The woman in this enterprise leads a highly domestic life. She has primary responsibility for housekeeping, family life, the care of children and husband. She may also link family to outside world through various boundary activities such as furthering her husband's career, working on a family farm or business, connecting the family to religious and educational institutions and to the local community. These activities take her outside the domestic sphere, where they connect her mainly to other women and children.

The basic principle of the Traditional Marriage Enterprise, and of the surrounding culture, is that women are homemakers, not provisioners—and that men are the opposite. When women enter the public work world (something they have done in all societies), this principle strongly shapes and limits their engagement in it. Girls traditionally are raised not to make a strong investment of self in a future occupation or career, and women are discouraged from full participation in the occupational system. When a woman takes a job, she generally engages in "women's work" that is relatively separate from and subordinate to the work of men. Her public life thus tends to have the same character as her domestic life—providing services, caring for others, fostering group integration and survival. It is often still a source of tension in the workplace when a woman has a position of authority over men, and a source of tension in the marriage when she is perceived as more successful or more powerful than her husband.

What is the meaning of the domestic world for its members? What part does it play in the lives of women and men? It is, in the most fundamental sense, a home base, a center for one's life. Outside is the public work world, with its heavy demands to meet external standards of performance, to enact more narrowly defined roles, to achieve success and avoid failure. The domestic world provides other satisfactions and stresses. It is the place that is most truly one's own: we build it for ourselves and for those with whom we are most closely connected; and in it we can be most fully ourselves. Ideally, it is the place where we rest, play, love, receive nourishment of many kinds, enjoy privacy and leisure, have strong affectional relationships with family and friends. In everyday language, we "work" outside and "live" at home.

But the domestic world also has its bleaker, more onerous, and often painful side. We experience the burdens (not solely the pleasures) of raising children. In it we suffer our own illnesses and despairs, as well as the illness and even death of spouse, children, and other close ones. Most women are faced with endless household and child care responsibilities in addition to outside work. The meaning of domestic life—the suffering as well as the satisfaction we derive from it—comes largely from giving and receiving care.

"Taking Care" Within the Traditional Marriage Enterprise

"Taking care" is a root issue in life generally, and especially in the domestic world. When a man and woman marry, they are agreeing to take care of each other, of their children, and of their domestic enterprise.

"Taking care" has three meanings: giving care to others (being a caregiver), receiving care from others (being taken care of), and taking care of oneself. All three are of great significance for our understanding of the Traditional Marriage Enterprise. Under conditions of marked gender splitting, the three ways of taking care operate differently for men and women.

In the Traditional Marriage Enterprise, a traditional man takes care of his family primarily by being a provisioner and head of household. He is required to work hard at earning a livelihood and establishing the family's place in the community. In order to take care of them, he must learn first of all to take care of himself: to be a hero within his domain—an independent, responsible, self-reliant adult who perseveres in his occupational struggles no matter how great the hardships. These qualities, so essential for his work life, markedly shape the kinds of care he gives and receives in his domestic life.

Within the family, a man is most likely to give care in ways that reflect the values of the work world: providing material benefits, managing money, maintaining discipline and order, being most involved with his sons in activities (such as sports, recreation, and other forms of male fellowship) that directly or indirectly prepare them for the adult occupational world. It is harder for him to give care in ways traditionally defined as feminine: being tender, showing his own grief and sharing openly in the grief of others, giving compassion rather than solving problems.

The kinds of care a traditional man can most readily receive from his wife reflect his images of the homemaker. He can appreciate her efforts to provide for his rest, nourishment, and comfort, to keep the household orderly and attractive, to share certain leisure activities and to allow him other activities that he prefers to do with men. He feels cared for when she inspires and supports his heroic occupational quest. She does this by admiring his intellectual and physical prowess, enjoying his successes, finding him a valued source of knowledge and authority, by being a supportive player but not a hero in her own right.

It is much harder for him to request and receive other kinds of care from her; for example, to talk about his experience of serious failure, disappointment, anguish, and confusion, and to ask directly for her understanding and concern. He finds it difficult to acknowledge these experiences to her—as well as to himself—because they involve a feeling on his part that he is failing in his deepest commitment as a man. Sharing such experiences is often difficult for her, too. To the extent that she participates in the homemaker-provisioner split, a wife has a tremendous stake in her husband's occupational success. Having limited her own involvement in the outside work world, she is almost totally dependent on him to provide for her and the family.

In short, it is urgently important to both partners in this enterprise that the man be a good provisioner, according to their standards. When his adequacy is in question, or when he fails in major ways, both of them often find it hard to share the experience and to engage in mutual caring about the painful feelings involved. For the wife this difficulty is compounded by the fact that, given the domestic-public split, she generally knows little about her husband's work world and finds it alien. The division that has served them well in many respects becomes an obstacle to empathic intimacy. Likewise, a man can take care of his wife in many specific ways, such as providing material support, helping with certain chores, participating in family events, appreciating her qualities as wife and mother. It is more difficult to involve himself in the intricacies of the domestic world and its meanings for her. The splitting of the domestic and occupational worlds thus produces a deep division in the marriage. Trying to bridge this division, and dealing with the consequences of not sufficiently bridging it, are basic tasks for every couple.

How is it, then, for women? Giving care, receiving care, and taking care of oneself are also important for them, but the forms have traditionally been different. For girls and young women, the primary emphasis is usually on giving direct care to others in the domestic world. Homemaking is, above all, about giving care: nurturing her children and husband; being chiefly responsible for the household; being a good daughter to parents and in-laws; maintaining ties with her own and her husband's extended families; being helpful to friends and a wider social network; dealing with crises stemming from illness, death, change in family fortunes, geographical moves, aging parents—ultimately, assuring the survival of the family. A woman's domestic caregiving usually takes the form of a service that directly meets another's needs: preparing and serving meals, child care, shopping for provisions, cleaning the house, comforting those in distress, nursing the ill, mediating family disputes.

A mother who gives care also receives care in exchange. She may receive care in at least three ways. Mothers vary widely in the degree to which they seek and obtain these forms of care-income.

First, a mother may receive important satisfactions directly from the bonding with her infant. She may experience great pleasure in breast-feeding and cuddling the baby. The infant's responsiveness to her may give her intense feelings that she herself is being cared for and appreciated. Her ability to meet the child's needs may give her a sense of great well-being as an effective, competent mother.

Second, in mothering her child she has an opportunity to re-mother herself—to give herself the love and care she wanted but did not receive sufficiently from her own mother. In her subjective experience, she is both the good mother caring well for her child and, simultaneously, the good child receiving the care she needs and deserves. The basic reality is the mother-child relationship. The mother often experiences this relationship from the child's vantage point as well as her own and imagines that the child is feeling what she feels in herself. The re-mothering possibilities are especially important for a woman who becomes a mother in adolescence or in the Early Adult Transition. Still very much involved in the relationship she had as a child with her own mother, she is likely to identify with her own infant and to feel symbolically that she is receiving care as well as giving it. However, such reliving and reworking of one's early mothering may occur at any age.

Third, a woman may receive care from her husband. While taking care of husband and children within the domestic world, she counts on him to take care of her and the children. He provides for her through his income, his position in society, his ties to other groups and institutions. He provides in a more personal way through his relationship with her and his participation in family life.

From one point of view, we can say that the traditional system requires her to give care in order to receive care. That is, she gives care to family and household as a means of receiving care from husband. But the opposite is also true: the traditional system requires her to receive his care — to stay home and be taken care of by him — so that she will devote herself to giving care as a homemaker. The traditional system attempts to engender in her the "feminine" qualities that make it highly gratifying to give and receive care in the home and, at the same time, that make it less gratifying to get strongly involved in the outside world.

A woman who freely chooses to participate in the Traditional Marriage Enterprise receives many benefits, such as comfort, security, the satisfactions afforded from being a "good wife and mother," but there are also great costs. She is an appendage to her husband, dependent on his care — be it beneficent, indifferent, or tyrannical — and subordinate to him within the home and in the larger scheme of things. She takes care of many others yet does not experience herself as a fully independent person who can take care of herself in the world. It feels dangerous to develop too strong a sense of self and too much interest in taking care of herself. If she did, she might then seek to enter the public occupational sphere and become a provisioner without a husband or on equal terms with a husband. To prevent this kind of independence, the traditional "good girl" generally lives in her father's home until she moves into her husband's home to embark on a domestic career. Indeed, her adaptation in this system is best served by accepting her place in it — not asking too many questions, not exploring alternative options, and not pursuing goals that would enable her to grow up as an independent woman. The homemakers studied here represent various forms of this self and mode of living.

The Gender Revolution

Since the onset of the Industrial Revolution about two hundred years ago, the human species has begun a major new step in its social evolution. Modern nations have grown astronomically in size and complexity. There has been a fantastic growth of institutions governing industry, finance, politics, education, science, technology, health, the arts and humanities. Many countries have moved from "pre-industrial" to "industrial" to "post-industrial" conditions. Some have moved farther than others, but the process of modernization is widespread.

One aspect of this historical process is the gender revolution: a transformation in the meanings of gender, the place of women and men in society, and the relationships between women and men in all aspects of life. The change is not the work of a single group or movement. It is both an effect and a cause of the social evolution of the human species. At the heart of the gender revolution is a reduction in the gender splitting and a modification of the Traditional Marriage Enterprise. It is not possible to maintain fully the old division of labor between female homemaker and male provisioner. Women can no longer count on having a permanent marriage and a life of domesticity. They are being impelled, by powerful social forces as well as inner motivations, into the public occupational world. And men are, much more slowly, becoming involved in family life and accepting the entry of women into all sectors of the occupational system.

Many social changes are reducing women's involvement in the family and increasing their involvement in outside work.

(1) *Human longevity has risen sharply.* In previous times very few members of any society lived beyond age 40. For the survival of the species this brief life expectancy was sufficient, perhaps optimal. Nature had provided a peak life season in early adulthood when people could meet their essential species requirements: they begot and raised enough children to produce a new generation of adults; they contributed to the society through productive work and maintenance of the community; and most of them died when their productive capacities diminished. Early adulthood was the crucial era in the life cycle. Only a small cohort of persons over 40 was needed for more specialized responsibilities requiring greater leadership and wisdom. Most adults over 40 would be impaired by illness, accident, and bodily decline; they would consume more than they produced and would thus be a drain on communal resources. Their early demise was thus a species requirement. The generation in early adulthood simply could not produce enough for itself and the children, if it had also to provide for middle-aged and older generations of any size.

We are now reaching the point where society must have a larger labor force in early and middle adulthood (roughly age 17–65) doing the productive work required to support themselves as well as the younger and older generations. We have not yet created effective, equitable arrangements for achieving this. Indeed, we have hardly begun to acknowledge the problems and to develop sound programs of social security, health care, retirement, and the like. The generation in this era bears a major responsibility for the survival and welfare of the species. The "aging" of the population increases the pressure on women in early and middle adulthood to be employed in outside work.

(2) *The demand for women's work in the family is decreasing.* The increase in life expectancy produces a decrease in the need for a high birth rate and in large family size. With the availability of birth control, the great majority of American women have their last child by the late twenties to early thirties. This decreases the intensity and duration of their primary involvement in a domestic career. It also makes them more available for work outside the home.

(3) *The incidence of divorce has grown.* A young woman can no longer take it for granted that she will enter a permanent state of matrimony and will have a permanent male provisioner. She needs some job skills so that she can "take care of herself" if she remains single or marries badly. The increasing divorce rate has propelled many women into the labor force. Many divorced women work both out of financial need and with the hope that occupation may provide a sustaining major component in their lives.

Today, homemaking is no longer a permanent, full-time occupation for most women. The domestic career occupies fewer years than before and is less demanding. Most young women live with the awareness that they may have to become the primary provisioner for themselves and their children. Those who don't actively want such work are often under great financial and social pressure to seek it.

The specific factors leading any individual woman to work are varied. They may involve external circumstances, such as her husband's low income or unemployment, being single, separated, divorced, or widowed, and emergencies of various kinds. They may also involve inner wishes and values regarding independence, ambition, personal growth, living on terms of greater equality with men, moving beyond the confines of a purely domestic life. Although individual situations and choices are extremely varied, the broad historical trend is clear: society is evolving to the stage where it cannot allow women to remain full-time homemakers. And, for the individual woman, full-time homemaking is becoming both less feasible and less attractive as a way of life: it does not offer lifelong tenure; it is less required by the dominant cultural values; and there is growing opportunity as well as demand for outside involvement. Women are increasingly impelled out of the family and into the occupational system. The character of both the family and the world is thus changing in fundamental ways.

Jobs, Occupations, and Careers for Women

More than 50 percent of all American women are now in the labor force—part-time or full-time, paid or volunteer, continuously or sporadically—and the figure is rising. Will women be employed? is no longer the question. The key question now is: What kinds of outside work will women do, under what conditions, with what benefits and burdens for themselves and others? It is useful to distinguish three categories of nondomestic work:

(1) *Unskilled or semiskilled jobs.* Most women have been employed in jobs, such as typing, clerical, sales, services, that involve little occupational training and identity and offer no long-term career path. These jobs generally demand little and give little in return. They provide limited pay, benefits, security, status, or prospects for advancement. They are explicitly or implicitly regarded as "women's work" and given solely or primarily to women. This practice creates segregated, all-female enclaves which exist as separate castes within a work organization. Women and men rarely work together on an equal footing. A woman's place in this system— working under a male authority, doing specific chores, providing services to those who need them—is much like her place in the traditional family. The economy needs to fill large numbers of such jobs.

This kind of work life is feasible for women who have a great personal investment in the family and a minimal investment in outside work. They can move more freely in and out of the labor force, with few problems of occupational training and long-term career management. Despite its limitations, this work increases somewhat the potential for gender equality. Women are moved toward greater independence and assertiveness when they earn money of their own, demonstrate competence in public, have public evidence of existing separately from their husbands, and participate in a nondomestic world that offers even minimal possibilities for advancement.

(2) The traditionally "female occupations" such as teaching, nursing, and social work are those in which roughly 70 percent or more of the members are women. They generally require more education and skill than the jobs above, and they provide a more clear-cut occupational identity. These occupations are predominantly in the fields of health, education, welfare, and culture, rather than in the production economy and the management of major institutions. They have to do with raising the young, caring for the sick, helping the poor, supporting the arts, teaching the young and the disadvantaged, providing services of many kinds. The kind of work they require has much in common with women's traditional homemaking work. The female occupations ordinarily require more education and

commitment than the less skilled jobs, and in these respects pull a woman more away from her domestic life. Still, they are often flexible enough in the demands they make on her time and energy that she can be employed to varying degrees while making her primary investment in family.

The entry and advancement of women in the traditionally female occupations are not a major source of social conflict and gender tension. The creation of "genderized" occupations helps to keep women segregated and subordinated. A high position in one of these occupations seldom represents a high position in the larger occupational world. Even when the female occupations become more professionalized, they tend not to be equal in authority or remuneration to the comparable occupations held by males. Women can attain prominent positions within nursing or social work, for example, but the health care system as a whole is usually headed by men. A woman can advance to a position of considerable authority in an organization where most of her subordinates are women; for example, director of nursing, principal of a school. But it is still rare for a woman to have a senior management position in which most of her immediate subordinates are men. Even in systems staffed largely by women, such as public education, the more authoritative positions of management and policy making are held largely by men.

Almost all of the women in the homemaker sample had outside jobs, regularly or sporadically. Most of the jobs were in category one above, the rest in category two. The women in the career samples, in contrast, were predominantly in, or moving toward, the third category.

(3)   The higher-status occupations, such as the professions, business, and management of work organizations generally, are regarded as "men's work" and inhabited chiefly by men. The issue of authority is crucial here. Women had virtually no access to these occupations prior to this century. In the United States, the first large-scale effort to reduce the barriers against women's entry and advancement in them began only in the 1970s. The process of change began a little earlier in some other countries, but the extent and depth of change are still quite limited everywhere. Small numbers of women currently hold professional positions in business, government, and other work organizations. For these women, however, advancement is often limited: they are concentrated in low- or middle-management levels, in staff positions without line authority, or in more consultative, free-lance work that provides greater freedom but less security and opportunity for advancement.

Over the past decades women have begun to enter elite occupations in more than token numbers, to have long-term careers, and to achieve positions of institutional authority. These are the kinds of work, and the conditions of work, that cause the rub. The entry of women into these occupations is much more problematic for work organizations, for the family, and for individual women and men than is their employment in semiskilled jobs or in traditionally female occupations. It violates the traditional division of labor between the genders: women are doing "men's work," very different from that of homemaking and caretaking. It undermines the segregation of women and men in the work world and "degenderizes" many aspects of life. It also violates the traditional division of authority between the genders: women are moving out of subordinate positions and engaging in the fuller exercise of authority—even over men who have considerable authority in their own right. Women's growing engagement in such work contributes to, and stems from, significant change in the Traditional Marriage Enterprise. It generates for many women a personal investment in career that may equal or outweigh their investment in family, and combining the two is extremely difficult. The career sample studied here exemplifies the diverse ways in which individual lives evolve within this context.

The Internal Traditional Homemaker Figure and the Internal Anti-Traditional Figure

I have identified the internal Traditional Homemaker Figure as one basic image of woman. It is reflected in the culture, the family, the occupational and other social institutions, and the psyches of individual women and men. Within the psyche this image exists as an internal figure, a self that may evolve in various ways. In the homemaker sample this figure often became the basis for the woman's conscious, valued self—the person she strove to become. Among the career women, too, the internal image of the Traditional Homemaker Figure played an important part, but she was opposed to another, antithetical internal image that I call the Anti-Traditional Figure. Subsequent chapters will document the place of these two internal figures in the lives of our subjects. For now I want simply to introduce them in three brief examples.

Virginia Woolf's Angel and Creative Writer

The English novelist and essayist Virginia Woolf was born in 1882, a product of nineteenth-century Victorian society and of the forces that transformed it early in the twentieth century. The Victorian form of the homemaker played a powerful part in Woolf's development as girl and woman, even as she struggled against it. She gave an eloquent account of this struggle in a lecture entitled "Professions for Women," given in 1931 as she was turning 49. It was a time when professional careers were becoming more available to women—not in large numbers, but larger than ever before and, as it seemed, ever-growing. Woolf was at the peak of her career after years of great struggle. She wanted to tell a group of younger professional women about the "inner phantoms" she had confronted in becoming a writer. Her name for the phantom most inimical to her literary dream was "The Angel in the House," the Victorian version of the Traditional Homemaker Figure:

> I discovered that if I were going to review books I should need to do battle with a certain phantom. And the phantom was a woman . . . I called her after the heroine of a famous poem, "The Angel in the House" . . . You who come of a younger and happier generation may not have heard of her . . . I will describe her . . . She was intensely sympathetic. She was immensely charming. She was utterly unselfish. She excelled in the difficult arts of family life. She sacrificed herself daily. If there was a chicken, she took the leg; if there was a draught she sat in it—in short she was so constituted that she never had a mind or a wish of her own, but preferred to sympathize always with the minds and wishes of others. Above all—I need not say it—she was pure. Her purity was supposed to be her chief beauty—her blushes, her great grace. In those days—the last of Queen Victoria—every house had its Angel. And when I came to write I encountered her with the very first words. The shadow of her wings fell on my page; I heard the rustling of her skirts in the room . . . She slipped behind me and whispered: "My dear, you are a young woman. You are writing about a book that has been written by a man. Be sympathetic; be tender; flatter; deceive; use all the arts and wiles of our sex. Never let anybody guess that you have a mind of your own. Above all, be pure." And she made as if to guide my pen. I now record the one act for which I take some credit to myself, though the credit rightly belongs to some excellent ancestors of mine who left me a certain sum of money—shall we say five hundred pounds a year?—so that it was not necessary for me to depend solely on charm for my living. I turned upon her and caught her by the throat. I did my best to kill her. My excuse, if I were to be had up in a court of law, would be that I acted in self-defense. Had I not killed her she would have killed me. She would have plucked the heart out of my writing. For, as I found, directly I put pen to paper, you cannot review even a novel without having a mind of your own, without expressing what you think to be the truth about human relations, morality, sex. And all these questions, according to the Angel in the House, cannot be dealt with freely and openly by women; they must charm, they must conciliate, they must—to put it bluntly—tell lies if they are to succeed. Thus, whenever I felt the shadow of her wing or the radiance of her halo upon my page, I took up the inkpot and flung it at her. She died hard. Her fictitious nature was of great assistance to her. It is far harder to kill a phantom than

a reality. She was always creeping back when I thought I had despatched her. Though I flatter myself that I killed her in the end, the struggle was severe; it took much time that had better have been spent learning Greek grammar; or in roaming the world in search of adventures. But it was a real experience; it was an experience that was bound to befall all women writers at that time. Killing the Angel in the House was part of the occupation of a woman writer . . .

Outwardly, what is simpler than to write books? Outwardly, what obstacles are there for a woman rather than a man? Inwardly, I think, the case is very different; she has still many ghosts to fight, many prejudices to overcome. Indeed it will be a long time still, I think, before a woman can sit down to write a book without finding a phantom to be slain, a rock to be dashed against. And if this is so in literature, the freest of all professions for women, how is it in the new professions which you are now for the first time entering?

Woolf's Angel is the Traditional Homemaker Figure as it existed in her historical period, class, and personal experience. For her, the internal figure of the Angel was locked in mortal combat with the internal figure of the Writer. Her inner Writer is a version of the Anti-Traditional Figure. Much of the drama in the following chapters derives from the struggle between these two figures: in the minds of individual women and men, in the family, in our culture and social institutions.

Virginia Woolf voiced the hope that the next generation of women would no longer be burdened by the Angel—that they would be free to have minds of their own, to know who they are as women and as persons, to participate in all domains of human life. That hope has been rekindled in every generation since hers. The Angel is, however, still alive and healthy.

For Virginia Woolf, the Angel was an internal phantom with which she had to struggle in search of a fuller life. For many other women, she is a valued ideal. Here is a contemporary homemaker who attempts to live in accord with her own version of the Angel.

A Modern Angel

Kay Ryan is a 43-year-old member of the homemaker sample. Her husband, of working-class origins, is now an executive in a medium-sized company. Despite some grievances she is generally satisfied with her 21-year marriage and life:

My parents divorced when I was 7. Life was hard for my mother and me after my father left. She had to work, and I'd be home alone, and we didn't have any money. She had all the responsibilities and worries that go with running a whole household by yourself. I knew what she wanted most was to be married and to be home with me. I learned from her predicament that a man needs to support the family and it's the woman's duty to do whatever is required to make the marriage work.

I never wanted to work. I went to college and expected to be married when I graduated . . . I wanted to stay home and take care of the house and raise the babies, and that's what I did. Oh, it was a lonely life. My husband traveled a lot on business and was never home, but he had to earn the living. I never wished I was out in the work world working, and he certainly didn't want to stay home and raise the kids.

I would rank my marriage as the center of my life. I have this image of men as being stronger and more capable than women. I always looked at my husband as being able to do anything and able to take care of me and the kids no matter what. I never doubted; I knew he would take care of us and we'd be all right.

When women work and have to run a house, too, it's very difficult. Magazine articles say that men still don't do half of the housework when the women are working. All these liberated women and their liberated husbands, wherever they are—the women still get stuck with two jobs, work and home.

I never was a woman's libber. I really think women have given up so much in order to gain such a little bit. I've always looked at men that it's their duty to take care of us women and children. That's their role: breadwinner. I expect a man to be the authority. I would never vote for a woman President. Luckily my husband's not a hard taskmaster, so I don't have a hard boss.

I asked him a few years ago if he wanted me to work. He said no, he wants me home. He likes to have me do his errands and pick up his dry cleaning. He's not domesticated at all. He wouldn't want to share the housework.

My husband's the disciplinarian, even though he wasn't around a lot while the kids were growing up. Our oldest son tells people that he really feels his mother raised him because his father was never home. I don't feel quite that way; they always knew that if they did something wrong their father would be back, and he would punish them.

My sons never help around the house—that's the woman's duty. My mother said my boys are going to have a shock when they get married because their wives will be liberated and will expect them to do housework. I say that's going to be their *wives'* problem.

I think that women have lost a definite advantage by giving up the double standard. Years ago it was very simple: a girl just said no, and that was what she was supposed to do; even the boys thought she was supposed to say no. Now they don't think that anymore; they think everybody is supposed to put out. All they want to do is go to bed. They sometimes don't even want to buy the girl dinner first. They are missing the chance to fall in love and get married. It seems a shame. I believe in the double standard. It's up to the girl to just say no to sex before marriage, and it's her fault if she doesn't. I know my boys are gonna take it if they can get it—how do those girls ever expect to get married? That old saying is true: Why buy the cow when you can get the milk for free?

The Single Successful Career Woman

Woolf's internal Angel, as we have seen, was the enemy of her internal Writer. For the Angel, it was unfeminine and potentially dangerous for a woman to become a serious writer—to have a mind of her own and to become a competitor and critic of men. Another aspect of the Angel theme is provided by Rachel Nash, from our faculty sample. Rachel's Angel carried the argument much farther. She gave a terrifying account of what would happen to a woman if she chose a career. Professional success, she made clear, could be gained only at the expense of marriage and motherhood. She conjured up an "appalling image" of the Single Successful Career Woman whose career success resulted in an empty, solitary life without a home or family. This internal figure is a weapon commonly used by the internal Traditional Homemaker Figure to combat the ambitions of the internal Anti-Traditional Figure.

At 26 Rachel had a husband, a 2-year-old child, and a new Ph.D. degree. She formed an Entry Life Structure as combined homemaker and faculty member. When interviewed at 43, she was a full professor and had just initiated a marital separation. She was becoming aware that, despite her strenuous efforts and relative success in pursuing a career, she had given first priority to homemaking and had placed major limitations on her career aspirations. In trying to decide how she would live in her next "growing up," she was engaged in a renewed struggle against the internal figure of the Single Successful Career Woman:

> Recently I had a major moment where the scales fell off my eyes—a revelation. One thing came back to me that I had completely forgotten, an article on "women's fear of success." When I first read it I rejected the idea. I didn't see it in my students and certainly not in myself. But in the last few weeks, in the midst of my marital crisis, psychotherapy, and self-examination, I realized that a fear of success was a big part of my reason for marrying and having kids.
>
> What I was really afraid of was the picture that my mother—and, I guess, society—painted of a single successful woman. It was somehow so threatening to me that I couldn't face it. I can still see it very vividly. It's a successful woman who goes home and cries at night because she has no

friends and no family, nothing, the bitter pinnacle of success. If I had remained single and pursued a career, I would have had to face that image. Even worse, my mother would have continually harped on that image—told me what a tragedy it would be and what a horrible life it would be and what I failure *I* would be. That picture was really what I was afraid of. I wanted to be sure I escaped that forever.

I had no image of a successful single woman who had happily made her career the center of her life. My image was that she had to be cold-hearted, she had to be grasping, she had to be cruel, she had to be embittered, frustrated, wishing she had done anything just to be sitting by the fireside knitting in the evening with children. The fear of success isn't the fear of succeeding per se but the fear of what consequences it would have. Success would bring total personal disaster. I had no way of imagining a person having a personally satisfactory life and being successful.

I never met any woman who made that choice and had a satisfactory life. The only single career woman I ever knew was an acquaintance of my parents. Once a year it was explained to us children that Poor Maggie is coming to dinner. We all felt sorry for her. We were so gracious to let her come and be a part of our happy family [laughs] for one evening a year.

My high school science teacher had a career and family. I felt she was marvelous. I asked her how she did it. She said, "By just not doing anything very well; I'm not as good a mother as I'd like to be, I'm not as good a teacher as I'd like to be, but it works out all right." I thought that sounded like a very good compromise. That was what I would do. I would be sort of a half-baked mother and a half-baked teacher and in a sort of cheery way I'd muddle through. That was the image I had for myself.

I knew that marriage alone wasn't enough to guarantee that compromise. It takes children. When you have children there is no way that you are ever going to have to be up there competing, succeeding, trying to carve out this kind of life that is so threatening to me. It took me out of the running in a certain sense. When you have kids, you've got a career handicap. It's a handicap that I was more than happy to have: I wanted it because I really wanted the kids and also because I really wanted a handicap. Then, any work I did was just pure extra in a certain sense. I wasn't a threat to anybody else and I wasn't a threat to *myself.*

I'm a full professor here. The kind of work I'm doing is successful at a certain level and very satisfying. But to be, say, at Harvard or Yale would involve a whole different order of demands that would be much harder to manage with a family. The choice to have children was not just a choice to have children, but also to avoid a certain career path that I found very threatening. If I had chosen to pursue a higher level of success the demands on me would have meant a real conflict in the family. To put my career first would have meant organizing my family life in a way that was foreign to me, or else not having a personal life. The image of the appalling single successful woman is so terrifying to me that I really couldn't face that. When I close my eyes I still see that image: this lonely, bitter person, isolated, a complete failure.

Moving Beyond the Traditional Marriage Enterprise

The splitting of female homemaker and male provisioner no longer provides an adequate long-term basis for a marriage enterprise, but no clear alternative has yet been established. All of us are finding our own way. Both marital partners face difficult questions: What is the nature of our enterprise? What part does each of us play in it? What is its place in each of our lives? What are the sufficient reasons for maintaining it or for ending it? How can we best modify it as we move from one season of life to another? Likewise, the occupational enterprise is changing. Women are entering new parts of the work world, but the terms of their participation are still often uncertain. Women who wish to live primarily as traditional homemakers face certain dilemmas; those who seek a new path face others.

The homemakers in this study entered adulthood with the hope of forming a Traditional Marriage Enterprise. They were prepared to work outside the home if necessary; however, for most, an outside job was a burden to be avoided when the husband was a good enough breadwinner. For others, an outside job held some attractions but had a clearly lower priority than homemaking. For all, there was something foreign about entering the wider occupational world and making a major investment of self in career. In their own worst-case scenario—being divorced, widowed, or never married—they would of necessity enter the labor market but with minimal expectations of doing satisfying, meaningful work.

The career women in business and academe took a different path. Like the homemakers, they formed an internal image of the Traditional Homemaker Figure. Like Virginia Woolf, however, they also formed a strong internal image of the Anti-Traditional Figure. This figure stood in direct conflict with the Traditional Homemaker Figure and insisted: "Become more independent, seek more in life than domesticity, acquire occupational skills, defer having a family until you establish yourself as a responsible, competent adult, able to take care of yourself, especially financially." Each career woman heard from within herself the voice of the Traditional Homemaker Figure and the voice of the Anti-Traditional Figure. She wanted greater freedom of choice yet found herself deeply rooted in the traditional pattern by virtue of her own personality development as well as the shaping influences of our social institutions. Numerous voices and social pressures from the external world pulled her in different directions but offered no clear-cut resolution of the conflict.

Every career woman asked herself: Is it possible to liberate myself from the narrow constraints of the traditional pattern? Can I participate in family life without being a traditional homemaker? Can I participate in the male work world with inner commitment and equality? How can I have a long-term occupational career without jeopardizing my femininity and my involvement in family? The homemakers had their own versions of these questions. The questions took different forms and received different answers in the successive developmental periods of early adulthood. We have as yet little accrued cultural wisdom that gives generally satisfactory answers to these questions or even guidelines to thinking about them. Women who try to build new careers, new marriage enterprises, and new life structures are pioneers in a new phase of human history. This book depicts the efforts of diverse women to deal with these questions in the course of their adult development. It does not offer answers but will, I hope, provide a deeper understanding of the issues. Chapters 4 through 9 present the lives of the homemakers as they traverse the developmental periods from ages 17 to 45. Chapters 10 through 15 give the corresponding picture for the career women. In every period I will examine women's lives from the combined perspectives of adult development and gender.

II *The Homemaker Sample*

4 Adolescent Life Structure: Homemakers

We begin now a series of chapters that carry the homemakers through the successive developmental periods of early adulthood. The first of these periods is the Early Adult Transition, which forms a bridge between childhood and early adulthood and is part of both. It follows the Adolescent Life Structure which, extending from 13 or 14 to 17 or 18, is the last period that falls entirely within childhood. The Adolescent Life Structure provides a base from which we begin the shift into adulthood, and terminating it is a major developmental task of the Early Adult Transition. I'll begin with a consideration of the Adolescent Life Structure and the familial-social context in which it is embedded.

Adolescent Life Structure

For the homemakers, the period of the Adolescent Life Structure typically extended through the high school years, occasionally a year longer. In every case it ended at 17 or 18. During this time all fifteen homemakers lived in the parental home and went to a public high school. The central components of their lives were the family, the high school, and the adolescent peer world. As graduation from high school approached, they began to think more seriously about leaving the parental home and beginning an "adult" life.

The homemaker sample represented a variety of social backgrounds and early life circumstances. Six women were Catholic, six Protestant, one mixed Catholic-Protestant, and two Jewish, and within each faith differed widely in religious views and involvement. Thirteen were white and two African-American. One woman had eleven years of education, four completed high school, five had vocational training, and five completed a four-year college degree right after high school. Although all of them lived in the New Haven area at the time they were interviewed, their regional origins were diverse:

five were born and raised in Connecticut; the other ten grew up elsewhere in the country, and moved to New Haven between the ages of 16 and 31.

There was variety as well in the socio-economic status of the family of origin:

(1)   Three women—*Emily Swift, Wendy Lewis, Claire Berman*—had college-educated parents who led relatively comfortable, middle-class lives. The family took it for granted that the girls would go to college, marry men of similar or better circumstances, and become homemakers in a Traditional Marriage Enterprise—as they did.

(2)   Six women—*Jenny Abatello, Elaine Olson, Beth Logan, Sara Cushing, Kay Ryan, Nan Krummel*—came from stable working-class or lower-middle-class homes. Their fathers' occupations included skilled factory worker, credit manager, schoolteacher. Fathers and mothers had twelve years or fewer of education, except for two who completed college. Four of these women got vocational training (as R.N., secretary, technician), and two went to college. All were preparing for adult lives as homemakers.

(3)   Six women—*Nora Cole, Carol O'Brien, Ruth Allen, Angela Capelli, Lynn McPhail, Vicky Perrelli*—grew up in conditions of poverty and hardship. Their fathers' occupations included hospital cook, handyman, local truck driver, mine worker. Their mothers were homemakers who often held full-time, unskilled jobs. Four of these women had no education after high school; Vicky Perrelli and Nora Cole got vocational training that enabled them to improve their lives. All six married by age 20 and quickly started a family. Five of the husbands had very limited occupational skills and inner psychological resources, so that the family lived in marginal circumstances. This group had an average of four children (range 2 to 7), as compared to under three for the others. They also had the highest divorce rate: two were currently in their first marriage; two were in their second, and two were divorced.

In our culture, the "normal" family is seen as a haven for all of its members. It is supposed to be a place where spouses come together to find loving, peaceful solace. Children have carefree lives, wrapped in the love and protection of the family. They receive the psychological and material sustenance needed so that they can develop into well-adjusted, responsible adults. The homemakers in this study generally did not grow up in such families or have such benign childhoods. Rather, they encountered a relatively high incidence of abuse (of parents as well as children), alcoholism, fragmented or "dysfunctional" families, and anguished adolescents stumbling into adulthood on the worst of terms. Standard survey research using brief methods and larger samples, and statistics gathered by various government agencies, generally give a more positive or blander picture of childhood and a lower incidence of the kinds of problems reported here.

Are the present findings unbalanced? Do they reflect an abnormally disturbed sample or an excessive emphasis in the interviewing upon problems rather than pleasures? Perhaps. No one study can be conclusive. In my opinion, however, the kinds of developmental difficulties and environmental stresses or constraints evident here—among the career women as well as the homemakers—exist roughly as often in the general population as in our sample. The frequency and severity of the problems, and the concrete forms they take, no doubt differ to some degree among classes, subcultures, and specific groups, but the basic theme remains: a very sizable minority of children and adults live under conditions that are in some ways inimical to their development.

Only a few homemakers gave a strongly positive account of their family life in childhood and adolescence:

❧ ELAINE OLSON

My parents were the most loving, wonderful people, very family oriented. We went to church every Sunday and on vacations together in the summer. We saw my grandparents every weekend and spent all the holidays with our large group of aunts, uncles, and cousins. My younger sister became a nun, and we are still very close. I still phone or visit my mother every day. I would be lost without that supportive family circle. I wouldn't consider moving far from New Haven.

Nora Cole gives a positive but more complex view of her childhood.

❧ NORA COLE

My father was a coal miner with four years of schooling. I remember running down the road to meet him coming home from work, his face covered with black soot. It was a very dangerous job, and they worked the miners like animals. We lived in constant fear of the whistle blowing that signaled an explosion in the mines. I adored my father. He was a proud man who loved his family and was involved in the community. We knew as children that our parents loved each other a lot. You would see them walking down that country road to church holding hands. I was raised very sheltered, which was good but didn't prepare me for a lot of harsh things I had to face in life. Our home was just a beautiful haven. I never heard my parents argue about bills, so I thought marriage was always like that [laughs].

My parents loved us children but did not spare the rod at any time. Boy, would they break our butts with the belt when we did something they thought was wrong or would get us into trouble. I still remember one Christmas: all of us children would go to the Company store to look at the toys. The store owner told us black children, "You go and you *look* but you don't touch the toys." The white children were allowed to touch. Well, one year I had had enough. I didn't care what anyone said, I was going to play with those toys. I got behind the counter and turned them on. The Ferris wheel started going round and round, and the train moved, and the plane whirred and spinned. The clerk yelled, "Okay, Nora, turn it off, and get back where you belong!" I knew I was in trouble the minute I did it but I didn't care. When I got home my parents had the belt ready. Boy, did my father give it to me that day. I said to myself, "I don't care, I've done what I wanted, and that's that." So I took my comeuppance. I knew that my parents were scared for me; they didn't want me to break the rules that would get me in trouble.

In high school I was a good student. I never had a white teacher. I was a big girl, almost 200 pounds, interested in sports. I was *definitely* not sexually active. Thoughts entered my mind that it would be great to be held in a boy's arms but the fear of God and Mama struck in my heart [laughs]. Religion was a ruling force in our home, and I was very active in the church. Summers I went to New Haven to work and live with my dad's brother and his family.

At 16 I graduated from high school. No job was available at home, so I moved to New Haven. My sister had done the same thing: finished high school, went to New Haven, got a job, and married a year later. I was hoping to work and earn money and do things for *me*. I lived with my uncle and his sister and worked as a secretary. It was kind of lonely coming home and finding no one there and no dinner made. Not like home! The guys in New Haven were faster and just wanted to have sex. I'd say, "No way," and that would be the end of that guy. He'd say, "You've wasted enough of my time—she's not about nothing." I got tired of their lines fast; it was leading nowhere.

My husband-to-be, Walter, lived on the first floor where I lived. He was twenty years older, and his wife had died a few years earlier. He worked in a factory. One thing that attracted me to him was his concern; he cared about how I felt and what I liked. His whole approach was different from the 18-year-old guys I dated. He was a very gentle person, experienced in life. He'd see that no dinner was ready when I came home from work. He'd say, "I'll bring you some food because you need to eat before going to choir rehearsal." He drank heavily at times; I wasn't used to that and didn't know what to make of it.

Walter and I admired each other from a distance for a while. Then in May we started dating. My parents got wind of it and made me go back home. I knew they loved me and were concerned about the age difference but I was certain that I cared enough for Walter to want to marry him, and he felt the same way. That's when I began to differ from my parents and make my own decisions. Finally, my parents just resigned themselves. I got married at 17 and had my first child at 18. There were a lot of rough times in the marriage when I wanted to give up and go back home but I knew that all my relatives were just sitting there waiting for the breakup. I stuck it out to show them I had not made a mistake.

In stark contrast to Elaine Olson and Nora Cole, the great majority of the homemakers painted a more negative picture of their parents and their own childhood lives:

ఆ CAROL O'BRIEN

My parents fought a lot, and there was an atmosphere of violence in our home. I just had a sense of chaos. My mother had a severe drinking problem and was verbally abusive. She told me that God would not give me kids because I was so bad—I didn't take care of her the way she wanted. When I was in high school things got so bad that I lived with my best friend's family for a year. At 21 I married the first guy who asked me. All I ever wanted was to get married and stop working and have a home and family of my own. I hoped to be rescued from the kind of life I'd had at home by becoming the perfect wife to a perfect husband; I would make him happy, he would make me happy, and we'd have perfect, happy children. Unfortunately, it didn't work out that way.

ఆ RUTH ALLEN

I grew up in the rural South. I was raised by my grandparents and rarely saw my mother, who was not married. We were poor but I always had food and care and the comfort of the black Baptist church. At 6 I went to live with my mother, her boyfriend, and their newborn child. We all lived in one room. Those were harsh, harsh years—a lot of suffering for me and my sister. My mother physically abused us. She tried to have food for us but that man just took it all for himself. We went hungry a lot and had no clothes and no heat. My sister and I just sat all day on that cold floor in that one room. At 8, I and my sister and my pregnant mother went back home with my grandparents, and life became happier. At least there was food, clothing, and heat. I didn't realize how poor we were because everyone was poor in that town. When I was 12 my mother married a man who was strict but kind, and things were better. He worked as a janitor in a nearby town and came home weekends. My mother was a cleaning lady for a white family.

In high school I was a straight A student. I had supportive teachers who made sure I had breakfast and gave me odd jobs to earn money for clothes. It was understood that I would receive a scholarship from my all-black high school to the nearby all-black college. At that time the integration of schools began on a voluntary basis. I wanted to stay in my high school but my stepfather insisted that I transfer to a formerly all-white high school even though I didn't want to, and even though it meant that I would not get the college scholarship. No way would a black student get a scholarship—it would kill the whites to recognize a black student like that. My parents said that if I wanted to go to college bad enough I could do it on my own, but there was no way. At 17 I graduated and went to live with an aunt in Boston.

In high school the girls began involving themselves in adolescent peer group activities, dating, working part-time, becoming part of the world outside of the family. They began, slowly, to feel more grown up, "not a child anymore." What is most striking is not that these changes occurred—they are well-known aspects of adolescent life—but that they occurred to such a limited degree. As high school graduation approached, these girls were minimally connected to the adult world and minimally prepared to take their place in it. Their parents wanted them to become more responsible yet did little to help them form a sense of the adult world and of themselves as adults. The adolescent peer world served more as a buffer against the adult world than as a direct link to it. Very few of the girls had a significant personal relationship with even one adult (teacher, friend, coworker, relative) who strongly affirmed their budding adult interests and identity. They generally studied hard enough to get grades appropriate to their educational-occupational goals. But, equally generally, they regarded schoolwork as a tolerable or oppressive *chore* rather than something of intrinsic value or interest. High school was not an intellectual treasure house, a stimulus to the imagination, an inviting world in which they could invest themselves with a sense of excitement and visions of the future. They experienced their teachers as alien: evenhanded and vaguely nice at best, unfair and vindictive at worst, but almost never friends, mentors, persons with whom they could have a meaningful relationship. This picture holds, I believe, for the great majority of American high school students. (Compare the experiences of the career women in Chapter 10.)

During this period the girls began to form personal relationships involving some degree of friendship, romantic love, and sexuality with boys. A few went steady for a year or more. In most cases the boyfriend lived some distance away and they hardly knew each other. The relationship thus had the advantages of giving her the prestige associated with going steady, of protecting her from the demands of more immediately pressing boys, and of having a like-minded boyfriend who could enjoy the romantic fantasy without having to deal with the day-by-day complexities of an intense relationship. All of the homemakers felt that it would be morally wrong to have sexual intercourse before marriage. They were also afraid of getting pregnant (in a time when birth control was not readily available to single women). Four young women violated this injunction, all with boyfriends they expected to marry. The stories of Vicky Perrelli and Angela Capelli exemplify many themes of the Adolescent Life Structure.

VICKY PERRELLI

I met Frank when I was 13 and he was 14. He was a good-looking, macho, high school athlete. Right away we started going steady. Once you did that no one else asked you out. He loved being part of my family, and they loved him. He was like a brother to me. When I was 15 he graduated, moved out of state, and visited me every other weekend for the next two years.

Frank put a lot of pressure on me to have sex. I lost my virginity in my senior year. I gave in only because he would go to someone else, and I didn't want to lose him. What a traumatic experience! It was against my religion, and I was terrified of pregnancy. To me sex wasn't that important; I never enjoyed it until after we got married. That first time I didn't know what he was doing until after it was done. I knew he wanted to "do it," but I had no idea of what was actually involved. It's really ironic: my daughter is now a senior in high school, and I said to my husband, "Do you remember my senior year of high school?" He smiled—he knew what I meant. I said, "Now, how would you like that to happen to your daughter?" He stopped smiling. I was really angry. I still am, in a way. The fighting about sex went on until we married three years later.

I had no one to talk to about sex. You didn't talk to your girlfriends because they would think you were horrible. We could never talk about sex in my house. Once I told my mother about a single girl who got pregnant. She said in horror, "Oh, whatever you do, don't disgrace me like that. If you want to get married out of high school I'll let you—but don't disgrace me like that!" I lived with that fear.

As graduation approached I had absolutely no ambition. I just knew I wasn't ready to get married. My friends were all becoming registered nurses, so I thought I might do that too. Nursing school was great. I didn't really leave home. I went to a nursing school seven miles from home and was still under the parental wing. The students were like family, and I loved taking care of people.

At 18 I started questioning my relationship with Frank and we broke up. I had never dated anyone else and wanted to try my wings a little bit, but I didn't get very far. I only got three dates. After six months I called Frank, and we got back together.

Vicky Perrelli's account indicates that her Adolescent Life Structure did not end at 17, when she graduated from high school. During the initial months of nursing school her life was still centered in family and school, and she had little sense of becoming an adult. Her Early Adult Transition began at 18, when she began questioning her relationship with Frank and wanting to "try my wings." Her foray into independence collapsed within a few months, and she returned to the fold. This is a fairly common theme among the homemakers. She and her husband-to-be scarcely knew each other. The relationship was formed in the Adolescent Life Structure, when neither had the inner resources nor the external supports to form a more adult relationship. It had a non-intimate, passionless quality. It was so limited that they couldn't discuss the sexual conflict, let alone reach some understanding and accommodation. Neither mother nor girlfriends were helpful. (Even now she does not mention the possibility that father or boys might have been confidants; this is an obvious example of gender splitting.)

✎ ANGELA CAPELLI

I met Harry when I was in the eleventh grade and he was in the twelfth. He really impressed me; he was so attractive and a good dresser. My family liked him and considered him a good catch. During my senior year he was in the service, stationed abroad, and we corresponded. He got back just as I turned 18 and graduated. We got engaged, though we hardly knew each other. Then I got a job as a typist in a garment factory where my parents were unskilled workers. I enjoyed the job and being out of school and having a social life with the people I knew at work. Harry was possessive and jealous of my relationships there. He also wanted to have sex before marriage. It was against my religious beliefs but he kept insisting, and I finally gave in, since we were going to get married anyhow.

I knew that the marriage would not work. Finally, I told my parents I wanted to end the engagement. They said, "Don't be foolish, everything will be fine." Once a wedding is planned you're too ashamed to call it off. How can you? The family has put money into it. In the long run it pays to lose the money but you don't realize it at the time. I was in a daze. Everyone I knew married by 20 — so young and foolish. You're at all your friends' weddings and all of a sudden *you* can't wait to be a bride, too. I married Harry at 19 and took it for granted that I would have a baby right away. I never thought about what it meant to be a mother; I was just going to be one. But I didn't get pregnant. We fought constantly. He had a bad temper and often hit me. I kept asking "What did I get myself into?"

The Internal Traditional Homemaker Figure and the Internal Anti-Traditional Figure

Several vignettes above show the emergence of the internal Traditional Homemaker Figure and the internal Anti-Traditional Figure. The former operated powerfully in all of the homemakers during the period of the

Adolescent Life Structure. They saw it as inevitable and, to varying degrees, desirable that they become homemakers in a Traditional Marriage Enterprise. Only a few young women questioned this destiny, and even they acceded to it after a brief, unsuccessful search for alternatives. Some would argue that the primary sources of these figures are biological, rooted in the genetic programming that prepared women for motherhood. At this point we simply do not know how strongly the genes shape women's primordial images of motherhood and family life. We do know, however, that a woman's images of femininity and womanhood are fed by her experiences within her own family and in the wider culture (via education, religion, the mass media, and so forth). From the stories these women tell of their own childhood, the mother also comes through as a primary source. Here are two examples from the homemakers.

✎ KAY RYAN

The predominance of the Traditional Homemaker Figure in Kay Ryan's adult life was described in Chapter 3. Here is a brief excerpt that connects her adult outlook and her childhood experience:

> I could never satisfy my mother. In her terms she's never been loved enough or appreciated enough by anyone in her life. She's very unfulfilled. My parents divorced when I was 7. Life was hard for my mother and me after my father left. She had to work, and I'd be home alone, and we didn't have any money. She had all the responsibilities and worries that go with running a whole household all by yourself. I knew what she wanted most was to be married and to be home with me. I learned from her predicament that the man needs to support the family and it's the woman's duty to do whatever is required to make the marriage work.
>
> I never wanted to work. I went to college and expected to be married when I graduated—which I did. All my friends went to that local college, too. But not many graduated—they'd quit to get married and start their family. That's what everyone did then.

✎ VICKY PERRELLI

> In my mother's day there was no divorce. Women just suffered alcoholic abusive husbands who were never home. She was a very traditional woman. She didn't have a great marriage or a great life, and I feel sorry for her. She always held a job because my father couldn't earn enough to support the family. They fought a lot. I always wondered where the families were like *Ozzie and Harriet* and *Father Knows Best*. But my mother never questioned her life. She always said, "The man is the head of the house, and the woman is the heart, and if you think you can live any differently, *you* have another think coming." And that's how she lived her life. Whether she agreed or not, the decisions always came from my

father. As a girl I always wanted my independence, but as a good girl in that family you could never speak your own mind.

Unlike Kay Ryan, Vicky Perrelli tells us that the voice of the internal Traditional Homemaker Figure was not the only one she heard as a girl. There was another, contrary voice within her, that of the Anti-Traditional Figure. It urged her to speak her own mind, to question the father's authority, to seek a different way.

5 Early Adult Transition: Homemakers

The Early Adult Transition is a cross-era transition. It is the concluding period of the childhood era and, at the same time, the initial period of the early adult era. It also brings about the termination of the Adolescent Life Structure and the initiation of the Entry Life Structure. In the homemaker sample it began at age 17 or 18 and ended at 22 or 23. It lasted four or five years, with a single exception of six years.

I'll discuss first the developmental tasks of this period, and then explore the major components of the homemakers' lives.

Developmental Tasks of the Early Adult Transition

The basic developmental tasks of all transitional periods are *termination*, *individuation*, and *initiation* (see Chapter 2), although the form taken by these tasks depends upon the place of the particular transition in the life cycle. The character of the Early Adult Transition is shaped by its place on the boundary between childhood and early adulthood. It is important to terminate the Adolescent Life Structure and the relationships with family, peers, school, and other significant parts of the adolescent world. It is important also to become more individuated—to modify the childhood self and move toward an adult self that is more ready to engage with the responsibilities, burdens, and satisfactions of early adulthood. A final task is to initiate and test out new relationships in the adult world, laying the basis for building an Entry Life Structure in the next period.

The Early Adult Transition of the homemakers generally began within a year before or after graduation from high school. Graduation did not in itself *cause* the developmental shift. Rather, the completion of high school was part of a broad array of social, psychological, and biological changes propelling the girl/woman into adulthood.

At the start of the Early Adult Transition each young woman was living within a life structure centered on her family of origin (or a surrogate). Over its course she moved toward a first adult life structure that was both continuous with and different from the adolescent one. In some cases the change was so great that we would miss the continuity if we didn't look closely at the actual relationships in each component. In other cases the continuity was so obvious that we might easily overlook the subtle changes. In every case, careful exploration revealed continuity as well as change in the various components and in the overall life structure. The major components of the life structure-in-transition usually included family of origin, home base, education/occupation post high school, love/marriage/family, other relationships, and community.

Family of Origin: Leaving the Parental Nest and Forming a New Home Base

During the period of the Early Adult Transition there is a growing recognition by the young woman, her family, and the surrounding world that she cannot continue living much longer within the family. She must begin the process of "leaving the nest."

The completion of high school usually instigated a change in the young woman's place in the family of origin and thrust her further into the adult world. Most parents now felt that she was getting beyond childhood. It was time for her to start becoming more independent, assuming adult roles and moving from the parental home to a new home base of her own. Parents differed widely in the degree to which they welcomed and dreaded this change. On the one hand, they gained great satisfaction from seeing their "little girl" blossom into young womanhood. They were relieved to be emptying the nest and ending the financial and psychological burdens of child-rearing. On the other hand, parents often wished to continue the old relationship with the daughter as little girl and to maintain the existing form of family life. Her departure meant that they, too, were moving on to something new and uncertain.

The move out of the parental home was generally a mixed blessing for the young woman as well. She usually wished to get out from under parental control and become more independent. Adulthood would, she hoped, bring great benefits, but the benefits were defined mainly as the absence of the things that made adolescence so difficult. She often had opposite feelings as well: "If my parents don't take care of me, who will?" To the extent that the parental home offered nurturing, protection, and structure, it was hard to give these up when the alternatives were so unclear.

I use the term "home base" to include not only one's primary place of residence but also its meaning as "home" and the functions it serves in one's life. A given residence—the parental home, a college dormitory, an apartment with husband or roommates—has different meanings and functions for different women, and for the same woman at different times in her life. In the Adolescent Life Structure our subjects had a home base in the parental home, which provided a center for their lives. During the Early Adult Transition the homemakers, even most of those who went to college or vocational school, remained closely tied to the parental home. Almost all of them had their home base with parents until they married. After marrying, they typically formed an adult home base that was geographically close to the parents and part of the extended family.

It usually takes a young woman five to ten years to depart fully from the parental home and to form her own, independent home base. The relationship of daughter to parents continues (with minor or major changes) throughout her lifetime. Her parents exist both as actual persons in the external world and as figures in her self. The daughter's developmental task in the Early Adult Transition is to transform the relationship to the family of origin from the childhood pattern to one that is more adult, not cut it off altogether. It is important to diminish certain aspects of the existing relationship; for example, those in which she is the excessively submissive or defiant child in relation to all-controlling parents. It is important also to sustain other aspects and to build in new qualities such as mutual respect between individuals who have separate (though still partially intertwined) lives. The parents, who are now usually in their forties, are involved in changing the character of their own relationships with offspring, spouse, and family, as part of their own development. If the relationships cannot be modified in a way appropriate to the developmental needs of both offspring and parents, they will become increasingly stressful and may in time wither away—a much more widespread phenomenon than is usually recognized.

Modifying the childhood relationship with parents is a major issue in the daughter's adult development. In the Early Adult Transition she can take, at best, only a small step in this direction. A young woman in these years forms a preliminary, tentative sense of herself as a female adult. She attempts to live as a woman while still feeling in many respects like a little girl. One of her crucial life questions becomes: Do I want to be like my mother and to live as she has, or do I want something different?

The homemakers generally answered this question without much conscious thought or conflict. The internal Traditional Homemaker Figure predominated. The young women saw themselves as homemakers in an ethnic-class-community context much like that of their origins. A little happier than their mothers, perhaps, or more "modern," but living the same basic pattern. Staying close to the family—especially the mother—implies a whole set of choices with regard to marriage/family, education, work, values, sense of self, and initial adult life structure. It limits a woman's possibilities for exploration and individuation, but it also promises greater stability, continuity, rootedness in a known community and tradition. Moving away from the family (as the career women usually did) generally leads toward greater independence, involvement in the occupational world, starting a family at a later age, and forming a different kind of Entry Life Structure in her twenties.

Education and Occupation

The end of high school is a major turning point that places one on the threshold of adulthood. The nature of this threshold is strongly shaped by education. It makes a huge difference in terms of life choices whether a young woman obtains further education and, if she does, what kind. In the homemaker sample, the women who did not go beyond high school were generally expected—by parents, community, and themselves—to take on adult responsibilities soon after leaving high school. Their main options were to get a low-paying, unskilled job and/or to get married and start a family. The homemakers who obtained vocational training or a college degree were not required to marry or to hold a full-time job while they were in school. Instead, they generally lived in the parental home, improved their prospects for a "better" marriage, got some skills and credentials for future work should the need arise, and envisioned an adult life as homemaker.

The young woman's educational level strongly influenced her course through the Early Adult Transition. The homemakers varied in the amount and kind of education they received after high school, and we can distinguish three groups on this basis.

Group A. No Education Beyond High School

Five women—Nora Cole, Carol O'Brien, Angela Capelli, Ruth Allen, Lynn McPhail—came from working-class or marginally poor families which had neither the expectation nor the financial means of providing for a daughter once she finished high school. Graduation from high school was considered the end of her childhood; it was now time for her dependence on parents to end. Her chief options were to get married or to take a low-paying, unskilled job and become a self-sufficient adult.

The parents usually allowed her a brief interim phase of several months to a year in which she could continue her financial dependence, perhaps work part-time, and get her bearings. The interim phase was seen by all as a kind of special parental gift: even though she ought to be an independent adult by now, the parents were providing an extra bonus of material and moral support. To live entirely on her own during the interim phase was not morally acceptable in her world and she was unprepared for that degree of independence. Her primary goal was to get married as soon as possible. This would enable her to form a new home base, stop working, and start a Traditional Marriage Enterprise. She was ready to work before marriage and, if necessary, afterward. Work was primarily an external necessity, of no intrinsic value. Still, it might serve various functions for her: to become more competent and independent, to get out from under parental control, to find a more adult peer world and, through that, a husband.

All Group A women married in the Early Adult Transition at age 17 to 21. The decision to marry did not emerge out of a long-term intimate relationship and a clear view of the future. It was based, rather, on strong pressure (external as well as within herself) to stop working and to extricate herself from the family of origin. The home situation was becoming unbearable. Several left home to get away from overt conflict or to prevent a suppressed conflict from erupting. They could not go on living at home as children but could find no way to live there as adults. The parents, usually with mixed feelings, acted increasingly to extrude the young women. Further education was not readily available, nor did they seek it. The only work available was in low-paying service jobs that offered few immediate satisfactions and no chance for advancement. These young women had no reason to expect more: occupation was not a potentially meaningful component of their world.

In short, early marriage was the most viable option available to these young women—the largest subgroup of American women—in the Early Adult Transition. They married before they had done much exploring of the adult world, of themselves as novice adults, of sexuality, of relationships with men in general and their husbands-to-be in particular. Their social environments did almost nothing to facilitate exploration of themselves and the adult world during the Early Adult Transition. They were required to act as responsible adults with little support for becoming psychologically adult. These premature choices complicated their entry into adulthood and left them with much undone growing up to do. It is not easy for anyone, female or male, to attain a reasonably satisfactory balance of dependence and independence by the end of the Early Adult Transition (or often much later).

LYNN McPHAIL

I quit school in eleventh grade at 16 because my father got TB and couldn't work. I went to work for the phone company. I enjoyed working and not going to school. I kept $5 from my paycheck each week and gave the rest to my family. When I was 17 I started going out with girlfriends after work, having a ball, innocent fun, dances, movies. I wasn't interested then in getting engaged and married.

When I was 18 you just start wanting to get married, I don't know why. In them days you get out of school, you get a job, now you find somebody and get married and become a Mrs. Somebody. I was having some friction at home with my mother and sister. Sometimes I think I got married so young just to get away from home and that friction, I really do. I got engaged at 18, married at 19, and had my first child at 20.

Group B.   Vocational Training After High School

Five women—Vicky Perrelli, Sara Cushing, Nan Krummel, Elaine Olson, Beth Logan—received one to three years of training for a vocation such as nurse, technician, secretary. They came from working-class or lower-middle-class families of somewhat greater stability, education, and income than those in Group A. The parents actively supported the daughter's decision to get more schooling. Most of these young women were the first members of their families to go beyond a high school education. The parents hoped that the additional education would contribute to their daughter's chances for a better life without taking her too far from her origins. Once the training was completed the daughter was officially "adult" and expected to become financially independent or marry. Like the Group A parents, they allowed her a brief interim phase in which to be partially dependent while seeking marriage and/or work.

The young women lived at home or in the supervised dormitory of a nearby school. They remained closely tied to the family of origin and had the continuing guidance of parents. The schooling thus provided a benign time in which to remain at home, mature a little, get some job skills, and seek a husband. The vocational training was clearly not for the purpose of having a long-term career. Rather, it gave her an occupation that would help her obtain a reasonably interesting, remunerative job before marriage and, should the need arise, later.

The tacitly understood timetable called for the young woman to marry and form a Traditional Marriage Enterprise soon after completing her training. Vicky Perrelli was right on schedule: at 20 she graduated from nursing school, married her high school sweetheart, and immediately started a family. Sara Cushing took a little longer: after finishing secretarial school at 18, she lived in the parental home, worked, and married at 22. Both Elaine Olson and Nan Krummel had a courting relationship that went awry; they did not marry until 28 and 25, respectively. Beth Logan completed the interim phase at 19, more quickly than expected: in the middle of her technician training program she got pregnant and married.

✎ভ VICKY PERRELLI

In the preceding chapter we followed Vicky Perrelli's turbulent courting relationship with Frank through the period of her Adolescent Life Structure. Let's continue the story now to her marriage at 20.

> I graduated at 20. I didn't care about a career. I figured it was something I could fall back on if necessary. I couldn't wait to get married and have a baby. If you weren't married and didn't have kids by 21 you were an old maid. You had babies right away because that's what you got married for. I thought at the time I loved Frank. I know now I wasn't ready to get married. I had never been independent of somebody, whether it was my parents or my husband. I was always a good girl and did what was expected. I got married at 20 and got pregnant on the honeymoon.

Group C.   Graduation from a Four-Year College

One of these five women, Jenny Abatello, was the first in her working-class family to attend college; she got there largely on her own initiative but with her mother's strong moral support. The other four women had college-educated, middle-class parents who assumed that their children would go to college and who fostered some degree of academic achievement. They wanted the daughter to have an opportunity, through attending college, to find a husband who would provide the kind of middle-class life that the parents had achieved or aspired to. In their minds, going to college was part of her "growing up" and thus something they had a parental obligation to provide. With the end of college she was officially on her own, except that again there was available an interim phase of parental support while she moved toward marriage or a more independent life.

Kay Ryan and Jenny Abatello went to local colleges and lived in the parental home, an arrangement that kept them close to their origins. Claire Berman went to college in another state and became somewhat more independent; but she had no strong academic or occupational interests, and the college provided little stimulus for change. Wendy Lewis and Emily Swift left home to attend academically excellent colleges that sought to expand their students' horizons. Wendy Lewis returned to the parental home and a local college after two years (see below), and Emily Swift did not develop occupational goals in college.

All five young women lived on the boundary between family of origin, school, and adult world. Going to college gave them the freedom, if they so chose, to neither marry nor enter the work world (except for occasional or summer jobs) until graduation. Nonetheless, the same basic understanding existed here as in the other two groups: this was the last time in which the parents would provide major support and buffering; when it was over, the daughter would have to get married or take a full-time job and establish her own adult life. The main purpose of the college education was to find a husband of appropriate education and prospects.

✺ WENDY LEWIS

I was a great achiever in high school. I was going to go to law school. My parents and I always felt I could do anything. I graduated from high school at 17 and went to a first-rate college. I was a good student and enjoyed college. When I was 18 I met my future husband, Hank, who was four years older. He was an unusual person and impressive: played the piano and had a brand-new Porsche. Two weeks after we met he asked me to marry him. I don't think I was passionately in love with him, but he was a good catch. We got engaged right away. He went to graduate school in my hometown. He really fell in love with my family, and they were crazy about him. When we got engaged he lived with my parents. In my sophomore year I transferred to a local college near home and lived at home with my parents and Hank.

I married at 19, the summer between my sophomore and junior years. Our parents paid for our tuition, and we got a one-bedroom apartment. He worked full-time and went to school nights, and I went to school days and got a job at night. We saw relatively little of each other the first few years of marriage. We were so busy going to school and trying to pay the bills that we sometimes only saw each other in passing. I got pregnant at 19 and had our daughter Gwen at 20. I was still planning to go to law school. Gwen was not an accident. I'd stopped taking birth control. Really, how stupid! I wanted a baby, and we thought we could do everything. I went to school only part-time after that, which was fine. My mother took care of Gwen. The next year the marriage was more difficult. We were both so busy. We had a lot of arguments. I don't even remember my twenty-first birthday at all; it's a blur: going to school, working, taking care of the baby.

In my senior year, I was 22, I applied to law school and was accepted. Then I got pregnant again. Neither pregnancy was a "mistake." We've never had a problem with birth control—when we used it, it worked. I just stopped using it. It was one of those half-conscious decisions: I knew what I was doing but I didn't. I made the decision before I consciously chose family and not law school. I was half-aware of the contradictions in applying to law school and getting pregnant at the same time. My parents were really hot for law school. I didn't want to disappoint them, and I couldn't tell them how I felt. I remember pretending that not going to law school was temporary, though I knew it was permanent. My mother had been taking care of my daughter and insisted that she could handle two children. She had never realized her own career dreams and wanted me to do it. But I was into having children at that point. I still think I made the right decision for me.

At 22 Wendy was a college graduate, the mother of one child and pregnant with another, and she had given up all pretense of wanting a legal career. She was ready to shift her home base from parents to husband and to build an Entry Life Structure around a Traditional Marriage Enterprise.

Graduation from high school had very different meanings in each of the three groups. For the young women in Group A, it marked the end of childhood and a fateful turning point in the life course. If a woman married at around this time, she started to take on the adult roles of wife (with motherhood soon to follow), homemaker, and perhaps jobholder—even though she still felt so much like a *girl*. For the women in groups B and C, high school graduation was a vivid reminder of things soon to come. The handwriting was on the wall: they had a year or two or four to enjoy their freedom from major responsibility but they had to use this time to prepare themselves for the adult life they would be abruptly thrown into after their next graduation. They were now placed, haphazardly, on the path to matrimony and family.

For men, educational aspirations are generally linked to occupational aspirations. They seek the amount and kind of education required for a specific occupation or a broad category of occupations. For the homemakers, in contrast, educational aspirations were closely linked to marital aspirations. They wanted the amount and kind of education required to marry an "appropriate" man. A traditional function of education for a woman is to enable her to marry a man who, by virtue of his education, occupation, and place in the world, can offer her a life consistent with her own interests and values.

In the traditional scheme of things, a woman who wants to be a member of the educated middle class has to attend an appropriate college: first, in order to associate with eligible young men; and second, in order to acquire the education, skills, and culture required by her future roles as wife, mother, homemaker, and member of the community that she will enter through the marriage.

Most homemakers married men of education and class origins roughly equal to their own. Women who sought only a high school education expected to marry a similarly educated man and to continue living in the working-class or lower-middle-class world in which they grew up. Those who went to college usually wanted to marry a man going into business or professional life, and all but one young woman did just that. They were in college, as several mentioned, chiefly to get the "MRS. Degree."

The three groups differed also in the support they had for doing the developmental work of the Early Adult Transition. Those in Group A entered this period with relatively the fewest resources and the greatest pressure to assume adult roles and responsibilities. After finishing high school they took unskilled, unrewarding jobs, often lived with parents in a state of overt or latent conflict, and saw marriage as the only viable option for adulthood. All five married soon after high school and four immediately started a family, acquiring the appearance though not the inner experience of being fully adult.

The women in Group B had a longer phase of parental support after high school. They had greater opportunity to form an occupation that would increase their potential income. Yet they, too, gave first priority to marriage/family and made only a minimal commitment to occupation. Three of the young women in this group married at age 19 to 22, soon after the end of their vocational training, and quickly started a family. Elaine Olson and Nan Krummel had courting relationships that didn't work out; in their early twenties they began building an Entry Life Structure as single, working, marriage-seeking young women.

The young women in Group C had parental support and protection during the four years of college. Wendy Lewis married and started a family while in college but continued to live within the parental nest. Jenny Abatello and Kay Ryan lived sheltered lives based in the parental home; they married at graduation and quickly started a family. To their regret, Emily Swift and Claire Berman were not married at graduation. They then became financially and residentially independent, marrying at 26 and 27.

Along with subgroup differences, there were common themes for the homemaker sample as a whole. All fifteen women went through the Early Adult Transition as an actual or a would-be homemaker. They knew—as a concrete axiomatic given, not an abstract belief—that they would lead family-centered lives built around a Traditional Marriage Enterprise. All of them accepted a timetable calling for marriage as soon as possible once education was complete. Eleven married by age 22, within a few weeks to a few years of their final school graduation. The remaining four married at age 25 to 28. All but two got pregnant within a year of the marriage; both of the others tried but did not become pregnant. The marriages evolved in diverse ways, as we shall see. Seven homemakers had divorced by the time they were interviewed: four in Group A and three in Group B. Of those who did not divorce, several barely weathered severe marital storms in the Early Adult Transition or later.

Love/Marriage/Family: The Path to Matrimony

Love/Marriage/Family is a component of the life structure which has many potential parts, not all of which may be present in a given life structure.

Love relationships ordinarily include marriage as well as other relationships that have romantic, sexual, or courtship aspects. The term "love" is commonly used in characterizing such relationships but is often misleading. There is little or no love in many marriages, courtships, and sexual affairs. And there may be a strongly loving quality in friendships and other relationships that are not sexual or romantic.

I will use the terms "courting" and "matrimonial" interchangeably to refer to those relationships in which marriage was the desired outcome for at least one person in a couple. The term "marriage" is meant to include legal marriage as well as psychological marriage. The latter is a relatively enduring relationship in which the two regard themselves as partners in many respects, sharing a household and/or other joint ventures.

A couple becomes a family when they have a child. The "nuclear family" includes parents and their children. "Family of origin" is the one in which one grew up as a child. "Extended family" includes the nuclear family and relatives who are part of a socially defined kinship system.

Love relationships, marriage, and family are usually interrelated in our thoughts and feelings, if not in actuality, as facets of a single broad pattern. They are often a single though complex component of the life structure. They may also exist separately. Even when they coexist within a single life, each has its own significance and meaning. In each life we must determine the nature of the facets that exist at a given time, how they are interrelated, how they fit within the current life structure, and how they evolve over time. For the homemakers this component was all of a piece in the Early Adult Transition. Having a romantic love relationship was closely linked with getting married, and marriage with starting a family.

Relationships with Males

During the Early Adult Transition these women knew a variety of males in family, neighborhood, work, school. In reviewing the early adult years, they did not single out their relationships with males as generally negative or problematic. From their actual accounts of various incidents and persons, however, we see that the relationships were for the most part limited, organized around specific activities and lacking in intimacy.

The father was rarely regarded as a valued adviser so far as major life choices were concerned, or a source of great encouragement. It was also rare that daughter and father were totally at odds or in a state of enmity. The daughter generally felt that she loved her father and was in some elemental sense loved by him. She seldom went beyond this opaque view to examine more closely the actual character of the relationship. The father was usually portrayed not as a major character in the life story but as a rather distant, ambiguous figure. The daughter had little sense of him as a person and did not expect to be known in any personal way by him. These bland relationships were ultimately depriving for the young woman. They contributed to her experience of the barriers that separate the genders and that hinder the development of mutually satisfying female/male relationships.

A similar distance was evident in their relationships with brothers. There were no instances of close relationships with brothers in the Early Adult Transition and beyond. Most young women were psychologically distant from their brothers and lived in a different, gender-defined world. A young woman might have the sense of a "family bond" with a brother, but the relationship usually played a minor part in her adult life.

This was also true of relationships with male relatives such as grandfathers, uncles, and cousins. A few women had a special relationship (good and/or bad) with a particular male relative, but for the most part the ties were minimal. Likewise, those who attended school in the Early Adult Transition rarely mentioned a significant friendship or *mentoring relationship* with a male teacher or other adult.

Most males in the woman's life during this period were age-peers—men of roughly the same age with whom she worked, went to school, dated, participated in social activities. These relationships had great significance for her evolving life structure. In them she was beginning to experience (or not experience) the possibilities for adult friendship, intimacy, sexuality, exploitation, collaborative work, romantic love, marriage. Partly through her relationships with men, she was forming (or failing to form) a more concrete sense of herself as an adult—friend, lover, student, worker, wife, mother, daughter, member of the community—in the domestic as well as public worlds.

Despite the potential importance of such relationships, they were remarkably limited in number and quality. The young women had contact with men chiefly in school, work, or social situations that strongly hindered the formation of personal ties. They sometimes had "crushes" and other forms of intense romantic attachment, but these were usually private fantasies involving someone who was unavailable or unaware of her feelings. Almost none had a close, enduring, nonromantic friendship with a man during this period (or after). Indeed, virtually the only significant relationships reported are the ones with the man they married and, in some cases, a previous love relationship.

The young women's stories of life in the Early Adult Transition give powerful evidence, as much by what is absent as by what is said, that women and men traditionally live in largely separate worlds. Even the women who went to co-educational colleges had minimal contact with men beyond seeing them in classes, around campus, and on dates that usually followed an impersonal, ritualized pattern. The young women who got vocational training were typically in segregated "female" schools and occupations. They met men in related occupations, but the status difference between the occupations was a great obstacle to the formation of more personal relationships. The women who worked in this period generally had unskilled "female" jobs or vocations. Gender segregation was (and is) pervasive in the workplace. Young men and women do similar kinds of work in offices, stores, and fast food chains, but women are generally paid less and promoted less. Women often work *near* men, rarely *with* men. Informal but strong social barriers separate "the girls" from "the men."

Dating, Courting, and Getting Married

Included here are all cross-gender relationships that are part of the path to matrimony. We have no standard name for these relationships. No single term adequately encompasses the full range of psychological and social qualities they may involve. They are often called "love relationships." I shall sometimes use this term—with the recognition that love may be present in many forms or may be entirely absent. Likewise, these relationships may or may not include sexual behavior, passion, emotional intimacy, affection, mutuality, or any other quality commonly thought to be part of romantic love.

Engaging in love relationships is an important though often painful part of adult development. It is also essential to our culturally preferred system of voluntary (rather than arranged) marital choice on the basis of romantic love. If a woman is to marry the man of her own special choice, she needs to explore a variety of woman/man relationships. These relationships enable her to learn what various men are like, what they may offer and want from her, what she may offer and want from them, the myriad ways in which they can love, admire, excite, sustain, and hurt each other. This learning may enable her to combine love and wisdom in choosing a husband with whom, as our cultural ideal has it, she lives happily ever after. The romantic ideal holds a magical promise and a heavy burden: it promises a marriage that is loving and fulfilling for both partners, but it demands great wisdom in choosing a mate and engaging in a marital relationship. We must be able to go beyond "blind" infatuation to a "seeing" love that knows the other and can make a considered judgment about the possibility of having an enduring, fruitful marriage. This task is difficult to fulfill in early adulthood.

The homemakers did remarkably little exploring and had extremely limited relationships with men during the Early Adult Transition. Most of them did some dating and had romantic fantasies about a loving male hero — fantasies nourished more by their private desires and the mass media than by the actualities of their lives. The men they knew were not especially loving or heroic. For the most part, they were politely distant or sexually demanding. Neither partner was ready for a more loving, intimate relationship. Marriage as a concrete way of life was still rather unreal.

Each young woman saw only two possible options once her schooling was completed: to get married or to become a single working woman. She thought of marriage with some mixture of anticipation, anxiety, and confusion. Still, whatever her misgivings, marriage was the preferred choice in her world and in her own mind. If she was not married soon after completing her education, she faced the greatest disaster of all: to "end up an old maid."

As their schooling came to an end, all fifteen young women felt a tremendous pressure to get married. Every relationship with a man occurred in the shadow of matrimony. A woman got involved in a relationship only when marriage seemed a likely and desired outcome. She could not afford the luxury of letting a relationship develop for some time before considering whether to marry.

Given the paucity of choices, one question was paramount: Is this an available man who meets my minimum requirements for a husband? The minimum requirements had to do with his role in the Traditional Marriage Enterprise — that he be an adequate provider, head of household, and link to a valued community. Some hoped for certain personal qualities: a man who was especially loving, admirable, and exciting; who was gentle or macho, ambitious or "steady," sexually passionate or restrained. In most cases, however, the relationship was so undeveloped that she hardly knew him as a person, nor he her. Eleven homemakers married between the ages of 17 and 22. Many young women had serious misgivings as they married but either denied them (until later) or decided to settle for what they had. None of the early marriers had had a significant personal relationship with a man other than their husband. Most got married after a courtship of less than a year. The decision to marry was based more on a sense of urgency to be married than on the quality of the relationship.

Two thirds of the entire homemaker sample were aware at the time of their marriage that they were *not* in love with their husbands:

> I fell into like with him. Everyone else was getting engaged and married. I wasn't passionately attracted to him, but he seemed nice.

> I didn't fall in love with him but I liked him very much. He was nice to be with and didn't put any demands on me sexually. He was a really decent guy. I liked his family very much, and my family liked him. Our families and backgrounds were similar. I thought I could have a nice life with him.

◄§ SARA CUSHING

After graduating from high school at 17, Sara Cushing took a one-year program in secretarial school and maintained her Adolescent Life Structure. At 18 she got a clerical job and made her initial foray into the adult world. She continued to live in the parental home, having few domestic responsibilities and receiving a weekly allowance in return for her paycheck—a system of forced saving managed by her mother. At 20 Sara began thinking seriously about marriage. Her first courtship relationship was with Larry, who was in the Army. She saw him only occasionally but had a special feeling for him and hoped they would marry. When she was 21 he asked that they have a sexual relationship. Morally outraged and disappointed, she stopped seeing him and began to think about living on her own:

> With the encouragement of an older girlfriend I found an apartment but my mother said I couldn't move out. Part of me wanted to go but another part didn't; girls didn't live alone before marriage back then. I'd had very overprotective parents and was a very good girl—I never did anything wrong or questioned anything they said.
>
> My biggest fear was being an old maid. I was a bridesmaid in three weddings and was really worried I'd never get married. At 21 I met and began dating Bill, the brother of a girl at work. He was in the Army, stationed in another state. I only saw him weekends and never alone; we always double dated. We got engaged six months later. I got married because I wanted to be married, and I wanted to be taken care of. I saw Bill as a sensitive, caring person who was attracted to me. He was a nice guy but I was not attracted to him. I never had a sense of what I wanted, only what I didn't want. I didn't want to live at home anymore, and I didn't want to be an old maid.
>
> We married when I was 22. The marriage was not good from the beginning. We didn't know each other. We had never been alone together and had never talked about what each of us wanted in a marriage. I wanted to be a mother and quit my job and stay home. He just wanted to have fun, fun, fun. His mother had always worked full-time, and he

wanted me to work, too. He had no ambition. He complained every moment he was home about how much he hated his job. It was horrible! I was unhappy and felt trapped—I had no place to go. I didn't want to admit to my parents that I had made a mistake. And I'd had such a fear of being an old maid that, no matter how miserable I was, at least I was married. I thought maybe if I had a baby everything would be fine in the marriage. I got pregnant after five months and had my daughter at 23.

Women Who Did Not Marry in the Early Adult Transition

In contrast to the eleven early marriers, there were four homemakers— Nan Krummel, Emily Swift, Claire Berman, and Elaine Olson—who did not marry by 22. The absence of matrimony did not stem from a lack of interest. All four had a courting relationship in the Early Adult Transition and were disappointed that it did not result in marriage.

✌§   ELAINE OLSON

After high school Elaine Olson entered a two-year program. She engaged in many social activities but did no one-on-one dating.

> My whole life changed at 20, after graduation—I lost 30 pounds and became a working girl and a dating girl, all at the same time. I was a bridesmaid in nine weddings from 20 to 21; all my friends got married at 21 and had a baby at 22. I met John when I was 21. He was a house painter, very tall, dark, handsome, very, very nice. I met him at a singles dance, and the attraction was very fast and very mutual. He was very nice to me. He was my knight in shining armor. I felt like a princess who had met her prince. I was in a whirlwind. It was wonderful. Everyone loved him. He loved my family, called my mother Mom. We dated a year and then John told me he was divorced and had a child! I was crushed! I told my mother but didn't dare tell my father. She told me I had to end the relationship. But how do you love someone and then just cut it off? But I really didn't want to get involved in all that, either. He had child support payments. He couldn't attend the Catholic church because he'd been divorced, and I went to church every Sunday. I started seeing him less and less.
>
> Then my father learned that John was divorced and confronted me and said I couldn't see him again. I told John we had to end. For six months I pined for him, didn't date anyone else. You don't just love someone and stop. It changed in terms of potential for marriage but not feelings. Everyone couldn't believe I'd broken up with him. "Elaine, how could you ever break up with him? He was such a good person, and he was gorgeous and he was a good dancer and treated you so good." But you know, still

today I can't imagine marrying a divorced man. For the next few years I dated but nothing serious.

Traditional Marriage Enterprise and Motherhood in the Early Adult Transition

What is it like to marry and start a family in the Early Adult Transition? For both spouses the actual character of the marriage was generally quite different from the anticipated ideal. A great hazard of marriage in the Early Adult Transition is that the relationship is formed, and the initial choice made, while one is still heavily embroiled in the process of separating from the childhood self and world. In getting married, a woman ordinarily moves out of the parental home and begins her official existence as an adult. Marriage in a Traditional Marriage Enterprise often limits her work on the developmental tasks of this period and locks her into a life structure not conducive to her further development as an adult. Although such marriages are not necessarily doomed to failure, they involve vulnerabilities that must in time be dealt with. As we shall see, some couples managed to do so in subsequent periods; a larger number did not, the consequence being divorce or an enduring yet unsatisfying marriage.

Problems arose during the first few years as the Traditional Marriage Enterprise took clearer shape. The division of labor between the spouses, and the splitting of the domestic and public worlds, turned out to be much greater than most of the young women had imagined. They were partners in a family enterprise but the partnership involved a minimum of direct collaboration or even contact. It was as though husband and wife were owner-manager-operators of a small business—the family—with a chronic shortage of help and resources. He performed the "outside" functions required to produce income and keep the family afloat. She in turn did chiefly the "inside" work of child-rearing and household chores. Her outside involvements were mostly with family of origin and neighbors, and were closely tied to her domestic concerns. If she had a paid job, it was mainly out of financial need and did little to bring her into the wider public world.

From the start, then, the spouses were leading relatively *parallel unconnected lives.* They had little time together, and what time they had was devoted largely to managing the family enterprise—dealing with money, housing, child care, schedules, details of all kinds. Even when the enterprise went well, the marital relationship tended to remain psychologically limited. For the most part they lived in different, barely overlapping worlds and were involved with different persons, groups, and activities. It was hard to find a common ground. Since the gender division was so widespread and "natural" in their world, they had trouble identifying the sources of strain and making a concerted effort to modify them. Many women, moreover, did not regard the lack of psychological connection between them and their husbands as a problem; they sought less from the marital relationship than from the relationships with children, extended family, or others.

Ten of the eleven women who married in the Early Adult Transition got pregnant within a few weeks to a year of marriage (one was already pregnant). Angela Capelli tried but did not conceive. The pregnancies did not stem from clear-cut, conscious decisions by the women or an explicitly discussed decision by the couples. The basic decision was not to use birth control. Some women objected to birth control on moral-religious grounds, but this did not seem to be the only factor, since they overcame the objection when they had as many children as they wanted or could manage. The most powerful reason for not using birth control was an unquestioned assumption that matrimony and motherhood were inexorably linked in the natural order of things. Reflecting on the "choice" to start a family, they found it difficult to identify specific motives or conscious goals:

> You get married at 19 or 20 and have a baby right away; I never thought about it then.

> I just thought it was God's will.

> We didn't talk about having a child; we just had sex and figured, "If it's meant to be, it's meant to be"—and it was.

> I grew up with the thing that if you didn't marry and have kids by 21 you were an old maid. Naturally, as soon as you got married you got pregnant—this was why you got married. Having kids was the point of it all.

The linking of matrimony and motherhood is axiomatic in the Traditional Marriage Enterprise: a woman and man join together in order to create a family. Having and raising children are not only her chief functions in the family, they are the justification for her existence. Any other work she does is in addition to, not instead of, the child-rearing. To become an adult is to embark on marriage and motherhood.

Despite the strong urge to *have* children, the homemakers had very mixed feelings about *raising* children. They wanted to be good mothers and made sure that their children had adequate food and bodily care. It turned out, however, that motherhood was much more difficult than they had imagined. They were young and poorly equipped for motherhood at the start, and they received little education or support as they went along. By and large, they succeeded in giving their children adequate custodial care—meeting their basic requirements for physical well-being, protection, and control. They did less well in providing psychological care—forming a differentiated relationship, understanding the child as a person in her/his own right, and fostering its psychological development. They did more *for* and *to* than *with* the child.

It was difficult at best—and conditions were generally far from "best"—for a young woman in her teens or early twenties to function with any maturity as a mother when she was still early in the process of separating from her own mother. Being in the maternal position in relation to her baby did not necessarily mean that, in her subjective experience, she was solely or primarily the mother. Indeed, she was often psychologically much more the little girl seeking to be loved than the adult mother in a loving, responsible relation to the child. These feelings were reflected in the young mother's experience of cuddling her small child, especially in the first two or three years. This was for many mothers a pleasurable and important part of maternal life. The cuddling also allowed the young woman to bask in a bodily contact that filled her with a sense of giving and receiving love. This experience did not involve an intimate sharing between two separate selves. It was more a fusion in which she was both mother and child, the holder and the one being held, filling the other and being filled herself.

SARA CUSHING

I loved cuddling my little girl. It gave me that feeling of being loved and giving love. Mothering is about being fulfilled. She was everything I had dreamed of. It was perfect. I loved cleaning my house and taking care of my little girl, being the perfect mother with the perfect child. I used to sit there for hours waiting for her to wake up so I could cuddle and play with her. It was just me and her. I didn't need my husband anymore—I finally had somebody to center my life with. She fulfilled the need of being needed, of being able to show your love and feel loved. I wanted the world for her. I wanted us to have more in our life for her, and I resented that my husband didn't earn enough money to give her that. I felt she was mine and not his; I never let him get really close to her.

Cuddling provided Sara Cushing (and others) an opportunity for remothering of self. It helped overcome her sense of loneliness in the marriage. In cuddling the child, she experienced herself as being lovable, fulfilled, "perfect." Her life now had a purpose. She could attribute her disappointment in her husband primarily to his failure as a father rather than his failure as a husband. Having these satisfactions from the child enabled her to need him less and to tolerate him more. As she realized only later, she had during her twenties very little sense of an adult self and of her own wishes, goals, and responsibilities in the adult world. She resented her husband's inability to give their daughter "the world" but felt no personal responsibility to see it as their joint concern.

The newlyweds were faced with great burdens as they began to form a household. The shift from couple to family intensified the burdens and the separateness between spouses. Every marriage was under severe strain during the first several years of family life. One source of strain was that matrimony took these young women away from the family of origin and required them to build a home base for which they had primary responsibility. They had to modify their relationships with the family of origin and to establish themselves in the husband's family. Some became outsiders in a new community, where they were dependent on husbands who provided little companionship. Some experienced the loneliness of great social isolation, others the loneliness of being a newcomer in an uncongenial, often frightening community and extended family. They usually did not form a marital alliance that would enrich their private life and facilitate their entry into a social world.

The young mothers were unprepared for the unending, draining rigors of domestic life. Children and household made unexpectedly heavy demands on them. It was fun to play with the children but oppressive to be continually faced with their neediness. Help was sometimes available from their mothers, relatives, or friends (rarely from husbands). In actuality, however, the young women had remarkably little guidance or assistance in their novitiate as homemakers. The problems were compounded for those who had to hold outside jobs or to make do under conditions of great material scarcity.

The severity of the problems faced by these young couples in their early marriage and family life is suggested by the incidence of divorce and major overt conflict. Of the eleven women who married in the Early Adult Transition, six subsequently divorced. Two divorced at the end of this period, four others in the Age 30 Transition or the late thirties. At the time of the interviewing some of the five intact marriages were in jeopardy (see Chapters 8 and 9).

≈§   RUTH ALLEN

After finishing high school at 17, Ruth Allen left her family home in a small Southern town to live with an aunt in Boston.

> I wanted to get a job and earn some money. Marriage was not on my mind *at all*. I hadn't found Ruth yet. I had lived in one room with three sisters for all those years, and we were so poor. All I wanted was a place of my own and to take care of myself. I knew what my goals were: I wanted to

get a job and earn my own money, have an apartment and fix it up my own way. I wanted to get away from home. I wanted freedom from being so poor. I wanted to find out if I could make it on my own. I wanted to know what there was out there that I hadn't seen yet.

Boston was a huge disappointment: a vast, uncaring, frightening city where the uprooted African-American girl felt utterly lost. She had no job, no friends, no prospects. Within months her life was becoming intolerable but she could not bear to go home in defeat. A few months after her move to Boston, a hometown boy wrote to her and proposed marriage.

Nathan was a small man, not attractive to me. He was ugly. But I felt he would make a good husband, and we could have a good life together. I began to think about it—maybe we could work things out together. He could work, and I could work, and we'd save our money, and then we could buy a home and then start our family. That's what I really wanted.

We got married the summer before I turned 18. Was I a virgin? You better believe I was a virgin! I had never seen a naked man. I was scared and ready to go home to Mama. What was this man going to do to me? I hadn't known what to expect with sex, and I was not sexually attracted to him. On our wedding night Nathan grew impatient with me and just forced himself on me. That was traumatic. I got used to sex, it was part of marriage, but I never enjoyed sex with him throughout the marriage.

We moved to Philadelphia into a one-room apartment. The city was huge and strange to me, and I was very isolated because I didn't know anyone there. That marriage was bad from the start. Nathan was extremely jealous. He said, "No wife of mine is going to work." Within a month he was beating me and drinking and had a white girlfriend. He lost his job, and we moved into his brother's apartment. Nathan was a mean, lazy leech. I got pregnant after three months of marriage and had my daughter at 18. All my plans went right down the drain quickly. Then we moved to his mother's farm in Michigan. We were one mile from the nearest neighbor. We starved. We had beans three times a day, seven days a week. It was horrendous. I couldn't take the isolation and the poverty. Nathan completely ignored me except for sex. I went into a state of deep depression. When I was pregnant again at 20, Nathan kicked me in the stomach, and I lost the baby.

I found the church, and it saved my life. There would be people and music, and I could forget my life for the few hours I was in church. The only thing I had in my life was the church and my baby. The best thing was breast-feeding her and feeling that cuddling closeness. She was my life and joy. I could talk to her, and even though she was an infant I felt she knew what I was saying, and I didn't get any back talk from her.

Then I was pregnant again! No way in this world did I want to be pregnant again. I was getting deeper and deeper into a state of depression and just stopped talking. I just sat there gazing at the bare walls and couldn't deal with what was going on. I felt my husband had taken me away from life and had just thrown me away. He didn't want to work and wouldn't let us go on welfare. He said, "I'm the man of the house, and I will take care of my family." But he didn't. He was a mean, mean man.

I returned home to live with my mother when I was 21 but Nathan followed me there. We got a place to live and went on welfare. My daughter Hanna was born that year. It was like a fresh start in our life trying to become a family. But then Nathan would get jealous, and all hell would break loose, and he'd beat me in front of the children.

I took a part-time job evenings. I got out and finally began breathing free air again; that's the way it felt. Once I went to work my children had clothes and never went hungry again. I'll never forget the day I got my first paycheck. I bought the children clothes. When I got home Nathan demanded the money. Why was I wasting it on the children? That was what I had to put up with.

I got pregnant again, and my son was born when I was 22. But I wasn't depressed anymore because I was back in my hometown with my family and friends and could go to church whenever I wanted to. Having all the turmoil in my marriage, going to church was very peaceful for me. It was the one place I could go without being screamed at and beaten. I went to church with black eyes and swollen lips. The church was my escape. As long as I was there I knew no one was going to hurt me. I felt safe there. At home there was no peace at all. But I never thought of leaving Nathan.

I kept wondering why this man kept beating on me. I'd never done anything to him. I wanted to be a good wife and a good mother. His clothes were always clean, his house was always clean. His food was always ready, and I wasn't out running around. He blamed me for his life. He admitted that he wasn't able to keep a job and take care of his family, but he said it was my fault because I didn't believe in him. How could anyone believe in anyone like that? He was taking my food stamps and selling them. I had to go to work so my children could have food. He wouldn't even baby-sit while I went to work evenings; I had to leave the children with a friend. I'd get home from work after midnight, and that's when all hell would break loose, and he'd start beating on me. The children were terrified of him because all they ever saw was him screaming and beating their mother.

I was beginning to realize that I could work and take care of myself and my children alone. After all those years I finally asked myself, "Ruth, what in the world are you doing? Why are you letting this happen to you?" I began to realize that it wasn't good for the kids to live in that kind of terror.

When I was 23 I came home from work one night, and the house was a mess, as usual. I went into the kitchen and started boiling water on the stove to wash the dinner dishes. Nathan was sitting on the couch with the

TV going full blast. He threw a cup at me, and something snapped in me. The cup whizzed past my head, and the next thing I knew I'd thrown the pot of boiling water on Nathan and was sitting on top of him with a knife at his throat. I told him if he moved an inch I'd kill him, and I would have. I'd had it. All those years of abuse just built up all this anger that finally exploded. I told him if he ever hit me again I'd kill him, and I meant it. I told him I'd taken too much shit off of him. He was burned pretty bad and begged me to help him. I told him the way he was burning then was how I'd been burning for years. I had no pity left for that man. I'd taken it for years, and I wasn't going to take anymore.

I didn't have sex with him after that; I didn't trust him. I gave him money for a bus ticket out of town my next payday, and I haven't seen him since. I felt good when he left, never missed him. It was just such a relief that he was gone. I felt like a brand-new person. I was a young woman, and I made a new beginning.

Participation in the Public World

A woman makes a place for herself in a community and forms her own social world within it. The community may be the one she grew up in, or another very much like it, or yet another that stands in sharp contrast to her origins. She may devote herself actively to certain aspects of public life or remain focused on home or work.

The eleven young women who married in the Early Adult Transition centered their lives in the family, holding outside jobs only when financially necessary. Their job experience was negative or only minimally satisfying. None made a major investment of self in forming an occupation. They retained strong ties to the family of origin and did little to expand their horizons. Most had few friendships with women, no friendships with men, and no mentoring relationships with either. For Nora Cole and Ruth Allen, religion provided both a sustaining personal experience and a means of participation in the public world.

Six early marriers left the parental home and moved to another community during the Early Adult Transition. They had difficulty in adapting to the new community. The move tended more to separate them from their husbands than to bring them together. They felt isolated and lonely in a strange place.

VICKY PERRELLI

I married Frank at 20. He worked and lived 300 miles from my home. I didn't want to move that far away but there was no choice! I think I cried the entire five years we were there. We never used birth control. We figured if it was meant to be, it was meant to be, and it was; I got pregnant on the honeymoon. I had Eric at 21.

I was alone in an apartment while Frank worked long hours. I was isolated, without friends or family. We had no money. I couldn't handle it. He and I fought constantly, and I demanded that we go visit my parents every weekend. We really didn't know each other; we had only seen each other every other weekend for all those years. I kept saying to myself, "What did I get married for?" It was just a legal way to have sex. And the sexual relationship was very limited. We had fought all those years about having sex, and then once we got married Frank never seemed that interested anymore.

I hated those years of my life. My son was a colicky baby and cried constantly. I hated him. I hated my life. It was horrible. Nothing had prepared me for any of this. If I hadn't been Catholic I would have divorced. I talked about divorce with my mother, and she said, "You can't come home; where will you go?" So I stayed. I was pregnant again at 22 and had Alice at 23.

✑ BETH LOGAN

I graduated from high school at 18, commuted to a local college, and worked part-time at a department store. I thought I'd try a two-year program and get through as fast as I could. I hated college. I didn't make any friends and never had any dates. I wasn't getting very good grades, either. In my first year I met Kevin on a blind date. He was a senior at a local school. He seemed like a very steady kind of guy. We only saw each other weekends. I was not passionately in love with him. We dated a year. I never dated anyone else, just kind of went along, and assumed we would marry. Kevin urged that the relationship become sexual, and I thought, "Why not?—We're getting married anyway." We never discussed birth control.

Then Kevin took a job out West and left. I think if I had not gotten pregnant we would have gone our separate ways. I phoned him when I learned I was pregnant, and he said he would marry me. I quit college but that was no problem; I never pictured myself with a career really or living alone and working and taking care of myself. I just assumed you got married and had kids and lived happily ever after [laughs].

We got married when I was 19. We had not seen each other except once in the last six months, and here we were married and pregnant and moving to the West together. Leaving my parents was no problem; I kind of went from being taken care of by my parents to being taken care of by my husband. We lived in a 10 by 12 trailer in an isolated area and didn't know anyone. Kevin worked long hours and was never home. He ate three meals at work, came home at 8 p.m., was asleep by 9 p.m., and left for work at 5:30 a.m., six days a week. We never fought because we never saw each other or talked to each other. All we did together was have sex, which I found pleasant enough. I kind of went along. There was very little cooking or cleaning to do, so I spent my time watching TV. We were very poor and had no money for anything other than the bare necessities. It was a very, very narrow life but I was happy enough. I felt that Kevin would be doing better and would take better care of me, and that's all that mattered.

When I was 20 I met Crystal, who was in her late twenties. She had a car and could take me places. She was married but didn't have children. She was very good for me because *she* was delighted that I was pregnant. When I was 20 Paul was born. Crystal had a great interest in taking care of the baby, which was very, very good for me because I slept a lot and wasn't too involved with the baby. When I was 21 Crystal moved out of state, and it was very lonely for me. I decided to have a second child so Paul wouldn't be an only child, and I got pregnant at 22.

Kevin had no connection to the babies, never held them or played with them. He only commented when they cried and disturbed his sleep. But I thought that was okay—Kevin worked long hours, and taking care of the kids was *my* job. But I didn't feel very close to the babies, either. I felt ill at ease with them and seldom played with them. I diapered them, and fed them, and kept them clean but I really didn't know what to do. Nobody teaches you how to be a good parent. I'd take a look at the baby and really didn't know what to do with it. I didn't know they needed to be held and cuddled. There was a definite lack there. It was ignorance more than anything else. I was a parent but I wasn't being a parent. I was a parent biologically, I was a parent by virtue of nature, but I wasn't emotionally a parent.

I look back on those years and it seems amazing. Where was I? I never questioned anything then. I just meandered through all those years without ever thinking about anything. It was like I lived in a fog. I was totally dependent emotionally and financially on my husband. Anything he said I went along with and never questioned any of his decisions. He took care of me, and that's all that mattered then. The image that comes to my mind of my twenties is like a cocoon. I sat by myself most of the time except for the kids, just kind of wrapped and cushioned against the real world. I sat there and waited for something to happen. I could have sat there a long, long time.

Developmental Crisis and "Rock Bottom Time"

Most of the women had a moderate to severe crisis during the course of this transition. They had a basic sense of being overwhelmed, of having no way to form a minimally good enough life as an adult. For some the crisis involved considerable turmoil and conscious suffering; others were not clearly aware of the extent of their difficulties. When the total mix of external problems and subjective pain is very strong, we speak of a "rock bottom time." Over half of the homemakers had a rock bottom time in this period.

◄§ NORA COLE

The story of Nora Cole's courtship and marriage at 17 is given in Chapter 4. Her motherhood began a year later.

> Being a wife was so new to me. There were things I had never really done and had to get used to: planning and cooking meals, making sure the laundry was done, cleaning, being responsible for the home on a very limited budget. There was never much money. My husband was twenty years older than me. He'd work all day in the factory and come home tired, and I'd want to go out. I had to learn to slow down my pace of life to his.
>
> I grew up real fast, real fast. I had three girls in three years, 18, 19, and 20. It was unbelievably hectic. One baby would be asleep, and I'd be feeding another, and then the first and third would wake up. Walter did not help with the kids. I was totally responsible for all those lives during the day, in the evening, in the middle of the night, seven days a week. It was exhausting. Sometimes they'd be crying, and I'd be crying right along with them. Those were rough years.
>
> My husband was drinking a lot and doing a lot of gambling weekends, and I'd be home alone with the children. There was a lot of loneliness. When he got drunk he got very angry. He was mostly verbally abusive. I'd try to ignore it, and then he'd fall asleep and when he woke he would be fine. When I couldn't ignore it we'd have screaming battles. He hit me once, but I hit him right back and sent him to the hospital, and he never hit me again.
>
> At about 20 I did leave him and go home with the girls. But I wasn't happy there. I was an adult, used to having my own home. My parents told me I could stay and get a job and they'd help take care of the children for me. But I talked with my husband and decided to go back.
>
> At 22 I had a son, my fourth child. When he was about three months old I began to feel an emptiness within. It was like there was a huge glass tunnel straight down the center of me that was empty—something missing in my life. It was a huge chamber of emptiness within me. I realized it must be a religious experience I was missing in my life. I wanted something true, I wanted something to hold on to that was real that would help me and not just take from me. I needed to be rejuvenated in some way. I just felt the terrors of raising four small children all on my own. I felt that I was expected by society, by my children, by my husband to do it all well. And I was having difficulty surviving, just plain existing was a

problem right then. I was going through a lot of changes and conflicts and depression. I was so burdened. I felt if I opened my mouth to talk I'd start screaming and not be able to stop. I was desperate.

I began to explore various religions. I went to a new church with my children. We sat down, and the children started fussing and whining and crying. One of the ladies from the church said, "Can I hold your baby for you?" Before the service was half over I didn't have any of my children with me. That was the first time something like that had ever happened to me. That church helped me a great deal. They constantly taught us how we could apply our spiritual experiences to our everyday needs, and how our religion would help us through whatever trials we had in our lives. If your husband stays out late, when he comes home don't argue with him. Make sure his food is cooked and his clothes are washed and ironed. The church helped lessen my burden.

Ending the Early Adult Transition

How do we decide when a transitional period in life structure development comes to an end? This judgment cannot be based on a single event, such as leaving the parental home, getting married, graduating, or making a major geographical move. Such events are important markers of a developmental process, but we can see its shape clearly only by placing the event within the larger life course. A given event may reflect the start or the end of a developmental period. It may also occur in the middle of a period and have a different developmental significance. Likewise, we cannot determine when a period ends by examining only one component of the life structure. A *transitional period ends when the tasks of terminating, questioning, and exploring have less urgency, and when first priority is given to the task of building a new life structure.*

The homemakers completed the Early Adult Transition at age 22 or 23. Where were they in their life structure development at this time? We can distinguish three basic patterns, each with wide individual variations:

(1)   Seven women had already formed a provisional structure as homemakers in Traditional Marriage Enterprises with a family of one to four children. As the Early Adult Transition ended, it was evident that this structure was badly flawed. All seven had major problems stemming from early marriage and motherhood and from stressful life circumstances. They were now trying to build an Entry Life Structure that would better support their adult aspirations.

(2)   Three women married and had their first child at 22 or 23. The marriage and pregnancy were marker events for the end of the Early Adult Tran-

sition and the start of the Entry Life Structure, in which they hoped to build a life structure as homemakers within a Traditional Marriage Enterprise.

(3)   Five women were single (four never-married, one divorced) and without children as this period ended. They began forming an Entry Life Structure as single, working, dating, matrimony-seeking young women. As the new period got under way, occupation was a major though not central component of the life structure, and family was the central, unfilled component.

The voice of the Anti-Traditional Figure could barely be heard in the Adolescent Life Structure and the Early Adult Transition, and it produced only a small blip in most women's trajectory toward a Traditional Marriage Enterprise. It was a little louder in some homemakers, inaudible or absent in others. In every case, however, the struggle and the balance of power between the two internal figures evolved through the successive developmental periods of early adulthood, as we shall see. The same kind of struggle occurred among the career women, though it differed in nature and intensity. In short, both internal figures exist, and develop in diverse ways, in virtually all women. One is not more "natural" or "basic" than the other. We have much to learn about their sources, about the conditions affecting their development, and about the possibilities for long-term change in both.

We will next follow the evolution of the homemakers' lives through the period of the Entry Life Structure.

6

Entry Life Structure for Early Adulthood: Homemakers

The period of the Entry Life Structure most often begins at 22 and ends at 28. The primary tasks of this period are to build and maintain a first adult life structure and to enrich one's life within this structure. Several other tasks derive from the primary ones. Work must be done on the various components of the emerging life structure. Within each component it is necessary to make major choices, to modify old relationships and to establish new ones. One or a few components will become central in the structure, others may drop out altogether, and still others may fluctuate in relative importance before taking a more stable place at the center or periphery. A woman must take a further step in her relationship to marriage, motherhood, family of origin, occupation, the wider community. She often has the illusion—so common at the start of every structure-building period—that if she just makes the right choices and forms the right relationships, she can create a satisfactory life pattern that will last forever after.

In the homemaker sample this period began at age 22 for most women, at 23 for two. It ended at 28, except for one at 27 and one at 29. For all fifteen women, marriage/family was the central component of the Entry Life Structure. There was no other component of major significance, except for a few lives in which family of origin or religion played a major part. Occupation was a central component only for Jenny Abatello, but it remained unfilled while she devoted herself primarily to family. Most women held outside jobs at times but none made much investment of self in occupation.

First Phase, Age 25 Shift, and Second Phase

A single life structure predominated in each woman's life during the entire period. There was, however, an evolution *within* the structure. The first phase of this period lasted from about 22 to 25, the second phase from 25 to

28. The move from initial to final phase almost always occurred at 25—not before late 24 or after early 26. Because of this age specificity I have called it the Age 25 Shift. It was discovered here by Judy Levinson in her careful biographical reconstructions of the lives of all forty-five women studied. I did not identify this shift in the earlier study of men, but it may exist for men as well.

The first phase is primarily a time of building—forming key relationships, strengthening commitments, and getting an Entry Life Structure in place. Some young women make their key choices before the period begins. In the initial phase they attempt to firm up each relationship and to integrate the various components. Other young women use this phase in a more tentative way, exploring possible choices and working on troublesome components. When a woman's life is externally stable and well ordered during this time, she still has inner concerns to deal with and changes to make before the new structure can be firmly established. When her life is relatively unsettled, she is trying to clarify her priorities and form a stable structure.

The shift that occurs at 25 is on a smaller scale than the transition from one life structure to another, but it is of decisive importance in bringing about the change from initial to final phase of this period. No one can fully establish a life structure before 25. The initial version of the structure is incomplete or poorly integrated in some important respects. There are problems of various kinds—a bad marriage or job, wanting marriage or children but not having them, the multiple pressures of homemaking, being too enmeshed with or too distant from parents, conflict between work and family.

At 25 a woman comes to a clearer recognition that her life has such problems and decides to make some changes. The changes are often highly specific: to get married, to end or stay in a difficult marriage, to have a child, get a job, go back to school, give a markedly higher or lower priority to a particular aspect of living. The specific choices are, however, rooted in more general concerns. She is taking a firmer position about the kind of life she wants to have. She is deciding which component(s) of the Entry Life Structure will be central, which peripheral or excluded. She is seeking a more stable order within which to pursue her aspirations. The change, in short, involves more than a single relationship or aspect of life; it is intended to make her life as a whole more integrated and satisfying.

The meaning of the shift is usually not very conscious or articulated, especially as it is happening. Some women make a dramatic change without much conscious reflection or planning, and recognize only later (or never) what their intentions were. For others the shift is more subtle and hardly noticeable. For example, a woman has a second child—an event that has no unusual significance to her husband or others. In her mind, however, the decision to have another child derives from a more fundamental life choice: to remain in a difficult marriage, or to put aside for a time her occupational interests. Another woman takes a new job not markedly different from an earlier one. From an external point of view, it is not a notable event. From a subjective point of view, however, it constitutes a major turning point: she is choosing not merely to take another job, but to become more independent, establish a more defined occupation, and give her family a less exclusively central place in her life. Her private intentions in making the choice may not become clearly conscious for many months or years. The impact of the choice on her life structure is evident more quickly.

Although the Age 25 Shift usually involves one or a few major life events, we cannot determine the nature and consequences of the shift by looking solely at the external events. It is essential to look as well at the personal meaning of the events and the life structure in which they occur. The Age 25 Shift crystallizes the Entry Life Structure and instigates the second phase of this period.

Some women have a relatively satisfactory life structure in place by 26 and then devote the second phase to enhancing their lives within it. Others decide at 25 to make a major change but need another few years to implement the choice. For example, a single woman may come to feel at 25 that her most urgent priority is to marry and start a family, but it takes another few years to marry, have a child, and establish a pattern of family life. Marriage/family was the central yet unfilled component of her initial phase and was gradually "filled in" during the final phase.

Let us now examine the various ways in which the homemakers' lives evolved during this period. I will group them according to the three patterns noted in Chapter 4.

Pattern A: Women Who Had a Family When the Period Began

Seven women were mothers of one to four children when they started building an Entry Life Structure. Family had been the central component of the provisional life structure they created in the Early Adult Transition, and it became the pillar of the new life structure. In many cases the external features of their lives did not change markedly in the new period. A closer look shows, however, that the Entry Life Structure differed in significant respects from the provisional structure of the Early Adult Transition.

One crucial change was in the character of the marital relationship. By the start of the period all seven women came to realize, with various mixtures of bitterness, depression, and resignation, that their marriage had severe limitations and was not likely to improve. The man they had married could not be the caring husband and responsible family man they had once hoped for.

Ruth Allen left her first husband at 23, immediately formed a stable relationship with another man, and started building an Entry Life Structure in which family was the central component. The other six—Vicky Perrelli, Nora Cole, Wendy Lewis, Carol O'Brien, Beth Logan, Lynn McPhail— decided that, despite the problems, the marriage was at least minimally adequate. It seemed better than the available alternatives—returning to the parental home or becoming for an indefinite time (perhaps permanently) a poor, employed, divorced mother and "single head of household." Each woman began making a sharper distinction between marriage and family. Her main commitment was to child-rearing and maintaining an intact family. Her husband was important as a provider, a public head of family, and in some cases a father, but the marriage now had a different place in the Entry Life Structure. She invested less of herself in the marital relationship and accepted less in return from her husband. If he had previously been somewhat unreliable as a provider and participant in family life, she demanded greater responsibility in these respects; but they lived in even more separate worlds and led more clearly demarcated parallel unconnected lives.

During the initial phase, then, these women formed an Entry Life Structure in which family was the central component, marriage was a necessary but limited component, and there was little else of any personal significance. For some it was a rock bottom time of acute suffering, for others a difficult time borne with acquiescence and denial but little conscious pain. For none was it a thriving or joyful time.

All seven women went through an Age 25 Shift. External events usually triggered the shift and gave it a particular shape. In every case, however, the woman responded to the events by strengthening the family as the central component of her life structure and by redefining the marital relationship. She also began to engage in outside activities that were satisfying in their own right and that supported her primary commitment to family. The Age 25 Shift thus produced minor but important changes within the Entry Life Structure, to some extent strengthening and enriching it.

Six of the seven women got pregnant and had another child at age 25 or 26. The pregnancy occurred at a time when the woman was feeling keenly the limitations of her marriage and her highly domestic life. Why did she have a child at this point? A major reason was that the new child helped her maintain the existing life structure by providing some additional satisfactions, strengthening her commitment to homemaking, and enabling her to avoid focusing more directly on her dissatisfactions. Four of the six women decided during the pregnancy or shortly after that this would be their last child; and in fact it was. They came to understand, usually in the Age 30 Transition, that with this child they were coming to the limit of their commitment to a predominantly family-centered life. In another few years this life structure would have to be modified. In effect, the child gave them a little more time—time to stay put, to avoid facing major problems, to continue a certain kind of domestic life.

The Age 25 Shift led to a final phase in which the Entry Life Structure was consolidated and stabilized. For example, at 25 Beth Logan and Vicky Perrelli both moved with their husbands and children back to their hometowns after several years away. They then established closer ties to their families of origin, and Vicky had another child. With the support of parents they remained in problematic marriages and shored up sagging life structures.

✺ RUTH ALLEN

After my husband left I got welfare and food stamps and stayed home with my children. I was badly hurt by Nathan and felt I would never trust a man again. I was 23 when I met Luke, who was 23 years older than me. I'd see him around and we'd talk, but I ignored his advances for months. Then one night he got upset and said, "I know you've been hurt by that husband of yours but all men are not like that. I'm glad your husband left because I like you a lot." We started a relationship. He was married with grown children. Divorce was never an issue. His wife knew that there was another woman but as long as Luke didn't divorce her she accepted it.

It was a much better relationship than my marriage had been. He drank but he never abused me. He was the kind of man I'd wished my ex-husband had been. He was a good provider. I never wanted for anything. He made sure I had an open account at the store in case I needed food or clothing for the children. People knew about the relationship. My mother never approved of my going with a married man. I would never take him to her house. But if my family came to my house and Luke was there then he stayed. That was my house; I paid the rent.

I had two children with Luke, Jill and Dean. I practiced birth control—foam and birth control pills—but it just never worked for me, not even the IUD. When I got pregnant with Jill at 24, to me it wasn't a sin. The church tried to throw me out because I was a married woman having a child with another man. I stood up in that church and I told them to prove it. "You don't take care of me; I take care of myself." They had no right to say anything; it was none of their business. They had never come to my rescue when my husband was beating on me. They never asked how I got those black eyes. They never asked me if my children were hungry. I just continued to go to church. It hurt me that they did that but I was not going to let those people get me down.

When I told Luke I was pregnant he was very happy. He was more of a husband to me than my ex-husband had ever been. He really was a good provider. He was very proud of his baby. He said all the spunk hadn't left him yet; he could still make babies. He was proud of that. It made our relationship stronger. I loved Luke, I really loved him. I'm not going to say that it was passionate as far as being sexual was concerned. It's just that I loved Luke for who he was to me, for his kindness, for his understanding. I wasn't involved with anyone else those five years. He never said he loved me but he said he had never felt that way with a woman before. He and I were very close, very compatible. We never argued. We enjoyed each other. We didn't talk much but we were very playful with one another. He often said he'd wished it was me he'd married. I'd like to have married him but I would never tell him to leave his wife. The way I see it now is: I had a fling that lasted five years, that two children I love came out of.

At 25 I took a nurse's aide training course for six months. I was in the top 5 percent of my class and got a job immediately. I worked there almost two years. I wasn't earning much money; I was still getting welfare supplements and food stamps but I was making it. We had food, and my bills were always paid. I even purchased things on the time plan. I tried not to rely too much on Luke. I never asked him for anything. I loved working as a nurse's aide. I began getting stronger. I felt that I had something within me that I wanted to share, and taking care of patients was a good feeling. Then I got laid off and drew unemployment. Then I cleaned houses and baby-sat, plus welfare.

I got pregnant, even with birth control pills, and had Dean at 28. After Dean was born I broke up with Luke. The reason I broke up was because I began to sit down and look at my life and to think about all the opportunities out there in this world that I wanted to tackle, and I just felt with Luke I couldn't do that. I had been to Connecticut on vacation and liked what I saw. My sisters begged me to move there. So I did. I have a lot of feelings for Luke even today; I think about him still. I'm sort of sorry things turned out the way they did. I got a job at a hospital as an aide and started a new life with my children.

The nonlegal marriage to Luke served a number of important functions in Ruth Allen's life. It enabled her to form a Traditional Marriage Enterprise of the kind she had always envisioned. He was a good enough provider, materially and emotionally, to ensure the survival and well-being of the family. He enabled her to be primarily a homemaker and to make family the center of her life. But the marriage was also flawed in several respects. It was not especially passionate. It created tensions in Ruth's relationships with her mother, church, and community. She continued to feel some guilt in relation to Luke's wife and family. She understood that, for all its seriousness and positive qualities, it was also "a fling"—a nonbinding, tentative relationship that could not permanently endure.

Paradoxically, these limitations were also advantages for her. She urgently wanted a husband/father who would take adequate care of her family but she was not ready to rely heavily on a marital relationship or to invest much of herself in it. The tentativeness and time-limited character of the nonlegal marriage were thus assets as well as liabilities for her. Being the "second" rather than the sole wife suited her quite well during this period. If Luke spent less time with her than he otherwise might have, he also made fewer demands and gave her more space to pursue her own interests. They had more time together and had a stronger relationship than most of the full-time married couples. Ruth gradually acquired job skills and became more able to take care of herself. At 28, entering the Age 30 Transition, she was ready to leave Luke and seek a new life, within which she would attempt to form a new marriage.

⤳   LYNN McPHAIL

I married Jim at 19 and moved from the Midwest to New Haven. I got pregnant right away and had my first baby at 20. We never used birth control—we just took what came. Jim had no ambition and didn't want to work. I found out I'd married a Mama's boy. He finally got a job, and we moved into our own apartment. Before that we lived with his family. He was never home. He worked nights, slept days, and visited his mother all the time. I kept asking myself, "What kind of life is this for me and the baby?"

At 22 I went to work full-time as a clerk in a supermarket, because we needed the money. I never wanted to be a working mother—I wanted to be at home with my daughter. I firmly believe that mothers should be at home unless it's a pressing financial need. I finally got pregnant at 23 and stayed home. I'd been exposed to German measles, and the doctor wanted me to abort. No way! I gave birth at 23, and she does have her problems; she is blind in one eye and has heart problems.

My first son, Barry, was born when I was 25. At that point I demanded that we get a house. I needed, finally, to have my own place. We got a house but Jim couldn't stand the pressure—the house, the kids, and the job. For about six weeks there were signs that he was nuts. He was talking to the TV and being physically abusive of me and the kids. He thought I was having affairs with everyone in town. We took him to the doctor, who gave him some pills. One night he tried to kill me [age 26]!

Jim was put in a mental hospital 25 miles away. He was there for almost two years, and I visited him twice a week. I didn't drive but I got rides. I never considered leaving him. I had a 5-year-old and a 22-month-old and a 5-month-old and all the bills, but I had taken a vow for better or worse. Well, this was worse, all right. We went on welfare and had a really hard time, but we made it. I finally got my driving license and was more independent. I raised the kids completely on my own, from then on.

When Jim was discharged he came home and went back to his job. I managed the house and the bills and kept all stress away from him. I didn't especially want more kids, but the hospital psychiatrist said it would help Jim's self-esteem to father more. That's how the last two kids were born. At 28 I got pregnant and had a miscarriage. When I was in the hospital Jim didn't even come to visit me. That hurt! I had visited him twice a week while he was in the hospital. I felt that nobody gave a damn about me. But soon I got pregnant again and had Dana when I was 29. [The pregnancies at 28 and 29 mark the start of her Age 30 Transition.]

Pattern B: Women Who Married and Started a Family in the First Phase

Three women—Sara Cushing, Jenny Abatello, Kay Ryan—married at age 22 and had their first child at 23, as they began forming an Entry Life Structure. The initial phase of this period was largely taken up with establishing a family and a new life structure. Becoming a homemaker was surprisingly difficult. The heavy burdens of life in this period contrasted sharply with the protected character of their previous lives.

All three women built an Entry Life Structure in which family was the central component. Each was faced with the multiple responsibilities of motherhood and home management, as well as forming and maintaining a marital relationship very different from the courting relationship. The husband worked hard, often overtime or at more than one job, and was minimally available for domestic work or pleasure. The splitting of the domestic and public worlds led the couple into increasingly parallel unconnected lives. Marriage provided an essential basis for family life, but the marital relationship was extremely limited.

Family of origin was an important secondary component in the Entry Life Structure. Although they wanted to become somewhat more independent of parents, these young women also looked to parents for various benefits: financial assistance, gifts, baby-sitting, emotional support. Mother was the key figure in the family of origin. The father had less presence and played a shadowy part. While seeking greater independence in some ways, the young women continued to seek maternal advice, to be highly vulnerable to maternal disapproval, and to have difficulty asserting themselves when they felt controlled or criticized. They took a small step from good girl/daughter in the parental home to good married daughter closely attached to the parental home.

Although mother gave concrete assistance and advice regarding specific problems, mother and daughter did not have a mentorial relationship. They did not talk about more fundamental issues for the daughter in becoming a wife, mother, adult; nor did she feel that her mother was a special source of wisdom and personal growth as she sought to make her way in the adult world. She felt, rather, that her mother continued to treat her as "my little girl" and to keep her in a dependent position. Despite a vague resentment about this, she found it difficult to separate emotionally and to take a more independent stand.

For Kay Ryan and Sara Cushing, occupation was virtually absent as a component of the Entry Life Structure. In the first months of the marriage they held routine jobs to help with the finances. After getting pregnant they gladly gave up the jobs and devoted themselves almost exclusively to home-making.

SARA CUSHING

I married at 22 and had my daughter Jane at 23. I was then on birth control pills until 25. Bill and I had lots of arguments. My daughter and I formed a pair, and Bill was not with us. I wrapped her in my world. My life revolved around her whether my husband was home or not. Bill wasn't part of disciplining her, either. He only reprimanded her if she got in his viewing field of the TV, only if she bothered him—which I didn't think was right.

In my twenties I was in a fog. I never expressed an opinion. My whole life revolved around my child and friends. But it was an okay life— everyone I knew was living the same way. When I was 25 I asked, "How can I better my life?" The only answer I could come up with was to have another baby—there were no other options. I wasn't happy with what I had. But I never tried to change *me*; I just felt sorry for myself. I was blaming my husband because he wasn't earning enough money. I didn't feel secure in my life as far as being taken care of. I saw my friends saving and buying homes but we couldn't. We were going nowhere.

Then Bill wanted me to go to work! I wouldn't even think of it. I wanted the kind of life my parents had: my father earned the money, and my mother stayed home and took care of the house. Divorce was a thought at 25 but it was put on hold. Bill was always more interested in being out with the guys than with me. I resented that. I always knew that I didn't want to live my whole life with him. Something wasn't right—I really hated being with him. There was a sense that I wasn't important to him. I knew he wasn't satisfied with our life, and it made me feel that it was somehow *my* fault. I hoped that having a second baby would make the marriage better and would make Bill change, and then he'd settle down and not need to go out with his male friends. I still wanted that storybook ending. Bill agreed to have another baby, and I got pregnant at 25 but had a miscarriage. I had another miscarriage at 26. That was very sad, and I was very depressed. I wanted another baby real bad. There was a sense of failure if you just had one—a failure to fulfill my dream of having three kids.

Another big change at 25 was that my parents moved to another state. I had a real sense of freedom but felt guilty about it. My mother had been helpful with baby-sitting but she was very critical and made me feel like a rotten mother. I had been very dependent on her for approval. At the same time I also had a sense of loss of the family. I felt abandoned, like an orphan.

Bill was making hardly any money. I nagged him into taking another job where he would make more. He took the job but he hated every minute there and complained every minute he was home. He made more money but we were still very poor. We were months behind in our bills and often didn't have enough money for food. I earned money at home, typing and baby-sitting. We bought groceries with the money I made.

Finally, after trying for three long years, I got pregnant at 28 and had my son at 29. That started a whole new time in my life.

JENNY ABATELLO

Jenny Abatello was the only homemaker with a Dream of having an occupational career. In this sense she was marginal between the homemakers and the career women. A major theme throughout her adulthood was the struggle to include both family and occupation as central components of her life structure:

As a girl I expected to have a life pretty much like my mother's. I certainly didn't go far afield of my family geographically or emotionally or any other way. By twelfth grade I knew what my future would be: I'd marry my high school boyfriend and have a family. I also wanted to have a career in teaching but I didn't see how to do that. I married Steve at 22, as I graduated from college. I worried about having this marriage and my career. I knew that Steve, who was 25, would want to have kids soon. I knew I shouldn't say that we should wait before having kids. We never discussed it. I thought, "I'll never get established in my career"—and I never did really. That first summer was boring at home, and I got to know how little there was to do there without children. When I started my teaching job in September I felt on top of the world: I'd made it! Birth control was frowned on; you took what God sent you. And my mother was pushing us to make her a grandmother. We lived in my old neighborhood a few houses from my parents. I got pregnant in the first academic year, finished out the year, and quit at 23 to have my family. I figured I wouldn't be able to return for ten or fifteen years until the children were older because it was unheard of at that time for a mother to work unless it was a financial necessity.

The first year of marriage was okay, no serious problems. I was going to be a good little wife. Steve was a pretty traditional man, and he expected a pretty traditional marriage—but he also respected my education and my desire to teach. The biggest problem was that he did hard physical labor, came home exhausted, had supper, and fell asleep watching TV. At first I didn't think it would turn out too well. He got up at 5:30, and I was just going to sleep at 1:30. When I got pregnant I was really upset. I remember crying all by myself when I came home from the doctor's, thinking, "I've not had a chance to really begin my life, and now I won't be able to do anything." Steve and my family and his family were delighted about the baby. It was pretty hard not to share their enthusiasm, but I just wasn't ready for this.

My first child, Guy, had a traumatic C-section birth. I felt like a total failure—couldn't have a baby the normal way, couldn't even nurse him. I had a horrible postpartum depression that lasted over a year. The next two years were horrible. Steve was laid off for a while, and my family had to take care of us financially. I was totally involved with Guy. No one had ever been so emotionally dependent on me before. It was draining. I felt so guilty: "Dear God, does this kid know I'd rather be someplace else, *anyplace* else?" I wasn't too domestic with the house, either.

I got engulfed! I was totally responsible for this child. I just felt cut off from any kind of social life, any kind of career. I felt hemmed in, closed in, afraid that I would never have an adult to talk to again. Steve's family thought I was a complete waste. I learned what being accepted by them meant—having coffee and talking at each other's home every day. How I envied my single friends! They were working, traveling, free. I tried all sorts of things to fill the void. I got Steve to join a bowling league and have some friends. He knew I was depressed and bitchy, and he tried to help. But after a year he had enough and stopped going out. I guess I was seeing my own needs and saying *he* needed to get out.

I still remember waking up in the morning and thinking; "Good grief, is this the way it's going to be, day after day after day?" I tried to discuss it with my mother and mother-in-law, but they were pretty tough on me emotionally and didn't understand what the fuss was about. After all, this was what marriage and motherhood were about. I'd see kids I went to high school with, pushing their baby carriages around. I thought, "I'm in the club now!" I was pretty sure I didn't want any part of it—but I stayed.

By the time Jenny was 25, Steve had a better job, the family had their own place, and things were more settled. Jenny could now take preliminary steps to enrich her life. She took an evening graduate course. She discussed with Steve the idea of having a part-time job as a substitute teacher. He agreed, as he generally did when she took a strong initiative around her educational-occupational interests. To her surprise, "It was horrible to sub — zooey, not a career." Within a few months she decided to have another child. "I thought, 'Why not?' I knew I didn't want just one child. If I was going to stay home anyway I might as well get it over with, though I wasn't very enthused about having another baby."

Jenny's second child was born just as she turned 26. The birth completed the Age 25 Shift and brought her into the final phase of the Entry Life Structure:

> Maggie was born without trauma. I felt like Mother of the Year — a typical American woman with my boy and my girl and my house. We were renting a better house by that time, right next to my parents. I really got into the domestic scene — entertained, took gourmet cooking classes. I felt, "Maybe this isn't going to be so bad after all." I also decided, soon after Maggie's birth, not to have more kids; two was just right. I never discussed it with Steve, and he didn't push it. As the kids got older they were like real people and much more interesting to me than infants. I took them places, tried to be Supermom. And Steve helped more: he loved them as babies but didn't do much with them, then after a year or so they began a close relationship. He's a good father. Thoughts of work were less in my mind until I was 28.

The conflict between the internal Traditional Homemaker Figure and the internal Anti-Traditional Figure was clearly a fundamental theme in Jenny's life. The former gave her the benefits of being closely attached to the world of her origins, but it also limited her exploration of other worlds and modes of living. The latter aspired to further education, a more "modern" outlook, and the pursuit of her own career aspirations. The two figures were absolutely antithetical in her mind and in her world. It seemed impossible to combine them or to find a middle ground. The basic choice, as Jenny experienced it, was to be a dutiful daughter, wife, and mother in a secure, well-defined world, or to risk losing all that that world offered in a search for something else that might not be available.

Among the homemakers generally, the internal Traditional Homemaker Figure was predominant and the internal Anti-Traditional Figure relatively unformed or suppressed at least until the late twenties. In Jenny Abatello's case, however, these internal figures engaged in three major struggles between ages 18 and 25. Each struggle was shaped by the developmental period in which it occurred. The Traditional Homemaker Figure won out in all three but the opposition kept gaining ground. Because they reflect so well the stability as well as the change in her life during these years, I'll review briefly the three choice points and the struggles they elicited.

The *first* choice point came at 18, the start of Jenny's Early Adult Transition. During high school Jenny had mentorial relationships with two female teachers who recognized her unusual talents and encouraged her to pursue a teaching career. Knowing of her family's limited means, they offered to assist her in obtaining an excellent college education. At graduation she chose, instead, to attend a less than excellent local college. While financial problems were a consideration, this choice stemmed in large part from her unreadiness to differentiate herself from the family and strike out on her own. Her anxieties about taking a teaching career path were intensified by the fact that both teachers were "old maids," thus confirming her fear that career and family were antithetical: to choose one was to lose the other.

The *second* turning point came at age 20, in the middle of the Early Adult Transition and the college years, when Jenny seriously questioned her relationship with Steve. This relationship, formed in high school, was a powerful link to her origins. It kept her on the proper matrimonial path and counterbalanced the potential in the college education to lead her to another path. Her basic conflict was not about the relationship with Steve; it was about what she wanted to do with herself and her life. After a few months' tentative separation she returned to Steve, got formally engaged, and had a "graduation" wedding. Again, after a brief digression, she remained in the fold.

What other options had she been seeking and why did she give up so quickly? The courting relationship was formed within the Adolescent Life Structure. In the Early Adult Transition Jenny had a glimmering of hope for a different life. But she was also afraid that ending the relationship would separate her from the family of origin and its familiar world. And there was the fear, strongly reinforced by others, that the search for something better would be fruitless: she would fail to gain a better marriage and, worse, lose her one opportunity for a secure life and end up with nothing. It would take an adventurous spirit, indeed, or a person who found the traditional solution intolerable, to seek so chimerical an alternative.

The *third* struggle lasted from age 22 to 25. Jenny had a severe crisis, a rock bottom time, in the initial phase of the Entry Life Structure. The conflict between family and occupation was becoming more sharply defined. Married life went well enough while she could maintain the illusion that she might continue indefinitely as wife and teacher but not mother. With the pregnancy she realized finally that she would be a mother first of all. With luck, she might start a limited career in ten or fifteen years.

The realization was overwhelming. She was entering a life that might well be intolerable, and she could see no way either to improve it or to leave it. Her condition was diagnosed as a "postpartum depression." In actuality, a depression of this kind is not simply about having a child. It can also be about the woman's life, as she lives it in the present and imagines it in the future. Jenny felt "engulfed," a member of "the club" of young mothers. She envied her single friends who were free to work and travel. At stake were her relationships with husband, child, extended family, friends, every key person and group in her life.

The inner struggle thus has to be seen in the context of her life structure development. The central component of her Entry Life Structure was homemaker in a Traditional Marriage Enterprise. This component supported various relationships consistent with homemaking and excluded virtually all others. Jenny had mixed feelings about everyone and everything included in this component, and she had a corroding sense of loss about the things that had to be excluded. The void she experienced was the absence of occupation, which included all the relationships and involvements that might be part of a flourishing career—intellectual stimulation, independence, travel, friendship.

Occupation was a central yet unfilled component. It was the vehicle for her vitality, her sense of excitement about adult life, her partially formed Dream of a career. Without it she felt empty and hemmed in. The internal Anti-Traditional Figure was drowning yet also struggling to survive. Jenny wanted in time to have a family and to maintain the ties with her origins, but her passion was in the occupation. Her depression stemmed from grief and anger over the loss of the occupational world and of the parts of her self that could not be lived out within a Traditional Marriage Enterprise.

We have two kinds of evidence that occupation was a central component. First, its absence was so painful. Second, and equally important, it had an inner presence that interpenetrated all the other components. It made her a "bitchy," demanding wife who was never satisfied, since her husband could not give her what she most wanted. It distanced her to some degree from the child for whom she wished to be a loving mother. It alienated her from her own mother, who, despite the mutual affection between them, could not understand what was gnawing at her daughter's heart. And it complicated the relationships with her friends and in-laws.

Family and occupation were central yet antithetical components of Jenny's Entry Life Structure. Family was actively lived out, valued in many respects, yet also oppressive when it took all her energies. Occupation, the unfilled central component, ate away at what she had. In its initial phase, from 22 to 25, the Entry Life Structure became almost intolerable.

The *third* struggle was resolved in the Age 25 Shift. The brief "zooey" job as substitute teacher enabled Jenny to set aside her educational-occupational aspirations and to have a second child. Occupation was still an important unfilled component but its absence was more tolerable. The family component became more satisfying. With the arrival of her daughter she could be a more competent, loving mother. The improvement in Steve's work and income allowed them to become more independent of parents. As the children grew beyond infancy, Steve got more involved in their care. The marital relationship did not become more intimate but they formed a more secure partnership in which each made a jointly valued contribution. She found ways to maximize the pleasurable aspects of motherhood, such as taking the kids to places that were educational for them and, equally important, stimulating for her. She learned to minimize the most deadening activities, such as household chores and small talk with the extended family. She felt like "Mother of the Year" and a good daughter, but much more on her own terms. The internal Anti-Traditional Figure had some breathing space and could be partially lived out. This figure came out of the internal closet, as it were, in the Age 30 Transition—a change that had enormous consequences for Jenny's further life.

Pattern C.   Women Who Were Unmarried and Childless Throughout the First Phase

Five women were unmarried and without children as this period began. Elaine Olson, Claire Berman, Emily Swift, and Nan Krummel were single-never-married; Angela Capelli had just ended her first marriage. All of them had full-time jobs such as nurse, teacher, or typist, but none had long-term occupational goals. They planned to work until they could find the right man, marry, and start a family within a Traditional Marriage Enterprise. In short, they were homemakers whose domestic career had not yet begun.

In the initial phase work was not a central component of the Entry Life Structure. The young women were ready to drop it as soon as they could enter a Traditional Marriage Enterprise. At the same time, work occupied a major place and served important functions in their lives. It reduced their dependence on parents (although three continued to live with or near parents and to remain firmly within the family orbit). It enabled them to develop some degree of competence and to experience themselves as active participants in the public world. In this respect they were markedly different from the women in Patterns A and B, who led more narrowly domestic lives during this period. Finally, work provided the basis for a social life through which they sought to meet prospective husbands. The job was thus of considerable importance for them even though they were not trying to build an occupational future.

Marriage/family was the central yet unfilled component of the Entry Life Structure. The concern with matrimony had a pervasive presence in their lives. Expecting to become homemakers, they invested little of themselves in occupation. They made a sharp distinction between potentially matrimonial relationships with eligible serious men, and other kinds such as casual dates. All five women had understood in the Early Adult Transition that it was important to marry within a year or so of completing their schooling. Four had been involved in a marriage or serious courting relationship that ended in great disappointment at age 21 or 22—a bitter outcome of their matrimonial efforts. Angela Capelli at 22 was coming out of a painful three-year marriage and was cautious about remarriage. Elaine Olson terminated with her "prince" when he told her of his ex-wife and child. As Emily Swift graduated from college, she counted on marrying the medical student with whom she had been going steady, but he broke off the relationship. Claire Berman was the only one who did not have an intense courtship relationship in her Early Adult Transition. In the initial phase of the Entry Life Structure she had a variety of dating relationships but was still not emotionally ready to form a courting relationship.

From about 22 to 25 all five women had full-time jobs and were financially independent. They had an active social life, dated, and looked forward to matrimony. While keeping busy on many fronts, they were not heavily engaged in any activity and generally felt that "nothing important" was happening. They had a sense of being in limbo until the key event—marriage and motherhood—would bring them into full adulthood. They were waiting for "Mr. Right" to come along but were often not internally ready to meet him. The initial phase was spent in a state of suspended animation—not doing much exploring of the external world and not being very clear about what they wanted.

In the Age 25 Shift they felt an urgent need to fill the unfilled component and embark upon a domestic career. All five young women got married at age 25 to 28 and were pregnant within a year of marriage; one had a miscarriage and remained childless. During the second phase they were engaged primarily in courting, getting married, and starting a family. Soon after marrying, they gave up their jobs and decided to work in the future only when they had the time or the financial need.

In the second phase of the Entry Life Structure the single working women became full-time homemakers. The change in social roles and circumstances was quite dramatic. When we examine the change from the vantage point of the life structure, however, we see changes within a stable framework. Four of the five women succeeded in forming the life structure they had sought from the start of this period. Family was the central component throughout, but it was unfilled until the Age 25 Shift or soon after. Work served important functions in their lives but was never a central component of the Entry Life Structure. It enabled them to survive on a more independent basis for a time, but was readily given up once they established a Traditional Marriage Enterprise. The fifth woman, Emily Swift, got married at 27, had a miscarriage soon after, and ended this period on a note of disappointment. In short, all five women maintained the same life structure during this period, a structure in which family was the central component, work useful but expendable.

✍ ANGELA CAPELLI

After I divorced at 23 I lived with my parents and worked at my old typing job. I wanted to get married and become a mother. I dated one guy for a year and a half. We were going to get married but he broke up with me because his mother didn't approve of his marrying a divorced woman. I was crushed. It hit me: I'm 25 and not a mother yet! I met with a priest about the issue of my divorce and my future as a wife and mother in terms of the Catholic Church. He gave me no hope. I could not remarry in the church! He made me feel that at 25 my life was over. All of a sudden I realized, "I'll never be a mother. If I can't get married I'll never be a mother!"

Then I met Jerry. He was divorced, too, and wanted to remarry and start a family. I was not passionately in love with him. I thought he had money because he brought me out to dinner and to the movies. He didn't push me to have sex before marriage, and that was okay with me. We got married when I was 27, and I got pregnant right away. I was thrilled! I was going to be a mother and stay home from work and have a family—that sounded nice to me. I had my son Bob at 27. He was colicky and cried all the time and was not my idea of a good baby.

The sexual relationship with my husband was not good from the start. Jerry was nonsexual and didn't pay any attention to me. In those early years of marriage we had sex maybe once every two months, and it wasn't the right way. He had problems. He couldn't keep an erection long enough. He would look for his own satisfaction and leave me out in the cold. I never saw him. He worked, had supper, slept from 6 to 11 and went to his part-time job. We were poor and never had any money.

I got pregnant again as I turned 28. Then Jerry was sick and out of work for a year. We had no money and the bills kept coming in. I kept asking him, "How could you do this to me?" There was a fear that I might lose the baby unless I got complete bed rest. I left and went to live with my mother. She took care of the baby while I rested in bed. A few months after my second son, George, was born, Jerry got better and went back to work. I returned to our apartment with the children, who were only 11 months apart. I felt like my life was going to start up now.

CLAIRE BERMAN

I graduated from college at 22 and never returned home to live after graduation. You know, you get away for four years, you have a mind of your own by then. It probably would have been hard on me and hard on my folks for me to return. We were very close but we didn't really talk. I never discussed anything with them about myself or my life or anything, ever. I was making my own money and living on my own. I wanted to be independent but not too far away from home. I lived in a town an hour away from my parents and went home a couple times a month.

I taught school for five years. Summers I was a camp counselor. At 23 I joined the temple and got active in the community and made friends and began dating. I had a good life; I really loved those years. I lived in a big house for a year with several other women teachers. That was a great year—we had parties and ate all our meals together. But then one by one they all got married and moved out.

At 25 I was dating Robert regularly and really liked him. I was also dating my future husband, Ben. Then Robert decided to move to another state. He asked me to go, too, and live with him. But this was not my philosophy in life. After he left I put all my eggs in one basket and just dated Ben.

I liked Ben. He was nice to be with and easygoing and didn't put any demands on me to have sex. He was a really decent guy. I didn't fall in love with Ben, but I liked him a lot. When I married him I would say I loved him—not crazy, head over heels kind of love, but I liked him very much. I thought he was a super guy. I thought I could have a very nice life with him. I liked his family very much, and I liked the way he was with my family. Our families and backgrounds were compatible. Ben was real formal when he proposed. He said, "Many girls won't date me because I'm not a professional." He told me he made a good salary working in his father's insurance business and would be able to support me.

I married Ben at 26. My first sexual experience was when we got married. I was too chicken before. I just didn't think I could handle it, to tell you the truth. Sex the first time was scary but not unpleasant, and I grew to enjoy it more.

I worked during the first year of marriage. Ben expected a very traditional marriage, expected me to make his breakfast and be home to make supper when he arrived home at 6 p.m. After several months of that I came to the conclusion that any idiot can make his own breakfast, and I stopped getting up with him in the morning. He'd leave for work early in the morning and get home late at night. He worked weekends and spent summers away at the reserves, so we didn't see a lot of each other.

I went back to summer camp the first summer after we were married. My husband thought that was ridiculous. He said, "Go ahead this summer, but not anymore." I understood; it was time to start a family, time to be serious. I stopped work at 27 with no regrets. We bought a house, and I spent most of my time fixing it up. I got involved in the local synagogue, and I had my son at 28. [Motherhood ushered in Claire Berman's Age 30 Transition.]

✑ ELAINE OLSON

After I broke up with John at 22, I dated a lot. Friends would arrange blind dates for me but many of them were too fast. I went out with one guy who gave me a corsage and then tried to have sex! I tore off the corsage: "I didn't ask for this, and I don't expect to have to pay for it!" I dated Chuck at 23. I was real close to his family, and he was like a brother. But then we broke up. There was just nothing there, no marriage encounter or anything. Then I began dating Sal. I gave up two years of my life being his therapist. All he talked about was his ex-girlfriend and how he had loved her, and she had died. I pitied him. There was no one else right then so it was okay.

When I was 25 I began to realize: "What am I doing? I'm 25 years old, there's no future with this guy. I would never want to marry him and have him the father of my children. He's a nice guy but nothing you would leave home for." So I ended the relationship. When we broke up he said, "You're ready to get married, Elaine. I wouldn't be surprised to hear in six months that you're engaged." And I *was* ready to marry, just not him.

I met Patrick at 26, and six months later I had my diamond. All my previous men were tall, handsome, and had big cars. Here was Patrick, five feet nine with glasses and a Ford, but I really liked him. He had a similar background, and my family liked him. He had worked his way up through the ranks at a local company and was now a manager. When I was 27 he was transferred to another state for a year, and we only saw each other occasional weekends. But that was okay—I was busy planning the wedding with my mother. Patrick and I got married when I was 28.

Ending the Entry Life Structure

As this period ended, fourteen homemakers were in an intact first marriage, one in a second marriage. Fourteen were mothers (of one to five children). Several mothers had decided to have no more children, and the one childless woman hoped yet to become a mother. All fifteen had built an Entry Life Structure within a Traditional Marriage Enterprise, in which family was the central component, although there were variations in sequence. None of them were well prepared for the changes that lay ahead in the next period, of the Age 30 Transition.

7 Age 30 Transition: Homemakers

The Age 30 Transition usually begins at 28 and ends at 33. Its developmental tasks are to terminate the Entry Life Structure, to explore new possibilities in self and world, to become more individuated, and to move toward the formation of a new structure. The developmental work we do in this transition is of crucial importance since its final product is the Culminating Life Structure—the vehicle through which we realize, in greater or lesser measure, the aspirations of early adulthood.

One impetus for change in this period is that the Entry Life Structure is necessarily flawed to some degree. As we enter an era, it is very difficult to form a life structure appropriate to that era. At 22 we are just beginning to establish our membership in a new generation. We are on the threshold of a new world and a new self but we know too little about either to have much wisdom in making the choices on which an Entry Life Structure is based. Limitations in the structure that were quite tolerable for a while become more oppressive, perhaps intolerable, in the late twenties. Even a structure that was quite serviceable for the twenties requires some modification for the thirties.

It is bewildering to discover, at around 30, that the life we so arduously constructed over the previous decade has major imperfections. There is an old cultural assumption—largely unexamined by the human sciences—that by age 20 or so people normally establish a life pattern that in broad outline will continue unchanged throughout the adult years. We are then shocked by the realization that our initial adult life structure is problematic in some ways and that we still have some "growing up" to do. If we had developed "normally"—so the reasoning goes—we would not be faced with such burdens. In actuality, everyone has them: they are part of the normal process of adult development. For example, a woman in the Age 30 Transition may become aware that she is in many respects still a "little girl" in relation to husband, parents, and others. She feels locked into a life structure that permits her relatively little room to participate in the world outside the home. She is not likely to know that many other women have a similar experience.

Changes in personality and in the character of one's relationships may occur at various times. In periods such as the Age 30 Transition, however, individuation is a major developmental task. People differ widely in the amount and kind of work they do on this task, but some concern with it was evident during this period in all the lives I have studied. To some degree, everyone asks: What do I want from life? What do I give to, and receive from, my marriage, my family, friends, work, leisure—every aspect of life that has significance for me? What do I need to change in myself, and in my situation, so that I can have a better life, according to my values? What are my values? What is most important to me?

A woman may be conscious to some degree that she is engaged in a process of questioning and change, but much or all of this process may occur without awareness. For example, she decides at 29 to get further education, largely on the grounds that it will give her some work skills or get her "out of the house" a little. She may realize only later, after considerable change has occurred, how dissatisfied she had felt with her marriage and/or motherhood and how much that small first step carried the potential—and often the unconscious or half-conscious intention—of appreciably altering her life path. To learn this, we must look at the sequence of changes in her relationships over time, as well as her retrospective understanding of the process of change.

It is now well understood that conflicts and anxieties originating in childhood often continue to plague us in adulthood. This is a specific example of a more general developmental principle: in every adult developmental period we are faced with the tasks of the current period as well as the undone developmental work stemming from all previous periods—those of adulthood as well as of childhood. In the Age 30 Transition we have to work both on the tasks of this period and on the undone developmental work of the earlier periods. Life would be simpler, though possibly less interesting, if in a cross-era transition we could adequately terminate our relationship to the outgoing era and do all of the necessary groundwork for the incoming era. Alas, no one can. After only a few years in the Early Adult Transition, we must settle for what we have and start building an Entry Life Structure for Early Adulthood. The Age 30 Transition provides a "second chance" to deal with unresolved issues of childhood and the twenties, and to form a life structure appropriate for the thirties.

In the homemaker sample, the Age 30 Transition was a period of great personal growth and development for many women. The Age 30 Transition typically began at 28 (with a range of 27 to 29) and ended at 33 (range 32 to

34). As the period got under way, all fifteen women were leading primarily domestic lives. The Traditional Marriage Enterprise was at the center of their sense of self, their view of adult life generally, and their first adult life structure. Ten had been mothers and homemakers for some five to ten years. Five had just recently married and, with one exception, started a family. By 28 or 29 they had realized their initial goals and seemed well on the way to becoming permanent, full-time homemakers.

During the Age 30 Transition the picture changed markedly: each woman began to reappraise her Traditional Marriage Enterprise, to limit her domestic involvements, and to expand her participation in the outside occupational world. As the transition ended she was forming a life structure different from that of the twenties. There were variations in the depth of the changes and in the degree of turmoil involved, but major changes occurred in every case.

None of the fifteen homemakers gave birth to a child after the end of her Age 30 Transition. This was a major life choice. Their lives until then had been predicated on being full-time homemakers and having at least one preschool child to take care of. In deciding not to have more children, they were deciding to make other changes as well, even though they usually had no clear idea of what they wanted or how to proceed. Some women had enjoyed feeling totally needed by, and giving essential care to, their preschool children; and they had felt obligated to be full-time mothers. This admixture of satisfaction and obligation was weakened when all their children went to school, became more independent, and required new forms of relationship and care. Other women had found that, despite their previous desire to *have* children, they did not especially enjoy *raising* children. Motherhood for them was more an obligation than a satisfaction. In either case, a woman's decision to have no more children meant that she was partially ready to limit her involvement in mothering her existing children. Motherhood continued to play an important part in her life, but she invested less of her self in it.

Let us now look at individual sequences through the Age 30 Transition. To highlight variations in sequence and outcome, I have distinguished three patterns on the basis of the life structures initiated during this period.

Pattern A.   Married Women Who Made Family and Occupation Co-central Components

During this period three homemakers made a remarkable transformation in life structure. As it ended Vicky Perrelli, Nora Cole, and Jenny Abatello were in intact first marriages but in qualitatively different marriage enterprises. Family continued to be an essential underpinning to their lives but was less dominant, and occupation was becoming more central. Their involvement with family of origin was reduced in subjective intensity and external connection. They became more competent and assertive in work as well as family. They saw themselves as "growing up" at last, making a qualitative shift from "girl" to "woman" that had not earlier been possible. The internal Anti-Traditional Figure was becoming more forceful and seeking parity with the internal Traditional Homemaker Figure in a life that included both.

✌ JENNY ABATELLO

At 22 Jenny Abatello set aside her occupational ambitions, married the boy next door, and established an Entry Life Structure within the world of her extended family. This life came into question at 28:

> When my youngest was 2½ I asked Steve if I could try subbing again. He said okay. I really enjoyed it: getting dressed up and going out and talking with people was wonderful. The next year I read in the paper that they were looking for full-time teachers. Steve said okay, and I got a sitter for the kids and went back to work. I took classes one night a week to finish my fifth year teaching certificate. It was too much to go on for my master's with the kids and working. But it makes no difference to me personally or salary wise; I've never regretted not getting my master's.
>
> It was not easy going back to work full-time. Steve helped as much as he could with the laundry and the housework and cooking and with the kids. He never resented it. Family is the center of his life. He has no other friends, and his work is important to him mainly as a means of creating a better life for his family. But he did work late, and we didn't have much time together. Teaching was exhausting. I'd come home and go to sleep with the kids many nights.

Jenny's family life affected and was affected by her occupational life. Her husband, Steve, was a factory worker who could not directly participate in the more middle-class educational and cultural world to which she was drawn. He was her "special man." She was in some elemental way "special" to him, and he could support her outside interests even without sharing them. He in turn was special to her. He provided a connection she strongly valued to the ethnic-class world of her origins, yet he also valued her upward aspirations and enabled her to create a place on the boundary between the two worlds. The primary bond between them was the family. They began forming a more Egalitarian Marriage Enterprise in which she shared the provisioning function and he shared child care and domestic responsibilities.

> The school was a male stronghold and very sexist. There were no women in administration or anywhere that policy was made. My starting salary was half the men's. But as my job became more and more important and

my pay went up I think my family looked at me with new respect. I was resentful of male teachers, and they resented female teachers. They thought teaching was just part-time for women. So I was always careful not to say I couldn't stay for a meeting because I had to go home to my family.

The first six years of work I never questioned anything. It felt like I was on probation in some way. Then I started looking around at the teachers, who really weren't doing well by these kids. I read a lot of liberal literature on teaching and learned a lot. I committed myself to become a more humane teacher. I decided that if I couldn't help the students at least I wasn't going to hurt them. I found the college-directed students less interesting than the kids who weren't making it, and I attempted to help the non–college bound kids. I introduced a program for kids who couldn't read, and it was very successful.

Just before I started teaching at 28, things started going better for Steve occupationally. The next year we started building our house, near our parents' homes but in a more middle-class neighborhood. We moved in two years later.

I had decided at 25 not to have more than the two children, but somehow the question came up again at 32—I must have missed a period—and this time it was final. I just didn't want to stay home anymore. I had gotten spoiled, feeling like a human being and having an identity. I had worked too hard to just throw it all away.

Tension between my parents had been escalating for several years. It was a time of bitter struggle between them with me in the middle of their fighting and the extended family taking sides. When I was 32, my 50-year-old mother left my father. My father was bereft by my mother's leaving and moved in with us. Three months later he died of a heart attack. It was a really difficult, sad time for me. I don't know what was the worst: the pain of my father's death, or being caught in the cross fire between different parts of the family, or the feelings of loss when that big clan fell apart and was no longer holding my life together. I had had great fondness for all my aunts and uncles, and all those relationships were so damaged. Outside of weddings I rarely see them anymore. It's like the family just disappeared. It's such a loss, still today.

There had been years and years of turmoil with my mother. At times I thought I should try harder to help her. But then I thought, "At what price? My own marriage and family?" I couldn't give up everything I had built as an adult just to remain the good daughter. Finally she remarried and moved to Ohio. Even before she moved away I knew I'd have to become more independent of her. She had been such an important part of my daily life. Now she was so full of hostility: her life was going to change, and she didn't care who or what she hurt in the process. I used to get weepy about it, but gradually she just became less important in my life. I think my work got me through all those losses.

Steve and I stopped going to church when I was 33, mainly on my initiative. With my parents' split and my father's death and dealing with my mother, I just couldn't take it anymore. I got a new attitude toward religion. It was about God taking care of you. I realized that, in the final analysis, you have to take care of yourself. It took me a long time to grow up.

Jenny's life was thus transformed in her Age 30 Transition. At 28 she had a seemingly stable life as wife, mother, daughter, member of a familial clan and local community. She hardly dared to think about the teaching career she had earlier set aside. By 33 she had made significant changes in every component of her life and in its overall structure. Occupation and family were co-central components of the new life structure. Occupation was the figure, the primary focus of her involvement, and family was the ground, the sustaining matrix and source of support. Family of origin, which had played a basic part in shaping her Entry Life Structure, became largely a shadow.

Accompanying these changes in her life were a number of changes in her self. At 33 Jenny had a clear feeling that she had been "growing up" during the past several years: becoming more responsible, self-reliant, ready to claim her own identity. She realized how little she had grown up in the twenties and how strong her dependence was on mother, religion, and traditional authority. She suffered the pain of separating from the major persons, institutions, and symbols of childhood and, at the same time, gained a stronger sense of self and a desire to live on terms of greater equality in the adult world, domestic as well as public. She began to form more mutual relationships and to limit or end other relationships in which she could not sufficiently be herself. She developed a sense of a competent self that could give something of value to the world and, equally, could legitimately expect to receive something of value in return. The adult individuation process was not completed. But she had made a decisive start that prepared the way for a further evolution in subsequent periods.

✒ VICKY PERRELLI

My pregnancy at 28 was a very happy time. I was never able to enjoy the first two; I was too young, there were too many pressures, we lived so far away from my family, I just couldn't cope. But we had moved back to my hometown when I was 25, and I felt ready for this child. My youngest was in kindergarten and getting very independent. I wanted something to cuddle. I remember thinking to myself, "Gee, they're in school now and don't need me anymore." I was close to my mother, and that was special, too. She spent a lot of time at my house. We had all these wonderful plans! She was going to be with me after the baby was born. But it was not to be.

Right after I delivered Edna, my husband's mother informed him that she was coming to live with us because she was having trouble with her second husband! When I got home, she had planted herself firmly in our house. I was in utter tears, and Frank was angry at me for being upset! We had just gotten our own home, we were getting involved with my parents and going out with friends our age and having a really nice home life. Earlier I had given in on many things without questioning Frank's right to decide but now everything was just churning up inside of me. The most traumatic thing was that I had no choice in the matter. I was thinking, "It's my home, too. I am your wife; at least discuss this with me." I had what was called a postpartum depression. It's a wonder I didn't flake out altogether.

I learned to live with it but I always resented it. I wanted to say, "This is my house, and I don't want her." But then I thought, "What if the tables were turned and it was *my* mother who needed help?" His mother was young, too, not even fifty. We were having a hard time financially, and I tried to convince her to go to work but she wouldn't. She wouldn't cook or help with the housework, either. I'd never been much of a housekeeper but she'd plan my chores every day: "Today we're (meaning *you're*) going to clean this room or that"—and *I'd* do the cleaning! That was a horrible life for five years.

As if things with my mother-in-law weren't bad enough, my daughter Edna was sick her first year. Every month she'd get croupy for four days, go into bronchitis, get well, and then, boom! It would start all over again. I thought she was dying because she looked so terrible, and I looked like the wrath of God from all the worry. That was a hellish time. To this day I favor Edna. I was afraid the other two kids would be jealous, so I'd wait until they went to school, and then I'd just hold her. I couldn't wait to have her. At a year it turned out that she was allergic to all the food I was feeding her. I was killing this kid!

For the first few years I called my mother every morning; she liked it, and I was generally glad to do it. One morning I forgot to call. When my father got home from work he called me, "What's the matter, your finger broke? You can't call your mother to see how she is?" It was smothering. Having to call my mother every day began to bother me. I never said anything but I thought, "If I wanted to call her, I'd call her. I have my own life." It wasn't until 29 that I started to rebel openly. My sister had married someone my family didn't like. All of them would kind of lean on me for an ear but I was supposed to keep my opinions to myself. One day my mother phoned and started in again with all this garbage. I said, "Ma, she's married now—why don't you just let her alone?" My mother absolutely blew up at me and hung up. I called right back, and I started crying, "I'm almost thirty years old, and I'm not allowed an opinion in this family. When no one else is around I'm the cornerstone of my family. Why can't I have an opinion of my own without being considered disrespectful?"

It became intolerable after a while. I didn't admit it even to myself until 30, when Frank got transferred to Connecticut. I remember a kind of relief settled over me as we planned the move. I was really looking forward to being far enough away from my family not to be involved in the day-to-day stuff. At 25 I had tried to go back to my earlier life when we moved back to my hometown, and it didn't work because I wasn't the same person anymore. I no longer wanted to be part of that life; I had grown out of it. I thought about the move to Connecticut: "Maybe now I'll be able to grow up and be a woman instead of a daughter or a wife. I have a chance to see if I can stand on my own two feet." I started a totally different life in the first few years in Connecticut.

I have loved it here in Connecticut from the time we moved. We started from scratch—no family, no friends, only high hopes. My mother-in-law came right along with us, though. Because of her, to this day we have this big financial albatross on our back; we had to buy a larger house than we could afford to accommodate her with an extra bedroom. Frank got a good position with a good salary. We had all these high hopes! But the prices of houses in Connecticut were totally out of our reach. After two months at his new job the company decided to let Frank go. He got another job right away but with a 20 percent drop in pay! We had bought this large house and geared our life to that higher salary.

That's not the worst of it, either. I had to go to work! Frank said he'd get a part-time job but I knew it would be too much for him. So I said I'd go to work. When I first got a job I definitely didn't want to; it was purely for financial reasons. But I didn't want to be saddled with the kids all day long and evenings while Frank worked part-time. I'd done that before, and I just felt stifled. I had kids constantly, constantly, constantly. I really did not want the constant responsibility—that's the main reason I offered to go to work.

It was scary to look for a job. I'd been out of nursing for so long, and so many things had changed. I went to a small hospital an hour away from home and was offered a job 3 to 11 or 11 to 7. We tried to get my mother-in-law to get a job but she refused. By that time she was crocheting, and we were buying her yarn! She was totally dependent on us and only in her early fifties. It wasn't natural. I pulled a nasty on her, though. I thought, "Oh, good. I'll work 11 p.m. to 7 a.m. and have a chance to get out, and *she'll* be home taking care of my kids!"

There were thirty pretty sick older patients on my ward, some dying. I couldn't stand it at first. For six months I got on the elevator each night with tears in my eyes. I used to pray it would pass. I was totally involved with those patients. To ask for another floor would have meant failure to me. I had never been in charge until then. I was ten years out of training, and all the wards had all this newfangled equipment I'd never heard of. After a month I called a nursing home and had a chance for a safe, cushy job. Then I thought, "What am I doing? I'll go back and stick it out, if it kills me." I was afraid of failure, didn't think I could make it. But I just had to do it—if I hadn't I would have wiped out my self-confidence and been totally stuck. Gradually I learned the new equipment. The confidence in myself, in my ability to learn whatever was needed, took longer. The really tough part lasted two or three years, though even now, at 38, I'm still learning. Only *I* know what I went through to make it where I am today.

My mother-in-law took care of the kids for about a year after I started working. I figured, "That's good; you're paying your way now." I was content to work: I was meeting people, I was getting out. So all of a sudden my mother-in-law takes off, and I don't have anyone to watch my daughter! My husband didn't say a word. After three or four months my mother-in-law comes back, and it's back to normal for a while, and then she suddenly takes off again for another few months. It was very difficult for me. When I got home from work I'd put Edna in my room and try to stay awake to take care of her but I just couldn't. I thought, "This can't go on." I put Edna in a nursery school afternoons.

When Edna started kindergarten at five, I hired a baby-sitter to watch her mornings and then get her on the school bus while I slept. My mother-in-law returned soon after but I kept the sitter. I remember huffing and puffing to my husband about it, "Listen, I hired this girl for a dollar an hour, and I'm not losing her because I don't know when your mother will take off again." My own mother was giving me grief, too: "Oh, how can you leave your children with a sitter?" But it was *my* life, and I didn't have a choice.

When my mother-in-law came back that last time, I was totally obnoxious to her. I had had it by then; I was just filled with animosity. We had housed and supported that woman for five years, and I never asked her for anything. Then, when I needed her, she took off. I was intentionally cruel for the first time in my life. I thought, "This is it. It's either her, me, or my marriage." I actually did not care which one. If I wanted to go out, I went out. I sat in my room alone and read, I worked, and I slept. She would start watching soap operas at 11 in the morning and continue until 4, all the time she lived with us. I just refused to keep her company that last time.

Soon after, when I was still 33, my mother-in-law left for good and went to live with her friend. What a relief! My daughter Alice was overjoyed to get rid of her. Frank was concerned at first but then he was pleased, "Well, that's good; she'll be able to get a job now." A few years earlier I wouldn't have been able to mount a real campaign to get rid of her and stay with it until she left.

I changed in some other important ways, too. When Edna was 5, I got that feeling again about needing something else to cuddle. When the youngest starts school she kind of leaves home and gets awfully independent. You need the feeling of being needed. But this time was different.

I said to my husband, "Get me a dog. I don't want another baby!" That was when I made the final decision not to have any more kids. Two years later I had my tubes tied. But the big decision was at 33, when I got more involved in my work and cut down on the household stuff.

I also started changing with Frank. Before that, if I disagreed with him about anything, it was like I didn't know what I was talking about; he always knew better than I did. Gradually I got more able to tell him, "I'm not your child, I'm your wife, and I have a right to my own opinions." Even now he sometimes reverts back to that old pattern, and I have to stop him. I also insisted that he get more involved with the kids. I wanted my family to be different from the way my family was when I was growing up. My father was never involved. I worried about what would happen in a few years with the pot, the drugs, the whatever else. I thought, "Well, I have a husband, what's he there for? It's not all going to be on *my* shoulders." I was afraid that, when the problems got bigger, something bad would happen and he'd say, "It's your fault; you told them they could go." So for any big decisions I'd tell them to ask their father and not let him put it all on me.

The basic change is that I was becoming more independent. Before that I figured that Frank would soon be earning more, and he'd tell me, "You don't have to work anymore," and I'd gladly quit. By 33 my salary was an important part of the family income, and I realized that I'll always be working. But it isn't just financial—it has to do with my independence, the kind of person I am. The same thing happened about managing money. I didn't know how to handle money and had to account to Frank for everything. At 33 I took out my own checking account. For the first time I could put away money, feel that it was mine, spend what I wanted. The checkbook gave me this immense feeling of power! I learned that it is hard for a widow or a divorced woman to get a credit rating in her own name, so I took a small loan from the credit union in my own name and paid it back.

I realized how important it is to work so you can take care of yourself and be less dependent on your husband. The work was interesting but didn't mean that much in itself; I had no big career ambitions. The big thing about work was the independence it gave me. Each year I'd get a raise and think, "Gee, I'm not doing too bad for a woman." Also, when you work you get out more and you see other people's marriages, and you start to question your own. I began to ask, "Is this all I want?" At first it was just a whisper but now at 38 I can ask it more clearly.

Pattern B.   Married Women Who Kept Homemaking Central but Reduced Their Involvement in Family

The four women in Pattern B, like those in Pattern A, continued throughout the Age 30 Transition to be homemakers in an intact first marriage while reducing their involvement in domesticity and doing more in the outside world. However, these women did *not* attempt to make occupation central or to modify greatly the Traditional Marriage Enterprise. Wendy Lewis and Kay Ryan started their families and became full-time homemakers in the early twenties. In the Age 30 Transition they sought more outside activities without questioning the basic terms of the Traditional Marriage Enterprise. Claire Berman and Elaine Olson were single working women until age 27, when they married and happily gave up their jobs. They quickly started a family with the intention of becoming full-time homemakers who rarely if ever held an outside job.

By the end of the Age 30 Transition all four had taken part-time paid or volunteer jobs. The job was not a path to a long-term occupation but it did provide significant immediate satisfactions: sociability, a sense of competence, a limited degree of financial independence, and, above all, escape from the domestic burdens. They considered their marriages moderately to highly satisfactory, but all had experienced keen disappointments in marriage and family life. They became more aware of their aversion to domesticity and more skilled in limiting their personal involvement in it. They made a firm decision not to have more children. As the children became more independent the mothers continued to provide general care but were less involved in the psychological relationship with them. In the Culminating Life Structure that followed, family was central but much less predominant and occupation became more important though still peripheral.

✌ ELAINE OLSON

Elaine Olson married at 28 and quickly got pregnant. She gladly gave up her full-time job in anticipation of a permanent full-time domestic career:

> My husband, Patrick, worked long hours but that was no problem. I was busy in my new home, pregnant, and near my parents' home. I talked and shopped with my mother every day. A lot of couples talk about liking to be together, alone, for a while, getting to know each other before a baby comes, but there wasn't that time for us. The big change came at 29 when my first child was born. Everything was new to me. No one teaches you how to be a parent—what to do when a baby wakes up screaming, how to clothe them and care for them and feed them. I had a really tough time! Three months later I was pregnant again! It was so soon after the first.
> Earlier I always said, "If it's God's will, I'll have a baby." After my third child, Chet, was born at 34, I said, "Now it's going to be *my* will: No more babies!" I stopped all the gourmet cooking, and I stopped enjoying to cook even. For five years before that I did all those homey things straight, and I got pretty tired of it all. Marriage full-time was less satisfying than I'd hoped. It was okay to take care of the kids when they were babies, but then they got loud and messy and fought all the time. That never happened in my family,

and I just didn't like it. I remember the time when I had three kids under 5, and there were rainy days when I couldn't get out and no one came to visit. The only thing that got me through it was knowing that Patrick would come home at 5:00 and lift this little boulder off my shoulders, and I'd have an adult to talk to. Then my husband started spending more time with them, and they adored him. He enjoyed being with them and could always think of things to do with them. I just never could. I worried too much and got overprotective, while he gave them more freedom.

At 34 I decided to go back to work as soon as possible, and at 35 I made it. Patrick saw this ad in the paper for a part-time job. Patrick was very good; he said it was fine for me to take the job—as long as it didn't interfere with my domestic chores or our home life.

So the provisional domestic life that started at 29 changed at 34, when Elaine began to form a Culminating Life Structure that included both family and outside work. Family provided an essential basis for her existence but was intolerable in large doses. Like other women who had worked for much of their twenties, Elaine strongly needed some form of outside life but did not want to work full-time nor to involve herself heavily in the work world. Work was primarily a diversion from homemaking. She enjoyed the sociability and the contact with the "real world." She felt fortunate that her husband was a good enough provider who helped with the child care and "allowed" her to work part-time as long as she fulfilled her homemaking responsibilities.

As the Age 30 Transition ended, then, Elaine was forming a life structure in which the various components remained relatively separate. Family (including family of origin) was central, occupation important but peripheral. No component claimed a large investment of self but together they made for a life of some contentment. She did little individuating in the Age 30 Transition. The relationship with her mother continued to provide an emotional grounding for her life, and she remained the dutiful caring daughter. She was a responsible mother to her own children but had no sense of their psychological development nor of her own development in relationship with them. Patrick's greater involvement with the children relieved her of a burden but did not bring the spouses closer together. She became aware of, and valued, only those aspects of self that could be lived out within this kind of life structure.

◄§ WENDY LEWIS

Wendy Lewis followed a more tumultuous sequence than Elaine Olson through the twenties and early thirties. At 22 she started building an Entry Life Structure as a wife and mother in a Traditional Marriage Enterprise. At

25 she consolidated this structure by getting pregnant with her third child. The second phase of the Entry Life Structure was a highly stressful time:

> My mother was dying of heart disease from my age 25 to 27. I took care of her but couldn't deal with my own feelings. I was not willing to give her up—and I didn't. It's like I've kept a room inside myself and not touched it. I still can't look at pictures of her. I avoided my feelings at the time by trying to cope with others' problems and hold the family together. I felt as trapped as any mother does with three children under 6. The eldest, Gwen, was an absolutely obstinate child. I couldn't handle it and got nasty with her sometimes. You feel like throwing her away and starting all over again. The most direct conflict was between her and her father, Hank. Hank was depressed about the problems of establishing his own computer business and the lack of financial help from his parents. He couldn't provide adequate discipline or love to Gwen. He would get into rages and sometimes abuse Gwen physically. It was terrible. Looking back, I realize that I devoted myself to taking care of people and mediating the father-daughter struggle, acting as though there wasn't a mother-father and mother-daughter struggle as well.
>
> After my mother died, my grandfather got sick, and we decided to take him in. It was a total disaster. He was absolutely stricken by the loss of my mother and had no will to live. He required constant care. This kept me from helping a husband and kids who were also hurting from my mother's death. I was coping with all this like a real soldier but couldn't deal with the extreme feelings that Hank was beset by.

From 25 to 28 Wendy's primary aim was to ensure the survival of her Entry Life Structure, and in this she was remarkably successful. As she says, however, she did not focus much on the quality of the relationships within the family. Her goal in mediating the father-daughter conflict was to keep it from splitting the family. She was less concerned with the destructive effects of the conflict and did not acknowledge her own contributions to it. In addition, she focused hardly at all on her self. A woman who lives in this way is often seen as "selfless"—devoted to meeting others' needs rather than her own. It is perhaps more accurate to say that she spends a good deal of her time taking care of others because she believes that this is the only way to ensure that others will take care of her. This way of living tends to break down when she feels that she is receiving too little care in return for the amount she is giving, or when she discovers parts of herself that cannot be fulfilled solely by giving and receiving care. In Wendy's case, the Entry Life Structure was quite suitable for the self that lived within it.

Things began to change as the Age 30 Transition got under way at 28. Hank had a brain tumor that kept him in the hospital for several months. In the aftermath of his illness, Wendy's situation changed from difficult to impossible:

> I had been coping before, but then it all fell apart. There was no way I could handle having Hank in the hospital, not knowing whether he would live or die, and having three small children and a sick grandpa at home. I phoned my father and told him he would have to find a home for Grandpa, which he did. The day he left I knew it would be the last time I'd ever see him—and three months later he died.
>
> Hank's recovery was disrupted by his being worried about the business, so I gradually took on more responsibility. I'd call customers, explain what happened, and place orders. I really took over his job. If I hadn't, the business would have gone under. He got increasingly depressed and angry. The hospital got him in psychotherapy for a while, and then we were in couples and family therapy. One big issue was my involvement in the business. He realized that I had to do it, but my taking his job made him feel useless, depressed, and angry. And I was angry at him for getting sick and making me perform the husband's role. But then I saw that I was capable of handling the whole thing, and everything changed. Before I married I had always thought of myself as independent and competent. Then I had played the housewife for a number of years and lost those feelings. Running the business brought them back to me. When Hank wanted the business back I wasn't that anxious to hand it back. This was the first time we came into direct conflict. He would try to build up his own confidence by pushing me down. But this time I wouldn't give in; I was determined to maintain my own strength. It seemed possible for only one of us to be competent.
>
> Soon after Hank's illness my third child was over 2 years old, and it was time to get pregnant again. I really wanted that fourth child. But if Hank died I couldn't raise four kids alone, and if he lived it would be too much strain on him. So I decided against it. At 30 my feelings of loss about not having the fourth child got stronger and more conscious. I used to think how it might have been with him, what he'd look like, and all that. But I was feeling the weight of so many problems! Every headache of Hank's worried me, and he used that to get me to do what he wanted. I had that *Why me?* feeling. Why did my mother die? Why did my husband get sick? Why wasn't my life going the way I thought it would? At about this time my daughter Gwen became more disturbed, and we had literally no peace when she was home. A year later we sent her to a boarding school. She was young to send away but *we* really needed it.
>
> By this time the youngest child was about to enter the first grade. I had enjoyed raising the kids when they were small, but there was no point in being at home without children to take care of—without something *real* to do. I was bored all by myself. The kids didn't need me, Hank didn't

need me, the house certainly didn't need me. I'm not a housewife-type person. It aggravated Hank that I didn't care about things like dusting and cleaning. He was home a lot but *he* didn't do the housework either. He really felt it was *my place* to do it—which increased my desire not to do it. But I didn't take a clear stand until my early thirties, and it was only in my late thirties that I got free of most household chores.

At 32 I started thinking more seriously about leaving the family business and getting an outside job. The initial push came from Hank: he could now handle the business by himself, and he wanted me to increase the family income. He complained that the ladies on the block were going to work, why not me? I had had it with his business—we couldn't find a way to collaborate. I needed a place where I would be free to be competent. It was time to get out—working together was threatening the marriage.

I considered going to graduate school but that wasn't a real option. The obvious reason was that I needed to earn money, not spend it. But the basic reason was that school would require devoting myself to something I had already chosen not to devote myself to. I wanted to work but I didn't want a demanding career.

At 32 I got a full-time job. I was afraid that the work would be totally different from what I had done ten years before and I wouldn't remember anything. At first it was a great job. I love working on my own, and it was exciting when I got a chance to learn. My boss instructed me about the project and then left me totally in charge of conducting it. Although I was doing high-quality work in an independent way, there were long periods when the work was routine and I felt like an assembly line worker in a factory. I wanted to do more interesting work but my desire wasn't strong enough to get me to move from a job to a career.

By 33 my life began to get more settled. We brought Gwen back home from boarding school. Making us an intact family again was important, especially for me. We also bought a wonderful house in a town with an excellent school system. Our troubles weren't over but we were at a new place in our life.

To get a perspective on her Age 30 Transition, let us compare her life at 28 and at 33. As she turned 28, Wendy was a harried but relatively contented housewife, a mother of three small children expecting soon to be pregnant with a fourth. At 33 family was still her first priority, yet she gave it relatively little time and involvement and was less invested in motherhood. The marital relationship was different. She got a job in order to avoid family-splitting conflict with her husband. The job did not demand as much or offer as much as a full-fledged career, but it gave her a greater sense of competence and self-worth than purely routine work. Occupation helped to compensate for the limitations of family but had little intrinsic importance to her.

As the Age 30 Transition ended, Wendy was forming a fragmented Culminating Life Structure. Its two major components, family and outside job, served to counterbalance each other but were virtually unconnected. Although family was essential, domestic life was in many ways oppressive and took up only a small part of her energies, feelings, talents. She regarded herself as primarily a homemaker yet was "not a housewife-type person." She felt a powerful need for "something more" in her life. The outside job served partly to meet this need, but she could not involve herself much in it. A "demanding career" would endanger her place in the family; and, at bottom, she felt that provisioning was the man's task, not hers.

Wendy thus used the Age 30 Transition to make modest changes in life structure and in self. As it ended she still had a good enough marriage. She was working toward a more egalitarian relationship with her husband, although he was not accommodating to her new demands. She was trying to develop a stronger sense of herself as a competent woman but had taken barely a first step on that path. Her outside job was similar to the one she had given up ten years earlier.

The internal Traditional Homemaker Figure and the internal Anti-Traditional Figure had fought to a standstill. The former was still predominant but the latter now had a small territory of her own. Wendy was creating a Culminating Life Structure that kept her firmly rooted within the domestic sphere. The new structure made life more palatable for the Anti-Traditional Figure without disrupting the Traditional Marriage Enterprise and the Traditional Homemaker Figure.

Pattern C.   Women Who Got Legally or Psychologically Divorced

During the Age 30 Transition eight of the fifteen homemakers came to feel that their marriages had failed. Three women initiated a legal divorce. Ruth Allen was not in a legal marriage and hence did not get a legal divorce, but the separation at 28 was the equivalent of a legal divorce. Five others, almost twice as many, remained in the marriage but began a psychological divorce. (Three of the five were legally divorced in a subsequent period.) Each felt that her husband had not met his minimal obligations within the Traditional Marriage Enterprise. Without leaving the marriage, she experienced herself in some basic sense as a single woman open to new marital possibilities though not likely to find them. She also moved toward some form of outside work that gave her a modicum of financial independence and might in time enable her to divorce. But none of these women attempted to establish occupation as a central part of her life. They hoped above all to find a better husband with whom to establish a more satisfactory Traditional Marriage Enterprise.

The eight women were diverse in background, history, and current circumstances. Emily Swift had graduated from an Ivy League college and was married to a relatively successful lawyer. Nan Krummel came from a middle-class family and worked as a secretary until she married a professional man. The other six were of working-class or lower-middle-class origins. Their husbands, of similar backgrounds, were generally not doing well enough financially or psychologically to meet the needs of their growing families. The wives functioned primarily as homemakers but often had outside jobs to help support their families.

Although the marriages had moderate to severe problems from the start, the women "coped" with minimal protest or inner questioning until the late twenties. The Age 30 Transition brought a sharp decrease in each woman's inner readiness to tolerate the hurtful marriage. She moved toward greater self-awareness, recognition of long-standing problems, and refusal to endure her husband's faults blindly.

What did these women want from their husbands, and what were the conditions that led them to seek a legal or psychological divorce? Their marital demands were surprisingly simple. They did not insist that he provide a high degree of worldly success, love, or involved participation in fatherhood or joint activities. While hoping for some of these, the women were quite ready to tolerate major deficiencies. A woman considered divorce only when she felt that her husband had violated the most elemental requirements of the Traditional Marriage Enterprise. She had agreed to take care of him and the children within the domestic sphere, on condition that he take care of her and the children. In her view, she had kept her end of the bargain but he had not. The most serious transgressions were: (1) he did not provide for the family (income, housing, place in the community) at a minimally acceptable level; (2) he was grossly unreliable (e.g., severely alcoholic, intolerably abusive of wife and/or children, not available for major emergencies); (3) he had extramarital affairs indiscreetly. These requirements were, indeed, minimal. It was remarkable how much the women *did* tolerate, as long as their basic expectations were met.

Transgressions of these kinds were the external conditions that led a woman to give up on her marriage. In her subjective experience the core issue was a deep sense of disappointment in her husband. She felt that he was defective as a husband, that he lacked the inner resources required to take care of her and the family. There was no basis on which they could build a life. The sense of disappointment—of having been let down or betrayed by the person who had promised to be the fulcrum of her adult life—was described in poignant though understated form by all these women.

✎ੀ BETH LOGAN

Beth Logan's marriage had been problematic from the start. Her husband earned a marginal income, was rarely home, and had little connection to wife, children, or household.

> We returned to New Haven when I was 25, and Kevin got a job. He worked 7 to 7, six days a week, but we were still very poor. The children were getting older, and he was still not involved with them at all. I think of my twenties as the "gray years." It was like I was in a fog. I wasn't aware of so much. I was very unaware of the molding a parent needs to do. I always made sure that the children went to bed on time and ate their meals and were washed and had clean clothes and went to school and did their homework, but that was the extent of it. I didn't realize how much *more* they needed.
>
> In my late twenties I could see that the children were not developing on the course I wanted. I wanted to be more involved in disciplining them and making sure they did the things necessary to become responsible adults. I could see that Kevin was not going to help me with that. When you have an infant and a young child you do everything for them. You assume that by age 18 you ought to have a fully formed adult who is totally capable of taking care of himself or herself. I was getting more and more resentful of these kids who wouldn't keep their rooms clean, wouldn't pick up their dirty clothes, wouldn't help with the dishes or anything. They had very little structure.
>
> My best friend April was a very involved parent, and she was a role model for my desire to be a better parent. I also saw April and her husband parenting together as a united front. His pleasure in life was his home and family. I could see the contrast between that marriage and my own. There began a time of subtle discontent when I realized how limited my marriage was. I really don't know how to explain the change in awareness. It just happened gradually, during my late twenties and early thirties. We were married almost fifteen years and up until the last couple of years the marriage worked okay, no thought of divorce until it happened.
>
> I felt that I needed to learn to become a better parent and help these kids before it was too late. At 28 I took a parenting course, which helped me become more aware. Then I began getting out of the house through volunteer activities. I volunteered at the kids' school and got involved in the PTA. From 30 to 32 I did volunteer work.
>
> When I was 32 I'd been on birth control pills for seven years, and the doctor felt I should stop. Kevin got a vasectomy. He warned me at the time that he would then have affairs. I heard him, it registered, but I didn't want to pursue it. I guess I could cope with it as long as I didn't know about it. We had gone long periods of time without having sex, and I guess I always

assumed he was having affairs. At Kevin's urging we started going to a neighbor's house to watch X-rated movies. Then Kevin wanted to swap partners sexually! I refused and stopped going to the neighbor's house, but he continued going there alone.

We were renting part of our house to earn extra income. When I was 32 a young man named Brent moved in, and we became close friends. I learned from him that a person can live alone and take care of themselves and not be dependent on another person to take care of them. He took an interest in the kids and spent a lot of time with them. He was more of a father to them than Kevin was, and he was a good role model. I was glad to have that. That relationship also helped me become more aware of the problems in my marriage. Kevin and I began having open arguments for the first time. I knew I needed to leave the marriage, but I had no place to go and no money. I'd hoped that one of the volunteer jobs would develop into a paying job, but it didn't happen. So then I stopped the volunteer work and pumped gas at minimum wage so I could earn money to buy my own car.

Kevin gave me permission to have a sexual relationship with Brent. I guess he hoped that that would get me more interested in swapping partners with his friends. Brent and I did begin a sexual relationship. It was all so new to me! The only man I had ever slept with was Kevin, and he had been so traditional, so rigid—no oral sex or experimenting. To Brent everything was free, and there were no boundaries. Once I started the sexual relationship with him I realized my marriage was hopeless. I needed to make a life for myself so I could leave the marriage.

Kevin and I began talking when I was 34. He opened up as much as he could, I guess. At first I felt that I had grown so much over the past few years that I could help him. But the more he talked the more I realized that he was past help and that I just had to get out. He was just too full of resentment at having to marry so early and having responsibilities he couldn't handle. Finally I looked at our relationship, and there was just nothing there. Nothing at all. Not anything at all. I think if there had been anything to build on—but there wasn't. At 34 I told Kevin to leave. He did, and we got a divorce. He rarely sees the children now, which is very hard on them.

I'm 35 now, and for the past year I've worked full-time as a typist. I earn less than $10,000 with no support from Kevin. I get food stamps but it's still such a struggle to make ends meet. I plan to marry Brent within the next couple of years and start a new life with him. No matter how difficult it is or what happens in the future, this life is a thousand times better than my marriage was.

⊷ SARA CUSHING

The marriage was terrible. I began to ask myself, "What am I doing here?" I felt we weren't living the way I wanted. Our ideas were so different about child-rearing; Bill couldn't care less. He started having really bad depressions. He hated his job and wanted to quit. He began bringing a male friend home all the time. I began wondering about Bill being homosexual but pushed the thought out of my mind.

I needed to get out of the house; I was changing and felt tied down. When my son was 2 months old I went to work part-time at McDonald's. I liked working and getting out. I had a sense of being a good worker and felt that I could do something. Bill liked my working for the money but he didn't want to baby-sit or help out at home. All he did was complain, "Poor me." I'd think, "Poor you? I'm taking care of the kids all day, doing the housework, making supper, going to work twenty hours a week, coming home and cleaning up the supper dishes and your mess, and it's poor *you*?" Then Bill started paying a baby-sitter so he could go out while I worked! I quit my job. That's when I realized I couldn't depend on him for anything.

The month before I turned 30 I got pregnant. That was a shock but I was thrilled. Bill got more depressed. He'd come home from work and stare at TV until he went to bed. I wanted a devoted husband who worked hard and had ambition, and Bill wasn't what I wanted in a husband. I still wanted that storybook ending. It was a big letdown at 30 to finally realize it wasn't to be. The unhappiness was getting bigger and bigger with Bill, and I was getting more and more tired of it all. By the time the marriage ended it was such a relief. He was getting friendlier and friendlier with this guy Bob. One Friday night they went out, and Bill didn't come home. The next morning Bill came home and wrote a note: "I have to go away and think about things and think about what I want." Something just snapped. That was it. I didn't want any more. I never yelled. I just left. I had a 5-year-old, a 1-year-old, and I was pregnant. I didn't know where I was going to go or what I was going to do, but I knew there was no going back. He'd disappointed me one too many times.

I went to welfare. Welfare took over the supporter role, and I realized I was better off. I was being taken better care of by welfare than by my husband. Bill rarely came to see the kids, which was very hard on them. He didn't give us any money; as far as he was concerned, we could have starved. Then Bill told me he was homosexual! He'd married me to hide his homosexuality behind me. I felt cold, empty, a total loss of trust. There was a sense that I'd never known this man, that I had been married to a stranger.

From 30 to 33 I was happier than when I was married. I was alone, but I was living more on my own terms. I was raising my three children; they were my life. My goals were very limited: to survive and raise my kids. I had my own plan to keep sane: I'd be with the kids until they were in school, and then I would go to work. My life was very constricted in those years. I blocked out a lot of feelings, sexuality, everything. I didn't give myself anything to get disappointed in.

✌️ ANGELA CAPELLI

Angela Capelli married Jerry at 27 and had her two children at 27 and 28. She then hoped for a better marriage and better life:

> I figured after the second baby was born it's time for a normal sex life. Life was so hectic—they were like twins, both in diapers. I was busy every minute: I did my chores, took them out for a walk, came home, and made supper. I wouldn't mind so bad if now Jerry pays some attention to me when he comes home from work. But he didn't. He would come home, eat, and sit in front of the TV with a beer. Time to go to bed: no go. He said we didn't have sex because he was worrying about the finances, but we were managing okay, and I took care of the money and the bills. He just didn't need much sex.
>
> Then it started to bother me more. I tried to keep myself up, keep myself neat. I kept wondering, "What's wrong with me?" I was feeling hurt. I enjoy sex, as long as I'm married. I was in my late twenties, and I was being neglected by my husband. I figured, "Hey, I'm starting to hit 30. I try all my life to be a good girl, and this is my payoff? I followed the rules, and this is my reward in life?" I never told any of this to anyone, not even my mother or sister. I kept it all in, always feeling hurt and rejected.
>
> In my early thirties I just decided, "Why should I get myself all turned on?" He was a man that was very selfish because he should realize my needs and he didn't. For somebody ten years older he acted like a child because he left me high and dry. I decided not to have any more babies.
>
> I thought about leaving the marriage but it was impossible. Where would I go? How could I support myself with two small children? Jerry was not really a husband to me, but he was a responsible family man, and he didn't abuse me the way my first husband did. Family life was important to both of us. But I was totally exhausted all the time. I had to find a way to keep the family even though the marriage was terrible. I finally did that by going to work. You might say I went to work instead of getting divorced. I told my husband I had to get out, get a break.
>
> At 33 I went back to my old typing job two days a week. I thought of trying for something better but I was afraid I didn't have the skills. After you have been raising children for a while, it's kind of scary to go back to work. Progress was being made in the outside world, and you've been away from it. But I really enjoyed getting out. I had a chance to get dressed up and have my hair done—I felt like a woman again! Jerry and I never went out Saturday nights, so this was my time out. At first I was only planning to work in the summer because I didn't want to be a working mother. Then my husband said it was okay to go on working two days a week, so I did. He worked weekends and was off the two days I worked so he could

watch the children. It wasn't what I expected, but I was starting a new life as a working mother. The marriage has never given me much, but it gave our children a home.

Legal vs. Psychological Divorce

More women got a psychological divorce than a legal divorce. This finding highlights a broader issue: some people deal with an oppressive situation (in marriage, job, career, religion, community, or whatever) by leaving or making a drastic change. A larger number who are in the same situation resign themselves to it and go into *psychological retirement*—doing a minimum, giving little of themselves, and obtaining little in return. The incidence of legal divorce is thus not an accurate indicator of the extent of marital conflict or distress in a population. The divorce rate underestimates the degree and depth of the actual severity of marital problems, just as the number of patients receiving psychological and psychiatric treatment underestimates the extent of severe emotional distress. The marriages that endure are as deserving of study as those that are legally terminated, but it shouldn't be assumed that just because a marriage has endured that it is necessarily a good marriage.

How does it happen that some women who have painful marital problems get a legal divorce, whereas others maintain an intact family while being psychologically divorced? One hypothesis is that the former group have more severe marital difficulties than the latter. This hypothesis is not supported by the evidence in this study. The conditions that lead to psychological divorce are as bleak and corrosive as those leading to legal divorce. A person does not take either step without strong, continuing provocation.

Another hypothesis is that the women who divorce have a feasible alternative—other sources of financial support, or the ability to support themselves—whereas those who remain simply have no way of managing on their own. Again, this is too simple a view. All eight women asked themselves, "How would I live if I left my husband?" None of them had a clear-cut, satisfactory answer. The three who left did not have better options than the five who stayed. Sara Cushing and Beth Logan initiated legal divorce knowing that their own earning power was minimal and that they could count on little financial support from husband or parents. Ruth Allen left her nonlegal marriage at 28 knowing that she could provide only marginally for her five children. The five women who remained married had similar prospects were they to leave their husbands. In the process of becoming homemakers none had developed the occupational skills or the inner sense of competence that would enable them to earn more than a minimal living.

No matter how destructive her marriage, each of the eight women found the thought of legal divorce even more distressing. Leaving her husband was an act of revolutionary proportions, threatening as it did her basic way of life as a homemaker. Unless she could quickly remarry or gain financial support from other sources, she would have to become the primary provisioner for her family. This involved a fundamental change in identity and way of life. She got a legal separation and divorce when she felt subjectively ready, as one put it, "to live on my own and take care of myself and my children." This was for every woman an enormous step. Three took this step in the Age 30 Transition. Of the five who remained in a failed Traditional Marriage Enterprise throughout the Age 30 Transition, Lynn McPhail, Nan Krummel, and Carol O'Brien got legal divorces several years later when they were more self-sufficient; Angela Capelli and Emily Swift at 45 still live in highly flawed marriages.

All eight women grew up with the absolute assumption that in adulthood they would live primarily as homemakers, and they established an Entry Life Structure on this basis. During the Age 30 Transition most of their initial expectations regarding marriage and family were violated. Before the end of this period the marriage was over or in shambles. They felt a need for something outside the home that would fill the void left by the flaws of the domestic life. As a result, occupation became an important yet unfilled or partially filled component of the emerging life structure.

Their initial exploration of the work world took many forms: full-time or part-time jobs, voluntary work, involvement in community groups, part-time courses toward a college degree or training certificate. Their aims were usually unclear. At first they were most aware of what they did *not* want; for example, "to go on being a baby machine," to live with an inattentive husband or rejective in-laws, to be forever cooped up in a small apartment. One elemental wish was simply to escape from domesticity for part of the day. Another equally elemental wish was to go places and do things and be carefree. Some women felt that they had lost, or had never formed, a connection with the adult world. They wanted an identity that being solely a mother and homemaker did not provide.

The move into the work world was usually a source of great satisfaction. They felt liberated, entitled to be treated as an equal in marriage and other relationships. Many women realized in the Age 30 Transition that they had been *in a fog* in their twenties, doing what was expected and required but without a clear sense of having a choice among real alternatives. They began to feel that they were coming out of the fog and beginning to know what they wanted for the first time. The strongest imagery was that of *becoming an adult*. It was exhilarating to begin, finally, a more adult life.

But the change was also frightening and difficult. The home that had seemed so great a source of security was starting to feel more like a domestic cage, but her wish for the old security and protection was still there. It was appealing to *be* an adult but hard to *become* an adult. The outside world was both inviting and repelling. It offered the possibility of developing greater independence, skills, participation in interesting activities and relationships — but it had drawbacks as well. She was totally responsible for domestic work as well as her outside job. The jobs for which she was qualified were generally boring and financially unrewarding. The opportunities for further education and advancement were limited. She had little support from others in the struggle for a better life.

The obstacles were not solely external; they were within herself as well. She was gaining some initial awareness of the costs of being the good girl and dutiful wife, but this was the only identity she knew. It was hard to go about learning what the alternatives might be and whether they would improve her life. What did it mean to be an adult rather than a child? How important was it to limit her domestic involvement, to establish a niche in the outside world, to become a more responsible adult? These women were literally forced to ask not only, "What shall I do about my marriage?" but the more basic question, "What shall I do with my life?" Despite the powerful stimulus to reappraisal and change, they did very little individuating in the Age 30 Transition. This added to their difficulties in the next period, as we shall see.

By the end of this period Carol O'Brien, Sara Cushing, and Nan Krummel had put some feelers into the public world but were not ready to take even a part-time job or to make an initial move toward financial independence. The other five had part-time or full-time jobs. While serving valuable functions in their lives, in each case the job offered relatively little to the self, and they were not able, for many reasons, to invest much of the self in the work.

All eight women in Pattern C would have preferred to live like the women in Pattern B: married to a good enough traditional husband, being a part-time homemaker with full responsibility for the household, and having a part-time volunteer or paid job for supplemental income and/or satisfaction. They began building a Culminating Life Structure in which family was the central component, marriage was a central unfilled component, and outside work was necessary but peripheral. The absence of satisfactory marriage was the key issue, and it cast a shadow over their lives.

It is not easy to assess the magnitude and importance of the shift made by the Pattern C women in the Age 30 Transition. In her subjective view, each one took several giant steps toward greater independence. From an external vantage point, only a small change occurred. In my opinion both views have some truth but need to be combined: the shift, though small in absolute terms, was nonetheless difficult and remarkable. To those who believe that life changes can be made simply and quickly, this was indeed a slow pace. As we begin to understand how difficult it is to modify significantly the structure and direction of our lives, we are impressed by even modest changes that evolve, sometimes with tortuous slowness, over a span of five or ten or more years.

8 Culminating Life Structure for Early Adulthood: Homemakers

Among women and men generally, the period of the Culminating Life Structure typically begins at 33 and ends at 40. In the present sample, it most often began at 33 (with a range of 32 to 34) and ended at 40 (range 40 to 41). In the early thirties we enter a new generation. We move from *novice adult* to *junior member* of the adult world. We take on greater responsibilities, make deeper commitments, and build a Culminating Life Structure for Early Adulthood. At around 40 this structure comes to an end. We begin the Mid-life Transition and the shift to a new generation and a new era. After 40 we can no longer be junior members; it is time to enter middle adulthood and to start forming our niche as senior members. The Culminating Life Structure is the vehicle by which we move from junior to senior membership. What happens in this period will strongly influence the terms on which we begin to establish ourselves in the next generation.

The Two Phases of the Culminating Life Structure

As noted in Chapter 6, the period of the Entry Life Structure is divided into two phases, which are separated and linked by the Age 25 Shift. The period of the Culminating Life Structure also has two phases, although the demarcation between them is less sharply defined.

The *first phase* of the Culminating Life Structure usually lasts until age 35 or 36. The task of this phase is to establish a new life structure. For some women, this structure involves much the same external setting and cast of characters as the Entry Life Structure: they live in the same community, with the same nuclear family embedded in the same extended family, working at the same job. Looking only at the externals, one might conclude that the woman's life is unchanged. A closer look, however, reveals significant changes in the character of her relationships and the structure of her life. For other women the structure is formed in relatively different circumstances: a new community, the start or end of a marriage, greater material affluence or scarcity, an increase or decrease in occupational involvement. Under these conditions the work of building a life structure is more obvious to the observer and to the woman herself. She has to ask more questions about what she wants, where she is going with her life, and how she will accommodate to new circumstances. Whatever the extent of the external and inner changes, a first phase of two or three years is needed to establish a Culminating Life Structure.

If a woman has tentatively formed the central components of her Culminating Life Structure by age 32 or 33, the first phase proceeds relatively smoothly. She can use the initial phase to establish her key relationships and weave them into a more or less integrated pattern. Going through this time with little strain has obvious advantages, but it may also mean that she has taken the easiest path rather than the one most suitable for an evolving self. The first phase may also be a time of great strain, even crisis. A woman may have great difficulty forming a new structure, or may feel stuck in an unsatisfactory structure. The struggle to form a satisfactory Culminating Life Structure is, however, well worth the pain involved. Once the second phase has begun, the structure is hard to modify.

In the *second phase* a woman attempts to form an enterprise through which to realize her major goals of early adulthood. The enterprise is ordinarily built within a central component of the life structure but involves other components as well. By their mid-thirties most women in this sample were no longer ready to be full-time homemakers. Instead, they tried to form a modified Traditional Marriage Enterprise that included a mixture of homemaking and outside work, not making a heavy investment of self in either component but giving first priority to family. At its best, the modified marriage enterprise allowed them to be "good enough" wives and mothers without feeling overly oppressed by homemaking, and to have the advantages of outside work without the burdens of a demanding career. Because gender differences are so important in the second phase, I'll speak first of the findings for men.

Becoming One's Own Man

In *The Seasons of a Man's Life* I called this phase Becoming One's Own Man. During the years from roughly 36 to 40 a man feels strongly the need to attain his youthful goals, to be affirmed by society, to speak with his own voice, to be taken seriously on his own terms. It is time to bring the efforts of the past ten or fifteen years to fruition. This phase might have been called

Becoming One's Own Person. I used the word "man" rather than "person" because a man's experience of this time is so gender-linked, so suffused with images of masculinity and manhood. A man is trying to become a full man and to overcome his sense of being still a boy. Within the context of the Culminating Life Structure, he seeks to realize his youthful goals and, in the process, to validate his "manly" self. At the same time, he is laying the groundwork for the change in era from early to middle adulthood, and for the change in generation from junior to senior member of his world.

At around 40 there is ordinarily a *Culminating Event* that marks the outcome of the entire process. The event may involve a promotion or demotion, the conclusion of a major work effort, a sharp change in marriage or family life, a geographical move. It may be a publicly dramatic change or something hardly noticed by others. Since the years around 40 are often eventful, the Culminating Event may be hard to identify. To recognize it and grasp its full meaning, we must consider its external as well as internal aspects. Externally, this event carries a strong message about the man's current place and future possibilities in society (particularly in his work world). Internally, he constructs from it a broader, more powerful message about the outcome of his youthful strivings and about his options for the future. This event ushers in a new developmental period, the Mid-life Transition, in which he begins to question and modify the Culminating Life Structure while also trying to maintain it.

A man's view of adulthood is suffused with gender meanings: he wants to be not solely an adult, but a man. Later, in the Mid-life Transition and beyond, he may attempt to integrate the masculine and the feminine, and to draw more on the feminine, in order to become a more complete *person*. To become a person in the fullest sense, each of us must to some degree overcome the inner gender splitting that makes it so difficult for a man to draw upon the feminine and for a woman to utilize the masculine.

Becoming One's Own Woman

Do women go through a corresponding phase? My findings indicate that they do. This phase for women is not identical to that for men, nor is it a simple mirror image, an inverse form of the male. We have to grasp the specific patterns that exist for women, in their own terms, before making cross-gender comparisons.

By age 36 or so, a woman has established a Culminating Life Structure and needs to consider the value of this structure: what it enables her to do for herself and others, what goals she can pursue within it, how it is constraining or oppressive. She has the desire, inchoate or clearly articulated, to be affirmed in her world, to speak more with her own voice, to be recognized in her own right and not merely as an appendage to husband, children, parents, boss, or anyone else. Some have suggested that a woman's main concern here is to gain a stronger sense of her own personhood, so that we might speak of "becoming one's own person." Women sometimes speak in these terms—about the wish "to be my own person" or "to be treated as a real person." My research suggests that, for women as for men, the word "person" is too imprecise. The issue is more gender-linked.

A woman at this time is engaged in a desperate struggle against her own sense of being a little girl and against being cast by others as a little girl (not just a child, but a girl). She is trying, not without difficulty, to move from girl to—what? Person? Adult? Woman? She herself is often unsure which word to use. My own sense of it is that she is trying to move from girl to woman. The most fitting name for this phase, then, is *Becoming One's Own Woman*. What is a woman? Concretely, a woman is an adult female. Both words, "adult" and "female," carry essential meanings.

First, she is trying to become an adult rather than a child—in the world and in herself. She wants to be independent, competent, responsible, taken seriously, in ways that distinguish adults from children. To become more fully adult, she must deal with the child in herself and with the cultural assumption (held by some women as well as some men) that an adult female is still a girl.

Second, she wants to be adult in a gender-linked sense—to be a woman. She wants to be affirmed for qualities associated with the feminine, however difficult this is to define. When she develops qualities commonly regarded as masculine (such as ambition or intellectual power), she wants these not to jeopardize her identity as a woman. These concerns are at least as hard for a woman to deal with as the concerns about femininity for a man.

In some respects the developmental tasks of this phase are similar for women and men, but there are important differences as well. For one thing, there is much in the meaning of being a girl that a woman has to outgrow before she can become "her own" independent, responsible adult—just as a man must outgrow the boy. Boys are under pressure to act like "little men" and to exhibit manly virtues such as bodily prowess, emotional control, rationality, respect for authority, and readiness in time to exercise authority. Girls are under pressure to be "good little girls"—charming, attractive, docile, eager to give care but less interested or able to take care of themselves. Whereas "manhood" is a valued ideal for males, the meaning and value of "womanhood" are much more ambiguous for women as well as men. In time, the good little girl evolves into the adult Traditional Homemaker. A good girl who fully incorporates the traditional values and images of the feminine is inclined to regard as masculine, and to reject in herself and other women, any proclivities she may have toward strong involvement in the occupational (male) world. It's all right to be smart, but not "too smart for her own good." It's all right to work, but safer to do "woman's work." If she works directly with men, it is best not to be conspicuously competitive, successful, or authoritative. The conflict is not limited to any specific age, but it often takes a distinctive, acute form in the late thirties.

For a woman in the process of Becoming One's Own Woman, the good little girl and the Traditional Homemaker Figure in herself is an implacable enemy. As she tries to become more womanly—independent, competent, taking care of herself, being responsible in a more adult way, having a mind of her own—she meets strenuous objections from the internal figure. The Traditional Homemaker Figure has a two-pronged argument: "First, it is more proper, secure, and pleasant to remain a child. Let a man take care of you. The burdens of independence and responsibility are greater than any benefits they may bring. Second, this new path is dangerous. If you follow it you will lose the feminine and enter forbidden masculine territory. Rather than become more a woman, you'll become a man—or get enmeshed in a struggle with men that will ultimately destroy you."

What does it mean to be a woman? We have few explicit definitions. The archetypal images in our culture are curiously vague and often negative. The most ubiquitous images are those of a young woman in her twenties who is engaged in romantic adventures or getting launched in her domestic career. Women's lives after age 30 or 35 are depicted much less often, and then typically in ordinary, everyday domestic situations or in major domestic crises. Modern culture has little wisdom to offer the woman in her late thirties or beyond who seeks to grow more as a woman—to form richer, more mutual relationships, to know more clearly what she wants, to gain a stronger sense of her own seniority and authority in the adult world.

A woman may develop to some extent within the domestic sphere. To develop more fully, however, she probably has to overcome the domestic/public split and become more seriously engaged in the public sphere. If she regards the occupational world and the personal qualities embodied there (such as competition, achievement, authority) as the forbidden domain of the masculine, she is not free to claim them for the feminine and for herself as a mature woman. As long as she splits off these allegedly masculine qualities, she can be feminine in ways permitted to girls and very young women (such as attractive, maternal-caring, mediative), but she cannot be womanly in a more adult sense. These qualities are not intrinsically masculine; they are given as potentialities in both genders. As she acquires them in the context of her own womanliness, she may be able both to enrich her own life and to make our social institutions less traditionally masculine and more humane.

I cannot emphasize too strongly that the foregoing tasks of Becoming

One's Own Woman are tasks in the development of the life structure. They are not simply motives—desires for greater autonomy, equality, and the like. A woman who has these motives to a high degree is likely to work harder at the tasks of Becoming One's Own Woman. However, the tasks are there in any case, even if she is not highly motivated to meet them, even if she is (as we all are) in some ways uneasy about meeting them. They are rooted in the nature of the life cycle, in the process of living and "growing up" during the late thirties. Women who earlier were content to remain quite dependent upon their husbands begin now to seek a greater measure of independence and recognition in their relationships with husband, children, extended family, work, community. Likewise, a woman who had been relatively independent becomes aware of many ways in which she was "not my own person" and devotes herself more assiduously to the tasks of this phase.

The tasks of Becoming One's Own Woman emerge and get worked on, or avoided, within the context of the Culminating Life Structure. A relatively satisfactory structure provides a basis on which a woman can expand her horizons and seek to live more fully than before. A less satisfactory structure impedes the developmental work. How a woman deals with the tasks will be influenced by her personality characteristics as well as her external circumstances, but these influences operate within the context of the life structure. In fulfilling the tasks, a woman gains a greater sense of meaning and fulfillment in early adulthood and a sounder basis on which to enter a new generation in middle adulthood. If she does not, she is likely to enter her forties no longer able to be a youthful homemaker yet unprepared for another mode of living appropriate to middle age. We shall see wide variations in these respects among the homemakers as well as the career women.

Within the framework of the Culminating Life Structure a woman attempts to be affirmed for doing what is most important to her. If she is involved in being a wife, she wants her husband to find her an attractive, interesting person and a competent partner in their joint enterprise. If she is involved in being a mother, she wants to earn respect and admiration for her maternal labors. If occupation is important, she wants to be affirmed as a worker and to speak increasingly with her own voice in the work world. She wants to become a senior member of her world.

When the effort to Become One's Own Woman goes badly, she has a sense of failure not just in one role but in her life. If things get bad enough she may undergo a developmental crisis and attempt to "break out" of the Culminating Life Structure in her late thirties. Unfortunately, it is difficult to change the structure in mid-stream; her efforts to modify it are not likely to go far until she enters the Mid-life Transition.

At around 40 the predominance of the Culminating Life Structure comes to an end and the Mid-life Transition begins. The shift is marked by the

Culminating Event of Early Adulthood, which represents the outcome of her early adulthood. She derives from it a message about her condition as a wife, mother, person, worker, member of the community. The most important events and messages are those that bear most directly on the central components of the Culminating Life Structure. If homemaking is the central component, she comes to a new sense of how well she has done as wife and/or mother and to new questioning about her prospects and preferences for the future. If occupation is a central or major component, she constructs a message about her prospects in the work world; for example, that she has the possibility of further interesting and rewarding jobs on the same occupational path, that the current path is ending but she has the possibility of creating a new one, or that her only choice is to continue doing work that gives her little or to leave the job market altogether.

Let's look now at individual sequences through this period. In Chapter 7, I distinguished three types of life structures that the women began to form in the Age 30 Transition:

Pattern A.   Married Women Who Made Family and Occupation Co-central Components

During the Age 30 Transition three women—Nora Cole, Jenny Abatello, and Vicky Perrelli—modified their relationships within the family and got increasingly involved in outside work. Family and occupation then became co-central components of the Culminating Life Structure. These women saw family as the essential grounding of their lives. If the chips were down, they would put the urgent demands of family before those of occupation. Yet they invested more of themselves in occupation, which became the major source of interest and excitement in their lives.

In the Culminating Life Structure the spouses formed a *Neo-Traditional Marriage Enterprise* markedly different from that of the Entry Life Structure. The marital relationship became considerably more egalitarian on the wife's initiative but with the effort and accommodation of both spouses. She made several things absolutely clear to him. She would continue to be primarily responsible for child care and domestic responsibilities. But having a job was essential to her. Outside work was about independence and identity even more than about money, though she was also proud to be contributing 30 to 70 percent of the family income. She wanted him to take a larger share of the household responsibilities. Many husbands did do more, but nowhere near 50 percent. The husbands largely accepted the terms sought by their wives. In time they met more than the minimal demands, especially by spending time with the children and becoming involved in the children's lives. The movement toward greater marital equality and a more equal division of domestic labor continued over the course of the Culminating Life Structure, but the basic pattern was set as the period began.

Like the women, the men had entered the marriage with a strongly traditional outlook. Each one took it for granted that he would be the provider and head of household. The changes did not come easily and were to some extent a source of marital conflict. Each husband, however, regarded his wife as "special." She represented something symbolically important, something he himself lacked. He appreciated her educational, occupational, and social accomplishments. He tolerated her less welcome departures from the traditional homemaker role. Each woman felt that her husband was mystified and to some degree alienated by the kind of woman she was becoming—so different from the kind of girl he had married. Yet she also felt an elemental bond that made the difficulties tolerable. Though two of the three women at times considered the possibility of ending the marriage, none came near to divorcing.

As the Culminating Life Structure began, occupation took on greater meaning for each woman. Nora Cole, who had started working as an untrained nursery school teacher only a few years before, took a full-time job at 34 in a nursery school. She started an occupational career that was scarcely imaginable in her twenties. At 33, after teaching high school for five years, Jenny Abatello committed herself to a long-term career. In her Age 30 Transition Vicky Perrelli took a nursing job largely to get out of the house and away from her live-in mother-in-law. At 33 she started to realize that the work was becoming an essential part of her life. Her occupational identity and career evolved much further over the course of this period.

Family of origin had a different meaning now than in the Entry Life Structure. Many women had limited relationships with parents and siblings by their thirties. Roughly 50 percent of the homemakers had friendships of some importance, and most of the others voiced a wish for friendships in their lives.

The life structure once formed tends to remain relatively stable in a structure-building period but significant changes often occur within its components. Every structure facilitates the realization of certain goals and hinders the realization of others. Structural stability and internal change were evident in the lives of all three women during this period.

⋑ VICKY PERRELLI

At 33 Vicky Perrelli was forming a life structure very different from that of her twenties. After twelve years of marriage she had three children, ages 11, 9, and 5. She had distanced herself, psychologically and geographically, from her family and community of origin. She worked three nights a week and work was, for the first time, her main source of satisfaction. She accepted certain limitations of the marriage while making changes in accord with her growing independence. Motherhood was still a high priority but she spent less time with children and household. She was starting to live out aspects of her self that had formerly been dormant or suppressed.

Occupation and family thus became co-central components of her Culminating Life Structure. There were heavy constraints, however, on making occupation central. The internal Anti-Traditional Figure had an uphill fight against the internal Traditional Homemaker Figure in herself and her world. Creating a structure that would include the disparate elements of family and occupation, and managing the tensions involved, meant an enormous struggle. Her relationships with parents and extended family gave her little, and she sought little for herself from them. Her relationship to religion became more internal and played a minor part in her life. It was hard to find time for leisure activities and friendships.

The overall structure remained quite stable from 33 to 38, when she was interviewed, but various changes occurred within it. A major incident was her possible pregnancy at 35:

> I knew I could not face another pregnancy—I'd wind up in a mental hospital. Having an infant felt like starting all over just when I was starting to get independent. My youngest was 7, and I wanted no more bottles and diapers. I loved working and didn't want to quit. I told Frank, "I'm afraid I'm pregnant." He said, "Don't say things like that!" Then I knew he didn't want another baby, either. But that didn't matter: it was *my* body, and I wouldn't have cared if he wanted the baby. I just told him my decision: "If I'm pregnant I'm getting an abortion, and if I'm not pregnant I'm getting my tubes tied." He didn't say anything. It turned out I wasn't pregnant, and I had my tubes tied. Before that I had qualms about doing anything against my religion. I felt that babies came from God, and if it was meant to be then I would have a child. I had gone from my mother's arms into my husband's and quickly had children and never really had time for myself. Now I searched my soul and knew what was right for me. I felt no guilt—never even confessed it to a priest because I figured it was *my* business. Since then sex has been much more enjoyable than it was because we don't have to use anything. All my hang-ups are lifted—I don't have to worry about an unwanted pregnancy, and that takes an awful lot of pressure off. It's so funny: now I can enjoy it more, but as you get older you don't have sex that often.

This story suggests that Vicky was entering the phase of Becoming One's Own Woman.

> Now my life is just work and family and the house. I'm 38 years old and finally grown up—but it was hard, and it took a long time. That's sad

when you think of it, it really is. Earlier I would have liked to spread my wings a little bit, but I met with resistance from my parents and then my husband. I feel very content at this age. I wouldn't want to go back. I like the way I turned out. I didn't like myself when I was just agreeing with everyone all the time, not being myself.

I only see my parents occasionally and talk sometimes on the phone. My mother is 60. To say that she's enjoyed her life, no. She accepts it, but it hasn't been good. The parents tell me what to do and will keep doing that until the day they die. Their relationship with me will never change. I just accept that. It's a good thing I don't have to put up with it that often. But I still love them.

I went to work because we needed the money. But I realized recently that I'd work even if we didn't need the money. The job has become a part of me, of who I am. I go to work, and it doesn't seem like a job to me. I care about the patients and their families. I just like it so much. I enjoy getting out. I feel useful. I feel important. The money is good, although it all goes for food and dentist bills. I am in charge, and I manage the ward well. I'm the head, the top. People come to me, and for the first time in my life my opinions matter. The doctors respect me, and the supervisor respects me. It's a completely different life for me there than at home or anywhere else.

Recently the head nurse job in my department became available, and I was really tempted to try for it. But I knew the time wasn't right because of my responsibility to my kids. Once I tried working full-time days, and after three days I was exhausted. Up at 5:30, home tired at 4:30, make supper, do dishes, laundry, housework, with no help from Frank or the kids—it was too much. Also, I'm not sure I want to be head nurse. Everyone talks about her behind her back. People don't like her because she's always in meetings, meetings, meetings, and she's lost contact with patient care. I like people to like me. I don't want success at that price.

But I am starting to wonder about the future. I'm not sure I want any big advancement but I probably can't go on indefinitely as I am. In a hospital it's either burn out or turn out. There is a big problem of burnout in nurses—it's constant tension and pressure, especially if you're in charge of anything. Also, to advance much I would have to get a bachelor's degree. I'm really not that ambitious. I should go to college but I don't want to. Actually, I might like to but it's not possible now; I have to think about the kids. The oldest is nearly ready for college, and the two others are not far behind. If I went to school, we'd lose necessary income, and the family would be under much more stress. I can't do that.

Still, I want to become a more respected person at work. As a starter, I have sent away for a medical book in my specialty. I plan to subtly read up as we get the cases. I feel very proud of myself when I give the doctors an opinion that turns out to be right on a difficult case—when I come through as knowledgeable and experienced. In the back of my mind I imagine being like a nurse in her sixties in the emergency room. Nobody, absolutely nobody, disputes this woman. She is the authority in that room. She's good at her job and she knows every cop, fireman, hooker, and clergyman in that town. She can deal with every problem, medical and social. I figure the only way I can stay on is to be as good as she is, so they wouldn't think of turning me out.

Though we have our problems, our family unit is basically very strong. Frank's greatest strength is that he is so committed to his family. He takes pride in his home, takes time every night to water and weed his garden, never goes to bars after work. He is so good with the kids, takes them everywhere; I love to see that. I don't spend as much time with them—I collect thimbles, embroider, and crochet. Frank used to be such a macho man but now there is more give and take between us. He has mellowed, whereas I've become a little more independent.

Yet the differences are still there, and they do bother me. Frank lives in a world of his own but he's content in it. He works, and he comes home and putters around in his yard and falls asleep in front of the TV—and that's it. He's content with his life as it is, and I'm not content with my life as it is. When he looks at me he still sees that 14-year-old girl who used to be, when we first met. He is used to making all the decisions. I have rebelled in some ways, but I've also learned to manipulate him—it's a kind of woman's strategy. Mostly I keep my feelings hidden so that he thinks he's making the decisions, but I usually get my way. All the same, I would like to have more discussion, more of a two-way street. I used to think he knew it all and I should do whatever he says, but now I realize that he doesn't know everything.

I'd like to spend more time alone with my husband but he doesn't seem interested. [This is a vivid theme for many married homemakers.] It is very frustrating. He won't go out with me, just the two of us. Nothing is spontaneous anymore. We never had time to enjoy ourselves alone together when we first got married, because right away we had the children and the responsibilities. When we were going together he couldn't wait to have sex, but as soon as we got married he was like an old man, still is. I don't mind the kids growing up because it leaves time for Frank and me to enjoy each other, but I'm not sure he wants that. I wouldn't want him to climb the ladder into middle management; he already has too long hours and too much tension. He recently got a little more money and a lot more responsibilities but no promotion. I'd rather he had more time.

I feel good about the kids. Their formative years are behind me now, they're nearly grown up. It's up to them now. I've taught them and given them good examples: they live in a nice house, don't hear their parents argue, don't see their father come home drunk, we don't go out without the other, we've always been there for them and open to them. My daughter Alice is a senior in high school. I'm very proud of her. She's an honor student, very independent. I'm ready to work hard to send her to college, even out of state, because she has the potential, and I wouldn't be wasting my money. I'm glad to see that she is not interested in going steady. At her age I had been going steady with Frank for three years, and I really did miss a lot. I would not recommend it to her, no, no! I tell her not to be in a hurry. I certainly don't tell her to go out and have sex, but it's okay to talk about it. In my day marriage was a way to legalize sex. Kids today are freer. I don't want her to get married until she's a little older. I'd like to see her enjoy her young life and travel, or whatever she wants to do. I have always encouraged her to be responsible and say what's on her mind. She works, manages her own money, buys her own clothes, has household responsibilities. I never had those things. If she had been raised the way I was she might have been more spiteful.

My son Eric's recent emergency appendectomy was an eye-opener for me. I got a call about 9 p.m. that he was in the emergency room. Frank was at a poker game and unavailable. I wondered, "Can I handle this alone?" But I knew I had to go. Eric looked up at me crying, "Mom, am I going to die?" Later I called Frank and asked him to come to the hospital, but he said no, he was going to bed. I didn't know that he had already talked to a nurse and learned that Eric was going to be all right. I absolutely could not believe that he would not come for me. At 2:30 a.m. I phoned again and said, "Please come, I need you," but he wouldn't. He really disappointed me. I sat there thinking, "Here I am, alone. If a man and woman can't share these times together, what else is there? There's nothing."

I have a lot of deep feelings about that night but I'm biding my time. I realize that he's always done this: when I really needed him he's never been there for me. He treats us like his underlings. It turns out to my amazement that I am stronger and more mature than him. I'm the one who holds this whole family together. He comes home from work and tells me about all his frustrations, and I listen. I look at him with my headache and think, "I've got a lot on my mind that I'd like to tell him, but he won't listen to me." I resolved that he's going to learn that I am my own person. I have my own opinions, and whether he likes them or not I couldn't care less.

The day after Eric's operation Frank told me that he had had too much to drink at the poker party and felt depressed. I just walked away. I'm not ready to have it out with him yet. If I do, I think to myself, one of two things will happen: either he'll wind up making me feel that I was stupid to have these feelings in the first place, or else we'll have such a row that nothing will ever be the same again. I don't want to risk that. You just don't throw 18 years of your life away.

I don't know if eventually I will leave him or not. For now I'm just letting it lay. I still love him but he does not see me as I am, he just doesn't. We don't have much in common except the children. I've grown away from him, and that frightens me. I don't know if I'd have the courage to leave him because the other possibilities seem worse. A lot of women at work are living with husbands who are alcoholics, husbands who run out on them. Or else they're divorced and having a difficult time making it alone. Maybe it's calculating of me, but I don't want that to happen to me. We still have a good marriage, compared to lots of others. The children have a good relationship with him. We have a happy home but it's the wife that has to keep the house together and make it run smooth. All in all, my life is not bad as it is right now. It's stagnant but it's not bad.

The themes of Becoming One's Own Woman were first evident in Vicky's Age 30 Transition, but the struggle is much more pronounced now. Without some form of advancement at work (in both her job and her own capabilities) she will suffer from "burn out or turn out." She needs an advancement as an affirmation of her blossoming self. If advancement is a burning question at work, it burns even more hotly at home. Vicky chafes under the weight of being "an underling" to her husband. She wants him to be interested in her as a woman and a person. She wants an advancement, domestically and occupationally, that would affirm her as an effective contributor and a person worthy of respect.

Her external circumstances support as well as impede her efforts at change. In work she is valued by others and has opportunities for promotion. Yet her domestic responsibilities make it extremely difficult to work full-time or to get the further education required for real advancement. Her husband both facilitates and hinders her growing involvement in occupation. He partially supports her wish for independence but does very little to reduce the burden of her domestic labor. External factors thus make it stressful but not impossible to improve her lot.

Likewise, we see within the self both an impetus to change and barriers to change. Vicky has learned to exercise the authority of night charge nurse but is not ready for a position of greater authority. She is still tyrannized by the need to be liked and the feeling that rejection implies catastrophe, obliteration of the self. These feelings hinder her efforts to become a more senior nurse and to confront her husband. She still has strong doubts about her legitimate right to exercise authority and seek advancement. She wants her husband to know who she is, yet is not sure herself of her own identity. She would like a more intimate relationship with him but finds it difficult to initiate greater intimacy with him or others. She does not recognize how little she knows Frank—what he wants from life and how he feels about her transformation from a 14-year-old adoring sweetheart to a 21-year-old docile girl-bride to a 38-year-old woman threatening to turn his world upside down.

She has no close friendships with women, and the idea of a friendship with men is so alien to her (and her world) that she does not mention the possibility. At the same time, she has shown a remarkable degree of self-development in adulthood.

Finally, Vicky's search is limited by her current developmental period. At 38 she is under an enormous constraint to maintain the Culminating Life Structure and to avoid drastic changes that might undermine it. Family and occupation are the central components of this structure. Occupation is a recent addition, whereas family is the foundation she will not jeopardize. To work full-time and/or go to college would risk splitting the family and breaking out of the structure. "Breaking out" in the middle of this period is a rare phenomenon. None of the fifteen women in the homemaker sample did so. Despite Vicky's serious grievances, the predominant forces are on the side of staying put. After all, as she says with such bittersweet directness, her life is "stagnant but it's not bad."

Pattern B.   Married Women Who Kept Homemaking Central but Reduced Their Involvement in Family

Four married women—Wendy Lewis, Claire Berman, Elaine Olson, Kay Ryan—were committed to the Traditional Marriage Enterprise but experienced considerable disappointment in their domestic life. Homemaking was, they found, not a full-time mode of living to which they could give a great deal and from which they could obtain much satisfaction. Their solution: they made homemaking the sole central component of the Culminating Life Structure but devoted themselves less to it and engaged more in outside activities.

One step was to obtain a job, part-time or full-time, paid or volunteer. For some women the job yielded income that was essential for family survival or for living at a standard the husband alone could not provide. For some it provided elective spending money outside the husband's control. They supplemented the husband's income without displacing him as primary provider. The job also gave them a legitimate escape from the domestic world, as well as activities that provided fun, contact with the "real world" of adults and public events, and the sense of being competent.

Although family was the fundament of the Culminating Life Structure, the relationships to marriage and domesticity were not as before. Without giving up the personal identity and public image of homemaker, these women reduced significantly the time spent on housework, preparing meals, managing children's and husband's affairs, and the countless errands of domestic life. They continued to regard the husband as "head of the family" and would not directly challenge his authority. Yet they were also increasingly prepared to make their own decisions and to manipulate him on decisions that were officially his. Although the family structure was patriarchal in a formal sense, a woman could exercise considerable influence in matters of importance to her. The relative lack of intimacy between the spouses was of great help in this regard. A woman could often make decisions without her husband's knowledge.

Motherhood, too, became a less involving part of the Culminating Life Structure. These women were strongly concerned with the well-being of their children, but the functions of motherhood were much less clear to them once their children passed the age of 4 or 5. They felt less "needed" by the children and obtained less satisfaction from taking care of them. The homemakers generally saw the kids off to school in the morning and received them at home in the afternoon. It was important to be sure that the kids were "well adjusted" in school and community, and to intervene if there were serious problems. But they were generally not very close to the children and did not know much about their actual life experiences.

The relationship to family of origin was different in this period from what it had been in the twenties. They maintained continuing contact with the family, even when they lived some distance away. They had a strong inner bond, especially with the mother. The Pattern A women, who had a similar relationship to parents in the Entry Life Structure, went through a conscious rebellion and separation in the Age 30 Transition. The women in Pattern B did much less to reappraise their relationship with family of origin. In the Culminating Life Structure they became somewhat less involved and felt less obligated to be the dutiful daughter. This change made life somewhat more comfortable but was not part of a larger process of individuation.

Family was still the pillar on which the life structure was built. The ultimate threat to their lives was divorce, since it would deprive them of the enterprise that allowed them to be homemakers. Family was, however, much less dominant than before. Despite their strong sense of obligation to be good wives and mothers, they got less involved in relationships with husband and children. These relationships were often more wearing than gratifying, especially with husbands and sons.

How *satisfactory* was the Culminating Life Structure for these women? In their own subjective evaluation it was quite satisfactory. Despite some complaints, they felt that life had been good to them. Their husbands were decent, reliable men who cared about their families and did a better than average job in taking care of them. Their children had a good home and, whatever their growing pains, usually seemed headed toward an adult life more or less consistent with the parents' values. The women themselves could meet their family responsibilities without much strain. They had a sense of security and order in their lives. All in all, they felt more content than most women they knew.

In my view, a life structure is satisfactory to the extent that it is viable in the external world and suitable for the self (see Chapter 2). For each woman in Pattern B the Culminating Life Structure was quite viable: it gave her a secure life and a general level of comfort at or above her initial aspirations. It was also suitable in the sense that it allowed her to live out most aspects of the self that she deemed important. She and her husband had created a good life according to her lights. She had worked hard to meet her end of the bargain. Now, in her late thirties, she was reaping the fruits of her labors.

It must be said, however, that this life structure is suitable only for a minimally individuated self—a self that can be content with a narrow, externally scripted life and does not seek to involve itself deeply in any aspect of living. The lives of these four women were almost entirely lacking in intensity and passion. Each woman saw her life as a series of disparate situations in which she coped or "got by" as best she could. She was not engaged in a search for meaning. She had little sense of a self that gave a distinctive character to her life at a given time and to her life course as a whole.

The relative lack of individuation was clearly evident in the phase of Becoming One's Own Woman. The Pattern A women in this phase struggled against the internal "little girl" and worked hard to establish themselves as competent women. The Pattern B women went through this phase with much less struggle. Feeling bored and restless at home, they turned to outside work for compensation and consolation. But they could not invest much of the self in an occupation nor use an occupation to help them develop the self and enrich their lives. While becoming less submissive to the husband's authority, they did not seriously question the basic terms of the marriage. They dealt with their dissatisfactions in the marital relationship by reducing their involvement in it, accentuating the positive, and making their lives more separate. To the extent that they succeeded in this effort—and, to a large extent, they did—the marriage became more tranquil, the marital enterprise was stabilized, and their lives had little substance. The themes of Becoming One's Own Woman are recognizable in their stories, but they appear for the most part in whispers, allusions, possibilities that the woman knows about but does not fully grasp or act upon.

✑ CLAIRE BERMAN

Claire Berman married at 27, gave up her teaching job, and started a family at 28. In the Age 30 Transition she explored the possibilities of a purely domestic life and concluded that it was not for her. Homemaking was the central component of her Culminating Life Structure but she could not obtain much satisfaction from it. Since her husband, Ben, made few demands and provided a comfortable middle-class income, she was able to reduce appreciably the time given to domestic duties. The second component of this life structure was recreation, primarily with women and children. Both components were necessary, but neither evoked an intense investment of self. At 34, when her youngest child entered nursery school, she took a job teaching swimming to small children two afternoons a week. "Working was great! The job was not challenging but it got me out of the house and meeting people. I loved it." She also played tennis. Since 35 she has had a weekly appointment with three other "girls" for tennis, coffee, and sociability. Since 36 she has been an unpaid coach:

> Four years ago I went to a game and immediately applied to be a coach. The minute I saw everybody yelling and those kids running around I thought, "This is where I belong." I'm too old to play myself but I am a kid again on the floor with them! I really love it. It has filled my spare time, and I am home when my kids get home from school. One year I coached the boys' team. I liked that better than the girls' but the fathers objected to a woman coach, so I had to stop.

Now, as she turns 41, Claire describes the present chapter of her life:

> I have been getting more assertive with my husband. I'd like him to do more around the house, but there's no way I'm going to change him now. We used to have picnics and I did *all* the work. Two years ago I told Ben, "No one helps me, so that's it, no more picnics!" He said, "Tell me what to do, and I'll do it." But he has eyes; he can see what needs to be done. My older son is just like him; his wife will have to do all the work. That kind of work was never demanded of Ben; to expect him to do it now I'd have to be crazy. I would discuss it with him if he had the time to sit that long and discuss something, but he's always working or reading.
>
> Ben has been working since high school in an insurance business owned by his father. I really get angry at his slow pace of advancement— very angry. He makes much less than his father though he works harder. He gets very resentful but won't stand up to his tough father. A few years ago he thought seriously about leaving but felt it would break his father's heart. In the end, they gave him an assistant and made him Senior Manager, but it's just a title. I tell his father, "Let Ben do more; you educated him for this, so use him." But he won't give up power.
>
> Ben is becoming more assertive from my pushing him. Last week for the first time in his life he spoke up to his father. His father told him to do something *right now*. Ben said he was doing something else and would help when he finished. His father didn't talk to him for two days. When he told me I was clapping: "All these years and you finally talked back to him!" I was so happy I almost baked a cake.

My life is quite separate from my husband's. He likes to read or play the violin in his little leisure time and doesn't like sports as I do. I no longer feel it's important to be home to make supper, which is okay with him. Whenever any questions come up he says, "Do what you want; just don't involve me." We don't see each other much before 8 p.m. every night. I have my coaching, friends, and the children's activities, and he is out a few evenings with a religious group and a music group. He's in his own little world. He has a nice relationship with the children but doesn't have much time for them. Sundays we spend the day together as a family. I'm very much the disciplinarian, not him. When he does, he's too strict and hits them too hard; I told him if he did that again I would leave him.

We have a good relationship but it was never intimate and is less so now. Everyone gets tired earlier now. Besides, I'm not the most romantic person. I don't have a sex drive, and he is not passionate, though he would probably want more frequency than I do. Often I go along because he's my husband. I have never discussed our sexual relationship with anyone. Over the years it has declined; most nights he comes home exhausted and goes to sleep at 9. All in all, I would say it's comfortable—I am comfortable and he is comfortable enough. Love takes different forms. I'm proud of him. He is smart and kind. I am glad I chose him. I'd choose him again.

I never had a relationship with anyone else, and I doubt that it would be different with anyone else. I will *not* have affairs outside of marriage. I have a sense of my own self-worth, whereas many of my girlfriends don't. They lead double lives, married and having affairs. One of my girlfriends has two kids and her husband wants to leave her. She has to go to work to pay her bills. She is just lost. She has no self-worth. Actually, she is as tired of him as he is of her; they've known each other since high school. I'd hate to be in that position. I have never been depressed. I guess I just roll with the punches.

How would I sum it all up? I like my life. I'm glad I got married. I have my kids, and we have our health. My husband has a good job. I have a lot of stability, and that's very important to me. I know he's coming home at night. I feel comfortable. I have never thought about whether my life was exciting or whether I would rather be doing something else. I just want to get through the day doing what I have to do. I get by, I'm not unhappy, I take life as it comes.

While emphasizing the positive aspects of her life, Claire also conveys a muted sense of disappointment. It is most evident in the story of her marriage. Ben is a good husband in all essential respects, a base on which she can securely build her life. He cares for the family but leaves everything to her. He lives in his own little world, which is not connected to her.

What of the future? Without actively seeking change, Claire recognizes that it is on the horizon.

Things don't stand still. The kids will be going into junior high soon. I'll have more time, and I don't want to just sit at home. I'd like to get out more and meet people. That means some kind of job. I never want to teach full-time again. I don't have to, financially, and I don't want to put up with this modern generation if I don't have to. In the fall I'll start working one day a week at a sports club, and that may lead to a paying job. I'd like something in the recreational area, maybe in an administrative position.

Claire senses that she is coming to a new time in her life. As is her wont, she is neither overjoyed nor devastated by the change, nor does she see it as an opportunity to seek greater meaning and purpose in her life. She attributes the change primarily to external events such as having more free time. It is evident, however, that her next life structure will be formed on a somewhat different basis than the current one. For one thing, she no longer wants to work with "this modern generation" of children. She is now becoming less animated by the child in herself and less able to make mutually enjoyable contact with the children outside. (This is not an inevitable consequence of age; a middle-aged person might enjoy working with children as a playful responsible adult rather than solely as a playmate.)

She is, in my opinion, on the verge of her Mid-life Transition. During the next four or five years she will move toward a new life structure. She may get more seriously involved in occupation, perhaps working with adults in the field of recreation. This work might give her a niche in the world of middle adulthood, while cushioning the shock by making it a world of play and a world comprised more of youthful than of middle-aged adults. Again accommodating to her own age and skills, she thinks of working as an administrator rather than a coach or youthful participant.

Although outside work is becoming increasingly important to her, Claire faces great obstacles, internal as well as external, in making it a more central component. She has in mind a relatively unskilled part-time job, which would soon bore her. An employer is likely to offer it to a younger, more energetic person who would hold it briefly and move on. A more appropriate job would provide more interesting work and a more senior place in a work world, but it would also require much more from her. She would have to take on more responsibility and authority with adults and involve herself more in the complexities of adult life. Without satisfying work, her life will be a round of trivial activities. To gain the capacity for such work, she will have to make creative use of the Mid-life Transition that is just getting under way.

Pattern C.   Women Who Were Legally or Psychologically Divorced

The eight women in Pattern C, who constitute more than half of the home-maker sample, experienced severe marital problems in the Age 30 Transition. As a result, they started the Culminating Life Structure either as a legally divorced head of household or as a psychologically divorced wife who maintained a household with her husband but was minimally married. The basic question was: How do I begin making a new life without a husband—or with a husband who is a highly inadequate partner in the marriage enterprise? Each woman's aim was to gain a good enough Traditional Marriage Enterprise, with homemaking as the central component of her life.

Women Who Were Legally Divorced

Three women were legally divorced mothers at the start of this period. Beth Logan, Sara Cushing, and Ruth Allen were all profoundly disappointed by the marital failure and terrified of the prospect of having to become financially responsible for their children and themselves. They had to find a new balance of homemaking and provisioning. Income was a crucial problem in each case. Their ex-husbands provided little or no child support. The women were high school graduates with limited occupational skills and experience. They had married early (at 18, 19, 22) and had the first of their children within a year. All of these women had worked sporadically at unskilled jobs that helped feed their children but were low-paying and had no meaning for them. The key question for all: Without a husband to provide for the family, how can I find other sources of help and/or become the provisioner myself?

Each woman managed to scrape together enough income from various sources to maintain her family at a subsistence level. Beth Logan had various unskilled jobs. Her parents provided a rent-free apartment. Her only prospect for improvement was to marry the man with whom she had started a serious relationship around the time of her divorce. When interviewed at 35 she was trying desperately to assemble the components of a Culminating Life Structure. Ruth Allen, at 39, was nearing the end of this period.

✑ SARA CUSHING

In my early thirties my life was totally my two daughters and my son. Then something snapped, and I wanted to do more with my life than just be a mother. I can't tell you what makes you wake up one day, and all of a sudden you just want to do something different with your life. Being divorced, being on my own, being responsible and making all the decisions all brought about a change. I became more independent and wanted more than being a mother. Gradually I began to emerge into the world. I needed something more than just the kids. I began by doing volunteer work for a political candidate. I was doing things I had never done before and learning to become more competent. I brought my landlord to small claims court, and I won. I joined the church and got active with my children in activities there.

Those years I was groping for who I was and what I wanted. I didn't realize I had blocked all these feelings after Bill left. How could this happen to me? How could I have married a gay man and gotten divorced and be stuck with three kids and be a single parent, raising my kids alone, on welfare. It was degrading. I never regretted my life of having my kids but it was very hard. I was blaming them for the kind of life I had. When you have no money and they need things, it's hard. All the burdens and responsibilities were overwhelming. I was angry about the mess I was in, and I blamed myself. How could I be so stupid to marry someone I didn't even know? How could I be so stupid to have three kids and not be able to provide for them?

I volunteered for a political action group. Getting to be with other adults was wonderful. The first meeting they asked why people had come. I said, "To get out of the house." Everyone laughed but then others said the same thing. I was with other people who weren't happy with their lives. By 36 I was heading committee meetings. It's like I woke up from a fog, this person who had no self-confidence was the person people were looking up to in the group. They started looking up to *me*, asking *my* opinions. I realized I was capable for the first time. Having these people take me seriously and respect me and listen to my opinion was a wonderful experience.

Then friends started divorcing. I realized being single wasn't so bad. I'd compare my life to theirs and appreciate mine more. All those years I'd had a fantasy of a knight in shining armor coming to my door who would protect me and take care of me. I realized there really is no such thing as a happily-ever-after marriage. I stopped having fantasies about meeting someone who was going to make my life better.

When I was 37 my sister married and moved out of state for a year and paid for me to go to word-processing school. She had contributed groceries and clothes and emergency money since my divorce. She felt responsible, and I felt resentful of her help. She used to tell me what to do. When she left it was like no one was bossing me anymore. Whatever I did, it was my own decision, and it turned out good. I became my own person that year.

Going to school at 37, I was petrified. How was I going to be able to do this? I went to school full time, did my homework, volunteered in the political action group fifteen hours a week, plus church. I think my kids haven't been first in my life since then. I was happy, and they were happy. I asked them, "What do you like about me going to school?" They said, "You laugh all the time now." It was a good year. I felt independent. I realized I could do it, and I was growing. I had a checking account and responsibilities and was managing.

I finished the one-year course, and my sister returned to Connecticut. There was great pressure on me to get off welfare and get a job but I was terrified. I was looking in the paper at 9 to 5 jobs and trying to figure out budgets. I became aware that there was no way I could better my life. It was overwhelming. If I went to work, I'd leave home at 8:30 in the morning and come home at 5:30 at night with my kids alone at home after school, and I wouldn't make as much as on welfare. Was it worth it? There was a $10 difference between working full-time and staying home and getting a welfare check and food stamps and being home with my kids. And if I worked I wouldn't have medical insurance for myself and my children. At 38 I took a job. I was thrilled, and I was petrified.

I'm 39 now. It's the happiest time of my life; I love my work but it's terrible when you work so hard and don't earn enough money to live on and take care of your children. My sister still buys the groceries and clothes for the children. After paying rent, heat, and electricity, there's nothing left. I know I can't make it financially, and it's a horrible feeling. I know a lot of women in my situation. Women just aren't paid enough. I'm so angry at my ex-husband. He hasn't paid a penny of child support in four years.

But my life *is* better. Sometimes I'm shocked with myself that I've come so far. Before I just thought about today. Now I'm starting to think about my future. I'm feeling very successful as far as the *outside* world is concerned. I'm happy about what I've accomplished in my outside activities like the political action group and church. I feel like a leader, like people look up to me. And I feel good and very confident and successful at work. All the things I tried to do trying to make a life for myself have been a success. But there are two sides of my life. One half is feeling that way, and the other half is feeling disappointed. I'm doing the best I can. I work six days a week, and I feel I'm a success there, and I've made something of myself but I realize it's not enough. I don't make enough money to support my family. There's no extra even for enough food from paycheck to paycheck, and that's very discouraging. Even ten years from now I'm not going to be earning enough. There's no way that I alone can support my family. So I feel successful but trapped as far as it's not enough.

I feel like I did when I was young, and I never thought I'd get back to that: looking forward to tomorrow. I spent all my adult life not wanting to think about tomorrow and what would happen next. Now I have a different outlook on life: I feel like there's hope. In my life now is a world, with people in it. I'm really with the world. When you're home, you're isolated, by yourself. I'm now in a world and involved with other people all day long and seeing how their lives are and realizing that we're all the same; we all have problems. The whole thing is that I'm a working person now. No matter what happens I have self-respect; I'm not on welfare. I think I have finally started to grow up.

✌ς RUTH ALLEN

Ruth Allen's first marriage, from 18 to 23, produced three children and great unhappiness. Her second marital relationship, not a legal marriage, yielded two children and a more satisfactory life. At 28 she moved to Connecticut in search of greater job skills and a Traditional Marriage Enterprise that would form the basis for a better life. At 33 she seemed on the verge of exactly the life she had been seeking. She was working as a hospital aide and raising her six children. For three years she had been in a stable relationship with Jesse, with whom she had a 1-year-old child. She was confident that they would soon get legally married—her fondest dream. The marriage would enable her to build a Culminating Life Structure around a Traditional Marriage Enterprise. At 34 she got pregnant for the second time with Jesse. But now the dream bubble burst, and she could not have the life that had seemed within her grasp. She was forced to form a Culminating Life Structure as a single working mother:

> When I told Jesse I was pregnant again, he said this baby would mess up his life, and he asked me to have an abortion. I said, "No way! I'm sorry your life is messed up, but what do you think you're doing to my life if you feel that way? You're single, you have no ties. I'm here with six children and another on the way, but I don't feel my life is messed up." Then I found out that he was going through some changes. He was seeing another woman and planning to marry her. I was hurt and angry. I told him to make a choice and not play between the two of us. I was hurt to the point of depression. But he wouldn't dissolve our relationship and I wouldn't either—I just loved this man too deeply. He'd come by and stay the night and then go back to his girlfriend. When I had the baby he visited me every day; he was still a loving father, and he brought money for the baby and me. Our relationship tried to build back up, but I couldn't take that chance, and I'm glad he didn't. I knew it would probably be a downfall for me, another bad hurt in my life.
>
> So we sat down and talked. I said: "I love you, and I guess I always will. But my mind is made up. I know what I want. I want a home, a happy home. I want somebody that's going to be here with these children and correct them when I'm not around and we work as a complete family unit.

I went through pure hell with my first husband, and I don't want that again." But it took two years to end the relationship. We just couldn't stay away from each other. He still takes care of his children with me, and all my children respect him to this day. He was the only father they knew for over six years. We stopped three years ago when I was 36, just before he married the other woman.

In a very real sense, then, Ruth's relationship to Jesse involved a psychological marriage and divorce. She decided that, if she couldn't have the homemaker life with Jesse, she would have it on her own with unemployment compensation as provisioner:

I'd always worked from the time my first child was born. I wanted to be at home and be a real mother for the first time ever. I wasn't sure I could stand being at home full-time but I needed to find out. My kids were shocked. I was baking cookies! I'd never been home other than a couple of weeks after each birth. I stuck it out for a year but then realized I couldn't take it. The whole apartment was closing in on me. I just had to get out—into the community, a job, seeing friends. I had to have my own work.

Finally I got a job with a community agency. It didn't pay much but I loved the work. I was the secretary-receptionist and spent a lot of time with the clients as an informal counselor. After a year at the agency, I was promoted to be office manager/bookkeeper. I earn only $9,000 a year but I really love everything about this job. It has given me the challenge I was seeking. I just have enrolled in a community college and want to go into accounting. Now that I see how numbers work I'm falling in love with them. [Interviewer: Your face is glowing.] Oh, yes! I really feel good about myself, my job, my family—about life itself and about what I'm about. It gets me to thinking more about the future. I've never been to college. I can't afford to go full-time, and I don't want to spend 30 years taking courses part-time. So I'll take enough courses in the next few years so I can advance in my work.

The nice thing about this job is that we are like a big family. They call me the mother of the agency. The director is a woman, but she is busy in her office all day. The main responsibility for the day-to-day work falls on me. I set the pace and the tone—the good feelings of staff and clients. I'm never too busy to talk with anyone. I feel very competent to do the job. I don't have any long-range plans of leaving this job but you never know. I want to be ready if another position came along somewhere.

Music has always been an important part of my life. Now I'm involved with the church choir. I love the music, and it gives me a place in the community.

My kids are still very important but most of them are pretty independent now. A few years ago the two oldest ones, both girls, gave me a hard time, but with a lot of prayer and meditation I left it to the Lord. They are 18 and 19 now with kids of their own. I'm a pretty old-fashioned mother, and we do have our differences. I have to realize that my 18-year-old is a woman, even though she's a child. I have to respect her as a woman. She has a mind of her own. I don't want to be the kind of mother that, what I was taught and what I did, she has to do. I did that for a while, and it didn't work. She's on her own now; she can take care of herself. When I was 16 I hadn't been on a date; these kids start at 12. It's a much different world.

A central theme at 39 is the disparity between Ruth's initial homemaking Dream and the realities of her current life as a single mother of seven:

What I've always wanted most is a comfortable home life, to raise my children to the best of my ability, to get them some kind of education. I've always dreamed that I would meet a person who could help me fulfill this dream. We would have a good partnership: he would help raise my children, or his children, too, and we would work together to be a complete family. But it never unfolded; it was a dream that stayed folded. My terms for a home back then was a place where I could say, "This is *my* home. I have a yard; my children have space." I've found out that a home can be wherever I make it, even a small apartment. But I haven't given up that dream, not even today, of trying to get out and buy a home.

I'm doing okay as a single parent, but one of these days all my children will be grown up and gone—and I'll still be a single parent, living at home by myself. A companionship is what I miss. I still want to get married again and provide a home for my husband and my children and his children. I want to be able to sit down with him and say, "I have this problem, and I need to talk to you about it." I am very strong but I need someone I can lean on every once in a while, someone that can pick me up when I'm falling down, that we can be a help to each other.

If I don't get married I'm strong enough to continue. I'm not going to give up. I'll just keep on working as long as I can, helping my grandchildren if possible. My life to me is beautiful. It hasn't always been roses, but to me it's beautiful because it's what I've made of it. No one messed up my life. Even with all the troubles of my first marriage, I feel good about myself because I did everything I could to make it work. That horrible marriage made me the strong person I am today. If I had let it just take over me, I couldn't have been strong for my children or moved across the country or sought out new opportunities.

The opportunities are much better for white women. It's very hard for a black woman, especially if she is classified as low income, a black woman by herself. Blacks have been dominated and down for so many hundreds of years, we are just getting to the point where we are trying to raise up. We're not letting our dreams go; it just takes us a little longer. A few single black women have accomplished some of those dreams, but most of them really can't do it. There's that color barrier—but we're still struggling.

Ruth's life from age 34 to 39 has been so tumultuous that it would not initially appear to form a single developmental period. Taking a life structure perspective, however, we see that she has been forming and maintaining a Culminating Life Structure. At 33 she was on the verge of marrying Jesse and having a Traditional Marriage Enterprise. At 34 the basis for her new life was suddenly destroyed. For the next two years she was in limbo. She knew that it would be best to terminate the relationship with Jesse yet was unable to do so. The difficulty lay partly in her love for him, partly in his inability to choose between the two women, and partly—perhaps most of all—in her unwillingness to give up the planned life structure to which she had become so deeply committed. It was as though she remained in the "psychological marriage" to Jesse while knowing rationally that it could not exist. His legal marriage to the other woman brought her out of the limbo: at 36 she gave up on him, quit her job, went on unemployment compensation, and became a full-time homemaker for the first time in her life. Then, finding domestic life increasingly burdensome in the ensuing months, she went back to work.

At 39 Ruth is at the height of Becoming One's Own Woman. She is seeking greater affirmation as a competent adult and trying to form a life more on her own terms. She is investing herself more in occupation but does not yet have defined occupational goals. Her symbolic title, "the mother of the agency," reflects the imagery of her current occupational identity. To become more professional, she will have to utilize additional aspects of the self—to be caring in new ways (as she is now learning with her adult daughters), to gain a stronger sense of her own authority, to become a responsible manager of an enterprise.

As Ruth approaches 40 she is coming to a turning point in every aspect of her life. Although motherhood and grandmotherhood are of continuing importance, she recognizes that they will have a qualitatively different and lesser place in her life. Her relationship with her adult daughters must be different from that with her child daughters. Family cannot be the central component of her next life structure. Likewise, she wants different things from a husband. In her twenties she regarded the husband chiefly as provisioner. Now she focuses more on the marital relationship, on having a man she can talk to and lean on in times of need—a relationship of greater equality and mutuality—for a new time in the life cycle. We also see a budding change in her relationship to outside work. Earlier she took a job to get essential income for self and family. Now her job and her involvement in the church choir have more intrinsic meaning and value of their own. She is on the verge of the Mid-life Transition.

Married Women Who Were Psychologically Divorced

Five women (Carol O'Brien, Nan Krummel, Emily Swift, Angela Capelli, Lynn McPhail) remained legally married as the Culminating Life Structure got under way but in some basic sense "gave up" on their husbands and became psychologically divorced. The men were providing for their families at a level ranging from bare subsistence to comfortable middle class, but income level was not the primary source of dissatisfaction. In each case, the husband was failing to meet at least a few of the minimal requirements of the Traditional Marriage Enterprise; he was, for example, severely alcoholic, irresponsible, physically abusive with wife or children, or tearing apart the fabric of family life. Emily Swift had no children; the others, two to five children. While planning to remain married for the indefinite future — though perhaps not permanently—each woman had to ask herself: How can I protect myself against the worst of my husband's excesses? How can I make myself less dependent on him and have some life of my own apart from him? How can I live as a married/unmarried woman?

The most obvious option for enriching her life was for the woman to become more involved in the public work world. This option offered the possibility of greater financial independence, self-esteem, and meaningful relationships with adults (including some that might lead to another and better marriage). But it was also experienced as antithetical to the Traditional Marriage Enterprise. During the period of the Culminating Life Structure, each woman struggled both to maintain her primary life as a homemaker and to move partially into the larger society. But the conflict was not fully resolved. The difficulty stemmed not only from the power of the internal Traditional Homemaker Figure, but also from the power of our culture and institutions, which operate to keep women in the home or in minimally rewarding jobs with low pay, no benefits, and no pathway to advancement. It takes a large effort for a woman in her thirties with little education and occupational training or experience to enter the public world, to form an occupation, and to expand her identity beyond that of homemaker.

During the initial phase of the Culminating Life Structure, these women made only small, tentative steps into the public sphere. Some could do no more than take a part-time job. Others explored occupational possibilities but made little progress. The pace generally picked up a bit at 35 or 36, as the women entered the phase of Becoming One's Own Woman. They were more likely then, as we have seen with Ruth Allen, to seek greater affirmation and pursue defined goals.

By around 40, as the period ended, the women were still living primarily as homemakers. All five had jobs and were capable of providing for themselves at a marginal level if necessary, but occupation was not a central or particularly satisfying component of the life structure. Two had divorced (Lynn McPhail at 38, Carol O'Brien at 40). Nan Krummel was more seriously questioning her marriage, which ended a few years later. Emily Swift and Angela Capelli were still married, though without hope that the marital relationship would improve. They had concluded that the alternatives were worse than the marriage and that they would stay put, albeit with a growing corrosive bitterness.

✑ EMILY SWIFT

At 27, Emily Swift married Chris, an ambitious young lawyer. She entered the marriage knowing that the relationship was a stormy one and that their fights were like "atomic wars." Her parents' advocacy of the marriage seemed in retrospect to be the main force overcoming her own misgivings. In addition, marriage offered the prospect of giving up her secretarial job and becoming the wife of a professional. An early miscarriage at 28, coupled with continuing physical and psychological abuse from Chris, led to her tentative decision not to have children in the marriage. When Emily was 30, the couple moved to Connecticut, where Chris became a partner in a law firm. By 33 she had reached a firm decision not to have children. She had no friends and no ties to the local community. The life she had hoped for was eluding her:

> Those first years in Connecticut were really hard. I had been doing office work so long that I was delighted not to be working. Chris was very involved in his work. I read, collected bushels of glass on the beach, strung beads, took pottery courses, but was not at all productive. I'd sit up all night watching TV movies and keeping a glass of brandy going. That's when my serious drinking started. Then I'd sleep until mid-afternoon. I was not lonely. I was doing things, exploring the area, driving around a lot. I enjoyed that. I took care of the house, but not very well. I was vegetating.
>
> At 33 I decided to get a volunteer job. I didn't want paid work again because I wanted to be more than a servant. At 34 I took a volunteer job at a newspaper, and I learned a lot about writing and editing. When I was 39, uncredentialed, unqualified me was asked to write an article. Over the next few years my work became more and more important, and I did a respectable job.

From 33 to 35, then, Emily went through the initial phase of building a Culminating Life Structure. Work and marriage were the two major components of this structure. Work occupied most of her time and absorbed as much of her self as she could invest in it. But she was not ready to make occupation the central component around which a new life might be formed. She remained a part-time volunteer, working in isolation and having no clearly defined place in the occupational world.

At first glance, it was hard to discern what part marriage played in Emily's Culminating Life Structure. She had very little contact with her husband, and their relationship was indifferent when not hurtful. Their sexual relationship ended at 35. She knew that he was having an affair but did nothing to oppose it. Why would she remain in so empty and destructive a marriage? When asked, she could not say. Yet it is clear that she would tolerate almost anything to remain in it. Marriage was in fact the central component of her life structure, the base upon which all else was built. In the most elemental sense, the marriage was terrible but being unmarried was worse—a void she could not contemplate. To prevent such contemplation and to remain numbed enough to go on, she became a heavy drinker in her mid-thirties and was still drinking heavily when the interviews took place at 45.

Marriage, work, and drinking were thus the major components of her Culminating Life Structure. Marriage was central yet almost meaningless. Work was important both as a refuge from marriage and as a form of self-expression. Liquor was the numbing agent that enabled her to maintain the life structure.

In her late thirties Emily made some small improvements within this structure and took a few steps toward Becoming One's Own Woman. She had a volunteer job that did not lead to a career path but did establish her as a competent worker. At 39 she overcame her self-doubts enough to write an article—a significant gesture of self-affirmation. During her late thirties, Emily had an extramarital relationship with a married man. She considered herself "in love" with him, but he made it clear that his interest did not lie in love or remarriage. It was yet another experience in mortification for Emily, and she ended the relationship.

> We had recently returned from a trip to France, three weeks of misery for me. I couldn't tell him what a terrible time I had because he spent so much money on it. He brought up the subject of divorce. He said I had ruined his life by not having children, and it would be best to end the marriage. I was horrified. The thought had never occurred to me; he just mentioned it out of the blue. Then we had a calm discussion—probably the only calm discussion we have ever had. Very calm, very rational, very sensible. How divorce would be much better for both of us. It made a great deal of sense. The same discussion would make a lot of sense today. We agreed that I would move out into an apartment or something—but

the time just went by and nothing happened. It was as if the discussion had cleared the air. Finally we talked about my not leaving. He said he was willing to accept things as they were because he wanted to keep me. Things subsided after that. I just stayed on but it's never been very wonderful—not satisfying, not even peaceful. Since then we go dutch when we go out to eat. We don't address each other by name. Everything has been different since that discussion.

The "discussion" was, I believe, the *Culminating Event* of Emily's early adulthood. The process of psychological divorce began in her early thirties but she maintained some sense, however vague and illusory, of being connected to her husband in a joint enterprise. At 40 their version of the Traditional Marriage Enterprise died. They came as near as a couple can to being divorced while sharing a residence and having minimal ties. While acknowledging that divorce would make "a great deal of sense," she was not ready to examine what kept her in the marriage. It was enough that "he wanted to keep me." Only the shell of the Traditional Marriage Enterprise remained. With this event her Culminating Life Structure came into question, and her Mid-life Transition got under way.

9 Mid-life Transition: Homemakers

The Mid-life Transition of the homemakers we interviewed got under way at 40 or 41 and was ending at 45. During this period they made the cross-era shift from early to middle adulthood. They ended the Culminating Life Structure of the thirties and created a basis for the Entry Life Structure of the new era. And they moved from the Traditional Marriage Enterprise to a new form of married or single life. The change in marriage enterprise at this time is rooted in the timing of the eras and developmental periods. It is also shaped by the evolution of motherhood and marriage, by the character of the occupational world, and by the shift from junior to senior generation in society. (For a fuller discussion of transitional periods generally, see Chapter 2.)

I'll discuss here the eight homemakers who were 42 to 45 years old at the time of interviewing and well into the Mid-life Transition. Of the seven others, five were under 40 and still in the Culminating Life Structure; and two, turning 41, were on the threshold of the Mid-life Transition but not yet far enough into it to say much about the changes just getting under way. This period thus brings us up to the present in the lives of the homemakers and to the conclusion of early adulthood.

Ending the Early Adulthood Form of the Traditional Marriage Enterprise

The Traditional Marriage Enterprise was the framework within which the homemakers built their lives in early adulthood, and it continued to shape their lives, to a greater or lesser extent, all the way through the Culminating Life Structure of the thirties. During the Mid-life Transition each woman began to question the Traditional Marriage Enterprise and her life as a homemaker. Significant changes were occurring in her relationships with husband, offspring, parents, occupation, self—with everyone and everything of significance to her. The process of change would continue, I believe, through middle adulthood. The core issue was this: caregiving would no longer be her chief function in life.

If caregiving had been the predominant theme of early adulthood, what did she hope for as the new era began? Two themes are prominent. First, she wanted to be more care-free. She wanted to exorcise her sense of obligation to provide care without limit, to feel perpetually responsible for others, to be self-sacrificing, to ignore her own needs. She was prepared to maintain her domestic responsibilities up to a point—but no further. Second, she wanted the right to be herself, to make her own choices and pursue her own interests.

In her youth the homemaker had made a bargain: she agreed to dedicate herself to the mission of wife/mother/homemaker. In return, she would be loved, taken care of, and made happy. In the Mid-life Transition, more acutely than ever before, she realized that she had been cheated. She felt as though she had sacrificed her youth and at great personal cost had fulfilled her part of the bargain and more. But she had received nowhere near the promised care and love. Now that the homemaking mission was largely completed, she felt that she had every right to be starting a more carefree life with fewer burdens and greater benefits. But the good life was, alas, nowhere in sight. It was becoming evident, moreover, that a better life did not exist "out there," waiting to be discovered. To enrich her life she would have to create a place for herself as a middle-aged adult in the public world—a world that was generally not welcoming or supportive. A major cost of the home-making life was a significant failure in the development of the self. She had become a homemaker without seriously considering what else she might want to do or be. It was difficult now to consider these questions, to explore her inner resources and to begin forming a life in which they could be well used.

Most homemakers went through a "rock bottom" experience of marriage and life in the Mid-life Transition. It was the predominant experience of some women for a large part of the Mid-life Transition and was experienced more fleetingly or obliquely by others. They felt that the marriage was stag-nant, arid. The husband, though not necessarily a bad man, was rarely involved with her and the children. There seemed to be no connection between husband and wife. They had sex infrequently, most often at her initiative. He had no apparent interest in making love or having genuine personal contact with her. It seemed that all he wanted from a wife was someone to cook his meals, do the housework, and give the public impres-sion of a "normal" marriage. She felt totally trapped. Her marriage was almost intolerable, yet divorce seemed worse—she had no place to go and no adequate way to take care of herself financially and socially. She asked herself, "What do I get out of this marriage?" The worst of her many answers was, "I feel old at 40. I'm utterly isolated and alone and used up. There is no love in my life. I'm too young to live like this. It's as though I'm in the middle of a dark hole and there is no way out. I can't go on like this much longer."

To various degrees, many homemakers became disappointed, bitter, resentful, disillusioned. There was resignation but also determination—they attempted to make new choices and to take greater responsibility for their own lives, even if this put them in opposition to significant persons and groups. Each woman learned that the right to pursue her own interests and make her own choices was not a given. It had to be earned through her own struggle and personal development. To be true to her self—rather than to an externally given authority—she had to form a more individuated self and a more internally defined relationship with self and world. This required her to ask, with greater urgency than ever before: Who am I? What is most important to me? How will I try to live in the next season of my life?

These questions are not asked or answered in a purely conscious, rational way. They involve deep, often amorphous feelings and images. They raise the possibility of drastic, frightening changes in a self and a life structure that, despite their limitations, are not readily altered. It is painful at around 40 to realize that I know so little of what I want and that it can at times be so terrifying to try to find out. Becoming more individuated brings new problems of its own. Living more on the basis of my interests does not mean that I have no appreciation of others' needs and no responsibility for them. Mid-life individuation involves a greater awareness of the other as well as self and a stronger desire for genuinely mutual relationships.

NORA COLE

In her twenties and thirties, Nora Cole raised her five children, worked extremely hard to establish herself occupationally as a nursery school teacher, and had a limited relationship with the man she had married at 17. In her Mid-life Transition the nest was emptying, and she wanted more from life. At the same time her older husband was in poor health, earning less money from his unskilled work, and having less presence in the home as husband and father. When interviewed at 43, Nora was starting to realize that her days as a homemaker were ending. She was reappraising the past and trying to imagine the future. Everything was in doubt. Her subjective experience is conveyed with poetic intensity:

> Two summers ago I realized that I was constantly being called upon to do things for others. Nothing was coming in to replace all that was going out. I just started crying and couldn't stop. The cry was coming from deep down within me. My husband said, "What's wrong? Why don't you take

a nap?" But it wasn't a nap I needed; I wasn't that kind of tired. There was no way I could make him understand what was wrong.

Our talk last time about my father's death brought up a lot of those feelings. I was tired of giving. I felt like an octopus, overextended. I felt tired and depressed and old. That feeling has been in there with me but I didn't notice it so much before. Most of the time I'm not even aware that I am giving a lot. It makes me feel good when I do something for someone else, like when I am singing in the church choir. When I'm not giving I feel guilty receiving; I don't know why. When I concentrate on doing something for me, I feel that that's selfishness and that I really don't need to spend that time on me. I have an awful lot of takers and need someone to be giving to me. Maybe I want the caring to come from other sources than my inner one doing for myself.

I have been working very hard lately. I really need a vacation—go somewhere for a week, check into a hotel and just relax. If I want to go out, go out. If I don't, lay in bed and watch TV. I need to do nothing for a while, just do nothing and have no responsibilities.

I had a dream last night: I was selling oysters at the store where I work summers. I was in a new department that didn't have much lighting. Lots of people were waiting for me to wait on them. I couldn't wait on them because I couldn't see prices on things and didn't know where things were. I got upset and started to cry quietly because I couldn't help all those people. There wasn't enough light for me to see what they were asking for. Yet they were not telling me what they wanted. They were just standing there looking at me, waiting for me to come over and offer my help. I remember looking from this new department that was dimly lit over to my old department that was well lit and that I was familiar with. I was getting angry because I had been sent to this new area.

Nora's dream depicts the sadness, anger, and confusion so common in the Mid-life Transition. She is moving from one "department," that is, era, to another. The new place is dark and unfamiliar. It is hard to see the new landscape. Her old skills seem less useful and relevant. People want help but they don't say what they want, and she has trouble knowing what it is. She doesn't know what she has to offer them. She feels lost—and angry at having to move.

This dream is about being forced to make an unwelcome change. Other mid-life dreams are about seeking change but not finding the way. Both kinds of dreams reflect an inner reality. We both welcome and fear the transition. We avoid it and seek it out. The external reality both requires and impedes the change. We must explore "dimly lit" places in order to enter a new place that may in time be well lit. The places are both in the world and in the self. The new place may be better and/or worse than the old. We cannot predict in advance what it will be. In time, a somewhat different self will have somewhat different relationships within a somewhat different world.

Let us now examine some of the specific changes occurring in mother-hood, marriage, occupation, and other components of the life structure during this period.

Motherhood

In the Mid-life Transition all but one of the homemakers were mothers. Those who had started a family at around 20 now had offspring ranging in age from the early teens to the early twenties. A few had started a family in their late twenties, and their children were now 10 to 15 years old. All were involved in the emptying of the nest, a process of family evolution that usually takes ten or more years. It typically begins before the first child actually leaves home and ends some time after the last child leaves. The meaning of this process for every mother is mediated by her age and developmental period. Its primary meaning for the homemaker in her early forties was this: she was approaching the time when motherhood would no longer be a central component of her life. She would continue to care about her adult offspring, but the relationship would have a different character for herself as well as them. They were becoming more independent, less in need of her care, and less accepting of her guidance and control. It was unclear what she wanted next with them and what they wanted or would tolerate from her. It was clear, however, that she would not be the maternal caregiver she had been in the past.

Early in this process most mothers had a sense of loss—loss of offspring-as-child and loss of homemaking as the foundation of her adult life. Provid-ing care had been her essential function in the Traditional Marriage Enterprise and her primary contribution to the world. What else could she do that would provide equivalent satisfaction and sense of value? Some mothers felt betrayed and abandoned by their near-adult offspring, who seemed neither to want much from mother nor to appreciate all that she had given them.

Others (or the same mother at other times) felt excessively burdened by offspring who continued to seek her care long after the age at which she expected them to become responsible, self-sufficient adults. Every mother had hoped that, by a certain age (typically, graduation from high school or college), her children would be well on the way to independent, well-adjusted adulthood. They would appreciate what a devoted mother she had been and what sacrifices she had made. They would respect her as a person and be caring of her in return for the care she had given them. These fond maternal hopes were violated by some or all of her offspring, who had a variety of problems: drug abuse; teenage pregnancy; mental or bodily illness;

poor academic performance in a family that valued higher education; excessive financial or emotional dependence; a conflict-ridden relationship with parents in which mutual caring and affection could find no place.

Another major theme was a growing sense of liberation. Each woman became more aware of the limitations and constraints of her previous life. She had experienced herself in part as the domestic servant, the self-sacrificing one who forever put the needs of others before her own. As the responsibilities of child care and household management declined, she enjoyed the greater freedom to pursue her own personal interests outside the domestic world.

The women thus had multiple, often conflicting experiences of motherhood in the Mid-life Transition. The loss of their maternal functions within the family freed them from much that had been burdensome, but it also required them to make major changes in their lives and their selves. In part they suffered feelings of abandonment, grief, dependency, rage, and guilt. In part they felt relief, welcoming and even hastening the offsprings' departure. When the departing daughters and sons were needy and requested (or demanded) further support, the mothers and fathers responded variously with responsible care, responsible independence, and diverse forms of dependency, guilt, indulgence, and rejection. The emptying of the nest rarely goes quickly and smoothly; it brings out the best and the worst in all of us. It plays an important part in the adult development of parents as well as offspring.

Marriage

The marriage, too, was questioned and modified. During the Age 30 Transition all the homemakers had experienced minor to severe marital problems and had succeeded to some extent in reducing the problems or in finding other satisfactions that made the marriage more tolerable. Most had then built a Culminating Life Structure around a marriage which, however limited or painful, allowed them to continue living as homemakers. Now, in the early forties, they were less tolerant of the marital problems. Each married woman felt entitled, as she completed the homemaking project of her youth, to reap the rewards of her arduous labors. One potential reward was a better marriage. She now had more time and energy to invest in the marital relationship. She had the hope that her husband, too, might give more to the marriage, since he was now more established in his occupation and did not have to work so hard to provide for the family.

What did she want to receive from, and give to, the marriage? Her emerging wishes and attitudes were not well articulated in her own mind nor readily communicated to her husband. At the least, she wanted him to accept less domestic labor on her part and to support her ventures into new, extra-domestic spheres. She wanted to be less subordinate in the decision making and to make personal choices more on the basis of her own preferences. At the most—something she hardly dared insist upon, and in some cases hardly dared imagine—she wanted him to be more sexual/romantic, to find her more attractive as a person, to care more about her actual interests and well-being, to have more fun with her in jointly pleasing activities. What they had done in early adulthood, while important in its own right, would be a prologue to the freer, fuller life that was now within their grasp.

In her mind, the changes she sought—spending more time together, taking more vacations, having a better sex life, "having fun"—were relatively minor. Actually, the entire pattern of change required a basic transformation of the marital relationship that had existed for fifteen or twenty years within the Traditional Marriage Enterprise. Although the marriage was the bedrock on which all else was built, it had not evolved much beyond its limited initial form. In attempting to improve the marriage, she was, in effect, trying to make it a more central component of her—and his—life. For both partners the present relationship was colored by disappointments, angers, voiced and silent grievances from the past. Changing it, or even initiating a joint effort at change, was extremely difficult. Their efforts to improve it usually brought minimal or negative results. Some couples succeeded in increasing the enjoyments and decreasing the irritants, but none was able to make the marriage a highly satisfactory, central component in either spouse's life structure.

As the eight homemakers approached the end of the Mid-life Transition, they varied widely in marital condition. Kay Ryan and Jenny Abatello found their marriages relatively satisfactory, though not without current problems. Nora Cole, Emily Swift, and Angela Capelli had extremely difficult marriages and lived in a condition of psychological divorce. Carol O'Brien, Nan Krummel, and Lynn McPhail got legally divorced in or just before the Mid-life Transition. Carol O'Brien and Nan Krummel were single working mothers in this period. Lynn McPhail divorced at 39, remarried at 40, and spent the next five years dealing with her Mid-life Transition while also forming a second marriage and family. The relative frequency of these patterns in a small sample is, of course, not necessarily what it would be in the general population, but each pattern is of wider interest and significance. I'll consider them in turn.

Women Who Had Long-term, "Good Enough" Marriages

Kay Ryan and Jenny Abatello exemplify this pattern. From a distance one might say that these marriages continued unchanged throughout the Mid-life Transition. There were no dramatic events to suggest any marked change. Looking more closely, however, we see that in the Mid-life Transition they formed a new marriage—a new relationship and new enterprise—with the same partner. The new marriage was better than the old in some respects, worse in others, depending partly on the vantage point from which it was evaluated. A single, overall rating of "better" or "worse" would hide the complexity of the actual changes. It is more useful to explore the many forms of change and the qualitatively different pattern that emerged in each marriage.

As the Mid-life Transition began, both women wanted to make some improvements but no major changes in the marriage. The marital relationship yielded some satisfactions and no excessive overt conflict. The spouses maintained an effective limited partnership as parents and as a couple in the community. The marriage enterprise had been experienced by both spouses as essential to their existence and worthy of the great sacrifices involved. Occasionally wishing for more, each woman reminded herself that she was better off than most women she knew. By the end of this period the tasks of the enterprise were not so demanding or so central in the spouses' lives. They had much less sense of being partners in a vitally important endeavor.

A key question of the Mid-life Transition: What new marriage enterprise, what new partnership committed to a shared mission, can we develop for the next season of life? Neither Jenny Abatello nor Kay Ryan had come to a clear resolution of this question at 43, when they were interviewed, but the direction of change was evident. They were not forming a joint new enterprise in which both partners were highly engaged. Instead, they would "make do" with a limited enterprise. In both couples, the two spouses regarded themselves as very different persons who cared for each other and would work hard to stay together. But they also understood that they would not be strongly involved in each other's lives. Each woman was forming interests and activities of her own, largely independent of her husband.

The marriage played a shadowy yet important part in the emerging life structure of both Jenny Abatello and Kay Ryan. It was a source of security and stability. It symbolized the couple's joint achievements in raising a family. It maintained the integrity of the family even as the adult offspring dispersed to form their own largely separate lives. Being part of an enduring marriage gave each one an identity and place in society far better than she could have as a single divorced woman. Jenny Abatello was strongly involved in her occupation and attempted to make it the central component of her life structure.

KAY RYAN

Kay Ryan was one of the two homemakers who had a Dream of a Traditional Marriage Enterprise, and she became an extremely traditional homemaker.

She was a middle-class housewife with no occupational interests or skills. Divorce for her would be an economic as well as a psychological and social disaster. She had friendly relationships with a few women but no close friendships; nor did she seek them. Since graduating from college she had been dedicated to raising her children, taking total responsibility for the household, and, starting in her mid-thirties, serving as "executive wife" who furthered her husband's efforts to ascend the corporate ladder. When she was interviewed at 43 this structure was clearly in process of change.

> Two or three years ago there was all this talk about women working outside the home, and I asked Peter whether he resented that I didn't work. He said no, he's glad I don't work. He likes me to be at home and do his errands. He wouldn't want to share the housework, and wouldn't want me to go to work. I don't want two jobs, an outside job and taking care of the house, too. Women who work have to take care of the house and the kids, too, and that's probably very difficult.
>
> Peter is a branch manager. Being the executive wife is less fun than it used to be. We have business visitors staying at our home most weekends, often for a week at a time, and it just gets to be too much. It's a lot of work changing the sheets, cleaning the bathroom, entertaining all weekend. But I don't have a choice—it's his job. I should change my attitude and just accept it. What would I be doing if it wasn't that? Sometimes it seems to me that I do more giving than he does, though.
>
> There have been a whole series of problems in the last three years. I'm not sure why they all happened in this short time. When I was 40 the doctor told me I'd been on the pill too long—13 years—so I talked to Peter about a vasectomy. As Catholics we felt it wasn't right but we certainly didn't want to start all over again with babies. The next year he suddenly decided to have the vasectomy. I didn't ask him why; as long as he changed his mind that suited me fine. A few months later he became impotent. He said he didn't know why; maybe it was because he felt unhappy with his job. That was not a good time for me either. I got depressed and irritable. I would fly off the handle for no reason and would get my feelings hurt for things he has always done, like bringing his business visitors home to stay with us. One night I woke up in the middle of the night and cried for no reason. I lay there feeling so sad and wishing that he would wake up. Finally he did wake up, held me in his arms, and said it would be all right. That was all I needed. It was just the vague feeling of being all alone. Our oldest son had gone off to college a few months before. I thought it was very nice having less work to do with him away, but I may have missed him more than I really thought. He's the son I can talk to the best. After nine months Peter's impotence stopped as suddenly as it had started. But he was pretty depressed about his job for a while longer and is still not sure what he wants to do.

He doesn't like a lot of the things he has to do as branch manager. He says it's a job with a million golden handcuffs—salary, perks, insurance, retirement, and survivor benefits—so no matter how frustrating it gets, it's hard to quit. The work is now less challenging, and there are no possibilities for promotion. He knows he won't ever be regional manager and doesn't want that anyway. He wants to be his own boss. I'd rather he stayed with the company. I have a certain loyalty to the company, which has been very good to us over the years and is probably better than most. Besides, I like our life the way it is. I like his job and the benefits we get from it, the expense account and travel and all that. If he just quit, it would threaten my well-being, my whole way of life. He considered starting a part-time business with a friend; if it went well he could then do it full-time and quit his present job without putting us in financial jeopardy. We and the other couple had a lot of fun imagining how well it would go and how we'd all be rich. But that has sort of died down. His sister says that he's having a mid-life crisis, and he'll probably get over it without changing his job. I hope so.

Last year I thought he was being too critical of me. He said he dreaded phoning me about bringing business guests home because I would grumble and make him miserable. And he was upset about the way I talked to our son when he was having trouble at college—I wasn't understanding or sympathetic enough. It all came to a head, and we had a fight. I said, "If I'm not any good as a wife and a hostess, and I'm not any good as a mother, then I'm not any good at all because that's all I am in this life. I have no other big career and nothing else I can do. If you don't think I do either of these well, then I don't do anything well!" We talked until 2 or 3 in the morning and I think we cleared the air. That's the longest talk we ever had. Peter said he appreciated me but just wished I wouldn't grumble so much. And I've been trying harder to be agreeable.

We're looking forward to the freedom of having our children grown. We don't envision having them around at 25, still freeloading off of Dad and having Mother do their laundry. A lot of our friends' children have returned home for financial reasons, and I really don't want that. I used to be afraid that when the kids left home nobody would ever talk to me again, because Peter is not a big talker. Recently we have spent a little more time together. I have this romantic idea of how love and marriage ought to be but he just doesn't seem to want or need time alone with me. We never go out alone, just he and me.

Peter, who is my age, firmly believes that he will die in his early fifties, like his father did. I try not to think about it because I can't do anything about it anyway. Statistically, men do die earlier, so lots of women face widowhood. I think I could cope pretty well by myself. I'm sure I'll be lonelier than ever I could imagine—but maybe not. I won't have to do so much housework and cook for other people and worry about what they want to eat and when they'll be home. Sometimes it's very nice to have only yourself to worry about. I'd build my life around *me*. There might be some advantage to living alone and being financially independent and doing what you want. I don't mean having to support myself and struggle financially. I mean living comfortably. I don't think I'll have any trouble filling my time. I'll sit around the pool and read all the books I haven't had time to read. I have always watched soap operas, and I am learning to embroider, and maybe I'll do a little volunteer work.

I'm worried about my aging mother, who is ill. She's always been very critical of me and bossed everything in my life. She thinks that if she doesn't run the world it will stop turning. I feel that I can never satisfy her. She's never been loved enough or cherished enough or treasured enough by her two husbands or anyone else, including me—at least not enough to suit her. Last summer was a nightmare. My mother was sick, and I spent a month with her. When I got home the visitors came one after the other, business guests and family and friends. No time could be as bad as last summer.

In the last few years I have become more aware of my own feelings. I don't necessarily like that happening, because the feelings get me upset and hurt me. I have always tried to ignore and push away things that bother me. I guess I've always been too busy doing whatever needed to be done right now to worry much about what I'd do later. But now the future looks uncertain; I feel like I'm standing at the edge of a precipice without knowing what lies ahead—what will happen with my mother's illness, with our sons, with my husband's job.

A key theme in Kay's story is the dilemma of the displaced homemaker. A chapter of her life is ending. The parental nest is emptying and mother-hood will soon be a peripheral component of her life structure. Marriage was always subjectively important to her, though she and her husband spent little time together. She had earlier imagined that, with the departure of the offspring, she and her husband might have a more romantic-loving-sexual relationship. It now appears, however, that this change is unlikely; for reasons she does not know, her husband does not seek that kind of relationship with her. While relieved in many ways about the termination of the homemaking phase, she has decidedly mixed feelings about the future. Indeed, her account contains two antithetical scenarios for the next chapter.

In one scenario she imagines a life of widowhood. Having a trust fund as provisioner she lives alone, carefree, building "my life around *me*." She is free of all previous obligations. She is also minimally engaged with other persons and with the larger social world. Indeed, it is not clear what place she might have in the generation of middle adulthood. Widow fantasies of various kinds are, I believe, held by many homemakers in middle adulthood.

In the second scenario, which is less detailed than the first, she tries to confront the still-unresolved problems of her current life: her mother's illness and potential need for daughterly care; her sons' extended process of entry into adulthood; her husband's uncertain career and personal development (which are in some ways more threatening than his early death); and the possibility—not yet consciously contemplated—of her own entry into the public occupational world. In this scenario she is "at the edge of a precipice." Other women in the Homemaker sample had their own version of the precipice and of the dangers and opportunities it contains, but the basic image is widespread. The scenario of the precipice is more frightening than that of idyllic widowhood but it also engages her more in life—in being a responsible woman, mother, wife, daughter, senior member of a community. To enact her part in this scenario she will have to develop a stronger sense of self as a middle-aged adult.

Women Who Were Psychologically Divorced During the Mid-life Transition

The marriages of Nora Cole, Emily Swift, and Angela Capelli, like the more satisfactory ones above, seemed from a distance to persist relatively unchanged from the women's thirties into their forties. In the thirties they found the marriage almost intolerable—empty, unsustaining, in some respects abusive—yet decided for various reasons not to divorce. During the Mid-life Transition there was a qualitative change in the relationship and in the Traditional Marriage Enterprise. The possibility of divorce became much more real. The woman no longer had a sense of marital partnership. She became more independent financially and relied even less than before on her husband's participation in their personal relationship, household responsibilities, and social life. The spouses spent very little time together and had little or no sexual relationship. They had no joint enterprise and no apparent basis for creating one. Their lives were almost totally separate. The marital relationship gave both partners very little and left them depleted, depressed, and disappointed. The women understood that they had more reasons to end the marriage than to remain in it. Yet none of them divorced.

Given so many reasons to separate, what kept them from doing so? The obstacles to divorce were remarkably strong. Although they worked full-time, none of the women earned enough to sustain herself at anywhere near the current level. Divorce would create severe financial hardship for her and the children still at home. The identity of "divorced woman" was frightening, for reasons both rational and irrational. Divorce would require her to invest more of herself in the work world and to make occupation a more central component of her life structure—a prospect that two of the three considered neither feasible nor attractive. All three feared that divorce would ultimately leave them isolated, vulnerable, marginal to their former community. They were terrified by the prospect of remaining single throughout middle and old age, with no one to take care of them and to share the tribulations and joys of those seasons. None had an alternative that would provide enough satisfaction and sense of personal value to counterbalance the losses imposed by divorce. All things considered, staying married seemed the least hurtful choice.

✌ ANGELA CAPELLI

The marriage had been bad earlier but when I turned 40 it seemed hopeless. For the first time I said, "Let's split up." My husband said, "There's the door." I knew I couldn't manage financially on my own, so I stayed. I decided to go back to work full-time at the one job I could do, typing. It would get me out of the house and supplement his meager earnings. Now, at 45, I like my job well enough. But it's totally monotonous, typing page after page after page of just numbers on insurance policies. You're more or less a robot. The other typists are girls in their twenties. They don't like the work either, but they don't mind it so much because they're just passing the time till they start a family or get out of a financial squeeze. That's how I used to be. Now I want more from work, and I'm not getting it. I have no friendships or social life with the girls at work. They are not interested in an "older woman" and I have no leisure time anyhow. It's hard to work full-time. I'm at the job from 8:00 to 4:30, come home, prepare a meal, do the dishes, do the laundry, iron, fold the laundry, do the housework. I go to bed every night at 1:00 exhausted and get up at 6:30 and start all over again. It's endless.

I get no help from my husband or sons. My husband and I don't exchange two words now. He works nights plus a part-time job weekends. When he is home he's asleep in front of the TV. We never had much sex and now don't have any. After 18 years of neglect I don't care anymore. As a parent I feel that I've done everything for my children. I've been a good mother to them. But I must have failed someplace. They have no respect for me; they call me foolish; they are undisciplined and constantly fighting. I can't wait for them to get 18 and leave. I work like a dog for them, and they don't appreciate me or give me anything in return.

At work I'm seen as happy-go-lucky but my life is in shambles. I can't keep the anger in anymore; I feel like I'll explode. I've given my life to take care of others, I've followed all the rules, and this is my reward? I've gotten nothing back—and never will. What will happen when I get older? Will I be able to take care of myself in my old age? I had a hysterectomy at 42 and a thyroid operation last year. I'm afraid of getting crippled and help-less, with no one to take care of me. There is no pleasure in my life. I often tell myself, "If I only had two hours a week of going out, having some laughs!" I'm in a semidepressed state all the time. I'll stay in the marriage because I have no place else to go. But I lost my life somewhere. Where did my life go?

Angela's experience of psychological divorce in the Mid-life Transition shows how marriage is part of the life structure, coloring and being colored by the other components and by the overall structure. Being at an impasse in one component is not so bad when another component counterbalances it and provides some of the things it lacks. When the life structure does not contain even one satisfactory component, however, a woman faces a middle adulthood of quiet resignation, depression, bitterness.

Women Who Divorced in or Just before the Mid-life Transition

Three women had remained in painful marriages during their thirties, unable either to make things better or to call it quits. After the divorce, Carol O'Brien became a single working mother, Lynn McPhail quickly remarried and began to form a second marriage/family, and Nan Krummel went back to school in order to start a career.

✌ CAROL O'BRIEN

Carol O'Brien had an unskilled job for three years after high school, married at 21, and had the last of her four children at 29. She started working again at 33, to supplement her husband's poor income and to find some relief from a failed, destructive marriage. In her late thirties she got financially more independent, and the marriage got even worse. She initiated a separation at 39 and divorced at 40:

I don't know what made me really decide to divorce. There was this incident when our son got in trouble with the law. I needed my husband but he was drunker than a skunk. I didn't care anymore if I hurt him or even if I hurt the kids. I just couldn't live like this anymore. My parents had divorced a few years earlier. I saw that my father was able to start a new life and thought that maybe I could, too. But it was pretty scary. There were so many obstacles to overcome. When I started talking about separating, my close Catholic friends encouraged me to divorce, and I learned that the Catholic community was much less judgmental than I had feared.

The divorce was the Culminating Event of Carol's early adulthood. It marked the end not only of her marriage but of her commitment to life as a homemaker within a Traditional Marriage Enterprise. How she would live next was very much in question. She describes her current life at 43:

> Since the divorce I have had a full-time job. My oldest daughter is in college. I'm very proud of her. I hope she'll have a career and not marry for a while. The second is a single mother, having a hard time. But we all make mistakes, and I'm not going to judge her. I see them often and try to help when I can. The two youngest still live with me, but they'll be out soon and aren't a big problem. Two years ago I met a divorced man with grown children. We don't live together because I don't feel right about that, but he is involved with me and my life, and I would like to marry him soon. We have a very comfortable relationship. I try to imagine my life after remarriage. I like my work well enough but it's not that important to me. I'd prefer *not* to work, just be at home and have time for different things. I'm a little embarrassed about it, because this time I'd be home for myself and not for my kids or my husband. And somehow I feel that if the second marriage works out, I'll be vindicated for the rotten first marriage. But I don't expect anything special: when you marry in your forties, what you see is what you get.

✑ LYNN McPHAIL

Lynn McPhail moved directly from the end of her first marriage at 39 to a second marriage at 40. She had psychologically divorced her first husband in her early thirties but decided to remain legally married to him until a better alternative was available. At 36 she began a serious extramarital relationship with Eric. She initiated a divorce only when Eric agreed to end his unhappy marriage and marry her. The basis for the second marriage was thus created in the Culminating Life Structure. At this time she did not question the Traditional Marriage Enterprise. Indeed, she took it for granted that she and Eric would have a child of their own, even though she already had five children and he two. It was only in the Mid-life Transition that Lynn decided not to have another child. In her early forties she tried to establish a second marriage/family very different from the first, while going through the intense changes of the Mid-life Transition—a large order, indeed. The phase in marriage/family development powerfully influenced, and was influenced by, the period in life structure development.

> The first three years of marriage [age 40–43] were tough. The biggest problem was combining two families. And let me tell you, we were no Brady Bunch! Eric's daughter was just plain nasty to me. She'd do the meanest things to me for no reason. And I'd see things like Eric yelling

more at my kids than his own, being stricter with my kids than his. It all put a horrible strain on the marriage. It was almost divorce time after that first year. After two years I decided that if the next year was that bad I'd get a divorce. It was out of one bad marriage and into another, trying to make two families one. We fought a lot, and he'd never tell me what he was feeling. I was going to the doctor's constantly. I thought I had heart trouble, a brain tumor, I thought I was starting the Change. But it was due to all the stress from the marriage. I hibernated a year, just stayed home, depressed. My doctor put me on Valium. It was a real low point in my life.

Eric's kids, who were 13 and 8, visited every weekend. The daughter treated me horribly, drove me right up the wall. I was as nice to her as I could be but nothing helped. This went on for two years. Finally I sat at the table and talked to her: "I am your father's wife. He picked me. I'm in love with him, and he's in love with me. When you grow up you'll have a life of your own, and you won't really care what your father is doing. I do not want to put your father in this position but if this bullshit goes on much longer he'll have to make a big decision: it's going to be you or me. I don't know what you think I did to you but let me know, and I'll try to correct it. But I'm not going to take this anymore." She wanted to come live with us, and Eric asked if she could. I said, "To be honest with you, you're not here that much, you're at work. I don't think I could start off with this girl who's too set in her mother's ways."

I brought myself out of it after three years. I just told myself this is a ridiculous way to live. I needed to speak up and have my opinions paid attention to. I said, "What the hell do you people, kids included, think I am, a robot? You get up in the morning, you just wind me up, you poke a button and tell me to be happy. Ha, ha, ha, I'm happy. Well, I'm not a robot. I'm human. I have flesh. I have muscles. I have bones. I have veins. I have a heart. I have everything you have, and I can get hurt, too." After I spoke my mind things got somewhat better. I agreed to take custody of Eric's son, and that has turned out okay.

There have also been a lot of changes with my mother. Four years ago she came to live with us, and for the first time in my life I realized I had a mother. I left home when I married at 19, and in those first 19 years at home we had not been close. It was like finding my mother; it was wonderful. Since then she has stayed with us for a year every other year. A few years ago I also began taking care of Eric's mother. She's in her eighties and has to be watched every minute. Eric works two jobs, so I watch her two full days a week. It's something that just has to be done, and there's no one else to do it.

The trouble between my mother and me in the past was my sister. I don't talk to my sister anymore; I can't stand her. There was always conflict between us. She uses my mother and tries to get her pension money. My sister used to write letters telling me all her problems. I finally got fed up and wrote her, "If you can't write a letter that just says every-body's fine, don't bother writing." Over all those years of terrible problems with my first husband trying to kill me and being crazy I never told nobody my problems. If I wrote I'd just say everything is fine. Nobody wants to hear other people's problems.

My kids are turning out well. Basically, I've got good kids. They're all hard-working and responsible, not like their father. Thank God, no drug problems. My son is 19 and very independent. He works 80 hours a week and contributes to the family finances. He has enlisted in the service and will be leaving soon. The girls ask me why I let him do things I don't let them do. I say because boys are different from girls. I don't want a Mama's boy, like my first husband was. I tell the girls not to have sex before they marry. Then out of the other side of my mouth I tell the boys to get it if they can but just protect themselves.

My oldest daughter, Molly, got married two years ago at 24. She asked if they could live with us for a while till they got on their feet financially. I said, "No, it's time for you to get your own life going." I knew she had sex before she got married. But I had sex with my second husband before we got married, too, so how could I say don't do what I did. People ask me, "Do you miss your daughter Molly now that she's married?" I say, "No, she's got her own life now." If she calls me, we'll talk. If she comes to visit, fine. If she don't, hey, she's got her own life now. My second daughter is 21 and has been going with her fella for a year. I told her, "If you decide to do it, this is your business. Just don't do it in my house or in my driveway, and by all means don't tell me. I don't want to know unless, God forbid, you get pregnant. Then I want to know it." My stepdaughter still wants to live with us. No way—she's 18 and should be on her own.

When the kids are 18 they are over the mountain. What they do then with their lives I am not responsible for. The top batch of kids are over that mountain now, and I've got three more to go. I'm trying to make the younger kids leave, too, and they want no part of it (laughs). I don't think kids belong with adults. I've got them trained good. My kids don't come two feet near me unless it's to say good night or to ask a question. They know where they belong, and it's not with adults.

I hoped our financial situation would be better by now but it's not. We have $200 a month in bills more than what comes in. It's tough. I've got $19 in my checking account. I'll have to struggle about money until the day I die, unless I win the lotto. Eric works two jobs just trying to make ends meet. He works his ass off, in plain English. If things don't get better soon I'll have to find me a job someplace. I'd like to work in the morning and be home when my kids get home from school. Eric says, "You will not work; you will be here with these kids and have my supper on the table when I get home from work."

Sex is seldom now. Eric's never home; sometimes he works six nights straight, 6 p.m. to 8 a.m. He usually falls asleep on the couch before going to work. Things change after marriage. Before we were married we'd be up until 2 a.m. having wild weekends. Now you come home, you sit there and watch reruns at 9 p.m. By 11:00 you're snoring. It's either have sex at 9 or 10 or forget it. It's that old marriage slack. You get that settled down pace, and that's it. I think it's a normal sex life for our age—we're not 20 anymore; we're getting old.

When we got married we didn't use birth control. We figured we'd have his, mine, and ours. But I never got pregnant. I just missed a period, and I'll have a pregnancy test next week. I never believed in abortion before but, to tell you the truth, if I'm pregnant I'll have it aborted. Eric said, "Five years ago having a child would have been fine but now it would be unfair to the baby, and you wouldn't be able to do what you want." I think so, too. I'm 45 and wouldn't have the kind of patience needed to raise a baby. It's time for me to be a grandmother.

In the years from now until the good Lord decides to take us, it's time to enjoy life a little. I've been doing things for others all my life. I want to do things for myself now. I don't want to take care anymore. I cook one meal a day. All the kids have household chores and earn their own spending money with paper routes. Everyone gets their own breakfast and lunch. I ain't cleaning up nobody's mess no more.

You know, we live for our kids. Every penny has always gone to them, and that's the way it should be until they're raised. But now it's about time we do something for Lynn and Eric. We'd like to go away for a weekend; to hell with the kids for one time; they can survive without us for one weekend. They love you but when they grow up they go, "Bye, Mom, bye, Dad," and that's it—they're gone. They love you, and they're concerned about you but not as much as you think they should be. So you don't give up your life for your children.

✍ NAN KRUMMEL

At 40, Nan Krummel was going through a crisis in her marriage and wondering whether to invest herself seriously in an occupation for the first time. During the Mid-life Transition she questioned every aspect of her life, got divorced, and embarked upon a new path. She is one of a growing number of women who return to college (or enter for the first time) in their thirties and beyond. Nan's chief aims were to move toward an occupation that would in some respects transform her life. She was fortunate in having resources, both within herself and in the external world, that could be used and developed further. Here is her story at age 44:

During my twenties and thirties I devoted myself to being a great wife and mother. I threw myself into my husband David's career and did everything I could to support it. David was a workaholic and was never around or involved with me or the children. I was totally responsible for the children and the household.

In my late thirties I began to look at my marriage. I was taking care of him and the children and everyone and everything else, and so someone was supposed to be making me happy. But I was not happy. I was exhausted. The marriage was stagnant. My husband was a workaholic and had always been emotionally distant from the children and me. He was quite alcoholic. There was almost nothing between us. He'd come home, we'd have a silent dinner, and we'd each go our separate ways. He'd go to bed first and be asleep by the time I'd go to bed. If I got to bed early, he'd stay up until he was sure I was asleep. We only had sex a couple of times a year, always at my initiative. He had premature ejaculation, and there was never any holding or feeling that he really wanted to make love with me. He was so withholding; he gave me very little. He seemed totally happy with the arrangement—and why not? He got someone to cook his meals, keep his house clean, and do the laundry. I felt totally trapped. I felt I couldn't divorce because I had no place to go, no job, no money. I got very depressed. I was in my late thirties, in a loveless, sexless marriage, and felt like an old woman who had been used up and thrown away. The future was clear: soon the children would be grown and moved away and I'd be all alone, isolated in that big mausoleum of a house. I'd be buried alive.

Throughout the years I'd taken courses to finish up my undergraduate degree. When I was 40 I got very focused on the need for me to have that degree so I could get a job and become self-sufficient if I decided to leave the marriage. Returning to college saved my life and gave me hope for the future. I was in a wonderful world of ideas and study, and I made wonderful friendships with other women my age who had gone back to school too. It was the best time of my life, and I never wanted it to end. Going to college helped me to stay in my marriage and earn a credential that would allow me to earn a living for myself and my children if I decided to leave the marriage. It also took my mind off my terrible marriage and gave me a whole new world full of interesting people who found me interesting.

As graduation approached, the marriage became intolerable. I decided, "I can't live like this anymore; I have no life. What do I get out of this marriage? I'm too young to live like this. What about love in my life? Am I supposed to have a sexless marriage or am I supposed to go out and have affairs? We live together but there is very little between us, and it has become intolerable."

I finished my degree and got my divorce. The divorce was very sad. We never fought; there wasn't enough between us to fight over. I did okay in the divorce settlement. I got enough money so that I should be okay as long as I also work. For the first time I've had a real interest in money and concern about my retirement and whether or not I'll be able to take care of myself and live independently when I'm old. I have a frightening image of an old bag lady which haunts me.

The pain of the divorce was almost unbearable. The pain came from the fragmentation of my life, the loss of the matrix in which I had lived for all those years, the sense of aloneness, the awareness of how much growing up I had to do in order to establish a better life. I had a lot of feelings of failure as a wife and person. I got into therapy, and I have made a lot of progress, but there is still so much to be done.

Dating for the first time after all those years was terrifying. The first few dates were really awful. I just sat there and cried, "I'm too old to be doing this; this is for high school kids." I hope someday to have a good relationship with a man and perhaps remarry, although I haven't met anyone special yet.

I am about to start graduate school. Going to graduate school at this age is scary. I started late, so I'll probably never have any great advancement. I have a lot of self-doubts and feelings of incompetence, but I am ready to take it one step at a time. I am much clearer about what I want now. I want a career that will grow for a long time to come. I need to keep growing, personally and professionally, and to make a significant contribution. It will probably take me another ten years to find my way and get more established, and I may not accomplish all I hope, but that's the road I want to travel. I feel lucky to be where I am now.

Occupation

As family became less central in their lives, the homemakers turned mainly to occupation for new interests, activities, and sources of satisfaction. I found three main patterns of change in the Mid-life Transition. The frequency of these patterns in this small sample is not necessarily representative of the general population. No doubt other patterns exist as well. But these are, I believe, relatively widespread and significant ways in which women attempt to modify their lives in middle adulthood. Let's consider them in turn.

Women Who Attempted to Become Senior Members of Their Occupational World and to Make Occupation Central

Three women had some education beyond high school. During their twenties they worked for a few years and formed a minimal occupational identity. During their thirties Nora Cole and Jenny Abatello worked regularly and made a growing investment in occupation; Nan Krummel was a full-time but discontented homemaker until she decided at 40 to return to college and earn a degree. At 40 all were mothers in an intact first marriage.

In the Mid-life Transition they recognized that homemaking would have a different meaning and play a much smaller part in their future lives than it had until then. They continued to care for their children, but motherhood was becoming less central. They had a problematic or limited marital relationship. Finally, they came to see occupation in a new light. Work was becoming the primary focus of their lives. They wanted to give more of themselves to the work, to receive more from it, and to participate in new ways within the work world.

During this period they were in the difficult shift from junior to senior member of the occupational world. They wanted to gain a more senior position, to become a legitimate, valued member of the senior generation, and to work in more independent, responsible ways appropriate to their new age and place in society. Making this shift is hard for men. It is much harder for career women (as can be seen later in this book). For homemakers it is almost impossible. The positions available to them at 40 are generally at entry or junior levels. To move higher these women had to overcome great obstacles in the work organization and in their own lives. At the same time they were beginning a process of mid-life individuation. They were forming a different and stronger sense of self. They were less ready to accept deprivations and constraints that had previously been tolerable or simply taken for granted. They were becoming more aware of, and attempting to shed, old illusions about themselves and about their relationships with significant persons, groups, and institutions. They were exploring possibilities for more satisfying relationships in the work world, with limited or poor results.

✌§   JENNY ABATELLO

Jenny Abatello spent her twenties as a homemaker and then made teaching and homemaking co-central components of her Culminating Life Structure. She had a special bond with her husband, Steve, who actively supported the teaching career that in some ways separated her from him and his working-class world. Her Mid-life Transition was highlighted by changes in marriage, family, and occupation. Here is her account at 43:

> When I was 39 my husband's business started to fail. It was a terrible time for the whole family. I really worried about him. It's pretty hard to make a man feel like the head of the household when he feels like the earth is falling out from under him. The next year he worked for a while in another state. We found out we missed him and really needed him. He has understood so much through the years and has been such a good father. I appreciate all he's given me. He is in a new business now; I don't know what he does exactly but he's doing very well. We are very different, yet we appreciate each other.
>
> My two kids are now in college, and I enjoy them more than ever. My son Guy is an average student. He thought he'd flunk out of college, but he has a C average and is feeling good about himself. He may transfer to

another college, where he can get training to work with handicapped people. I'd like to see that; he has a lot to offer. Maggie just started college. She's an honor-roll student, class officer, cheerleader. We are very close. She's independent and knows what she wants. I raised her that way—don't limit your options. I get so angry with girls in my classes who have abilities but don't want to go to college. They say they'd rather get married. I tell them, "How can you say that? You have so many opportunities, so many options!" When I was young I was going against a lot. I *hope* things are changing, but I don't know.

My mother was a good, supportive mother and made sure I went to college, the first in the family to do so. She divorced my father and remarried. I told her recently, "I don't know if I could ever do what you did—go away and make a new life that makes you feel better." Recently an uncle died, and I was anguished over whether to attend the funeral. My mother insisted that I go. She was really upset when I said no. But there has been so much petty conflict in the extended family since my parents divorced and my father died. I hate what they did to each other, and I felt it would be just too hypocritical of me to attend the funeral. I had to do what was right for me. It has taken me all these years to finally say no to my mother. After I told my mother I wouldn't go, I sat and cried and cried. My daughter sat with me and said, "Ma, I know how you feel." Guy was upstairs and Steve was in bed. Maggie was wonderful: she knew it was a crisis for me, and she was with me.

My career has been an essential part of my life, and I have worked hard to become a competent, humane teacher. During my late thirties I was recognized as a person who could help the kids, especially the ones who weren't doing well. At 39 I wanted to accomplish more and thought about becoming a guidance counselor. But I realized that that's a pretty limited role, and I'd have to go back to school for more training, so I decided against it. At 40 I was asked to be department head. That was a tough choice but I finally said no. I'm really not interested in being an administrator; I like teaching. I realized that they just wanted a yes man to represent the status quo, and I couldn't do that. I love teaching, but I started late, and there is no real career path beyond administration, counseling, and burnout.

At this point work has come to everything I ever wanted it to be with my colleagues and my teaching. I trust my judgment. I feel comfortable as a senior-level teacher. I have earned a reputation as an educator. The students talk to me; I can say I'm sorry if I make a mistake. I have good relationships with other teachers, too. I really enjoy helping the younger ones progress. They call me "mother" and ask me to read papers they write for graduate school. I've become more assertive and take a stand for myself with administration and colleagues. Last year I proposed an intensive remedial English program to help prepare the weaker students for college. It was a good idea but it was rejected. Maybe I'll resubmit it next year.

There is not much joy now in education. The sheer number of students can really wear you down. We send ill-prepared kids off to college. It's a societal problem; nobody reads or writes. Teaching eats you up; it's all-consuming. I often come home exhausted and go to sleep at 9 o'clock. My work now is not very exciting, but I don't know what I'd be doing if I weren't in education. I'd like to continue teaching for another ten or fifteen years, but I wonder if I'm going to be like my colleague who was smart enough to take early retirement—or if I'll just burn out.

Two Culminating Events at 40 marked the onset of Jenny's Mid-life Transition. One was in the marriage: her husband's business failure and his brief departure from home. She recommitted herself to the marriage, but on different terms. She no longer regarded him as the primary provisioner and herself as the primary homemaker. The second Culminating Event was the offered promotion to department head and her refusal of it. The offer told her that she had reached the pinnacle of her youthful occupational strivings. Becoming a department head would bring her to a higher level in the system and a qualitatively new place in her career. It might also give her a chance to make the system more effective and humane. Yet she feared that she would be co-opted into becoming an administrative "yes man" and doing work she hated. This dilemma is not uncommon for innovative educators.

Jenny's decision to refuse the job offer had major consequences for her own life. She was committing herself to "stay put" in a teaching situation that was already pinching and might become intolerable. It was not clear how many more years she could go on as a teacher and whether she, like so many others, might not drop out or be pushed out in her fifties. At 43 she feels that "work has come to everything I ever wanted it to be," yet there is "not much joy now in education." She is faced with difficult questions: Where can I go from here in my career? How can work be a source of greater fulfillment? If at some point occupation can no longer be a central component of my life, what else is there? These questions are the stuff of which the Mid-life Transition is made.

Women Who Attempted to Give Occupation a Moderate but More Significant Place in Their Lives

Like the women above, the three women whose lives followed this pattern sought more from occupation than they had earlier. Since they had a more limited occupational history and a more limited investment of self in occupation it was virtually impossible for them to attain a more senior position.

Carol O'Brien and Angela Capelli were high school graduates of working-class origin; Emily Swift had graduated from an elite college and married a lawyer. All three women got psychologically divorced during the Age 30 Transition. In their thirties they worked on and off at unskilled, entry-level jobs, trying to make some kind of life outside the home. By 40 they understood that the marriage would never improve. Carol O'Brien got legally divorced at 40 and became a single working mother. Angela Capelli and Emily Swift remained in the marriage but got more involved in the job, hoping that the work world might compensate for the bleakness of their domestic life.

In the Mid-life Transition they realized that their jobs could not provide more than a bare minimum of satisfaction. They resigned themselves to work for the indefinite future in low-level jobs with no possibility of significant improvement in income, responsibility, or personal reward. It is not clear how much longer they could, or would, remain in jobs of this kind. Very little is known about the work lives of women in such jobs after age 50. It is my impression that many women drop out, or get pushed out, well before normal retirement age. Those who remain are seen as "older women" in junior positions usually occupied by "younger women" in their twenties or early thirties. The disparity between high age and low rank becomes increasingly oppressive. One solution commonly taken by women (and men) is to enter "psychological retirement" (an analogue of psychological divorce), continuing to hold the job but receiving and giving very little. It is especially difficult for women who are unable to validate their seniority in either family or occupation, as we have seen in the case of Angela Capelli. Emily Swift exemplifies this theme in another context.

✃ EMILY SWIFT

Emily Swift approached her Mid-life Transition in a hollow marriage, existing with her husband in a state of almost total separation. She had never formed a specific occupational identity or developed skills:

> We don't have a happy marriage or a normal home life. My husband is a very violent person. I can't believe I'm saying this. We've had many fights over the years. He says hurtful things to me, often makes physical threats, and has hit me occasionally. Nobody else in the world has seen this side of this man. Everyone loves him and thinks he's wonderful. He is a wonderful man—except for the temper and the moodiness.
>
> When I was 40 he said that he wanted a divorce, but then he said that he was willing to accept things as they were because he wanted to keep me. In some funny way I do love him, and I believe he loves me. I mean, I can't stand him half the time; he's a horrible person to live with. But can you imagine living with me? I don't know whether anyone else could.

We lead very separate lives in the same house. We share all expenses even though he makes a lot more money than I do. I'm totally responsible for keeping the house clean. We have no interests in common and do very little together beyond an occasional dinner. Most of the time we're in opposite parts of the house. We do not have sex. He has affairs and sometimes tells me about them. I really don't care what he does; if he's with other people then he's not yelling at me.

We both know we shouldn't be married. I put up with a lot because it would be very difficult for me to be on my own. I just control the anger and keep away from him. It would be a scary thing to separate. Neither of us could live with anyone else. Things are as bad as at 40, but there is no talk of divorcing now. We don't live together very well but it's the best each of us can manage.

I drink a lot every day. I've been close to being an alcoholic, if not an alcoholic, for a long time. I drink mostly in the evening but also in the afternoon if I'm alone. I think I'm killing myself. I've often asked myself why I do it. I have thought of seeing a psychiatrist but don't do it. I just can't imagine that what I have to say about myself could be interesting to anyone. I feel that way about these interviews. My husband has been having a hard time, too. He says he's depressed and lonely, and he takes Valium.

In my thirties I volunteered about twenty hours a week at the newspaper. At 40 I took a paid clerical job there so I could earn money in case my husband and I separated. I didn't like having a paid job. Lots of women are in low-paying clerical jobs but work in more or less professional capacities. Every male was "Mr. Somebody" and given respect, but the "girls" were not. I was in a more respected position as a volunteer than as a clerical worker.

When I was 43 a position was created for me at the newspaper, and I still have it. I get a half-time salary and volunteer the rest. I never get around to doing the work I'm officially paid for because I spend so much time functioning informally editing. All I have in my life now is my work. That's it—there's nothing else. I'm very pleased with my current work. I feel that after ten years I have somehow arrived at the right end. I have a certain body of knowledge and am respected for that knowledge. The work I do is professional. It's a great feeling, and high time at the age of 45 to have finally arrived at the right end with my work. But I also feel like a fraud in a sense, as I did in college. I'm in a pretend, pseudo-professional status. I enjoy the work but work on my own with no colleagues and no credentials, no title and little pay. I'm in a powerless position, and it is not clear whether I can continue in it indefinitely.

At 45, then, Emily is starting to build the most fragile of life structures. Her life is, one might say, impossible yet tolerable. She continues the marriage in a state of psychological divorce but on different terms than in her thirties. She understands (and so, apparently, does her husband) that they are held together by an invisible thread that may last indefinitely. To end the marriage would be a liberation if she had the external and inner resources to make a new beginning, and a catastrophe if the resources were lacking. Occupation is now the central component of her life structure. She is at the "right end" of a decade's work. She is also at the start of something new, but the prospects for becoming a senior member are slim. She can have more challenging, meaningful work in middle adulthood only by overcoming severe external barriers and by developing a more individuated self.

Women Who Attempted to Expand Their Leisure Activities without Pursuing an Occupation

This pattern is exemplified by Kay Ryan and Lynn McPhail. During their thirties they lived as full-time homemakers and maintained the ideal of the provisioner-homemaker split. Their occasional experience in unskilled, routine, low-paying jobs strengthened their aversion to the occupational world and their commitment to the Traditional Marriage Enterprise.

In the Mid-life Transition their children were in the teens or early twenties and had partially or totally left the parental home. The women recognized that the existing marriage enterprise was coming to an end. They considered getting an outside job and were relieved when their husbands insisted that they stay at home. Having a job was not part of the life they had envisioned for middle adulthood. At the same time, they became increasingly resentful of the domestic labor still required. Chores they had formerly done without question now seemed excessive. Motherhood required less of their time and involvement, but they found themselves increasingly intolerant of the problems of their adolescent and young adult offspring. They were disappointed that, despite the partial emptying of the nest, the marital relationship did not improve.

As they approached the end of the Mid-life Transition, both women continued to hope for a more carefree existence yet found it elusive. Kay Ryan could imagine it as coming about in her fifties when her husband's early death might leave her a solitary widow with ample resources and only herself to take care of. At the same time, she feared that she would continue to be burdened by the unceasing demands of husband, adult sons, mother, and mother-in-law. Her miscellaneous leisure interests allowed her to pass the time, but she had no sense of a self that might be more intensely engaged in living. Lynn McPhail, too, wanted a more carefree life within the context of her working-class world. She longed for the time when she and her second husband could enjoy each other more, once the last of her five children finished high school and left home. She didn't know what kind of life they would have in the future, except that it would be very different from the past.

Ending the Mid-Life Transition

The homemakers in this sample were pioneers in the transformation of the Traditional Marriage Enterprise. From them we learn about the high incidence and durability of this enterprise, as well as the many powerful forces that are transforming it. These women had entered adulthood expecting to live as unemployed homemakers within Traditional Marriage Enterprises. In their early forties, they entered the Mid-life Transition and the shift from early to middle adulthood. Only one homemaker was in her first marriage and unemployed. Fifty percent of the homemakers were divorced or in a second marriage. Motherhood was becoming a less central component of the life structure, the terms of the marriage enterprise were changing, and the marital relationship had to be modified. Eighty percent of the homemakers were in the workforce. It was not yet clear what new marriage enterprises these women would create in the new era of middle adulthood as they struggled to create better lives for themselves.

The Career Women Samples: The Businesswomen and the Faculty Members

We interviewed two samples of career women: fifteen businesswomen in the corporate-financial world, and fifteen faculty members at several colleges and universities. Corporate and academic careers are highly demanding and require strong personal commitment, but they offer the promise of great personal satisfaction. Both careers are situated in institutions largely populated and controlled by men. At the same time, they differ from one another in several major respects. An academic career, compared with a corporate career, requires a longer period of post-college education. Its culture is somewhat less hypermasculine, offering women slightly more opportunity to advance beyond entry-level positions. It is financially less rewarding, but it provides women with a little more support for combining career and family. How these similarities and differences are reflected in the lives of individual women is one subject of our inquiry.

In the following chapters I shall explore the commonalities among the career women generally, the differences between the two career samples, and the similarities and differences between the career women and the homemakers. Perhaps the most general findings are these:

(1) All three samples have certain features in common, features that underlie the variations in personality and life circumstances among them. All forty-five women go through the same sequence of periods in life structure development, albeit in different ways. Likewise, all forty-five must deal—again in their individual ways—with the same basic issues of gender: maintaining or modifying the gender splitting in society and in self; maintaining or modifying the Traditional Marriage Enterprise; forming the internal Traditional Homemaker Figure and the internal Anti-Traditional Figure, and dealing with the conflict between them.

(2) Women with corporate or academic careers have much in common that differentiates them from the homemakers. They traverse the developmental periods in somewhat different ways. They make a stronger effort

to overcome the splitting of feminine and masculine. They form a more developed internal Anti-Traditional Figure who plays an increasingly important part in their lives. They attempt (with various degrees of success and failure) to achieve a more even balance of occupation and family. They develop a greater variety of alternatives to the Traditional Marriage Enterprise.

(3)   The businesswomen provide the greatest contrast to the homemakers. The academics are intermediate: when they differ from the businesswomen, it is usually in the direction of the homemakers.

(4)   Finally, and perhaps most important, is the *diversity of individual lives.* Along with the common themes, there are remarkable individual variations within each sample and across the entire spectrum. "Homemakers," "businesswomen," and "faculty members" are not unitary categories with no internal variation. Likewise, "female" and "male" are not unitary categories. The differences between male and female are important, but so are the similarities—and so, too, is the tremendous variety of individual lives, female as well as male. Even when a theme is characteristic of a particular group, there are still individual variations—as shown by the case vignettes—that enrich our collective lives.

The career sample was diverse in social background and early life circumstances. Two businesswomen were Catholic, ten were Protestant, and three were Jewish. Fourteen women were white; one was African-American. Three faculty women were Catholic, eight were Protestant, and four were Jewish. All fifteen faculty women were white, as no African-American faculty women volunteered to be in the study.

One faculty member withdrew from the study after she had been interviewed. We have used her case in data analysis, but we have not quoted her directly in this book.

10 Adolescent Life Structure: Career Women

The Adolescent Life Structure typically extends throughout the high school years from roughly age 13 or 14 to 17 or 18 (see Chapter 4). The central components of the career women's Adolescent Life Structure were the family of origin, the high school as an academic/social world, and the adolescent peer world. Most women in both academic and corporate careers grew up in relatively well educated, middle- or upper-middle-class families. Some 80 percent lived in the parental home while attending a local high school; the others went to a residential preparatory school but maintained strong ties to family. The parents generally placed emphasis upon the daughter's academic success and social adjustment.

The career women in the sample were born between 1936 and 1947. All thirty women were currently living in the Eastern corridor within two hundred miles of New York City, but their origins were extremely diverse. They came from large cities, small towns, and rural areas in various regions of the country. Many attended colleges and graduate schools far from the parental home. The parents, too, were diverse in social and economic background. In short, this sample is not narrowly local or regional; it contains a rich variety of American lives.

Family Life

Few of the thirty women gave a picture of a relatively uncomplicated, enjoyable childhood and adolescence within a relatively uncomplicated, happy family. As with the homemakers, several referred to television programs of the time, such as "Father Knows Best" and "Leave It to Beaver," as portraying a traditional happy family life that they found attractive but alien to their own experience. But since the television programs portrayed families widely believed to be standard normal American, the girls had hoped and expected that their own adult lives would fit this pattern.

About 15 percent of the career women gave a brief description of the childhood family containing little that was especially positive or negative. They sometimes alluded to various problems of family life but did not make explicit the full extent of their experience.

◄§ NINA DALTON

It was a quite happy childhood. My mother was always an important role model for me in the sense of someone who had combined marriage and children and a career successfully so I never had conflict about that. I knew I was going to have a career, and I was going to get married and have a family, too. I wanted to find a husband who was supportive.

◄§ EMMA BEECHWOOD

I had a fairly close relationship with both my parents. I had a woman relationship with my mother, which in effect meant we'd go shopping together. My father was very patient but not home much.

In subsequent interviews it became evident that Emma was actually not close to either parent. Moreover, she had strong grievances that she could not discuss with them nor examine fully within herself. One of them concerned her maternal grandparents. When Emma was 10, her mother became a teacher, and the retired maternal grandparents moved in. At first they did much of the child care. Very soon, however, they became increasingly ill and difficult. Mother's energies went almost entirely to work and grandparents, rarely to the children:

I didn't like my grandparents because they used to fight terribly with each other. My grandfather took drugs for his illness and abused them. I remember many, many evenings when my mother would go upstairs to my grandfather's room. My grandfather had fallen down because he was doped up; they had terrible fights about the medicine. I just very seriously disliked my grandfather because of that. The grandparents didn't get along either; they just coexisted, fought all the time, didn't even sleep in the same room. Today maybe they would have divorced.

Emma clearly felt great fear and anger toward her grandparents. The criticism of her mother was muted and would probably not appear at all in a questionnaire or brief interview. Even now, in her late thirties, she finds it hard to examine those early relationships and their relevance for her adult life. She distanced herself emotionally from the destructive, frightening grandparents, the concerned yet absent mother, and the distant absent father—but this made it difficult to have more genuinely intimate relationships with loved ones.

The great majority of the career women gave more explicitly negative descriptions of their adolescent experience within the family. Many said that the family looked very good to the outside world but was actually quite destructive for its members.

✍ JULIA HART

It was a devastating marriage all around. I have never known why my parents hang in. They are not a compatible couple by any stretch of the imagination—lots of fights and high frustration on both sides. My father would come home exhausted and probably wanting to be looked after himself, not sympathetic to the fact that my mother had to deal with three brats running around all day making demands. She'd become quite expert at nagging. So all hell would break loose, each being needy and not able to give to the other. I thought it would be much better if they stopped bitching and moaning at each other and separated. My father was a patriarch, very domineering, the head of our family and large extended family. He argued strongly that we children should have a profession, as he did, so that we could be master of our own life. Academic achievement wasn't that important to my mother, especially for girls, as long as we behaved. She could find a place for herself in a patriarchal family: in her view a real mother cooks very well and cleans even better; her life is her children and even today she relates to us as *children*, not adults. In her way she, too, was domineering: you didn't do things for yourself, you did them for *her*; everything was done for her. There were constant expectations from both parents. They weren't always articulated, but they were made clear.

I always respected my father, but I didn't have a close relationship with either parent. Quite early I led my own life. Beginning at 11 or 12 I'd go off on my bike for the day and come home at bedtime. Even now I go home purely as a duty. Growing up, I was just dying to get away and have my own life. When I left for college, I wanted to get away so badly that I didn't even want my parents to drive me there.

✍ MICHELE PROTO

Marriage has always represented control to me—like my parents' marriage. My father was domineering. He never respected my mother. He belittled her, called her stupid in public. He was rich, but he made her account for every penny. My mother was a very generous, kindhearted, good person, but she basically did whatever he told her. I couldn't stand that. I always thought, "Who wants to get married?" If I'd have to ask somebody whether I could buy a blouse, like my mother did, I'm not going to do it. I have a tremendous desire to be independent and a tremendous fear of control. My mother once told me that she was never in love with my father; she married him for security. I wanted to be able to take care of myself so I wouldn't need that kind of marriage.

Both parents made sure I was well fed, given material things and a good education. But they didn't really give me their interest or guidance. My father, with his eighth-grade education and his great ambition, wanted all three kids to attend good colleges and become professionals, and we did. He brought us up to be independent, to never rely on anyone. To this day, at 43, I still seek more success trying to prove to my father that I'm a person and worthy of his recognition. My sister suffered the most; she has been in a mental hospital several times.

✑   KRISTIN WEST

My parents fought all the time. My father didn't treat my mother very well. My mother was retiring and quiet and shy and could be stepped on by my father. It was a very cozy-looking family to the world, but it was destructive as well. I thought my mother was stupid because she didn't realize my father had affairs. Later I just felt sorry for her, but I didn't have any respect for that woman. My strongest sense was simply that I wanted to be free of my family. I wanted to be as independent as I possibly could. I appeared to be outgoing and confident. I never had a problem that I let my parents know about, and I had no relationship with my brother growing up, either.

✑   ELLEN NAGY

I had a miserable childhood, I did not have a good home life, I did not like my whole situation, I felt out of it, I didn't belong.

My parents have had a very difficult marriage. They never adjusted to each other and to their different views about how to live their lives. They were fighting all the time, and they still fight. As far as I can see, there is no evidence of personal growth in either of my parents. My mother has never forgotten or forgiven; she's an incredibly bitter woman. It's just the intensity of the bitterness. It's tragic. My father was very focused on his work. I rarely saw him while I was growing up. My idea of family is that at best they don't cause you any problems, and at worst they're a terrible drain and cause all kinds of problems. If you need help, you don't go to your family.

✑   AMY YORK

I was an only child. My parents never fought or yelled but also never showed much feeling. I was an army brat and moved almost every year. I never had any friends. I just felt so all alone.

My father was never home, and my mother was always volunteering someplace. My most vivid memory of our family is this: I would come home to find my mother going out the door to do some volunteer work while my father was sitting in the darkened living room, staring at the TV and eating dinner on a tray. In high school I just stopped talking to my parents beyond a "yes" or "no" answer, but they didn't seem to notice that that had happened. I never wanted to get married or have kids.

Amy York did not elaborate on this brief statement, but more words could not make more powerful the image of three isolated figures living in the same household yet unable to form a family. Given her childhood experience of family life, Amy found it difficult as an adolescent and young adult to imagine herself as a wife and mother. She also found it difficult to imagine an alternative option.

Relationships with siblings were rarely brought up as a major concern. The life stories, however, provided an unexpected finding: some 75 percent of the career women—like the homemakers—mentioned that their relationships with siblings were negative or very limited from childhood through adulthood. Often, one sibling became the "good" daughter or son while another was identified as the "bad" (deficient, wayward, disappointing) child. More focused study is needed to test this finding and to learn more about its meaning and consequences.

Relationship with Father

By social origins and current circumstances, the fathers of our sample can be divided into two fairly distinct groups: about 70 percent were business or professional men who had attended excellent colleges. About half of these had a postgraduate degree. Some were from affluent families. Others were of working-class or lower-middle-class origins and had worked hard to reach a higher educational and occupational level than their parents. By the time the daughter entered high school, the father was usually established in a comfortable life. Having attained his version of the American Dream, he considered it part of his legacy that his daughter should have a fine education (though not a career) and material advantages comparable to his own.

The remaining 30 percent of the fathers were less educated and less professional. One father had only an eighth-grade education, some had no education beyond high school; others had completed part or all of college. All were of working-class or lower-middle-class origins and had "raised themselves by their own bootstraps." Their occupations included small business owner, contractor, real estate dealer. Some had modest incomes; others had become wealthy. Virtually all wanted their daughters to have a college education and a life comparable to or better than their own, though these fathers' aspirations were generally more limited than those in the first group.

Two themes were prominent in the career women's accounts of their relationship with father in childhood, particularly during the high school years. The first had to do with the emotional aspects of the relationship. In most cases, the girl felt some degree of love, respect, and appreciation for father. He was in certain ways caring and supportive, and he was portrayed in less dramatically negative terms than mother. He was also often a distant or absent figure in the girl's life. The daughter had major grievances against him, although they often did not emerge clearly into awareness until some years later. The most common theme was that she experienced a marked ambiguity in father's feelings toward her. Did he really love and appreciate her? Did he find her disappointing? Was he basically just indifferent? She was left with a pervasive uncertainty about where he stood emotionally.

The second theme was about the future: How did father envision her life as an adult? Almost every girl experienced her father as strongly wanting her to do well in school, to attend a good college, to become a bright and accomplished person. At the same time, he was quite negative, restrictive, or ambiguous about her occupational future after college. He wanted her to have some work skills so that she could have a job if necessary. But he also steered her toward the female occupations and discouraged her from getting so heavily involved in a career that it might interfere with a stable marriage and family life. She understood by high school or college that father's emphasis on her intelligence, talent, and academic performance had mainly to do with her matrimonial prospects. Homemaking, not career, was the primary goal. He could take pride and pleasure in her high grades, her artistic gifts, her cleverness and charm, her being smarter even than most boys. But he could not imagine a girl following in his footsteps. In envisioning her life as an adult, he did not give her a full place in his (male) work world—participating as an equal with men and making an important occupational contribution. Although he prized her as a girl, he could take her seriously as a woman only within the domestic sphere. For the girl who was beginning to form an adult identity and to consider possibilities other than that of traditional homemaker, that was indeed a blow. However much father appreciated and encouraged her, even he was steering her toward a future very similar to mother's. In her conflict with mother (partly over having a different kind of life), father did little to protect and support her or to mediate the struggle.

❧   HELEN KAPLAN

My father was very warm, really a nice guy. He was a more positive figure for me than my mother. He was not interested in how we dressed or whether our hair was combed. He spent a lot of time talking with us, working with us on interesting projects. He was a very involved father, although he was busy with his work, too. He'd leave for work at 7 in the morning and come back at 6, but then he was pretty available. He didn't work weekends. He was professionally and financially secure by the time I was a child. He was able to be so interested in us as people because he wasn't out scrambling so much occupationally. He was a pretty satisfied, happy person. I felt gender wasn't really very emphasized in our relationship with him at all. He didn't try to make us into boys. He treated us like persons. We did a lot of fishing and carpentry on boats. He was very interested in our being competent and did a pretty good job at that. But he and my mother expected I'd be married by the end of college.

◆§   SALLY WOLFORD

I only saw my father weekends. I admired him and thought he was wonderful. He was glad to have a girl. It was taken for granted that I would go to college. In high school I wanted to be an accountant like him, but he discouraged me. He said there were very few opportunities for women, and they got stuck doing boring work. He thought I should go out and get married and be pretty and have fun. That was what a girl should do in those days. Nobody wanted me to have a career—nobody. I vaguely thought about it but couldn't take it seriously.

◆§   EMMA BEECHWOOD

I remember my father telling me in high school that if I were a man he'd have me become a lawyer, following in his footsteps. But since I wasn't a man that wasn't such a good idea because lawyers sometimes had to work late on jobs and go to parts of the city where they'd be going home at midnight and it wasn't safe for a girl. And therefore I couldn't do that. At the time I thought he was being very protective.

◆§   TRISHA WALL

When I was a year old my mother died giving birth to twins. I have only a negative image of family life and being a mother. Father raised the three children with a succession of housekeepers. None of them stayed long because we kids were too rowdy. When I was 11, my father stopped having housekeepers and did most of the work himself. As the oldest, I moved into the mother's role. I was the most responsible and obedient, but I also bore the brunt of my father's authoritarian discipline. He sacrificed himself in extraordinary ways to keep us together as a family. My grandmother lived with us a lot, but she, too, was an austere, harsh disciplinarian. She favored boys, didn't have much use for girls. We had to spend summers at her farm. It was like hardship duty, but it gave Father respite.

I have only a negative image of family life and being a mother. I never yearned to have children like a lot of women do. I was troubled with the burdens and hassles that come along with children, and I saw none of the good parts. I'm sure I picked up my attitude of not wanting kids from my father. I saw him coming in at 7 or 8 p.m. after a long day at the office, cooking dinner for us, helping us with our homework, putting us to bed, and not having any of the evening for himself. Then I saw him getting up early the next morning, making our lunches, cooking breakfast, driving us to school, and calling in the afternoon to make sure we were okay at home alone. For him and my grandmother life was not fun, but he never complained. Work was the be-all and end-all of life; play was frivolous.

In high school I started thinking that that was too narrow a way to live. I wanted time and money for myself, and I still do. My main interest in going to college was to get away from the family. I didn't care what college it was, as long as I got away. In those days a girl went to college with one of two goals: to teach or to find a husband and get married and have children. Since I wasn't interested in the latter, I figured I had to do the former. I had no sense of what a college might offer me. Nobody told me, "Trisha, you can be anything you want to be; you can go to law school or get an MBA." I had an interest in art, but I saw no way to pursue it. My father wanted his *son* to have a career, but not his daughters. He kept saying that I should return home immediately after college, get a job, and take care of him.

It is noteworthy that, although Trisha Wall lost her mother at age 1, she nonetheless formed an internal Traditional Homemaker Figure who sacrificed herself to children and household. This figure was created in part out of her experiences with the succession of housekeepers and with the grandmother. It was perhaps influenced as well by her mother's death in childbirth—powerful evidence of the dangers of motherhood. Her internal Traditional Homemaker Figure derived, too, from her father. In addition to being the provisioner, he was also the primary homemaker—an Angel in the most self-destructive, frightening sense. He did the domestic/maternal work, but it remained women's work and a form of suffering, not joy, for him. It understandably had much the same meaning for Trisha.

✎ ABBY MURPHY

The basic truth about me is that my father raised me to be a boy. This meant taking care of everyone from the time I was 10: my mother, my sisters, my relatives, my father's business, everyone. My father would continually say, "If something happens to me, you have to take care of the business and the whole family." He expected me to carry on his small business exactly as he wanted it—that's all our relationship was. He never listened to me or my ideas; he just wanted me to listen to him. There was absolutely no praise. I always felt strong but unspoken pressure to achieve. So I became an achiever, but I did not enjoy my achievements. In my father's book, feelings were ridiculous. He kept giving me a strong message: "Get yourself a good background and good training so you'll be able to take care of yourself and not be stuck with a man who can't take care of you." I responded by being independent and competent like my father. I know now that this is a strength but also a weakness; I have a hard time letting anyone do anything for me. I feel very much that, if I gave in to the feminine part of me, I'd be just like my mother: weak, ineffective, totally dependent, things that I consider bad. As it is, I need to be there for others and not need anything for myself, and that's no better.

I worked in my father's business through high school. We'd do the payroll together. He was the salesman doing the outside work, and I was going to be the accountant. By high school it was understood that I'd go into the business with my father. I liked the status and recognition I'd get from that, but there was also the deep feeling, "I've got to get out of here." He was domineering and authoritarian. On the rare occasions when I stood up to him, he'd freeze me out emotionally for two weeks, and I'd just be destroyed. I felt I had a right to be heard, but he wouldn't allow it. To make things worse, my mother would not stand up for me or for herself. I had a hard time dealing with puberty; I gained weight and had a poor social life. I often got angry inside, but I was always the well-behaved daughter.

When I was finishing high school, my father proposed that I not go to college but remain at home and work with him. He offered me a new car and other things. I didn't seriously consider the offer. I wanted out, and college provided that opportunity. I just wanted a college as far away from home as my father would allow, a big anonymous place where I would have great freedom and a chance to start over. No one at home or high school helped me with the choices for college; I just bought a book and made my own decisions. I felt deserted by my mother because she had absolutely no interest in helping me select a college. It's like she punished me for deciding to leave home and becoming unavailable to her. Our relationship was different from that time on, and I began to see how limited it had been earlier.

Still, there was a good side to my relationship with my father. I admired him, idolized him. I saw him as a lot of fun, knowledgeable, outgoing, a good businessman. Despite all the problems, I felt that if I got enough distance for a while and developed my credentials, I could work with him after college on a different level. I followed his advice to major in something practical at college, to plan on a business career, to not get married in college but try for a more interesting life. It took me many years to get more independent of him.

Relationship with Mother

Almost all of the subjects' mothers lived primarily as homemakers in a Traditional Marriage Enterprise. About half of the mothers came from middle- to upper-class families. The mothers had been sent to excellent colleges by parents who wanted their daughters to have a liberal education though not a career. Education had broadened their horizons and spurred their desire to have some kind of outside work in addition to a family. After marrying, however, they had settled into a relatively traditional homemaking pattern for which they were overqualified. Some of them later had jobs, but only a few made occupation a central component of their lives. The remaining half of the mothers had less education (usually through high school) and had seen themselves as traditional homemakers from the start. When the children were in school some of these mothers worked part-time or full-time, but occupation was rarely a major source of satisfaction or self-esteem.

While the daughters were growing up, almost all of their mothers had what they regarded as comfortable, secure lives. Each one had reached or exceeded her youthful aspirations: her husband was a good provider, materially and socially; she lived in an attractive home and neighborhood, according to her lights; her children went to good schools and had bright prospects for the future; she was not burdened by poverty, heavy domestic responsibilities, or demanding outside work.

In the midst of this comparable freedom and abundance, however, many of the mothers had an inner sense of oppression and scarcity. Seemingly free to do anything, they didn't have any viable alternatives to the Traditional Marriage Enterprise. Their lives, though busy, sometimes felt empty and trivial. A succession of activities held their interest briefly, but no activity had special importance or meaning. They knew that something was wrong, yet couldn't identify what it was or find ways to make it better. Many were chronically depressed. They often blamed specific others such as husband, children, parents—and ultimately themselves for not enjoying what was obviously a "good" life. They were too much the products of a cultural and familial system to recognize that the system itself, not any few individuals, was the primary source of their malaise. And they were too isolated to see that many other women had the same problems.

Betty Friedan's *The Feminine Mystique* was published in 1963. It vividly portrayed the lives of this generation of women and gave voice to their experience. It also placed the problem in broad social-cultural perspective and identified goals for collective action. The book both reflected and helped to generate the Women's Movement which began in the 1960s and crested in the 1970s. Its greatest impact was on women who saw themselves as homemakers stuck in a domestic life that was stultifying even in its most affluent form.

The career women in the present study were, so to speak, "daughters of the Feminine Mystique." For many subjects, this book gave a vivid picture of her mother in particular, her mother's generation, and what she herself might easily become if she did not struggle actively to prevent it. Her imagery grew out of her own direct experience by the late teens, independent of any book. She wanted desperately *not* to become a homemaker like her mother: caught in a domestic cage, an appendage to a husband in a bland or corrosive marriage; emphasizing the importance of motherhood yet unable to give or receive much in relationships with her children; lacking the resources, independence, and competence to make a richer life of her own. Each girl had her own specific forms of this imagery, her own ways of accepting and opposing it, her own evolving views about a better life, and her own difficult search for a better life.

The girl's experience of family life and relationship with her mother strongly shaped her evolving sense of what it meant to be a woman. The imagery of the Traditional Homemaker Figure was conveyed to the daughter in every aspect of her world, but the relationship with mother was the primary medium through which she made it part of herself. Mother wanted daughter above all to develop the feminine virtues of a homemaker: she should make matrimony and family her primary goals. She should accept male authority in home and workplace. She should be an excellent student but not so smart or so intellectual that the brighter boys (and more attractive potential husbands) would be put off. The daughter should, in short, form an adult life much like her mother's. To some degree, each girl incorporated this aim and tried to develop many of her mother's traits and values.

But there was an underside to this. Mother also represented qualities quite different from those of the happy, admirable homemaker. The girl saw that mother's life was much less satisfying than she publicly made it out to be. Mother wanted a family but felt restricted by the domestic labors. She wanted a hardworking, "successful" husband but felt unappreciated by him. She pursued interests outside the home—through a paid job, volunteer work, community groups—but often had no sense of direction. While accepting the dominance of men in family and work world, she resented her own subordination in both. She experienced psychological scarcity in the midst of material abundance, inner oppression in a world that seemingly gave her great freedom.

The daughter thus received two contradictory messages from her mother:

The predominant, "official" message: prepare yourself to become a traditional homemaker like me. Be a good girl, and accept your place within the patriarchal system. Otherwise you will be without a family to take care of, without a man to take care of you, and, worst of all fates, alone.

Beneath this was often an opposite, muted yet powerful message: escape as best you can from this limited life. Don't lose yourself in it and become a powerless victim. Learn to be independent and take care of yourself. Become a stronger woman and live a better life than I was able to—though I don't even know what that might be and can't help you seek it.

In most cases the daughter regarded her mother's life as tolerable at best, a total disaster at worst. She experienced mother as a victim of a deprived childhood, of a hurtful marriage, of external circumstances that kept her from being happy. In part she could sympathize with mother-as-victim and blame others for her misfortune. By the high school years, however, her sympathy was strained. She felt that mother was herself largely to blame, that she had colluded in her own victimization. Rather than using available opportunities and fighting against the restrictive, oppressive forces in her life, she had been passively submissive or actively self-defeating.

In their daily relationship, daughter often experienced mother as an extremely needy person—disappointed in her own life, vainly hoping to revitalize her aborted aspirations, unable to "find herself" and have some control over her own fate. Mother's neediness was often directed toward daughter. The girl felt stifled by the intensity of the demand that she be her mother's selfless, loving, dutiful daughter: a source of consolation for mother's sufferings as well as an alter ego who would capture the good life that had eluded her. It was important to be helpful, talented, well adjusted—not defiant, needy, or selfish. But dutiful conformity was not enough. She had to provide the emotional gratification that mother could not otherwise obtain. It was necessary to make mother feel loved and lovable, to meet mother's wishes out of an evident desire to please her and be her good girl.

Mother tried to form a re-mothering relationship (see Chapters 3 and 5) in which she could experience herself as the "perfect" mother: loving, caring, meeting the child's needs in every way, and thereby making her the "perfect" daughter. At the same time, mother identified with the daughter and experienced herself as the beloved child, healed of all hurts and basking in the nurture of a devoted, bountiful mother. In this way, the actual mother tried to provide for her child/self all that she had missed in the earlier relationship with her own mother. In imagining herself as both mother and child, mother gained the uniquely satisfying experience of giving and receiving love entirely on her own terms. The re-mothering relationship offered mother (and in her mind the daughter as well) an opportunity to be loved/loving, admired/admiring, protected/protector. She regarded herself as an altruistic mother who did everything possible for her daughter's welfare and happiness. She could not believe that her mothering was in any way "selfish" or that she might be pursuing her own agenda more than her daughter's. Indeed, she could not imagine that daughter might be a separate person with her own agenda, except out of malice or selfishness.

This relationship posed a great dilemma for the daughter. If she violated mother's demands—by open defiance or, what was perhaps worse, by conforming without seeking to please—she feared that mother would feel betrayed, deeply hurt, even destroyed, by a bad, unloving daughter who was unworthy of her loving care. To disappoint mother was to run the risk of losing entirely the emotional connection between them. Given the strength of her attachment and dependency, the daughter feared that the loss of this connection would jeopardize her existence as a person—would destroy her self. On the other hand, if she selflessly served mother's needs, there would be no space for her own. She would lose her self, just as mother had. Participating in an enduring, intense re-mothering relationship with a psychologically impoverished mother thus holds both a promise and a danger for the daughter. The promise is largely illusory, the danger enormous. Such a relationship is very different from that with a *good enough mother* (to use child psychologist Donald Winnicott's expression), who creates a space within which the child can become herself.

There was a second, related theme in her experience of the relationship with mother. The daughter was supposed to be not only a source of re-mothering but also an alter ego who would have the kind of life mother had hoped for—and missed. The goals mother had always wanted for herself, especially in adulthood, the daughter should now desire and attain. Anyone can take satisfaction in seeing a loved person enjoying the successes she herself had dreamed of. But in this case it went much further. The girl came to feel that in mother's eyes she was not a separate person, that mother was living vicariously through her. To be a good daughter was to have no self of her own. She would follow a script written and directed by mother, enacting the part mother had wanted to play. To the extent that she adhered to the script, any choice she made or any success she earned would be more for mother than for herself. Indeed, she would have no independent self to make a choice or to enjoy the fruits of her own efforts. As several subjects later asked themselves, "Whose life is this, anyway?"

Mother thus came to be experienced by many daughters not only as a victim but also as an actual or potential victimizer. She sought to control her daughter not through her strength but through her weakness, her emotional neediness. By mid-adolescence the girl felt it imperative to protect herself by limiting their relationship, erecting strong emotional barriers between herself and mother, and pursuing an independent course. Failing this, she would be engulfed in the relationship and become a victim, no more able than mother to find herself and make her own way in the world.

Varieties of Daughter-Mother Relationships

Let us turn now to some individual vignettes that exemplify the various themes and variations discussed above.

A few girls succeeded in gaining some emotional distance from mother.

They established a relatively bland relationship with minimal conflict—and with minimal substance as well. At best, this relationship was quite "nice" but was limited to specific activities such as shopping and household chores. At worst, mother and daughter were separated by an emotional chasm that prevented open conflict but also permitted no genuine contact.

For the great majority, however, the mother-daughter relationship was more turbulent, with an uneven mixture of involvement and withdrawal on both sides. These relationships were usually part of a family pattern characterized by overt conflict between the parents and between subgroups, each containing a parent and one or more children (and perhaps members of the extended family). The daughter sometimes had partial allies in this struggle, but for the most part she felt alone and unable to count on anyone for enduring support or protection. Mother was her chief adversary in the family conflict.

✌ᢒ   HELEN KAPLAN

In my family I had it all—smart and attractive. It was very bad for my sister. My mother was more complicated than my father. She was hard on my sister, couldn't find things to approve of in her. I was the special one for my mother. I was the one who could possibly fulfill her fantasies about everything. I should be socially popular, beautiful, graceful, charming. I should do well enough to marry properly; both parents believed that. I was a good student.

I think my mother always had many dissatisfactions with her own life. She seems always to be trying to manipulate things in some way that will make things different or better in her view. She blows hot and cold as far as her feelings are concerned. She is not very reliable emotionally. She is superficial. She seems not to have very deep attachments to anybody or anything. She doesn't have intimate relationships with people or with her self. What you see on the surface is about what there is.

I think she was very attached to my father. There was no question that she was deeply grieved and depressed and felt her world had come to an end when he died. But it wasn't clear to my sister and me how much of that had to do with our father as a person whom she appreciated and how much it had to do with her status in life, which was entirely tied up with his. They did enjoy many activities together, like bridge and tennis and golf. We're just not sure how much real sharing and intimacy and companionship they had.

✌ᢒ   ELLEN NAGY

My mother placed a great deal of personal investment in her daughters, and I became aware of that at a very early age. My mother was always very needy of our attention to her. She constantly played me and my sister against each other, and we were very competitive for many, many years.

My mother will still do it; if she has something positive to say about me she'll have something negative to say about my sister. But now I understand what's going on.

My mother felt that she was a success if I was. I have great ambivalence about receiving recognition because I never know if it's for me or for her. It was vicarious pleasure for her. She was living through us, and ultimately that was damaging. We went to college, which she had never been able to do. We had careers, which she had never been able to do. We got divorced, which she had never been able to do. When we got divorced she was very bitter: "I never could leave my husband, why should you?" She never consciously understood what she was doing or saying.

Here is this woman who is terribly unhappy. Her children always came through with awards, grades, very polite, very good. We did all the things we were supposed to do—and it did not make her happy. I thought, "I'm not gonna live through my child. It's damaging to the child, and it doesn't make you happy. I'm gonna live my own life."

ABBY MURPHY

I have a hard time talking about my childhood because it was so unhappy. I was shy and awkward, felt there was something wrong with me. Nobody had any fun in my family. My mother's mother lived with us and was a real bitch. My father's sisters lived nearby and were part of my life growing up. My mother hated them, and they hated my mother. My mother was depressed and emotionally absent all through my childhood. When I was 10 my sister, Jeannie, was born. I was her mother—my mother just copped out. I'd have to get the baby up and change her diapers and bring her to my mother to be breast-fed. I felt robbed—my mother never did her job. I can paint a picture: my mother would scream, "Abby, the goddam kid's crying, will you please shut her up?" So I did. My mother would never tell me I did a good job, but she wouldn't scream, and there'd be less tension in the house if I did what she wanted. I never had free time after school or on weekends. I had to take care of my sister and the housework. I felt so burdened by all the responsibilities.

I created a fantasy that I had a perfect family and everybody was happy together. In my fantasy I had a great mother, and she took care of all of us, and she was always there, and it was perfect, the way it should be. And, in fact, my mother *was* always there. She fed us and kept a nice house. But there was no emotional involvement with anyone in that family. My father went off to work, made a nice living, and we had a nice place to live. Nobody beat us, but there was just no emotional involvement ever. Since my mother had no friends, I was her friend—and had no time for friends of my own. Together we would cook, decorate the house, go shopping. That was the only way I could get attention from her. But she was so caught up within herself that she couldn't take much stimulation. She never listened to me or anyone else. She didn't know *me* as a separate person. I used to think: "Everything's so wonderful here. What's wrong with me? Why am I so unhappy? Why do I feel this way?"

I've always just needed to be there for other people and not have anything for myself, like in my relationship with my mother. That's a hard role, and I haven't been able to break out of it totally. I have a lot of unmet needs from childhood, often feeling scared and overwhelmed because I couldn't cope with all those demands and responsibilities. I felt that if I gave in to the feminine part of me I'd be just like my mother—weak and ineffective and totally dependent. And that to me was all things bad.

GRACE TOBIN

I regarded my mother as a fantastic role model: an independent woman who was a fine teacher, a really fine mother, a really fine wife. I would never have taken as much for granted about myself and what I could do if she hadn't allowed me to take it for granted. Nobody ever said, "You're a girl and you can't do that." She never showed that she didn't enjoy what she was doing. She worked because my father didn't earn enough money.

I have come to understand that my mother has always been sort of a Pollyanna. She always makes the best of any situation in a cheery sort of way. She is about to retire now and finally admits that she never wanted to be a teacher, but I would never have known that from anything she ever said. If you mentioned a problem, her typical response always was, "Don't worry, you'll work it out." She did that on a visit recently, and for the first time [age 36] I told her that it bothered me, that it showed a lack of interest in my problems. I guess a young girl expects her mother to be the one who helps her through the turmoil of adolescence. But my mother never asked me one question about my personal life. I never volunteered any information or told her about my problems because she never seemed to have any interest—there was just a constant silence. I made all my own decisions about my life and where to go to college. I always wondered why my parents, and particularly my mother, never got involved in my personal life. It was like you weren't supposed to admit that you had problems because somehow life is not supposed to be problematic. There was quite a distance between me and my parents. It would have been nice if I could have had a little more help growing up. I remember when I was a teenager my mother would tell us at length at dinner about the particular problems of some student who had just spent two hours crying on her shoulder. I would sit there resenting it, thinking, "You can get so involved in the life of this kid, why can't you get involved in *my* life?"

HOLLY CRANE

In spite of being a successful physician, my mother had very traditional ideas about sex roles. A boy was to be a sperm producer, and a girl was to be pretty, to be a wife and mother. It's such a paradox. I remember her saying to me when I was a child to stay home and have babies because the work world is hard, and she had missed too much. She felt she had never had time to stay home and bake cookies. She had a lot of conflict between home and work. We had housekeepers who came and went, and that was very hard on me. My mother would come home at night chronically exhausted. She tried to be a superwoman, but in fact she failed badly. She was not a great mother. She was not good in my adolescence, and she probably wasn't good when I was a baby. Being a mother was just not what she was good at. Her energy went into her career. There was this huge gap between the ideology of motherhood and how wonderful it was supposed to be for the child and what I really experienced as a child. Family life was painful although it looked happy from the outside.

My mother has never taken me seriously. She never encouraged me to develop my intellect the way she did with my brother. She is very surprised now that I am where I am professionally.

JESSICA HALL

I didn't have a very pleasant childhood. My family had tremendous conflict, and nobody got along with anybody else. My mother took care of me—fed me, washed and ironed my clothes—but she was terribly depressed and didn't like me very much. The main thing in life for her was to be a fine cook, to keep her house immaculate, and not spend money. Somewhere along the line my parents had a falling out. She got to the point where she wasn't talking much and kind of lobotomized herself. She felt abused and exploited. She could not act. When I was 9 we moved because my mother couldn't function very well. Then I had four mothers: two maiden aunts, my mother, and my grandmother. My mother got squashed between these powerful female personalities. The four of them were very unattractive role models for me. They relied on each other, but were always bitching, moaning, lying, shitting all over females. They felt that the women suffered from the horrible men, who had all the fun while the women did all the work and had a miserable existence.

The women in my family presented a pretty unattractive picture to me, whereas my father was much more appealing because he was doing something and was active. I didn't want to stay home and be like them. I thought they were what it was like to be an adult female—and I wanted out! My interests were clearly not conventional female—I liked what my father liked. Even as a child I liked playing with my brother's toys but was discouraged because I was a girl. When I wanted a chemistry set for Christmas I got another goddamned doll. When I looked at those women I just screamed, "No, no, I don't want to be like that!"

At 14 I decided that I wanted to come to New York City more than anything else on the face of this earth. From the pictures in magazine ads

I thought it must be very exciting—and very different from my life at home. I wanted to be a good student. I wanted to know things and have things and do things differently from what was being done at home. There *had* to be something else out there.

Actually, I didn't really think about wanting a career. In high school and college all I wanted was to be married and have a child and stay home. I knew I was in college to get a husband, but it just didn't happen. Finally I knew I had to have a career because my family kept telling me that I had to be able to do something when I finished college if I was still single.

Jessica Hall provides a classical example of the conflicting internal figures. Identifying with her mother and female relatives (with the support of her father and the surrounding culture), she formed an internal Traditional Homemaker Figure: a woman living under the control of her husband, taking care of children she did not particularly want or enjoy, having a miserable existence. To have an adult life of this kind was for Jessica a living death, yet she could imagine no alternative. In high school she began forming an internal Anti-Traditional Figure who yet wanted to marry, raise a family, and have no career. In contrast to the Traditional Homemaker, however, she would be an enterprising, knowledgeable person who refused to be exploited by others. In Jessica's mind, the women in the New York magazine ads had exciting lives but apparently did not have careers that would jeopardize their domestic obligations. The conflict between the two internal figures evolved but was not fully resolved by Jessica's late thirties. One major reason for the difficulty was that her internal Anti-Traditional Figure was created largely from *masculine* sources—especially her father, and in contradistinction to her experiences with women. As she put it, this figure's personal qualities, such as competence, responsibility, self-respect, were "not conventional female." In actuality, these qualities are not intrinsically masculine. A woman can develop these qualities without becoming less a woman, if they are not identified as antithetical to feminine by a gender-split world.

Two career women reported incestuous childhood relationships, one with mother and one with godmother. Both girls grew up to become highly achieving women with complex but not markedly pathological personalities. Since we know little about incestuous relationships in relatively "normal" populations, I shall present one woman's story without further identifying data. This is an extreme form of a relationship between a needy mother and her daughter. It highlights some of the themes that exist, to greater or lesser degree, in such relationships generally, even if they do not involve incest or other kinds of gross abuse.

ANONYMOUS

My parents divorced when I was 7, and I rarely saw my father after that. My mother and I lived alone. The next few years were for me a total disaster: a mother, barely coping, with recurrent depressions and excessive drinking. She was a very giving, caring person, but it's hard for me to think of that time without the bad things coming out. We had a terrible relationship, and yet I feel a tremendous pity for this woman who was extremely bright and had no formal education—a primitive, powerful personality without any moral or intellectual control. She could be very strong, but at this time she was worried and frightened and alone, with an overwhelming neediness.

She took me to sleep with her. It was sexual. When it first happened it wasn't horrible; I was a child and didn't grasp that much. The sexual relationship was positive at first, but she simply could not allow room for me to develop past a child. That was what she wanted permanently. My rage at her has a lot to do with the way she just used me. She fastened on me as something to meet her needs and got angry at me if I questioned that. I felt very attached to her but also hardly existing. The incest practically wiped me out. I felt that I was her daughter, mother, and husband all at once. I just couldn't do it all. She had all the cards because I had strong feelings of obligation to take care of her. I finally left and lived at a private high school.

When I was 17 she was driving me out of my wits by trying to reclaim that physical relationship. She would get drunk and aggressive and try to get me to go to bed with her. The more advances she made the more repelled I felt—yet also guilty because I wasn't able to give what she wanted. She really got to me where it hurt: I felt obligated and horrified and had no one I could talk to about it. One way of coping was to switch things off. Often I didn't really know what I was feeling. I didn't know how to differentiate erotic feelings from other feelings. I experienced myself as split—at a great distance from my body, watching my body go through the motions. I kept busy, and my mind functioned beautifully, but I always had headaches and other signs of stress. I was sort of dead—going through life in a trance. I couldn't intensely engage in a relationship with another person. Gradually the world took over for me. But I was on ice for a long time, and to some extent I still am.

By 18 I was in open revolt against my mother. I marginally delivered the care but resented it more and more. There was an acute struggle within me to end the sexual relationship. I was getting ready to break the relationship and accept the consequences, which had always been carefully laid out to me: I would be killing her; she would die. It was a life-and-death struggle. I left at 19, and I never lived at home again. Leaving was a start, but I still had a long way to go.

At college over the next few years I was a desperate person. I drank a lot, and I was acutely depressed and made a serious suicide attempt. I had an extremely important relationship with a married man; it probably couldn't have been that intense with someone who wasn't married. I had never met anyone who wanted from me only what I was able to give. I had experienced erotic feelings as too dangerous and didn't get close to people because I was afraid of experiencing that split self. He was the first person I was ever totally together with. It was a profound physical and emotional relationship: passionate, gentle, liberating in all sorts of ways. It was a great gift, my first experience of someone seeming to really care about how I was feeling.

The Academic/Social World of High School

Almost all of the career women were college bound from early childhood. It was taken for granted by parents, school system, community, and themselves that they would be academic achievers and attend a first-rate college. Almost all did, indeed, follow this course, though it was usually more problematic than expected. About a third of the girls went to prestigious high schools, public or private, that prided themselves on the large number of graduates they placed in elite colleges and universities. The others went to less "academic" schools whose graduates were generally not college bound. These girls were often, as a few put it, "big fish in a small pond"; they had outstanding academic records and were strongly recommended for admission to excellent colleges. A few had supportive mentorial relationships with high school teachers. For the great majority, however, teachers served only limited mentorial functions and played a minor part in their lives. All of the girls performed well in high school, and several were stars: senior class valedictorian, National Merit Scholar, class president, newspaper editor, soloist in the school orchestra.

Virtually all of the girls were highly motivated to attend college. As we have seen in several examples above, there was strong family support and often "incessant pressure" for academic achievement. Doing well in school meant, in part, "being a good girl." But the academic effort was also driven by the internal Anti-Traditional Figure, who wanted to become a competent, independent adult. Attending a good college was thus the ideal next step after high school: it served the paradoxical double function of meeting parental demands and of leading to an adult life on the girl's own terms. In the short run it offered a legitimate way out of the oppressive parental home.

Despite the importance they gave to education, the girls were remarkably undifferentiated in their academic interests. They tried to do well in every-thing—required courses, electives, extracurricular activities. When they got involved in a particular activity, the choice was based more on their ability to perform well (and thus to elicit admiration and praise) than on their intrinsic interest in that activity. An exception for some was dance: several girls experienced dancing as something special that they did for themselves more than for others; yet most received no support to regard it as a serious occupational option.

Thinking seriously about an adult occupation was especially problematic. The internal Anti-Traditional Figure wanted ideally to become a competent adult who participated on equal terms with men within the family as well as in the public world. The girl rejected the traditional life of her mother as well as the traditional female occupations. But she was not entirely free, for internal as well as external reasons, to consider a wide range of occupations. There were heavy pressures against entering fields such as mathematics and the physical or biological sciences, which were in a sense too "masculine" and thus unacceptable to the internal Traditional Homemaker Figure. Some girls considered a career like their father's (in law, medicine, business) but gave it up when father said no. Most girls sought a middle ground between the overly "feminine" occupations (which were subjectively intolerable) and the overly "masculine" (which were neither externally supported nor internally desirable).

In high school the girls were just beginning to think about the balance they wanted between family and occupation in their adult lives. Most girls gave first priority to family while also wanting occupation. They planned to marry only after completing college, probably in the middle or late twenties, when they would be resourceful enough not to become "just a housewife." While not ready to pursue the ambitious career of the male-provisioner, they would do serious, meaningful work. Molly Berger gave a serio-comic representation of this dilemma in her image of Madame Curie, imagining the workplace as an appendage to the kitchen.

≈§   MOLLY BERGER

In high school I admired Madame Curie because she made a significant contribution and worked with her husband. That's the concept I had in my mind. I figured she was boiling up that stuff in the back of her kitchen, and in that way she combined work and family [laughs].

Peer Relationships in High School

Half of the career women reported having close friendships with girls or boys in high school. However, noteworthy by their rarity were accounts of intense, enduring friendships or love relationships that gave life a special excitement.

ABBY MURPHY

I didn't date much in high school, always went to dances in a group. I was a good girl who got along with everyone and didn't make waves, but I didn't get close to anyone. I couldn't bring kids home because my parents would criticize them and embarrass me.

TRISHA WALL

In high school I had no friends and no dates. I was pretty skinny and strange-looking. I didn't feel in the mainstream in terms of family and social life and looks.

GRACE TOBIN

In high school I was socially insecure, couldn't make myself popular; no boy in the school was going to hang around with me. Boys usually don't like girls who are taller or smarter than they are.

ELLEN NAGY

I came to think that I was the original ugly duckling; born in the wrong pond. If I could just get into the right pond I'd look like everybody else. I really wanted to get away from home.

We were being raised to go to college, there was no question about that. The clear object was to go to the best college possible. The reason was to have a career to fall back on after one got married and perhaps the spouse died. Or one might not get married, especially since one was not exactly the most popular kid in town.

My parents were very achievement oriented, and I internalized all that. However, once my parents realized I was doing well enough academically to get into a good college, the message changed. "Now wait a minute, boys don't like smart girls. Boys like to feel strong and dominating. If you're smart, you'll shut up and stop answering all the questions in class." I received that message pretty early on in high school, but I liked learning. So I figured if I went to an all-girls college I could be as smart as I could be. I could keep my social life separate. The boys wouldn't need to know how smart I was.

Beauty and intelligence became important issues in the girls' relationships with boys. Physical attractiveness was an asset and, even more, it was a great handicap to be unattractive—"strange looking," too fat or thin, too tall, no sex appeal. For many girls beauty was an aspect of the feminine, intelligence of the masculine. Given the basic gender splitting, this meant that beauty and intelligence were in some sense mutually exclusive.

❧   MOLLY BERGER

I'd like to think that you can be both intelligent *and* attractive, but they seem like opposites to me. I have always thought that smart people were not good looking and that good-looking people were not smart. Since I considered myself smart, I didn't consider myself good looking. It's as though you can't be both feminine and successful. Being accepted and liked has always been important to me. In high school I worked hard to get all the marks of acceptance: I was Prom Queen and got straight A's and had lots of friends. The last two years I dated a boy from another town. He wasn't that special but going with him allowed me to concentrate on grades and not worry about dates for dances. I felt it was such a liability to be smart that I had to make up for it by balancing. I always felt the danger of being one of those people who are real brains and don't have any friends, and it got worse in college.

Ending the Adolescent Life Structure: From High School to College

The final year of high school was colored above all by the prospect of going to college. The question was not whether to attend college. Parental values and pressures, combined with the girl's academic interests and performance, made that virtually inevitable. The great majority, as I have already noted, looked forward to college as a liberation from the family.

Most parents did not push for a particular college; they simply wanted their daughter to attend one from a pool of the best. The parents were rarely emphatic, lively participants in the daughter's efforts to imagine and deal with the exciting yet frightening next step in her journey. Of the thirty girls only Florence Russo applied to a school chosen for its convenience or low tuition. Even when the parents were not affluent, a way was found to provide educational advantages appropriate to the daughter's abilities and the parents' values. College was a serious business. The girls' own feelings in high school about going to college are conveyed in these brief recollections:

❧   EVA PITCHER

I was expected to go to college. I assumed you would work a few years and get married, and that would take care of your life plan. That was an attractive image to me: married and having children. Unlike lots of other girls, however, I didn't think that the point of going to college was simply to snare a husband and get married. But I also wasn't clear about the future, and I certainly had no idea of a career.

◄§ PAM KENNEY

I always had a vague sense that college was important and that I would work. I did well in high school but had no subjects or teachers of special interest to me. I liked English and history, and I would never major in chemistry or science. I knew what I *didn't* want to be, like a teacher or nurse. But I had no idea of what I *wanted* to be. I gave no serious thought to having a career or lifetime work in the sense of earning my own living and taking care of myself long term.

◄§ FLORENCE RUSSO

I knew in high school that we didn't have the money to send me away to college, but I could go to the local college. I didn't know too many options for future work for women other than teacher, nurse, or secretary. I didn't want to be a nurse, or secretary, so that left teacher.

◄§ KRISTIN WEST

There was never a question that I would go to college and get married and years later have children. I would be like my mother. She was married, she had a college degree, she taught, she had children, and that was what I was going to do. My strongest sense in high school was simply that I wanted to be free of my family, that I wanted to be out on my own. I wanted to be as independent as I possibly could.

Over 80 percent of the career women went to a residential college more than one hundred miles from home. They generally went to elite colleges and universities: women's colleges such as Wellesley, Vassar, and Radcliffe; private co-educational institutions such as Oberlin and Vanderbilt; and excellent state universities such as Texas and Minnesota. These schools traditionally placed their *male* students on a track that led to a professional or business career and their *female* students on a track that led to marrying a man with such a career.

11 Early Adult Transition: Career Women

The basic developmental tasks of all transitional periods are termination, individuation, and initiation (see Chapters 2 and 5). The particular form taken by these tasks in a given transition is shaped by its place in the life cycle. The Early Adult Transition forms a boundary between childhood and early adulthood. In it we must terminate the Adolescent Life Structure and the relationships with all significant parts of the adolescent world. The task of individuation is to move toward an adult self that is more ready to undertake the responsibilities, burdens, and satisfactions of early adulthood. The task of initiation is to test out new choices and explore new relationships in the adult world, laying the basis for building an Entry Life Structure in the next period.

The Early Adult Transition began at 17 for half the career women, at 18 for the others. Its onset coincided roughly with the move to college. Several women who had strongly dependent ties to their family of origin started the period only after completing part or all of the freshman year. A few others began the Early Adult Transition during the senior year of high school as they chose a distant college and planned their escape from the parental home.

✒ DEBRA ROSE

You had to get your driver's license, had to learn to play bridge, and buy yourself some clothes so you could go off to college and get a man. Going to college wasn't leading anywhere. It was just something you did to become an educated adult. It was not anticipated that you would use your education to earn a living. You were supposed to use it to be an interesting wife and raise your children and have a certain kind of home life. You should get a teaching certificate so you could earn a living if you had to because of catastrophe, like you didn't get married or you got divorced or your husband died. Having a career was not viewed as positive then.

Entering College

As we have seen in Chapter 10, the senior year of high school was a time of *combined departure and arrival.* The girls were aware that graduation would bring a departure from their childhood world. Most of them experienced the impending departure as a blessing—a welcomed opportunity to leave a difficult family situation and/or a relatively unsatisfying high school life. At the same time, the girls were imagining their arrival at college—a promising new world that would offer increased freedom and an opportunity to be oneself. But the young women had only the vaguest idea of what this world was like and how one might live within it. Only a quarter of them had a fairly positive experience of college life during their freshman year.

JULIA HART

Going to college was a kind of liberation. It was sort of like getting out of prison in a way. I think it was the first time I was free to be myself and not have to be what anybody else wanted me to be or to be used as my mother's handmaiden. Now I could really do what *I* wanted. I think what I wanted at the time was a chance to find out what I could be. I don't think I had anything concrete in mind, but I wanted to be able to dictate to some extent the total events of my life and not be constrained. I had a feeling that this was a chance to show what I could do. I was determined to do well, and I did. It was like wiping the slate clean and starting over. As a child I had a passionate interest in dancing. It's a very powerful experience for me that evokes a broad range of feelings. But my father would not allow it. In college I had an image of teaching dance. I knew it was too late to become a dancer, but it would be pleasing to be able to teach it. The college experience was broadening and constricting at the same time, though. The broadening was that I was really on my own at last. But it was constricting as well because it was an all-girls school in an isolated area.

HELEN KAPLAN

I chose a wonderful college. I got more socially and politically liberal and had great friendships. My parents wanted me to be a good student but never had any vocational aspirations for me. They just thought I'd marry some nice professional man like my father and live in the suburbs. My mother was happy if I had the right boyfriend and wore the right clothes. My father was happy if I was a good student and enjoying myself. I kind of felt that I was making everyone *else* happy—that that was my task in life—but I don't remember having very strong feelings about any of it myself. In college no one pressured me to decide on an occupation or major, so I was free to wander around in various departments and see what I wanted. I made the dean's list and developed a lot intellectually. I worked with some wonderful faculty members on their projects. But I never thought about going to graduate school and had little imagination about what I could do after college. Wanting a career was considered "ambitious" for a woman at that time. I didn't want to be just a housewife, but I didn't confront the dilemma. It took a few years after college, and a lot of moral support, for me to seriously consider graduate school.

Three quarters of the young women experienced a "transition shock" occasioned by the actual shift from the world of their origins into the college world. The process of combined departure and arrival continued in a new way. The work of departure from childhood went on throughout the freshman year. With few exceptions, the young woman experienced the satisfaction of being more distant from family but also found it unexpectedly difficult to disengage. The parents usually encouraged participation in family life; in addition, she often missed the benefits of the earlier home base and sought to remain connected to it.

It took time, too, to depart from high school, peer group, and community. Some college freshmen recalled high school with surprising fondness. Though often stressful or boring, it had provided great rewards for rather effortless achievement—in sharp contrast to college. The young women were also terminating relationships with significant friends and groups that, for various reasons, could no longer be a part of their lives.

The arrival at college brought its own complexities. Each young woman had a residence, ordinarily in a college dormitory, but it was only in the most limited sense a home base. The process of forming one's own home base went on throughout the college years. It was only after graduation that the young woman had the sense of creating a true home base of her own, apart from the parental home. To some extent she lived in a kind of limbo between college residence and parental home; each served certain functions, but neither offered sufficient support in her journey toward adulthood.

The college was a strange new world full of opportunities and dangers. It offered much but was often demanding, lonely, and alien. In high school the young women had imagined college as a wonderful alternative to their current lives, but it turned out for most to be in many ways worse. In college the high school "small pond" became a turbulent, unfathomable ocean, populated by diverse species of larger fish, many of whom seemed indifferent, unfriendly, predatory. Most newcomers experienced themselves as "different" and "out of place" without realizing how widespread these feelings were.

✌§   JESSICA HALL

My parents didn't know any college-educated people, didn't know one college from another. On the advice of my adviser I picked the choicest school where people went from my region. It was full of social butterflies—the opposite of what I was. You *had* to be in a sorority, and you had to have references to get in. But my mother didn't know any women who could give me some. I was scared shitless and could barely utter a peep and was not exactly the most desirable candidate. I did get in, thank God—I would have died if I hadn't. It was a lower echelon sorority, of course. My first roommate was from a very wealthy family. Every night she and her sorority friends would come into my bedroom and slash apart other people whom they perceived to be lesser, including all of my friends. It was ugly, terribly cruel. I was miserable. The second year I got a room of my own.

✌§   RACHEL NASH

College was a disaster. There were 3,000 students on the campus, and life was pretty rugged. You were basically on your own. The dorms were impersonal. It was difficult to make friends, I had few dates, and I was very lonely. There were lots of pregnancies, lots of abortions, and lots of drinking. At least half the girls I knew dropped out and never finished college. It was brutal, the anonymity and the fact that nobody cared what happened to you.

In most courses I got A's without putting too much thought into it. But the pressures of being a woman were strong. If I had been a genius they would have recognized me and encouraged me—there's really no discrimination against geniuses. The difference comes at the second level, where the men get pushed ahead. It was assumed that the boys could do better. I was ignored and not considered to be important. My relationship to my work was very equivocal, too. I wasn't really sure what I was doing or what I wanted to do. The teaching was atrocious. There was no one who took me seriously. So I was nowhere.

But there is something in me that keeps me going; it never dawned on me to drop out. Something kept me going, fighting negatively rather than positively. I knew what I didn't want: I was *not* going to be like my mother.

✌§   GRACE TOBIN

Entering college was a trauma. I was certainly not prepared to confront a lot of things that happened there. I wasn't up to the level of academic work and just barely got through. It was a very isolated campus. There weren't any women I could identify with. There was a strong pressure to lose your virginity as soon as you got to college. A lot of girls got really upset when they realized that there was no feeling involved from the guys. Young women all around me were falling apart. Almost 50 percent left and didn't finish. Everyone was living on Valium. My roommate got pregnant and left junior year. My first sexual experience was a one-evening thing with an alumnus who was back for one of the games. I explained to him that I wasn't very experienced, and he was very kind. I never saw him again. I was miserable the whole time there—I just wanted to graduate and get out.

The Internal Traditional Homemaker Figure and the Internal Anti-Traditional Figure

The meanings of gender played a key part in each young woman's Early Adult Transition. As we have seen in Chapter 10, the internal Traditional Homemaker Figure and the internal Anti-Traditional Figure were emerging in adolescence. These images became more articulated in the Early Adult Transition, and the conflict between them played a major part in the young woman's academic and social life during the college years. The Traditional Homemaker was usually predominant and more directly represented in awareness, but the Anti-Traditional Figure often influenced the young woman's plans and choices.

The Traditional Homemaker Figure had some clear-cut values and goals. She wanted to be a good student, but not too good a student. She sought to impress men with her attractiveness and general intelligence, but not to compete directly with men. She made strong (though usually implicit) distinctions between the traditional masculine and the traditional feminine, choosing the feminine and avoiding the masculine whenever possible. She hoped to be engaged or married by the end of college to a man of similar education and social class who would be a good partner in a Traditional Marriage Enterprise. She was not interested in high occupational achievements or a demanding career.

The Anti-Traditional Figure, in contrast, wanted to develop her own independence. She bridled at the thought of being controlled or taken for granted by a man. She sought to free herself from the traditional feminine/masculine divisions, be they in college major, occupation, family, or lifestyle. It was important to be feminine in certain basic respects, but not excessively so. She wanted to marry and have children, but not within the framework of a Traditional Marriage Enterprise. She knew what she wanted *not* to do but found it more difficult to determine what to do in a more positive sense, and there were few alternative models available to her. One compromise was a modified Traditional Marriage Enterprise. The young women who chose this route were by no means rebels who sought to overthrow or drastically change the traditional gender system. Each young woman wanted to become an independent, resourceful person who had an interesting life. She was prepared to accept the basic homemaker/provisioner split and to stay home when the children were small. More than half of the career women began forming an *Anti-Traditional Dream* during the Early Adult Transition. This was not an occupational dream for most. The young woman hoped to have some occupational skills but not a demanding, long-term career. She hoped to live on terms of greater equality with men, in work as well as family. She would, in short, be a homemaker with many "modern" advantages.

Although the Anti-Traditional Figure was seeking a reform of the existing gender system rather than a revolution, she nonetheless coexisted in basic conflict with the Traditional Homemaker Figure. Like Virginia Woolf's Angel and Writer, they were engaged in a struggle to the death. From the Traditional Homemaker Figure's point of view, the Anti-Traditional Figure represented a fundamental challenge to the Traditional Marriage Enterprise. The Anti-Traditional Figure wanted to form personal qualities—such as initiative, responsibility, ability to engage in a nonfemale occupation—traditionally regarded as masculine. To develop in this direction was to violate the basic rules of gender splitting and to stray into the masculine domain. The Traditional Homemaker Figure reminded the young woman that the world has its ways of punishing those who "try for too much." The path she sought would jeopardize the traditional order and undermine the security of all women within it. She would be in danger of being destroyed by men (and women), of losing the feminine satisfactions of motherhood and family life. The conflicts between these internal figures generated new opportunities and problems in successive developmental periods as the career women attempted to have more equal relationships with men, a caring family life, and a satisfying career.

Forming the Anti-Traditional Figure and the Anti-Traditional Dream was a first step in moving away from the traditional ideal—but only a first step. While defining what they did *not* want, these young women did little to define a "new woman" with new goals and relationships, liberated from the old constraints of gender. Moreover, society provided a scarcity of images, role models, and concrete options that might guide their quest. The young woman had many unanswered questions: What kind of marital relationship and marriage enterprise do I want (if any)? What occupation do I prefer? What are my long-term goals? How will I balance my involvements in family and work?

Most young adults have trouble focusing on these questions, let alone answering them. The women in the homemaker sample generally managed to avoid or minimize the questioning by keeping the internal Traditional Homemaker Figure predominant. For the career-oriented women, the questions were problematic from adolescence on. What distinguishes these women is not that they had difficulty with the questions, but that they persisted in the struggle to find new answers to the questions and to deal with the opposing internal figures in their effort to seek fuller lives more on their own terms.

The College as an Academic/Social World

In high school most of the young women had been academic stars. Each girl had assumed that, although college would be more difficult, she would work harder and thus continue to excel. Being a highly intelligent, achieving student had been the foundation of her adolescent identity, her self-esteem, and her hopes for a good life as an adult. It had made her feel "special" in the eyes of important adults (notably parents and teachers). It had also provided a basic sense of competence, an assurance that she could attain whatever goals she might choose to pursue in adulthood. The problem of *choice* — of deciding more specifically what she wanted and how she would live — lay vaguely in the future.

In college this assumption of omnipotence came into question. The change was triggered in part by the young woman's academic performance, which was often variable and below her expectations. For the first time, some got grades lower than A or B. After being big fish in high school, they now felt like little minnows or, even worse, like "a fish out of water."

For the first time the young women had to make major choices and to clarify their priorities. Perhaps the most important problem academically was to choose a major field of study, which was closely tied to the question of future adult occupation. Most went through a series of two or three or more tentative choices of major before settling on one. Choosing a major was difficult primarily because it required self-exploration. It was necessary to sort out and clarify one's abilities, which were reflected in the effort required and the grades received in various courses. It was also necessary, but more difficult, to clarify one's interests: What subjects do I most enjoy learning about? What fields are especially important or valuable to me? Although many asked these questions, very few arrived at clear-cut answers. Most discovered that they had no special interests. Several fields were "interesting" in a general sense, but none excited an intense or passionate involvement, a feeling that "this is what I really want; this is right for me."

The choice of major was strongly influenced by the *masculine/feminine split*. In choosing a college major (and a potential adult occupation), most of the career women carefully avoided narrowly "feminine" fields such as education, nursing, social work, and the like. At the same time, most could not bring themselves to enter strongly "masculine" fields such as the natural sciences, business administration, medicine, and law. It was clear, even in the women's colleges, that literature and art history were female-appropriate majors, whereas economics was seen as marginal, and science was an option only for the foolhardy. The women in co-ed colleges had qualms about majoring in a field with only a few other women. They regarded the women who took such majors as "unattractive" and "not very feminine."

Majoring in a predominantly male field carried a further danger for the young women: it placed them in direct competition with men. Even for those who had earlier missed the message, it became quite clear in college that a woman could be too smart for her own good. A certain degree of success was all right, but a woman who outdid most men at their own game ran the risk of being seen as unfeminine, of being rejected as a woman, and of being seriously hurt in the competitive struggle. It was the esteem of men that the young women sought most. The "attractiveness-intelligence" dilemma came into play here. They wanted men to find them attractive and worthy of respect as knowledgeable, interesting persons. They resented it if a man did not take them seriously. Yet they often hid their talents and skills out of a fear of being seen as too smart or too accomplished. Chapter 10 gave Molly Berger's experience of this dilemma in high school. Here is her account of the college experience.

◆§   MOLLY BERGER

In college I led a double life. During the week I would go to classes and concentrate on my work. I'd be friendly with the more intellectual students who were unacceptable to the sorority and fraternity people I hung around with on weekends. The more intellectual men were my buddies; even if I was interested in dating them, I didn't. I would quietly do my work and try to get A's, but it was a real conflict, a high-anxiety situation. I figured that if I was too smart the men wouldn't like me or date me, so I just played dumb. The sorority women who seemed to be successful with men didn't work hard. I knew that the main objective of going to college was to get engaged; in my sorority, only two of us were not engaged at our final senior dinner.

I can picture myself walking down the campus around the fraternity area. I didn't comment on things I knew about. I didn't want to be conspicuous for my brains or my assertiveness. I couldn't stand being the only woman in the economics class I took in my junior year. In my senior year I thought of going to business school at Harvard or Wharton but, my God, I didn't want to be one of the few women with all those men.

❧   ELLEN NAGY

My major was a purely vocational choice. My parents' message was: once you are in a good college just be socially acceptable. I realized that my parents didn't care about what grades I got, and the only person who was disappointed in me was me. I did as well as I could, which was fairly well. I commonly lied to the men I went out with about my grades; I told them I was doing terribly. But the men I spent the most time with valued women who were more intelligent. I experienced it as a split in my personality—to be intelligent or to be attractive. It took quite a few years for these two personalities to fuse, the smart one and the attractive one.

In choosing a major, most of the thirty career women selected a field that represented a middle or neutral ground between the traditional feminine and masculine extremes. Only a few majored in traditionally female fields such as home economics and education. Over half of the young women majored in the social sciences, arts, or humanities. A quarter chose more "masculine" fields such as economics or business administration, but most saw their major as academically interesting rather than as preparation for a professional career.

❧   JESSICA HALL

In my sophomore year I started thinking seriously about what I wanted to do after college and what I should major in but had no idea of what I wanted to do. I really didn't want a career and kept hoping to get engaged, but it didn't happen. My family kept telling me I had to be able to do some kind of work after graduation. They thought I should become a teacher, but I knew I didn't want that. I was miserable. I kept saying, "What do I want to do? What do I want to do?" I really liked economics and should have majored in that, but it seemed less appropriate for a woman, and there was no one to advise me.

❧   KIM PRICE

At first I thought of becoming a teacher, but when I took a few courses in education I realized that I'd die of boredom. Three quarters of the students who came out of that women's college were teachers. I was a great student and valedictorian at my small high school but fell flat on my face my first year in college. I was devastated but got through. In my sophomore year I took an anthropology course, and that was it: I had a major in a much smaller pond that fascinated me. I still struggled, but I started picking up right away. The head of the department was a very stern woman but very bright. We had a good student-teacher relationship; it wasn't very personal, but she gave me a lot of guidance and encouragement.

Most freshmen had a difficult time in the social world of the college. Things improved in the second or third year as they made a place for themselves either in the mainstream or in a subgroup of like-minded peers. Most now look back on the college years as a time of more sociability, friendship, and fun than any other time in their lives. Their social world was populated mainly by other young women, and their personal relationships were almost entirely with young women. Yet, despite the abundance of casual friendly relationships, there was a dearth of more enduring, intimate friendships. About a quarter of the career sample spoke with great pleasure and nostalgia of such friendships, but the rest commented sadly about the lack of significant friendships.

✎ϩ   GRACE TOBIN

I had a group of six or seven girlfriends, and we were rather close. But after graduation we just went our separate ways. I very often regret that I've never really established deep or long-term friendships with women. This whole question of friendships interests me. One or two of my friends from college are important to me; they still play an important role in my mind even though I haven't seen them since graduation.

The relative absence of men in the career women's lives is not surprising for those in women's colleges. Men were more available to the women in co-ed colleges, but they got together chiefly in collective situations such as a dance, informal dorm party, formal date, classroom.

Some women spoke of a close, nonromantic friendship with a young man. This friendship had a "special" quality for the young woman. The two liked each other and felt very comfortable in a relationship not burdened by sexual tensions. They engaged in casual leisure activities and were free to discuss their more complicated relationships with others. Both enjoyed a moderately personal relationship based on mutual regard, without strong feelings, obligations, and demands.

✎ϩ   ABBY MURPHY

The relationship I liked best was with Charles. We saw each other a lot, all through college, but he was not my boyfriend. He was always around if I needed someone to go out with, and I didn't have to worry about sex with him. We'd talk about the girls he dated, or about my dates or my home or sorority. He was a good listener.

Relationships with Teachers: Mentoring and the Dream

The largest number of adults in the students' world were faculty members. One might suppose that the faculty would not only teach the young women in courses but would enter their personal lives in significant ways. Not so. With few exceptions, the teachers played a remarkably limited part in these life stories. Some women made no reference to individual faculty members, but it was clear from their accounts that the faculty remained a distant, shadowy group in the experienced reality of college life. Others stated explicitly that they had very little contact and no significant relationships with individual professors.

✑ STACEY LANE

My first exposure to women role models at my Seven Sisters college was two professional women, but they had limitations in terms of being role models for me because they were single. I don't think I had any female teacher who was married with children.

✑ PAM KENNEY

I had a lot of trouble deciding about a major and no idea what I would do after graduation. I had an adviser who was sort of there, in his office. If I ever wanted to ask his advice I could, but I never particularly did. There were lots of women teaching the lower level courses, but men were the full professors. I was not exposed to any female role models at all. The general feeling was that you got out of college and got married and raised a family.

Some career women mentioned an incident in which a faculty member gave special encouragement, offered advice about graduate school, or recommended them for an award. Only a few, however, described a relationship of some duration and personal significance.

✑ TRISHA WALL

In college I majored in education. I had a couple of women teachers who were models for a well-rounded life: they worked and had families and were active in their communities. But neither had a real career. They were like family to me. They told me what would be best for me after college: teach high school for a few years, then get a master's degree out of state so I could come back and teach there. I did what they suggested. I didn't think about any other field, nothing.

⌁ EVA PITCHER

I don't think I ever had anybody who stood over me and was very influential. I have never had many friends, mainly acquaintances. I did have a series of people in college and after who were very supportive and encouraging—but no personal relationship. I never liked the word "mentor." In college there was a young male faculty member who had to keep his distance from the female students but also encourage them. He'd write nice comments on my exams and tell me I should think about going to graduate school. A few others encouraged me in the same way, and they certainly influenced my decision to attend graduate school.

These relationships provided benefits that most of the other students received from no one. The helpful teachers gave support, advice, and sponsorship for graduate or professional school. Some of the good female teachers were "like family": maternal figures who were caring but not emotionally imposing. Other female faculty and the male faculty were helpful in other ways. Each relationship served a few mentorial functions, enabling the student to realize specific goals, to feel appreciated, to cope with stressful situations. However, very few served the most crucial function of a mentorial relationship, namely, the development and articulation of the young woman's Dream.

In its primordial form, a Dream is a vague sense of self-in-world, an imagined possibility of one's adult life that generates excitement and vitality. Though its origins are in childhood, it is a distinctively adult phenomenon: it takes clearer shape and is gradually integrated within (or, often, excluded from) the adult life structure over the course of early adulthood. A Dream formed by the internal Traditional Homemaker Figure is likely to portray the woman in a Traditional Marriage Enterprise as a nurturing mother and/or someone supporting her husband's achievements. The internal Anti-Traditional Figure, in contrast, is more likely to form an Anti-Traditional Dream of living in independence and equality, perhaps engaged in both work and family.

A life based upon a Dream has a special, vital quality; any other is at best a compromise and at worst a defeat. A Dream that does not develop, or that has no place in one's life, may simply die. In some cases the Dream is pursued through early adulthood and then modified or given up in the forties. Pursuing a Dream is risky, since the outcome may be grievously disappointing, but life without it is less intense and exciting.

A major task of the Early Adult Transition is to begin crystallizing a Dream and forming a life structure around it. Unfortunately, the obstacles are usually formidable and the sources of support limited. In the simplest (though not most frequent) case, a Dream evolves and is articulated into specific, consciously planned goals. To achieve the goals is to realize the Dream. Some persons, however, pursue goals that do not stem from the private Dream. A young woman may have a clear Dream yet renounce it, temporarily or permanently, in order to pursue other, more pragmatic goals favored by her family and social world. She may have an inchoate Dream yet be unable, for various reasons, to give it conscious meaning and to translate it into concrete goals. She may never have felt free to ask, "What do I really want for myself?" A person cannot afford the luxury of a Dream if she is totally occupied with survival in a barren environment or with conformity to a life scenario that leaves no room for personal choice—a widespread experience of young women.

A full, complex, mentorial relationship supports the evolution of the Dream. A true mentor fosters the young adult's development by nourishing the youthful Dream and giving it her or his blessing, believing in the young woman, helping her to define her newly emerging adult self in its newly discovered adult world, and creating a space in which she can move toward a reasonably satisfactory life structure that contains the Dream.

Mentoring cannot be understood in purely individual terms, as the activity of a single person. It is a relationship which the two participants conjointly initiate, form, sustain, exploit, benefit and suffer from, and, ultimately, terminate. The nouns "mentor" and "mentee" identify the participants. But the verb "to mentor" is essential in identifying the drama they are engaged in. The essence of the drama is the evolution of the mentorial relationship. The relationship is fostered and hindered in various ways by both parties; it is significantly colored by the social context in which it occurs. The relationships between the young women and their special teachers can usefully be examined from the perspective of mentoring and the Dream.

✌§   KIM PRICE

During the college years Kim Price had a powerful though barely articulated Dream: to move out of the world of her origins and become a respected member of a more educated, affluent world. How she would live in this world was still a mystery. Education was the key. Her Dream, still quite vague, was to enter the educated middle class on terms of personal dignity and equality. Her relationship with a professor stimulated her academic involvement and achievement, provided student jobs, and supported her flagging self-esteem. The relationship helped much less in developing her Dream. At the end of college she sought a job in the business world but had no sense of career direction. Although the relationship with this teacher supported Kim's entrance into the job market, it apparently did not help her to imagine and then plan an exciting adult life. We do not know enough to identify the major obstacles involved. Presumably they lay partly in the teacher's limitations as a mentor, partly in Kim's inner difficulties in forming a mentorial relationship of greater intensity and in pursuing a Dream, and partly in the state of society, which made it hard for any young woman, especially an African-American woman, to form and live out an occupational Dream.

Debra Rose was the only career woman who had an articulated occupational Dream in the Early Adult Transition.

✐   DEBRA ROSE

I always wanted to do something special with my life. I had a sense of destiny since I was very young. I had a sense that I was going to do something special, that I was not going to lead an ordinary life and be an ordinary housewife. I felt I was going to be a painter. My husband was very unhappy with that activity; he definitely did not like the idea of my becoming an artist and staying home and painting because I got moody and depressed; I don't think that was an unreasonable action on his part. Painting was something that took me away from my husband. If I had become an artist I wouldn't have stayed married to my husband. It would have been going away from my parents. It would have been a different life. I want to be free, but freedom is dangerous; I do not want to be alone.

For a long time as I went through life I had the idea that ultimately I was still going to become an artist, but I think it was too difficult for me to choose that path. I don't think I was willing to face the consequences of becoming an artist. It would have been upsetting to my family, my parents, my husband. I think it's connected to the struggle that I've always felt that I wanted to be free and independent. I think the occupation I chose as an adult kept me in society and in the family, whereas if I had become an artist I would have devoted much more of my life to myself. I've always been responsible. I felt it was too selfish to be able to do what I wanted to do.

✐   TRISHA WALL

Being a good student was Trisha Wall's primary source of self-esteem, and being financially self-sufficient through work was the essential groundwork of her planned life as an adult. During college, with the help of her major professors, she planned to become a teacher. Within the narrow confines of her childhood and college worlds, this occupation made perfect sense. It was secure work for which she had high aptitude. It would enable her to get a job right after graduation and thus to make a quick getaway from her father's enveloping neediness. It was acceptable to both the internal Traditional Homemaker Figure and the internal Anti-Traditional Figure within herself. Her occupational plan unfolded with a kind of inevitability over the college years. It was jointly created by the eager student and her beneficent teachers.

Only later, in the Age 30 Transition, did Trisha realize that "nobody ever told me about possibilities for a real career connected to my special artistic interest." The biggest problem was not that no one told her about *external* possibilities. It was, rather, that no one asked her about *inner* possibilities— about her private interests, fantasies, preferences. And Trisha could not ask herself, could not listen to the timid inner voice that wanted to tell her about artistic rather than purely practical interests. The college student could barely hear that voice. The teachers had no inkling of it and perhaps took for granted that they knew what was best for Trisha. And their social-institutional world placed no value on the secret work aspirations of its young women. Had she come to hear and at least partially embrace that inner voice, she might have been more able to explore the occupational options through which her interest could be lived out. As it was, the seeds of a Dream lay dormant throughout a developmental period in which, with a little nurture, Dreams may blossom.

During the Early Adult Transition, only a few women had mentorial relationships that contributed more directly to the formation of occupational goals. These women were among those who became faculty members, not businesswomen, and the mentoring relationships occurred in graduate school, not college.

Relationships with Parents

During the Early Adult Transition all thirty career women went through some degree of psychological separation from parents. The young women were trying to establish a center for a new adult life. At the same time, the parental residence was still in a basic sense "home"—the one place to which they could return if all else failed. In many ways, they still felt like little girls in relation to powerful parents. They continued to experience their parents as important sources of emotional nurture and moral authority, even as they strove to gain greater emotional independence.

By the end of the Early Adult Transition, most career women were starting to form a new home base. It was important and satisfying to be on their own—yet the parental residence remained their symbolic home base for some years longer. Not until the Age 30 Transition, or later, did the career women struggle in a more conscious way to get beyond the inner sense of being the "good little girl" in relation to parents whom they endowed with powers of authority, benevolence, and malevolence. While seeking greater psychological (as well as social and geographical) distance from parents in the Early Adult Transition, they also sought to maintain emotional ties and to avoid any actions that might rupture the relationship. They struggled to become more separate and to remain attached.

Love/Marriage/Family

In the Early Adult Transition each young woman began to experience herself more as an adult in her relationships with men. The key questions were: What do I want with men now, and in the future, with regard to sexuality, intimacy, friendship, work, marriage, family? The internal Traditional Home-maker Figure and the internal Anti-Traditional Figure took strong yet contradictory positions on these questions. The actual choices made by each young woman were sometimes closer to one extreme, sometimes the other, and they evolved over the college years. In their choice of boyfriends the young women were increasingly put off by young men who were highly "macho" or who made strong sexual or emotional demands. The young women did not want to be seen as dependent or as sex objects subject to male control, and these feelings were evident in their relationships with men.

Fourteen career women married in the Early Adult Transition, eleven from the faculty sample. Almost all of them married within a year before or after graduating from college. Twelve of these women completed college and went on to a job or graduate school, and the marriage was often in the service of the internal Anti-Traditional Figure. None had a child before age 25. The other two women became mothers as their Early Adult Transitions ended: Stacey Lane at 23, at the start of graduate school; and Holly Crane at 21, just after college graduation. Both of the mothers then formed an Entry Life Structure in which homemaking was the central component.

Love/Marriage/Family: Businesswomen

During the college years all but a few businesswomen wanted to marry and have a family. The internal Anti-Traditional Figure reminded them in the strongest terms, however, of the dangers of premature marriage and motherhood. The safest course, she advised, was to complete college and then spend several years proving oneself in work or graduate studies before starting a family: "Through work you will develop the ability to take care of yourself as an independent, competent adult. You can then have children with less risk of being consumed by domesticity. It is all right to marry earlier, provided you find a husband who—unlike most men—will give you space to work and become independent before having children."

✍ JULIA HART

In those days most women had the idea of getting married. I just wanted something to do in the interim that wouldn't be a chore. Having an occupation or career really didn't mean much to me then. I wanted to get married and have children, but I wasn't overly optimistic about my chances of getting married, that I'd meet someone whom I'd want to marry who would want to marry me. For some reason I never found any of the men I met particularly interesting. I kept thinking, "Is this all there is available?" A lot of my classmates were "rock gatherers": They'd rush out and get engaged and flash their diamond rings. I had sort of contempt for them, for the fact that they were so keen on getting married that they'd do it at any cost.

I wanted to find a different kind of man. Somebody who would have some respect for my innate capabilities and treat me like an equal. He'd be fairly well directed and motivated, a doctor or lawyer. I wasn't too specific. But we were not going to make the mistakes our parents had. I thought about what we *wouldn't* do as opposed to what we would do. We would bring up children differently than our parents had. Less pressure on academic accomplishment and more on allowing the child to develop at his or her own pace. And certainly a much better relationship between mother and father: more talking, more sharing, less fighting. But I didn't find that kind of man in college.

✍ ABBY MURPHY

I had two serious dating relationships in college. I went with Dennis for most of my freshman year. It was mainly social dating; I liked having someone around so that I could go out like the other girls and not be alone. Looking back, I don't think I was ready to really get to know someone. I had strong sexual feelings toward him but they scared me. I was a good Catholic girl. If you had sex before marriage you were a bad girl. Even limited sex was frightening because there was the danger of loss of control. I was afraid of the demands of someone who would want sex. With my parents I felt that I gave so much and got so little in return. If I actually got something out of the relationship, what would the other person want from me? But with Dennis I could set limits—just petting. The thing he really did to end it was want to get married. When he proposed, I said *no*. That was it; I cut it right off, never saw him again.

I always felt I'd get married someday, but it was not my first priority.

The main thing was to get through college and work awhile. I couldn't even get on the wavelength of marriage. Being in love with someone was not the big issue. I just wasn't ready for a permanent commitment. I didn't want to be like most women I knew: a weak pretty thing who goes with the tide. That doesn't fit my image of myself. Through my relationship with my father, I suppose, I see myself more as a man: strong and purposeful; someone who has to do what she has to do. I really didn't like women very much for many years.

All through my junior year I was pinned to Kevin, a good-looking graduate student. I liked having a date every weekend. We did some heavy petting, but I was still afraid of sex and pregnancy. We didn't really talk—all those relationships were pretty superficial. But then Kevin got very possessive and wanted my total attention. I went out once with another guy, and Kevin got furious. I couldn't understand that, and I certainly wouldn't tolerate it, so I just quit seeing Kevin.

Birth control was not readily available to this generation of young women. Of the twelve businesswomen who did not marry in the Early Adult Transition, only Amy York and Melissa Howard had sexual intercourse during this period. For both, the sex was not part of an intimate love relationship. It represented, rather, a futile effort to overcome the rigid emotional-social barriers that separated females from males. In some elemental way, each young woman was trying to form a relationship in which she could give more of herself and receive more from the other. The relationships in which sex occurred were not better than those without sex. (This phenomenon may be more common today, when premarital sex in the Early Adult Transition is more widespread but often not part of a more intimate relationship.)

AMY YORK

I basically hate thinking about the college years. I had no sense of what I wanted as an adult. I knew I didn't want to be married and have children. I wasn't into studying and skipped classes a lot. I made some friends but always felt outside of the group. I made two girlfriends, boozing buddies. We would hang out and drink and smoke grass. In those days I'd never talk about myself to anyone because I didn't know much about myself. It never occurred to me to discuss how I *felt* about anything.

I wanted a boyfriend but didn't know how to go about getting one. I thought maybe if I went to bed with them then a relationship might follow. I decided to lose my virginity and hopefully gain a friend at the same time. I went out with a virtual stranger and went to bed with him. It was really awful. He just climbed on top and pumped away. I had a lot of one-night stands like that.

I don't want to discuss it further because I just want to forget it, but I was raped walking home late one night. He came out of nowhere. I was so terrified I didn't know what to do. It was horrible. I don't want to discuss it further because I just want to forget about it. But getting raped taught me one thing: to fight back. It was one of the major decision points of my life. I would fight to the death if I had to, but nobody was ever going to get the better of me again.

◄§   MELISSA HOWARD

I didn't date much until senior year. Four of us shared an apartment. I wasn't dating much, but then I had sex with the guy upstairs. I wouldn't say the first sexual experience was bad; it was just stupid. We had spent most of the year exploring the petting scene. I'd been raised Catholic, and everything was no, no, no. So we were petting, and we really got down to it, and he said, "You just can't stop now." I said okay, but I wasn't going to help it along. It hurt like hell and was very unpleasant. I just went downstairs and never talked to him again. So I had lost the dreaded or heavenly thing virginity without having any of the great excitement. I just said, "Oh, well, I got rid of the damn thing." To be 21 was pretty old to be a virgin. But I think you do wish for a bit more. I said, "Is that all there is?" It was years after that before I really cared much about sex, and I've never been orgasmic.

Three businesswomen married in the Early Adult Transition. For all three young women, the marriage was in the service of the wish to become independent of parents and defer parenthood. The young women consciously chose men who supported their wish for autonomy and agreed not to have children until later.

◄§   DEBRA ROSE

I met my husband at the beginning of my freshman year of college. We married when I was 20. I think I had just reached that stage in life where I was ready to meet someone, to fall in love, have romantic connections and sex. It was just a question of finding someone my age and my general socio-economic position.

Wallace has a lot of very special qualities, and there was certainly every reason for me to fall in love with him and marry him. He was exactly the kind of young man who fit into what my parents' ideas were about who I should marry. It wasn't a terribly exciting romance, but it was fine. We didn't have a sexual relationship until after we were married.

The marriage was never very good for me sexually. I have always had strong sexual feelings but rarely had an orgasm. I remember on my wedding night, getting undressed and having this feeling of total panic. "What am I doing in a hotel room with a stranger? I married this man, and I don't even know him!" Which was true.

The marriage has always lacked passion on my part. I have never been fulfilled in my marriage. I have a collection of personal needs that I don't think my husband is capable of meeting or maybe I'm not willing to let him try. There is definitely a holding back on my part as well as lack of sensitivity and interest on his part.

Being married at that age in my generation was really very liberating. Getting married was a way to get out from under your parents, your dorm and do what you wanted to do. The thing I value most in life is independence. I was not looking for a man who was going to be my boss. I was looking for equality.

⋘ ELLEN NAGY

During my sophomore year I would have said that I was not going to marry for quite a while. I was going to get the career stuff settled. I wanted more freedom. I did expect fully to get married and have children after a while, but I needed to be somewhat independent first.

I met Carl, my first husband, the summer before my junior year. He was one year older and went to college in another state. We had this lengthy correspondence that got more passionate and more involved over a several-week period. Carl was drawn keenly to me precisely because I was intelligent and had ability. He was the first man I ever met who valued those qualities and who saw a woman not as a possession or a housewife but as a partner. His mother worked, and he wanted a woman who would have a career. I would not get married until I found someone who liked a wife that had a career. I also fell in love with Carl (I behaved irrationally twice in my life, and I married both of them). Carl proposed in the fall of my junior year, when I was 18, and I said yes. I had a very busy senior year at college, very social, and I did well academically. Carl and I spent my senior year, the year before we got married, largely apart; we only saw each other one week at Christmas and one week at Easter.

In June at 20 I graduated and got married. I felt that getting married was not very important. At the same time, it was important to get married so I could go out and have a career. I wasn't conscious of all that, especially the contradiction. I didn't have the internal self-confidence to be on my own, and I didn't have the social self-confidence to believe that there would always be other men out there for me. Sexuality was a real problem. I didn't know what to do with my sexual drive; it was trying to burst out all the time. I thought nice girls don't. Also, I was afraid of getting pregnant. So I did the obvious thing: I got married.

In looking for a marriage partner, I was companionship-oriented and willing to scrap a lot of other things for a person who would be a good friend, which Carl clearly was. What I left out in that rational equation was sex. Ultimately that was a pretty serious mistake because sex never really clicked between us. The whole relationship was founded on companionship. I thought of Carl as protective, strong, and capable. I had found someone, instead of my father, who would look after me, protect me, and let me do my own thing. That's what I needed most at the time.

The sexual part was not overly passionate. If the person you share your life with is a good steady friend and companion, I figured, then sex will work out reasonably well. It's not the most important thing in the world. But sex never did work out reasonably well for us. It was tolerable for a brief time. We had not been totally intimate before marriage, and it was a total disaster when we started. It took a long time to recover from that.

The bondage part of the marriage hit me at the beginning of the ceremony, and I had great difficulty going through with the wedding. I stood there thinking, "My God, what have you done with your life? You're locking yourself up!" And that feeling persisted. I remember waking up the next morning with a sense of emptiness, thinking that my whole life was over. "Well, what do I do now? I'm the good little girl who does all the things I'm supposed to do. I do them better than anybody else and get A's and get married and that's it." Getting married was the pinnacle of success for a woman, but what were you supposed to do after that? I was 20 years old. What was I going to do with the rest of my life? It was obvious that I was going to graduate school and to work. We agreed that we would postpone starting a family for several years while my husband finished medical school. Later when he was established I would work part time while I raised three children.

Even though I'm divorced now I refuse to look at that marriage as a mistake. It helped me get some physical and psychological distance from my family, which enabled me to become more independent. It was very much what I needed at the time, but I grew a great deal, and Carl grew in another direction.

Love/Marriage/Family: Faculty Members

Most faculty women were more "academic" in orientation and values than the businesswomen. Being a good student and having an adult life in an intellectual world became essential aspects of their identity. They felt more at home in the academic environment and received more encouragement from teachers and peers. By the senior year of college they could think seriously about going to graduate school, even though they had little sense of a long-term career.

This strong academic orientation was also reflected in marital choice: almost every faculty woman married a faculty member or a graduate student. Eleven faculty women married in the Early Adult Transition, the rest by 28. The courting and early marital relationship usually had some mentorial qualities: he believed in her potential and helped her form an Entry Life Structure in which education-work was a central component. However, the mentorial aspects created pitfalls as well as strengths. Although the relationship initially nurtured her occupational aspirations, in the long run the inequality was hard to outgrow and became a source of painful tension.

KRISTIN WEST

As I look back on the college years, I was amazingly divided in my plans for work and family. My strongest sense was that I wanted to be free of my family and become as independent as possible.

I met my husband-to-be in my senior year, and right away I told myself, "Jack is someone I can give myself to completely, and he will make something of me." He had graduated four years earlier and was teaching high school while deciding what to do next. He was the first man I had ever talked to who talked back. For some reason I just started talking to him, and we discussed existentialism. A month later he asked me to marry him. Well, he didn't actually ask me to marry him. He said, "You can marry me and become or you can marry someone else and become." He was putting it like I had the potential to become *his* idea of what I should become. I'm so mad about this now, but at the time that idea was attractive to me, just what I wanted to hear. I thought about it and said, "Yes, I really do want this." We got married that summer, as I graduated and turned 22.

Jack was entirely right when he said I could become what he wanted me to become. I had done as much with myself as I knew how to do, and I was looking for someone who could help me do more. I was getting into a more artistic and intellectual world but had no sense of direction. No woman I knew had ever done anything. Jack was offering me something beyond my previous experience—opening up a whole new world for me. My father was the first person in my family to get even a high school education. When I finished college he said, "We're really proud of you, but you're not going to do any more of this education stuff, are you?" I said, "No, of course not." It didn't matter what grades I got; in my parents' view, I was successful when I had dates.

The first thing Jack and I wanted to do was go abroad, discover more of the world, and get more perspective about ourselves. It was a very romantic idea: we would go to France, where I would draw and paint, and Jack would write.

Going abroad was really a big leap for us. We had never thought of it before, and we didn't have any money. So we taught high school for two years, and I got a master's degree in education. I didn't want to be a teacher in the long run, but it was the most remunerative kind of work I could get then. My mother had taught, and she was not what I wanted to be. Teaching was a way to save money for Europe. During the first year [22–23] we worked out our plans and settled into our marriage. We agreed not to have children for several years in order to have this great adventure.

I wasn't in love with Jack until we decided to go to Europe, and then I was definitely in love with him. I put myself entirely in his control, I wanted to behave the way he wanted; I wanted him to be pleased with me. Here's an example: soon after we married I spent a lot of time at a party having a friendly talk with another guy. After the party Jack completely withdrew his affection for three days. I was a complete nervous wreck. I knew I had done something wrong but didn't know what. Finally Jack said that I had spent too much time with this man at the party. The man was a fool, and my talking to a fool was a bad reflection on my husband. Through incidents like that I came not to do anything Jack wouldn't like. Before we married he supported my painting and sculpture, but I gradually cut down because he couldn't stand the mess I made around the apartment.

Since our marriage ended I have thought a lot about what happened in it. The way I see it now is that he was very controlling—but I put myself completely in his control, willingly, stupidly. Actually, it wasn't so stupid because he did direct me to a point so that in my early thirties I was doing what I really wanted to do and starting an academic career. Jack really educated me. He was the first person I had ever known who saw outside the local community. The odd thing is that by now, at 43, I have accomplished much more than he has.

HOLLY CRANE

I went to a co-ed college that had a good dance department. Then I discovered that I couldn't dance; my body just wasn't right for it. That was very hard for me; I was mourning psychologically for my lost dance during my freshman and sophomore years. But I liked school and got hooked on history. That's when I began to feel that there might be something in my head instead of my body, and I got very involved in school.

I'd been very interested in boys and sex since high school. The clear message from my family was that you don't have sex before marriage. It was such a charged area: full of guilt, full of excitement. I petted and kissed and fooled around, but I wouldn't have intercourse. I managed to stay a virgin technically.

The summer after high school graduation I met Eric. He had an apartment, and we had intercourse. The first time was weird. I had thought bells would go off because it was so terrific petting. But intercourse was such a disappointment. I didn't really feel anything, and I certainly didn't have an orgasm. I thought, "Is this all it is?" But I kept thinking this is what you're supposed to do, and maybe it will get better. After having intercourse you can't go back to just petting, so the next four or five guys I went out with before my husband I went to bed with. They were not very good experiences. Sophomore year of college I got pregnant! I wasn't using birth control; somehow I never thought it would happen to me. I had an illegal abortion. It was very painful. I went in alone, came out alone. Then I went back to school. I was so mixed up and unsure at that point.

Then I met Ralph, who was separated from his first wife. He was a professor at the college and a very high status figure. I never took courses with him, but I knew who he was and thought he was wonderful. We had a good sexual relationship. I saw that I could learn a lot from him. It was so ridiculous! Here I had this professional mother, all these models of independent living. Why did I want to get engaged and married my senior year of college? But that's what I did. I felt an urgency to get married. I was looking for a man for some of the things that I'd wanted from my mother. I wanted someone to take care of me. The thought of graduating was very threatening because I didn't know what the hell to do with my life. I knew I didn't want to go to graduate school. I'd tried a stint during summer vacation in publishing to decide if I wanted to do that. But I discovered that in publishing women become secretaries, the men become editors. All I could do with a B.A. in history was become a secretary! It was jolting to me.

At that point my relationship with my mother was very strained, and getting married was a way of getting away from her. I didn't feel I could live by myself at that point. So there were no options other than to get married. I wanted to nail down security, and marriage was a way of doing that. I wanted what my family should have been and wasn't. I would create with Ralph the family I never had. I was coming to the end of my college career and didn't really know what I wanted to do. Ralph was very supportive, and he got me out of a very difficult family situation. So it was like I could attach to this strong academic man and be his good little wife and live in an interesting academic world.

We married during my senior year when I was 21. My father disowned me for marrying a non-Protestant. My mother did not like Ralph at all. When he and my mother were together in a room there was a lot of tension: two narcissists sitting in a room and not liking each other.

Ending the Early Adult Transition: Post-Graduate Paths of the Career Women

The Early Adult Transition usually ended at age 22, occasionally at 21 or 23. It lasted four or five years for the great majority, six years for a few. Graduation from college served as a powerful marker event for the completion of this period, a reminder that life was about to begin in earnest. Most career women needed some additional time, however, before they could conclude the transition and start building an Entry Life Structure. The world of childhood was slipping away, and the world of adulthood lay just beyond the next bend in the road—inevitable, not quite visible, attractive yet frightening. As graduation approached, each young woman was under some external pressure to begin a new life on a more independent basis, outside the parental orbit. She also felt some internal pressure and desire to "grow up," to decide what she wanted with her life and to start living it. At the same time, there were many external and inner pressures to delay her entry into the adult world. She found herself on the threshold of adulthood—yet often separated from it by an "abyss." She was often not clear how to get there from here, or whether it was even possible in her case.

✺ AMY YORK

At graduation I had no idea what I wanted to do. I was kind of surprised that a mantle of adulthood didn't just drop over my shoulders at graduation. I never thought you actually had to work at a lot of things to get to a certain point. No one had ever advised me on anything. I just assumed that there would be a line of college graduates and a line of management representatives who would grab you off the production line. So I sat there. And it didn't happen.

✺ SALLY WOLFORD

At graduation I thought, "What am I supposed to do with my life? Someone tell me what to do!" It was like looking over the edge of a vast precipice. I didn't know where to start. I felt the world was coming to an end because I wasn't getting married like the other girls.

In the senior year of college each young woman was faced increasingly with the question of how to live after graduation. Once again, the voice of the internal Traditional Homemaker Figure relentlessly urged her to marry, start a family, and limit her occupational interests. The internal Anti-Traditional Figure, in contrast, insisted upon deferring family until she became an independent, competent adult. Each young woman worked out her own initial compromise between the two internal figures. There appeared to be a bewildering array of concrete choices. In actuality, the young woman had only a few basic options. Some of these were intolerable to her; others were possible but not unequivocally attractive; and even the one or two options she could consider were not clearly defined in her mind. The conscious sense of confusion often covered a more elemental sense of having no truly satisfactory or viable choices.

Since the external circumstances and internal motivations were so different for the two samples of women, I'll consider them in turn.

Post-College Paths: The Academic Women

Most of the future faculty members had strong intellectual interests and felt at home in the academic world. Some were encouraged by college faculty to go on for higher degrees. Their self-esteem was rooted in the identity of "excellent student." Going to graduate school was the most obvious, attractive, and feasible next step after college, and this was indeed their choice. Most became graduate students without having long-term career goals. Half entered master's degree programs that gave modest training and credentials, while ignoring or leaving open the possibility of continuing for a doctorate. Even those who entered a doctoral program were often uncertain about the desirability and the feasibility of a long-term academic career.

The faculty members usually needed a year or two after college graduation to complete the Early Adult Transition and make the choices around which an Entry Life Structure could be built. They graduated at age 20 to 22 and ended the Early Adult Transition at 22 or 23. During the interim phase they tentatively made and modified major life choices, especially those relating to love/marriage/family, education, and work, and tried to form the basis for a first adult life structure. This was an especially difficult time for many, and for some a *rock bottom time* in which it often seemed impossible to find a satisfactory way to live as an adult.

As the Early Adult Transition ended, eleven of the academic women were married but only two had children. In almost every case the husband was a graduate student or faculty member. There was often a mentorial aspect to their relationship: he was three to fifteen years older, further along occupationally, and supportive of her interests in graduate work and deferment of motherhood. She often experienced him as a "special man" with whom she could have a relationship that would enable her to develop more fully. Many had a sexual relationship before marriage, but the relationship was not very passionate. The qualities of the relationship that seemed most important to the young woman were the mutual appreciation and the vision of a future life in which both could realize their fondest hopes.

In most cases the woman came to realize later that she initially had an idealized view of her husband and of the relationship. His feelings for her were more ambiguous, and in some respects more negative and controlling, than she had recognized. He wanted an interesting, educated, accomplished wife who would have some involvement in intellectual work, but he also assumed that she, rather than himself, would take primary responsibility for the home. They agreed that she would do outside work but colluded in avoiding the question of her "career." Some women were later surprised to learn that their husbands preferred not to have children or would agree to having children only if she would be totally responsible for their care. Ten of the eleven Early Adult Transition marriages ended in divorce, usually at the woman's initiative.

✑ NINA DALTON

In my senior year, turning 22, I applied to all the best graduate schools and was accepted by all. I chose a university, not because it was necessarily the best, but because my boyfriend Jay had decided to go to a school near there. Both of my parents were professionals. I always assumed that I would do as my mother had—find a supportive husband and combine family and career.

My graduate school was highly unstructured, and for the first time I was living by myself in an unsafe neighborhood. I kept having anxiety attacks—it was like the whole environment was closing in on me. At mid-year I left school and returned home to live with my parents. I was depressed and slept all the time; it was a really bad year. My whole idea of what I had wanted to be came crashing in on me. Until then my life had been smooth. I had always been very successful at everything. It was my first run-in with the real world.

That spring I decided to apply to a different graduate school. At about the same time Jay proposed marriage. I didn't feel especially happy about marrying him. Our relationship was not passionate. It certainly wasn't the optimal circumstances under which to make that kind of commitment; it was really a way of being safe again. Marrying Jay seemed like the right thing to do, but it wasn't as joyful as it should have been, and I certainly recognized that at the time. On the day I got married I did not feel especially happy.

We married that summer, when I was 23. We had applied to the same universities, and in the fall we both went to the same one but in different departments. Once again, I made a choice on the basis of *his* preference. That was the beginning of a relatively stable but not exciting time. We had our own separate worlds and friends. We didn't fight, but we didn't have much of a relationship either. Though I enjoyed graduate school and did well enough, I still didn't know where it was leading.

At 23, a year after college graduation, Nina Dalton settled on her initial adult choices and began forming an Entry Life Structure as a married childless graduate student, still unclear about the place of family and career in her future life.

✎§   HELEN KAPLAN

When I was 20, my boyfriend Tim graduated and was going off to the service, so we decided to get married. It was crazy, looking back on it now. I think I felt insecure about his going so far away, and a lot of people were marrying early at that time. I think I was in love with Tim, although I certainly have been much more in love subsequently. We had known each other for so long. It didn't turn out very well. We didn't have a sexual relationship at all premarriage. It was a kind of security relationship above everything else, but it wasn't a passionate physical relationship. It seemed that our lives would fit together very well because we came from the same kind of family, went to the same kind of school. I wasn't questioning too much at that point.

I graduated in January at 21 and joined Tim in the Midwest. I lived on the base there, which was the first time I'd lived by myself. Tim lived at officers' school, and I only saw him once a week. So it wasn't much of a relationship at all at that time. I was not emotionally involved with Tim. It was a very difficult life for me, and I was very lonely. The upperclassmen picked on the lowerclassmen, and the wives mimicked that. We were supposed to be very competitive with each other over who could serve the most elaborate teas. When my husband's group became upperclassmen I invited all the wives together for a tea. I opened a box of Hydrox cookies and said, "I think it's time we changed things around here." It was a real revolution [laughs]!

After a few months we moved to a different base and got an apartment off-base. I decided I was not going to sit there and be a lieutenant's wife. I was not going to serve tea and cookies. I got a job three days a week and took graduate courses two days a week. When I was 22 Tim left the service.

Although I'd been an honor student in college and learned a great deal from some wonderful women teachers, they did not particularly encourage me to have an academic career. I had no career plans and assumed that after working a few years I would settle down and start a family. During that first year after college, however, I learned that life among the housewives was not for me. I still didn't know what I wanted to do, but I got very clear about what I *didn't* want: I would not be an unemployed housewife, nor would I spend my life in a routine, intellectually dead job.

By chance I got a job in an academic department at a nearby university at 22. I went through a tremendous change and got clearer about my life goals. I really loved the work. After a few months I was contributing enough so they made me a co-author of articles. Two of the senior faculty treated me with considerable respect and made me feel I was very promising. They enthusiastically urged me to go to graduate school. The wife of one of them was a graduate student and mother, and her example was a big help. That's when I really decided to establish some kind of career for myself.

I started graduate school at 23, and my husband started graduate school, too. My record was so good that I was offered scholarships at several top schools. In the application process I got a real education in sexism. Several male interviewers interrogated me about my career plans. One professor, politically very liberal, told me what a problem women graduate students were: "They never do what the men do; 75 percent of them don't finish the doctorate, and those that do might as well not have." I said, "I assure you, if I come here I intend to finish." He answered, "That's what they all say." In graduate school one of my advisers told me, "Look, you're married, why don't you go home and have babies?" They thought it was okay for a female to be a good liberal arts student because that would make you a better mother, but this professional stuff didn't make any sense to them.

So age 22–23 was a really important time for me. My first job brought me into an academic world. Some of the senior people there taught me a lot and helped me get a clearer sense of what I wanted. I still wanted a family, but it became essential to try for both family and career, which I have in fact done. When I went to graduate school at 23 I was starting a whole new life.

Helen Kaplan's story reflects several themes of wider importance. Her relationships with the two male faculty members and the wife/mother/graduate student were mentorial in several respects: they provided guidance, moral support, sponsorship, an example of a woman attempting to combine career and family, and a work situation that fostered her intellectual development. Few young career women received mentoring to this degree. At the same time, we should note that these were *partial* mentoring relationships and that certain crucial qualities were minimal or absent. One ingredient missing in Helen's account was love. I am not referring here to sexual love, which I believe is usually more a hindrance than a help in the evolution of a mentoring relationship. I am referring to the personal character of the relationship, the experience of emotional attachment, involvement, identification. The mentors were helpful primarily in an instrumental sense. They did a lot to foster the mentee's interest in and admission to graduate school, but the relationships seem not to have a highly personal quality.

A second missing ingredient has to do with the Dream. Although the mentors helped her in setting occupational goals, they appear not to have helped her in forming a Dream and in giving their blessing—something much more powerful than support—to the pursuit of it. Moreover, her account of applying to graduate school gives clear evidence of the anti-mentorial, sexist qualities of many male faculty members who do not truly welcome a woman as a full participant in the academic world.

Only two faculty members got pregnant during the Early Adult Transition.

HOLLY CRANE

We married during my senior year, when I was 21. I had my first child nine months after we got married. I had wanted a family, but not quite that fast. I was pregnant when I graduated. So I moved right away into a comfortable niche—or I *thought* it was comfortable at the time. I was just wanting to crawl into somebody's arms and have somebody take care of me. I was willing to do whatever a woman was supposed to do to get that. It's pathetic to look back on now. I was a product of my culture; that's what women did when I went to college. All my friends were getting married.

I had three children in four years—21, 24, and 25! I loved being pregnant. The first baby was very responsive, and I really enjoyed nursing her and cuddling her and caring for her. But it was very demanding, very draining. There is no harder job in the world physically than being a mother. It's too many hours of unrelieved time. It's just impossible. And Ralph didn't give me any relief; he just would not help. He distanced himself emotionally. He was never around. He was off giving speeches and writing books. He had a lot of trouble with the baby except as a toy. When it cried he would get angry, and I felt caught in the middle. I didn't know any better. I thought this is what marriage was. It seemed like what most of my friends were doing. I tried very hard during that first year to be a good faculty wife and mother. I had had all these fantasies of being different from my mother—staying home and giving myself full-time to a baby and a house and cooking, and I did that with real gusto.

Ralph was writing his first book that year. I began to read, critique, and rewrite it. An important part of our early marriage was that I in effect was Ralph's research assistant. There was a lot of me in his work. I certainly did a lot of work that would be recognized as co-authoring. I began to feel I had intellectual power which came via Ralph. I was learning intellectually from him as a student does from a teacher, but it never changed and became equal. It was a real exploitation. Graduate students do the same thing and get a Ph.D. for it, but what do wives get? I really feel I got ripped off. I was responsible for getting Ralph's career started, and he has acknowledged that.

Ralph really wanted to leave the college. He was beginning to become very ambitious, and I shared his ambition. A year after we married he got an appointment at another school, so we moved. We had had a nice life at the school. It was a community, and there was an intellectual/cultural life, and I took courses. But I went where my husband went. Leaving was a big transition for me. It was a very different life in a small apartment in a strange city.

Four future faculty members remained single throughout the period of the Early Adult Transition.

GRACE TOBIN

I decided to go to graduate school. I didn't know quite what else to do. I decided on a master's program because I wasn't sure I wanted to do this at all. I never thought I would go all the way for a Ph.D. I knew very few women who went on beyond college. I imagined I would teach at some college, but not as a scholar at the university level. Perhaps a small college. It never occurred to me that I wouldn't work or marry and have a family. I had a lot of friends in college who desperately wanted to get married and start families. I didn't have either of those urges. I assumed that sometime down the road I would find someone I wanted to marry and have some kids.

I got my master's degree in three semesters. Academically I was very successful, but personally I was kind of flopping around, trying to find direction socially and personally, trying to figure out which way I was going and what I really wanted. I was involved in a bunch of one-night stands, just running around being rather promiscuous and not really liking it but not finding anybody that I could get interested in. I met a gay guy whom I decided didn't have to be that way—I could change him with love, kindness, and understanding. Only after several months, with no success, did I realize that it wasn't as I thought. It was the most frustrating, upsetting relationship I have ever had. I was in agony, a total wreck. It was so destructive that I finally broke up with him.

After getting the master's degree I put all that stuff behind me and started a new life in England, where I got a job teaching American soldiers for a year. I immersed myself totally in the little community there, which was a lot of fun. There was a lot of partying and having meals together and socializing. I learned a lot about myself, and I learned I could teach.

Post-College Paths: The Businesswomen

Going to graduate or professional school was a possibility for virtually all of the businesswomen. Further education offered the opportunity of developing a clear-cut occupational career and, for the unmarried, of finding an appropriate husband. A few took this course but the great majority decided against it. In college they had typically been good but not outstanding students. In most cases the young woman saw herself as a "solid but not brilliant" student, oriented toward practical work rather than academic work. MBA programs were just beginning to admit women, and several young women considered going on for an MBA but quickly rejected the idea. It seemed unappealing to be one of a few "token" women in the highly competitive masculine business world. While wanting greater freedom, they were not prepared to storm the Establishment bastions. (Some women got an MBA or similar degree later, when they had a more secure base of operations and knew better what they wanted.)

The option actually taken by the great majority of these women was an entry-level job in the business world. For a variety of reasons they were drawn to New York City, the center of the corporate-financial world, even though their colleges and parental homes were usually some distance away. A few obtained an entry technical-professional job in a field such as accounting or finance. Most got a job that was held by women only—computer programmer, research or editorial assistant, general office factotum and gofer. They were clearly overqualified. In filling these necessary but minor positions, corporations gave special preference to Ivy League and Seven Sisters college women applicants. Men with similar education would not have taken the jobs or even been offered them.

As she graduated from college, each young woman urgently wanted an opportunity to prove that she was entitled to a place in the work world. Her first job (and often her second and third) was by no means the first rung of any career ladder. Rather, it gave her the only available starting point from which she might in time get to the bottom rung of a ladder leading upward in the organizational hierarchy. At that point, she hardly knew what a career was or whether she wanted one, let alone how to get it. Through an admixture of chance and motivation, she found this starting point and diligently used it to gain greater competence and advancement. A career path came later, typically in the Age 30 Transition.

A few businesswomen concluded the Early Adult Transition a few months after graduation and then devoted themselves to building an Entry Life Structure. The great majority needed an interim phase of six months to two years to complete the Early Adult Transition. During this phase the young women explored the possibilities for a more independent adult life while maintaining the ties to parents and the structured life of the college student. For some 25 percent of the women, the initial year or two after graduation was primarily a time of hopefulness and adventure in an exciting new world. For others, it was a time of both excitement and difficulty as they tried to make their way along a rocky path. For more than half, however, it was a rock bottom time that offered few immediate satisfactions and no clear basis for a better future. Here are a few examples of life in the senior year and the interim phase after graduation:

JESSICA HALL

At graduation I was miserable. Only five or six women in my class didn't get married within six months of graduation. Secretary, social worker— they all had ditsy little jobs, not a career. Leaving college, thinking about what I was going to do next, I was in *terror*. In my senior year the head of the Placement Office invited us to a meeting. For the first time the reality began to set in that I couldn't do anything I wanted. She told us that females had to type or teach; no other jobs were available. She was a frustrated spinster who fully believed that if you did anything other than type or teach you would not get a man, and your prime aim in life was to get a man. I said, "Screw that!" I'd interviewed with a foundation and learned that they had erased my name from the list because I was female. I made a scene and went to the head of my department, but they had never seen one of these creatures like me. They were afraid the companies would stop recruiting there.

I wanted to go to New York City. The only job title I'd ever heard about was analyst, so I decided that's what I would be [laughs]. I sent out sixty letters to companies and got four appointments for interviews. It turned out they didn't hire women as analysts. A few wanted to make me a computer programmer, but I knew that didn't lead anywhere. My aunt knew a man who got me an interview at a brokerage firm, and I ended up there.

My parents wouldn't let me loose in New York City, so they got me into a residence for women. The residence ran a tight ship, with curfews, but I liked it. I didn't mind the restrictions and enjoyed the group of ready-made friends. I got there as I turned 22 and stayed almost a year. I loved New York City, though I had a terrible time adjusting to it and becoming part of it. I got there never having had a taste of wine, never any cheese other than American, bread other than white, steak other than well-done.

The job itself was terrible. I worked for a nice 60-year-old man who couldn't function very well. As a "kindness," the firm had made him head of this small department. I was finished with my week's work by noon Monday and had nothing to do the rest of the week. My boss and his secretary spent all their time crying about their troubles. It was very depressing for a young woman.

I wanted to advance, but I didn't fit in with the crowd there. The people who did best had both brains and money. I mean, this was the most handsome set of Ivy League types you ever laid eyes on. Preppie, real preppie. Whereas I was real cornpone, a fish out of water. There was a big difference between this 22-year-old thing from the Midwest, who barely knows how to wear shoes, and a 26-year-old woman who was educated in the East and has lived in a sophisticated milieu all her life. I was terrified of the women there, couldn't integrate with them, didn't have any friends. I was too intimidated even to phone these people for lunch. And I certainly didn't know how to function in New York cafe society.

Things improved slightly after six or eight months. I made friends with Bev, who helped me learn the ropes. She is still my best friend though I don't see her very much. I asked for a job as an analyst, and they said they'd give me a try. My parents put great pressure on me to keep the first job, bad as it was, but I finally took a stand. I began to blossom a little with men, too, became somewhat interesting to them. I was not popular, but I went out with some singularly interesting and intelligent men. Finally, after nearly a year [almost 23], I became an analyst, moved into my own apartment, got my life in some kind of order, and began to have a sense of the future.

PAM KENNEY

I graduated at 21 and had no idea what I would do. At that time, you got out of college and worked, but you didn't have a long-term career. I had no models of what women did after college beyond secretary and teacher. My parents said, "Wouldn't you like to go to graduate school?" and I said,

"No, thank you." So I decided I might as well come to New York City and try it. I didn't have anybody I was going to marry. Going back home wasn't an option. So I decided that I really wanted to work. The standard question at job interviews was, "Can you type?" At the time women were secretaries and men were other things, so I went to secretarial school to get job skills. I lived at a hotel for women. It wasn't exactly a college dorm but it was very protective, like an extension of college.

KIM PRICE

I wasn't sure what I wanted to do when I graduated from college. I didn't want to become a teacher; it just seemed too dull and traditional. After graduating I moved away from home immediately and got my own small apartment. It was an exciting time! I was free, on my own, independent, making my own decisions. I was ambitious and wanted to get ahead. I wanted to be taken seriously for my intelligence, competence, and abilities.

I went out searching for a trainee job and ran right into prejudice. Many doors I walked in just offered typing jobs, clerical jobs. Because I was black they used the excuse, "You've got too much education; you're overqualified." But *all* the women then were overqualified. An employment agency got me a job as a typist. I worked my way up to administrative assistant and went back to school nights to work towards my master's degree.

I had my first sexual adult-type relationship. It was with an older man. That lasted for a while. It was an important experience because I had finally made that big step, and it was with somebody I trusted and liked. I was in love with him. Sex is giving of myself. That is a side that is very private to me, and I don't treat it very lightly. I don't feel that it should be available to just anybody because I have an urge or they have an urge. It's a need, but a more controlled need. It's connected to my feeling of being independent, of being able to take care of myself.

ABBY MURPHY

I moved to New York City right after graduation and moved into an apartment with three other young women who had been at my college. That was comfortable. By the fall I started making friends at work and really started to enjoy it.

The company I went with was not large, but it was the only offer I had, and it was in New York City. That was probably the best thing that ever happened to me because I did make that break from home. It was a difficult year because I realized the total lack of support from my family. Just none, zero. How difficult it is to make a transition without that. My father's reaction to my job was, "What kind of an idiot would pay you that kind of money?"

I got wonderful experience, and it worked out very well. My job was actually very good: two years later I went to a Fortune 500 company, which is what I wanted to do in the first place.

❧ ELLEN NAGY

I went to an all-women's college. It was very supportive reinforcement, very protective. They taught you to be a first-class citizen, to develop your maximum potential, to be supremely capable. The message was that there's no reason why you can't do anything. But the men who went to equivalent colleges were aiming for the top jobs, every one. *They* would be the best and the brightest in their professions. By rights we women should have been the privileged too, but we were not.

In the fall after graduation I went to graduate school. I didn't have any money, and my parents would not pay for anything; on college graduation day I was on my own. Going to graduate school was job-motivated. I knew I couldn't get a good job unless I had a graduate degree.

Career was just a vague thing for me then. I had selected my major because I thought I could get a high-paying job. It was not a dream, this career; it was an idea to do something interesting. I was sure that work was going to be boring, and I was trying to get myself an interesting job. More than that, I wanted to earn money, and I wanted it to be *my* money.

I got half a fellowship because they said I would waste a full fellowship that could be used by a man. The faculty was very explicit about their discrimination against women, and so were the students; I was the only woman. The idea that I would go into the business world rather than academia made me a double leper. I did a two-year program in nine months and got the master's degree. It was just sheer hell, that's the only word for it. My husband, Carl, was getting out of the service in June, and we would move to wherever he could get into medical school, so I had to hurry. Carl and I did a lot of entertaining, and we had tons of people over all the time, which was very nice. That went on through Carl's medical school, too. I did a lot of the traditional things—cooked, kept the house reasonably neat and clean, did all the housework stuff myself.

I did not have a clear sense of what I would do after graduate school, just that I would get a job in the business world. The business world was where you could make money, and I figured that they would be willing to hire a woman in my field because they needed that. I had enough sense not to become a programmer, which was the standard career choice at the time for a woman.

I was very career-oriented and motivated, but I think a career represents an underlying conflict for women. Men know that they are going to have a career; it is a given. They don't contemplate a career of raising children or being a spouse. Women who believe men will do that are swimming against the current. And most women who were trying to do just the career were probably swimming against their own current and probably questioning what they were doing on some level. I think there's an underlying conflict about having a career for women. For most women, jobs were what you did until you did the real thing of getting married and having children. You might go back and work later if you wished, but that's not a career.

Carl got into medical school in NYC, and we moved there just as I turned 21. My sense of where I was going was extremely confused. I knew nothing about the business world, got no encouragement from anyone about going into it, and ended up there for negative motivating reasons: money. I was pressured to get a job right away because our economic survival depended on it. I wrote to all the companies in NYC who hired women, about fifty of them, and I got a fair number of replies. I started calling and banging on doors. Everywhere I went people thought it was a very, very strange thing for a woman to be applying for those jobs. I got three job offers. I was very well suited to my field from my education and abilities, and it turned out to be a very good job and a stepping stone to increasingly responsible jobs. I was ignorant but not dumb. I actively sought more responsibility. I had help along the way from men who liked having a capable, hardworking person work for them and would champion the cause for you.

A constant toll was exacted from women, a general putting-down, not taking them seriously, treating you like a sex object, downgrading your work role and not expecting you to stay. Until I came back after my baby was born at 29, they never expected me to stay—sooner or later I would get pregnant and leave. People would say to me a lot, "Aren't you going to have children?" There were two other women in professional positions. One left and got married, and the other woman, very capable, is now a senior person at that company. She's very traditional but not married. If your aspirations outpace your progress, then you're still reaching and probably dissatisfied. If your progress exceeds your aspirations, you're always rather pleased; you've come further than you expected. She was in the latter category, and I was in the former. Initially I had no thought of advancement; I just figured that if I could have an interesting job at a relatively decent salary for the rest of my life, I'd be pretty happy. My concerns with advancement came later.

My husband was very proud and supportive and tolerant when he was in medical school; he took an active interest in my work, and I took an active interest in his work. Here I was working with all these men, so I thought it was a good idea to make sure they met my husband. Carl would come down to the office and meet everyone as my husband, confirming me as a married and unavailable women. That was very helpful, allowing me to form work bonds with male colleagues.

Without knowing it, both groups of career women were pioneers: they were part of the first generation in American history in which a significant number (though still a small minority) of women were attempting to move beyond the bounds of the Traditional Marriage Enterprise. With few predecessors, they had to find their own paths. In the academic world, women had been on college faculties but largely in small colleges and in "women's" subjects. Few women held senior positions in most fields at the major colleges and universities. In the corporate-financial world, very few women had been employed in positions above the entry level. The corporate world was more gender-segregated than the academic, but both presented severe obstacles to the hiring, daily work satisfaction, training, and promoting of women. As the Early Adult Transition ended, most of these young women were groping their way, not at all clear what career path (if any) they might eventually come to.

12 Entry Life Structure for Early Adulthood: Career Women

The primary tasks of the Entry Life Structure are to form and maintain a first adult life structure and to establish a place for oneself within the generation of young adults (see Chapter 6). For the career women it began at 22 or 23 and ended at 28 or 29. Its onset was usually six months to two years after graduation from college. As it began, fourteen of the thirty career women were married, and two had a child. For the nonmothers, the love/marriage/family component of the life structure was of subjective importance in the early twenties but was overshadowed by the concern with work. A few career women had a broadly defined occupational direction such as accountant, analyst, academic scientist, or economist, but most had no clear vision of a long-term career. The great majority of young women were simply seeking a foothold in graduate school or the work world, a place from which to start. The Dream was not highly formed in the early twenties. The internal Traditional Homemaker Figure played an important part in setting family goals and in limiting occupational horizons but did not generate an animating Dream for any of these women. For most career women the rudimentary Dream was carried by the internal Anti-Traditional Figure. The key image of the Anti-Traditional Dream was that of an independent, competent woman who was taken seriously by herself and others, who was not mindless or selfless, and who would have a reasonable balance of work and love/marriage/family in her life.

First Phase, Age 25 Shift, and Second Phase

Since I have already discussed the evolution of the Entry Life Structure in Chapter 6, a brief summary here will suffice. The first phase of this period, from about 22 to 25, is devoted to building, testing, and consolidating an Entry Life Structure. Even if the main components of the structure are well defined at the start of the period, a few years are needed to create a more integrated structure. For many young women the life structure at 22 or 23 is rather fragmented, incomplete, or unstable. They are just beginning to explore the possibilities for living as relatively independent young adults. A few years are needed to learn a little about what the world offers, and what they want, with regard to work, love/marriage/family, home base, and other components of the life structure.

In the Age 25 Shift a young woman attempts to correct the major limitations in the Entry Life Structure as she experiences them. It is *not* a shift from one life structure to another. Rather, it is an attempt to improve the structure formed during the first phase. It may take various forms: setting clearer priorities around work and love/marriage/family, filling a major unfilled component (by getting married or starting a family or entering a new occupation), becoming more independent of parents, firming up the existing structure. There are wide variations in the relative success of this effort and in the nature of the resulting life structure. The shift ordinarily begins at 25 — rarely before late 24 or after early 26.

The Age 25 Shift begins the second and concluding phase within the period of the Entry Life Structure. If a relatively stable structure was formed in the first phase, a young woman tries now to enrich this structure and to protect it from major change. If the initial structure was fragmented, she tries now to fill an unfilled central component and to form a more stable, secure structure. The shift is often dramatized by one or more marker events such as a job change, a geographical move, getting married or divorced, having a child. An event is part of the Age 25 Shift to the extent that it serves to stabilize the life structure and to instigate the second phase, which lasts until the period ends.

Whether they were married or single, work was the central component of the Entry Life Structure for most career women. Love/marriage/family was usually an important but partially filled or unfilled component for much or all of this period. The career women's engagement in both components was, however, deeply compromised by the conflict between the internal Traditional Homemaker Figure and the internal Anti-Traditional Figure. The women were pulled in various directions by their own inner aims and by external social pressures. They were eager to work but often reluctant to get heavily involved in a career, which might keep them from having a family. Most of the single women wanted to marry, but not too soon nor to a too-traditional man. Motherhood was important, but again not too soon, lest one become overwhelmed by a Traditional Marriage Enterprise.

None of the career women was able to establish an Entry Life Structure containing occupation and love/marriage/family on terms that were very satisfactory to her. All of them spent much or all of the second phase trying to fill an unfilled component or to make improvements in a component that had somehow gone awry. Let's look now at the evolution of various components during this period.

Relationship with Family of Origin

During the period of the Entry Life Structure the career women became more distanced, financially and psychologically, from parents. All but two young women lived away from the parental home, usually in another city, and took primary responsibility for their own life decisions and sustenance. Parents came to play a less central part in their lives, with occasional moments of pleasant contact or great tension. The greater emotional and social distance was important to the young women. It is generally not feasible or desirable for adult offspring to make the relationship with parents a central component of their lives; at best it is a highly valued and satisfying peripheral component.

The growing separation was usually brought about by parents as well as daughter. The parents generally supported daughter's decision to work and live elsewhere. At the same time, they wanted her to live at a higher level of comfort and social class than her initial income permitted. Most parents partially subsidized their daughters by providing a regular allowance or specific gifts for rent, furniture, visits home. The parental help was usually a mixed blessing and burden to the novice adult struggling to find her own way. The parents of an unmarried daughter offered help intended primarily to improve her chances for appropriate matrimony. They wanted her to have an apartment, neighborhood, job, social circle, and lifestyle that would enable her to meet a prospective husband with a good career potential. They were investing in their daughter's future. The daughter often felt that her parents were offering help with too many strings attached, or for their own purposes rather than hers. For these and other reasons, she moved with deliberate speed toward reducing (though not eliminating) her dependence upon them. Her move toward separation was usually more active and more conflicted in the second phase of this period. Mother was often more involved in her matrimonial progress, father in her work. Father regarded her work as a source of independence, a bulwark against a bad marriage or a lack of marriage, but not as an achieving career that might interfere with her primary career as homemaker. He was thus both a support and an impediment to her budding occupational aspirations.

Over 75 percent of the career sample had little contact with siblings during the Entry Life Structure and beyond. Few had formed a good enough relationship with a sibling to want to continue the relationship into adulthood.

Occupation in the First Phase

For almost all of the career women, work was the central component of the Entry Life Structure and the primary basis upon which the other components were formed. The work of most businesswomen was an entry-level job in a corporate firm. The work of most academic women was to attend graduate school to earn a master's degree or doctorate, in preparation for a future academic profession. Being a graduate student is very different from being a college student: the primary aim of graduate school is to transform a novice into a skilled professional capable of doing mature work in a particular discipline. Graduate school is the first step in a professional career; "graduate student" is an entry-level position within the academic career. In this context, then, the term "work" includes not only a paying job but also graduate studies and any other activities through which we form an academic occupation.

As the period began, each young woman found herself lacking in occupational skills and in her sense of who she was and what she wanted with occupation. Most of those who were married had chosen a husband who was in no hurry to have children and who generally supported his wife's interest in occupation. Those who were single had usually terminated one or more potentially matrimonial relationships out of the fear that the man would insist upon a Traditional Marriage Enterprise and/or that she was overly susceptible to becoming a traditional homemaker. It felt essential to the young woman to form an occupational identity and, through the medium of work, to develop a competent self who could have both family and occupation in the future. Work was seen as a vehicle to a modified Traditional Marriage Enterprise in which the young woman would give first priority to family while still having some serious outside involvements.

How did the thirty career women progress occupationally in the first phase of the Entry Life Structure?

Roughly a third of the career women were at 25 on a well-defined path leading to an academic or professional-managerial career. The future faculty members in this group were graduate students making substantial progress toward the Ph.D. degree. They obtained the doctorate at ages 26 to 29 and began an academic or professional career. Examples among the businesswomen include: analyst at a major firm, accountant in a medium-size accounting firm, technical job in a corporate finance department with good credentials and prospects for promotion. In the Age 25 Shift these career women strengthened their commitment to occupation, though their long-term goals were still vague.

Another third of the career women, most of them faculty members, were at 25 on an occupational path other than business or academe. They were usually teaching high school and/or obtaining a master's degree that had limited career potential. Only after age 25 did the young women enter a doctoral program or corporate job with some prospects for career development.

A final third of the career women had jobs that led nowhere in particular and had no sense of an occupational future. Most of these were in the business sample. Their primary aims were much more immediate: to make a first niche for themselves as competent members of the work world and to get clearer about their occupational and matrimonial interests. They generally expected to start a family in a few years and then have interesting work but not a career. They had job titles such as editorial assistant, research assistant, administrative assistant. In the corporate world these jobs were given primarily to female graduates of excellent colleges who were educated, middle class in background and orientation. The women were bright, hard-working, and had few expectations. They had the skills to perform specific office functions such as typing and editing. They had the literacy, culture, and decorum to carry out other responsibilities such as talking to clients, going on field trips, reviewing technical literature, and assisting the work of a highly professional team. The young women were often overqualified for the job as officially defined but well qualified for the work actually required. They were also underrewarded in terms of job title, pay, and prospects for advancement.

These jobs were "women's work." Men were rarely offered them and would generally not accept them. They were usually jobs held by transient workers: young women who would work for a few years, get married, and become homemakers. The young women often made a limited investment of self in the work, and the organization invested little in them. This scenario probably held for the majority of young women who held such jobs. The women studied here exemplify the minority who remained in this world beyond their early thirties and later entered a more professional career path.

Whatever her job and occupational orientation, every young woman became a member of a work world: a work organization contained within a larger network of academic or financial-corporate institutions. She was for the first time an adult member of an adult world. To some extent, both the academic and the business world invited her to demonstrate that she was a competent, interesting adult, able to function on equal terms with other adults. To a greater extent, both worlds (especially that of the corporation) also did the opposite: they treated her as a girl, limited her to women's work, kept her in a subordinate position, and denied her the opportunities available to men of equal or lesser qualifications. The same contradiction existed within the young woman. While seeking the freedom to develop her skills and pursue her goals, she was also constrained by the internal Traditional Homemaker Figure who kept reminding her of the dangers of getting too involved in career.

The work world also played a major part in shaping the young woman's social world: the people she came to know at work and elsewhere; the social circles within which she participated; the social circles she could not join because they were above or below or simply outside of the ones accessible to her. At its worst the work world rebuffed her attempts at affirmation and made her feel like an alien being in male territory. At its best (which sometimes coexisted with the worst) it made available an exciting social and cultural milieu that broadened her horizons, stimulated her intellectual and artistic sensibilities, gave her strong affirmation as person and worker, and encouraged her to develop her skills. She often experienced the corporation/university not as an impersonal bureaucracy but as an integrated, caring community in which she was a valued member. People saw each other for meals, celebrations, dates, recreation. Work thus provided a positive quasi-family for many young women: a context for personal/social/occupational development that facilitated her separation from the community and family of her origins.

⊷§   MICHELE PROTO

My first good job (at 23) was as a computer programmer in New York City. That was one of the happiest periods of my life. It was a very exciting place to work. I felt a part of the company and identified with the people in my section, who were bright and hardworking and fun-loving, mostly in our twenties. We worked sixty hours a week and loved it. Everybody's social life revolved around the people in the company. There was a lot of spirit, camaraderie. I was project leader and the only woman on my team, and they made me feel good to be there. I was exposed to sales, proposal writing, a lot of customer interface. It was a five-year period of self-development for me; I learned a lot and contributed a lot, and I felt competent. But after five years I had no way to progress further in that company.

Mentorial Relationships

In this period about a third of the career women had mentorial relationships, almost entirely with men. These relationships existed within the work world and were concerned primarily with occupational development. They were somewhat more frequent in the academic than the business sample. Most mentors provided moral support, helped the newcomer get oriented to the work and the work world, took her seriously, recommended her for minor promotions. They "brought her along" to become a more competent and valued group member. She was clearly better off with them than she would have been without them. But the degree of mutuality in the relationship was often limited. Although he liked her and enjoyed being helpful, the male mentor usually found it difficult to regard a woman as becoming like him and perhaps surpassing him in the future. He usually did not have an intuitive sense of the novice's Dream, however articulated or inchoate it might be. He had difficulty giving his blessing to her highest aspirations and making her feel truly welcome within his broader occupational world. Most women, in turn, found it difficult to entertain such ambitions. The barriers to empathy and identification often prevented the development of a fuller mentoring relationship.

↩ ELLEN NAGY

I was working and supporting my husband and myself financially while he attended medical school. I was advancing steadily at my company. By 22 I began to feel more grounded in my work and could begin to think more clearly about having a career. Lou, one of the managers above me, was promoted. He thought I was promising and got me promoted to his group. The promotion occurred when I was 23, after a year's preparation. With Lou's encouragement and support, I was able to think more ambitiously and to look for lines of advancement. I started to figure out that I wanted this job, and then that job, and then—I was always about three jobs ahead of where I was, and I began to shoot for places beyond my grasp. Lou was a good mentor. He took a "push people off cliffs, and they'll learn to fly" approach. I always felt I was operating on the edge of my abilities, and that's an exciting way to grow. He took risks in promoting me in the first place; he sponsored me, went to bat on salary and job level, sent me on business trips overseas. Of course, this proved to everyone that we were sleeping together, which we were not. He had to be very self-confident to deal with that.

At 23–24 I began to do more international travel; I'd be out of the country for a week at a time. I loved traveling and still do, although business travel is very hard. It was very unconventional for a woman to be traveling at that time. Everyone said, "You can't send a woman to France; the Frenchmen won't put up with it." That was totally untrue. But there were inherent sexual difficulties in being the only woman in groups of men—the oddball, reserved and distant. I was often the youngest in situations where I was naive and ill-at-ease. I'd never been to Europe before, and I didn't know anything about anything. Your typical male business stuff would happen: sitting around a table of men, and they lapse into telling jokes. And, of course, they apologize to you for telling them, but they keep right on because they really don't want you to be there. A lot of male bonding stuff. But people *do* listen. If you're representing an American company you could be pink with purple feathers, and they'd listen. They realize you're intelligent and making a contribution; the fact that you're a woman is not a big deal. Also, you're not competing directly with them. But you are a woman in a man's world. They made the rules, and it's their club, and you are the odd person out. That is very formative for women in the business world.

The lack of female mentors was mainly due to the scarcity of women in more senior positions. An entry-level woman generally worked for a male boss or faculty member, or on a team containing few or no other women. When she had a relationship with a senior woman it was, however, often quite negative. She experienced her female boss or supervisor, rightly or wrongly, as "a poor role model": a woman who had been promoted but was not very professional; an ambitious career woman who was no help to younger women; a manager who seemed harder on female than male subordinates. The problems were more severe in the corporation than the university, but they existed in both.

In every relationship between a junior person (apprentice, beginner, student) and someone more senior (boss, supervisor, teacher), there is the potential for a relationship that serves some mentorial functions. Very often, however, the potential is not realized. Instead, the two develop an *antimentorial relationship*: they are not simply indifferent to each other but are in some basic sense oppositional. The senior person finds the junior inept, unmotivated, ungrateful, rebellious. The junior, in turn, finds the senior indifferent, exploitive, overly critical, or imposing.

❧ JESSICA HALL

At 23 I got a seemingly attractive job as an analyst. My boss firmly believed that a woman's place was doing statistics. You can't be a real analyst until you call on companies. The men started doing that the first week, and I just sat there. I worked really hard and learned a great deal about the company, but I wasn't getting anywhere. After two years I told the department head I wanted my group changed. Six months later, when I was 25, they put me in a new group with a new boss. He wasn't terrific, but he was a lot better, and I had a chance to call on companies and do the whole analyst thing. They tried to do more for women, but it didn't go very far. At first there was one woman in each group, and later there were two. They call that "a gain of 100 percent" [laughs]. We were paid less than men in the same job and were hired only in research, not in investment, which was the key organizational function. It's hard to describe my feelings at that time in my life: the mixture of excitement about becoming part of a whole new world and frustration over the obstacles to be overcome for women.

Occupation in the Second Phase

The *second phase* of the Entry Life Structure was a time of personal development and growing occupational commitment for most career women. They had been responsible workers for several years and had gained a sense of independence and competence, and they wanted to establish occupation as a major part of their lives. They became more intolerant of dull, demeaning, or unrewarding work and took greater initiative in seeking advancement within the current workplace or elsewhere. As the period ended at age 28 or 29, most of the young women had taken at least a modest step forward. We can distinguish three broad levels of occupational advancement.

Women Who Were Embarking upon a Professional Future

Almost half of the thirty career women—six businesswomen, eight academics—were at this highest occupational level. Each woman had made significant progress in pursuing the Dream of her Anti-Traditional Figure. She was forming an identity as a professional woman capable of living independently and making her way in the work world. While knowing that she had the ability and the desire to advance further along this path, she was still unsure of how far she wanted to go and how far the world would allow her to go. The occupational progress made it seem safer to the young woman to have a family without excessive danger of becoming a traditional homemaker. The danger was by no means gone, but she felt strong enough to take the risk.

The six businesswomen had by 28 advanced far enough along in the corporate-financial world to set longer-term goals, although most did not yet envision a long-term career.

The eight faculty women in this group were on the threshold of an academic career as the Entry Life Structure ended. At age 26 to 29 they earned doctorates in fields such as literature, philosophy, the social sciences, and economics. A few went directly from graduate school to a full-time faculty appointment in another university. Others, following a common practice for new Ph.D.'s in their discipline, took a postdoctoral fellowship for a year or two and then became faculty members. Still others took one or more transitional jobs before getting on the academic ladder. The factors contributing to this "in between" time were varied: accommodation to the husband's career, which had first priority in her mind as well as his; institutional discrimination, through which women are more likely to be offered part-time instructor or "adjunct" positions; and the young woman's inner concerns about trying for an academic career and finding a balance between work and family. For all eight young women, the end of the Entry Life Structure brought with it the search for a new structure in which she was a more mature professional, usually with a husband and children.

DEBRA ROSE

After graduate school I went to work. By 25 I got strongly involved in my work because my marriage was less satisfying to me. My first job was such an important part of my life and my development. It was an opportunity not usually given to a woman, and I was really good at it. I formed close friendships with my colleagues and supervisors. It was like a family. It was exciting work and had great spirit, and I was pleased being a leader of a group of thirty whose collective work was really better than the work that each of us would have produced individually. We had a terrific esprit de corps.

One of the reasons why I got to a position of leadership there was that I was competent and exercised authority well. The manager thought of me as a favorite. I was always very ambitious; I wanted to go as far as I could go. It was a six-year period there, and I was promoted several times. I had always been very used to being at the top of my class in school, and I was always very good at what I did, and that was acknowledged right away. I felt admired and felt that people liked and cared about me. During that period of time I had two children, my first at age 26, so I was pregnant and out having children, and people were just very nice to me, very protective and caring.

Women Who Were Just Getting onto an Occupational Path

Eight career women were at this middle level—three businesswomen, five academics.

The businesswomen were all single and had worked in nonbusiness jobs (usually teaching) for five or six years before entering master's degree programs that led them into the business world. While recognizing that their late start was a handicap to further progress, these women were excited by the new turn in the road. The Dream of the Anti-Traditional Figure was taking clearer shape and holding greater promise of realization.

During their late twenties, many of the married faculty women became involved in the Women's Movement. The young woman's experience in the Movement became a consciousness-raising experience for the internal Anti-Traditional Figure. The young woman met and formed friendships with other, like-minded women who were also questioning the traditional way. The Women's Movement provided badly needed role models for a different path and supported the young woman's movement out of a too-traditional life and into the world of graduate school.

JULIA HART

I was 26 or 27, teaching high school and dating a man attending business school. We had a sexual relationship. He was the person who suggested that I go for my MBA. I always had a strong sense of independence, a need for equal respect. I felt there was something wrong with all the relationships I had in that in one way or another I always ended up being someone's handmaiden; it wasn't a partnership of equals. The relationship with this fellow ended, and he moved away. I think we both realized that the foundation just wasn't there for having any longer-term relationship.

I began to realize that I probably wouldn't marry, and my main thoughts were to get work that would be sustaining over the long term, both intellectually and economically. At 27 I applied to business school and began at 28. I started business school with no clear idea of where it might lead. I was not "liberated" and wasn't aware of the Women's Movement until I got to business school. Then it hit you like a sledgehammer, the *need* for a Women's Movement. I'd never been particularly aware of discrimination, but there were 28 women in my class of 500, and you really felt a minority. Where I had been teaching I might have been paid $3,000 less than my male counterpart, but I didn't know it, and at least there were quite a few women around. But at the business school I got derogatory remarks about taking a man's place, that I'd come for my MRS. degree as well as my MBA. The most blatant example was the marketing professors. They made their resistance to women quite obvious. They'd always call on me to give comments on the "consumer's point of view"! So I went from being totally unaware to being militant in about three months [laughs].

The five faculty members in this group were also delayed in getting started on an academic career. Stacey Lane exemplifies several common themes.

STACEY LANE

I graduated from a Seven Sisters college and went on full time to an elite graduate school. I don't think I had a sense of a career as a college teacher, although that would be the only thing to do with a graduate degree in my field. I felt one goes to college to pursue interests, and graduate school was an extension of that.

I met my husband, Tyler, at 22. I was in love with him. We were graduate students in different fields, working for our doctorates. I was very serious about graduate school, but I got pregnant, and we got married. It really was a screwing up of the works. If abortion had been available there would have been no question. I think Tyler felt trapped. It was a painful time for me. I became a mother at 23; I liked the mothering part but never loved it. In my mind—and everyone else's then—women were separated into those who would have families and those who would have careers. It never felt all put together into one happy package. I decided to get a master's degree and run. I finished my thesis at 24, I don't know how; there wasn't much joy in the writing. I did it to get the credential but had no plans to do anything with the degree except a little part-time teaching.

The first three years of marriage were a very hectic, isolated time for me. I organized my life around my husband's career. He and I were very separate; he was totally involved in his work and not interested in intimacy. I always had the feeling that if the house was burning down he'd grab his work first before the children and me. My idea of marriage was that it was supposed to be on an even keel at all times and at all costs. I thought that fighting would open up all sorts of irreparable damages, so I stored all my bad feelings underground. I had my hands full with three children and no help. I was totally exhausted. I thought about going back to graduate school for my doctorate . . . some day . . . if . . .

We lived in this ghetto faculty housing. The women identified themselves as, "My husband teaches in the Math Department." I was floundering. I became a part-time instructor at the local university, but I couldn't feel part of the academic community in any real sense. It was a community of scholars, and no one saw *me* as a scholar. I was being exploited by the department, too. Their attitude was, "Give her the work we don't want, pay her as little as possible, and *don't* put her name in the catalog!"

At 27 I began to have a constituency of women who were trying new directions for themselves. We met once a month. Many were faculty wives. They were the most interesting women: vigorous and intellectually stimulating and wonderful people. I began to think that maybe it was possible to strike out and do these things, do everything. Through the group experience I started to think about going back for the doctorate, although it took me a year to get myself ready to try to apply to graduate school.

At 28 I became a doctoral student and started a new life. It was very hard for me to believe I could really do it. Going back was one of the few big decisions I ever made in my life—that and getting divorced later on. It meant that I was making a long-range commitment and not just going year by year. I wanted my own identity and a life outside my home community. The decision had a lot to do with the Women's Movement, which was just coming into my life. My husband, Tyler, was very supportive of my wish to return to graduate school. He was the most liberated man I knew. He also saw me needing less from him and leaning on him less because I got support elsewhere.

Going back was a great reclaiming of a community I had left behind years before. My graduate school department was very helpful to me all the way along. They gave me the confidence—which I didn't have on my own—to apply for a fellowship. My aim was to become a college teacher, but my specific goals were unclear. I knew that it would take three years of commuting to complete the courses, one or two a semester, before I could start my dissertation, and that's what I did. I finished the coursework at 31 and the Ph.D. at 37.

Women Who Were Not on an Occupational Path

Eight career women were in this group—six businesswomen and two academics.

The businesswomen were still working in entry-level jobs such as bookkeeper, computer programmer, editorial assistant. They were feeling acutely the limitations of their current work and the need to enter a field of greater interest and potential for advancement. Despite their relative lack of external success, they had made significant progress with the Anti-Traditional Dream by demonstrating that they could take care of themselves without a male provisioner. Few were married and none had children. All wanted work to be a major component of their lives, even if they had a family. They were, however, just beginning to form an occupational identity and did not yet know what they wanted to give and to receive through their work. They were also faced with massive obstacles in their specific circumstances and in themselves.

The two academic women in this group were on the fringes of the academic world throughout their twenties.

ERICA WARREN

The crunch came in the marriage when I got the master's at 25. I was exhausted—working full-time and doing all the domestic things with no help from my husband. I felt a lot of guilt and anxiety. I decided, "Maybe I should stop trying to be Superwoman and just stay home." We tried to get pregnant for two years and finally had a baby when I was 27. Our daughter was a real delight, but my husband would not help at all with the child care and housework, and he was very resentful when I occasionally left the child with him. I stayed home full-time the first year and found it very tedious. I loved my child, but I didn't want to be home all the time.

I had a real conflict about whether I wanted a career or a family. There were a lot of problems in the marriage, and I blamed everything on myself.

Love/Marriage/Family in the First Phase

The love/marriage/family component of the Entry Life Structure was problematic for virtually all thirty career women, but the problems were somewhat different for the married and the unmarried. I'll discuss the two groups separately.

Women Who Were Married as the Entry Life Structure Began

At the start of this period fourteen career women were married and two of these were mothers. The two mothers built a Traditional Marriage Enterprise, and the other twelve married childless women attempted to build a modified Traditional Marriage Enterprise of the young, professionally oriented, dual-working, childless couple. (I use the term "dual-working," rather than "dual-career," because it was not at all clear whether the women would go on to a long-term career.) The chief function of the modified Traditional Marriage Enterprise was to provide a vehicle for both spouses to pursue their separate occupational goals while enjoying the benefits of marriage without children. For these young women legal marriage had a number of advantages. It made their relationship more legitimate in the eyes of parents as well as work organizations. It took them out of the competitive struggles of the single dating game and reduced the sexual pressures faced by many single young women in a predominantly male work world. Life is simpler for a married than a single woman in these circumstances. The marital relationship, and the apparent assurance that it would later evolve into a stable family, allowed the young woman to devote herself more fully to work.

In most cases, however, the promise of this scenario was largely unfulfilled. The spouses generally did not know each other well as they married, and the level of intimacy rarely increased much in the next few years. Like the traditional homemaking couples, though on different terms, most of these couples lived parallel unconnected lives. The partners were primarily involved in their separate occupational enterprises. They had a joint home base (for which she took entire or major domestic responsibility) and usually gave each other some moral support, but they had little or no joint involvement around which the personal relationship might develop.

During the first phase of the Entry Life Structure, most early marrying career women had a difficult, often rock bottom time. They came to realize that their marriages were in jeopardy. Very few women were initially "in love" with their spouses. The relationship had much more to do with affection and mutual support than with passion or strong sexual interest. In the first years of marriage, many young women found their sex lives increasingly unsatisfactory. Also, her husband was more traditional and less supportive than she had earlier imagined. In most cases, he assumed that, once the children arrived, the wife would be primarily responsible for child-rearing and housekeeping. Though appreciative of his wife's talent as student or novice worker, he often had difficulty in accommodating to the demands of her career.

Within this general pattern, there were some notable differences between the two samples of career women. I'll start with the businesswomen.

Only three businesswomen, as compared to eleven academics, were married as the Entry Life Structure began. The married businesswomen generally came from more conservative, restrictive backgrounds than the married faculty members. They were emotionally and sexually more constrained in their relationships with men and more concerned that marriage/family would be engulfing, and their Anti-Traditional Figure was more anxious about her survival in adulthood. In college the businesswomen became part of a more conventional social world and associated with more traditional men. The men and women in this world took it for granted that the husband would ultimately be the main provisioner for the family. However competent and enterprising the wife might be, she was not "going anywhere" in her work and could not be his equal occupationally or financially. Even though they were currently equal in many ways, the imagined future placed a stamp of inequality on the relationship. Perhaps the strongest tie between them lay in the value both placed on being emotionally separate; they had chosen partners who would neither demand nor offer great intimacy and involvement.

The married faculty members usually had a more intellectual, liberal background than the businesswomen. They were part of a more scholarly world in college and especially in graduate school. As students the young women could participate more freely in this world and gain greater affirmation for their knowledge and creativity, and some male students and faculty in the academic community supported their aspirations. These young women thus had available a larger number of men with whom it felt safe to have potentially matrimonial relationships, and more of them had enduring premarital affairs and early marriages.

The Anti-Traditional Dream of virtually all the academic women had evolved into the Dream of a modified Traditional Marriage Enterprise within the academic world. Her place in this world would be assured by a husband who had an academic career. Even if she did not have a full-fledged career herself, the young woman assumed she could still be part of academe and have an intellectually stimulating life. It was also important for her to obtain some form of graduate education. The publicly stated purpose of this education was to have an academic career. Her chief aim in the Entry Life Structure was, however, to be a graduate student and to develop a competent self, so that in time she could be a homemaker with a less traditional marriage and an opportunity to do interesting work. Usually she did not envision an achieving career as professor/scholar in an institution of the caliber she was currently attending.

The eleven early marrying faculty members believed that their marriage would, indeed, serve these functions; however, all but one experienced severe disappointments in the first phase of the Entry Life Structure. The husband was more absorbed in his own work, and less interested in her, than she had originally supposed. The limitations in their sex life weighed more heavily upon her. Ten of the eleven early marriages ended in divorce.

Women Who Were Single in the First Phase

Sixteen career women were single throughout the first phase of the Entry Life Structure. Four businesswomen and four faculty members hoped to marry (though not to start a family) within a few years of college graduation, if Mr. Right came along, though they were cautious in their relationships with men and gave high priority to becoming self-sufficient adults.

The four businesswomen had a difficult time establishing an initial Entry Life Structure. Most of the single businesswomen, whether they sought or avoided marriage, lived in an apartment with one or more female roommates. A roommate provided company and shared domestic costs and responsibilities, and she was often part of a common social circle that was a medium for dating and recreation. She was usually a friendly acquaintance who quietly passed into and out of the others' lives. The home base was thus a stable domicile for transient "revolving roommates." The domicile might continue indefinitely, but the cast of characters changed every year or two. The most desired and most frequent scenario was that a woman lived there briefly and then left to marry. Failing that, she left for a better job, a more independent living arrangement, or in search of new options. The succession of roommates was a constant reminder to each of our subjects that her current life was transient, that its main purpose was matrimony.

◄§ PAM KENNEY

I graduated from secretarial school at 22 and chose a secretarial job. It wasn't a career, and nobody there was particularly interested in saying, "You graduated from a Seven Sisters college; why don't you do something serious?" That summer I got an apartment with two girlfriends who were also secretaries. There were a lot of parties, and we knew various men in the business world. Soon one of my roommates got married and then the other, but there were always others to move in during the four years I was in that apartment. It was like revolving roommates.

At 22 Pam Kenney began forming an Entry Life Structure as a single, working, marriage-seeking woman. She was a member of a readily identifiable category: well-educated women, overqualified for their jobs, yet glad to live independently and to have an opportunity to meet eligible men of appropriate background, education, and prospects.

Sally Wolford and Molly Berger were the only businesswomen who lived in the parental home after finishing college. They suffered many problems of the single adult daughter vis-à-vis a traditional mother who wanted the matrimonial best for her:

⋍§   SALLY WOLFORD

Age 23 was a really low time in my life. I had been living at home with my widowed mother for the two years since finishing college. I took care of her and did volunteer work as she had done, not getting into any serious paid job. I was dating but nothing much was happening that way either. Then this fellow came along. My friends seemed to like him, and he was pleasant. I was bored with my volunteer job. I figured, "I've been too fussy. There isn't anything to do in life except get married anyway; then everything will fall into place, and I'll have children and be busy with family life, and that will be it." So we got engaged.

Then a friend got me a job at a bank. I was so excited about that job! Meanwhile, my mother and fiancé kept charging ahead with the wedding plans. I kept digging my heels in further, saying, "I know that I just never seem to want to get married, but this time I *really* don't." Three weeks before the wedding I broke it off (age 24). My mother was at her wits' end. I thought, "What kind of mess am I getting myself into? Here I am breaking off this engagement for a job!" I felt very guilty, but I really got into my work.

At 25 I moved out of my mother's house. I'd never been away from home except for college. It was frightening to leave and hard to break with my mother, but it was clear to me that I wanted to be single for a while—to work and travel and have fun and be independent.

The single matrimony-oriented businesswomen exemplify one version of the basic conflict between the internal Traditional Homemaker Figure and the internal Anti-Traditional Figure. The voice of the Traditional Homemaker Figure predominated in the first phase of the Entry Life Structure. The young women told themselves that they were working only because, as it happened, they had not yet married. They tried earnestly to get on the matrimonial track and to avoid a deep engagement in work. The Anti-Traditional Figure, though not strong enough to win the battle, could nonetheless force a stalemate. As a result, the women were partially involved in both work and dating yet deeply involved in neither. The Anti-Traditional Figure was terrified at the possibility of being swept off her feet by a man who would then enslave her in domesticity. In the Age 25 Shift the Anti-Traditional Figure came more into her own.

The four single, matrimony-seeking academic women gave first priority to education/work but had at least one significant love relationship in the first phase. Eva Pitcher and Alice Abel each formed a matrimonial relationship with academic men, and both married at 25. Both husbands had similar values and took their wives seriously as persons and professionals. The initial modified Traditional Marriage Enterprise supported the academic pursuits of wife and husband, while deferring parenthood. Megan Bennett and Grace Tobin, on the other hand, more fully acknowledged their interest in occupation at 25 and gave themselves permission to defer marriage.

Eight single women, all in the business sample, were not very oriented toward matrimony in the first phase. Most expected to marry, perhaps in the late twenties, but not soon. Their immediate goals were to establish themselves in work and to create an inner basis for later marriage and family life. In this group the internal Anti-Traditional Figure predominated, and the internal Traditional Homemaker Figure operated surreptitiously to gain limited objectives—the mirror image of the matrimonial women above. But there was also a common theme that held for the career women as a whole: neither internal figure was truly in command; partial victory, compromise, and stalemate were the most common results of any conflict between them. Only three of these eight young women had sexual relationships with men during the first phase of the Entry Life Structure.

ABBY MURPHY

I met Nick at 22. The relationship was warm and pleasant while it lasted. I was impressed: he was very good-looking, a young star in the company, and he noticed me. I liked having someone to go out with. I never thought of the relationship as long-term; I didn't love him but I liked him. Marriage never entered my mind at that point. It was my first sexual relationship. I really didn't enjoy that part of it at all, and I never had orgasms. I felt that at some point I am going to have intercourse, and it might as well be now. He used condoms. I was physically attracted to him and wanted to do it, but it was scary, not enjoyable. Afterwards I felt, "Why did I do that? It's sinful." That's my Catholic background, which I still had to work through. It didn't stop me from having sex, but it kept me from enjoying it. Six months later, out of the blue, Nick married someone else! That really hurt me because I wasn't ready to let him go. That was the first time anyone had ended a relationship on me. I was angry at him but more angry at myself for getting so vulnerable and not being aware of how it would end.

The second relationship, from 23 to 25, was with Larry. He was a confirmed bachelor, clearly unattainable, and that was fine with me for a while. We were both out for a good time. We'd go to dinner, drive in his Corvette, go to the beach, have parties with his friends. We had a sexual relationship, but it was no better than the one with Nick. I could do it as long as I didn't enjoy it. I did like the cuddling part very much; it would have been enough for me, but he wanted more. After sex I felt lousy, let down, deprived. I never consciously dealt with the meaning of being a single, sexually active woman. I didn't even deal with the issue of contraception; I'd been on birth control pills because I had an ovarian cyst. At 25 I started wanting a more permanent relationship, a promise of commitment, but Larry didn't. He had been up-front about that all along. The difference in commitment created tensions between us, and the relationship just fizzled out. In the process I got clear that marriage was a top priority for me.

The other five single, anti-matrimonial businesswomen had no sexual experience and very limited relationships with men during the first phase of the Entry Life Structure. They did little dating and came nowhere near forming a relationship that might lead to marriage. All of them were "late bloomers" in social-sexual development. Although they enjoyed working with congenial male colleagues and being part of a mixed social group, they were ill at ease in situations that had a more erotic-sexual potential. For some the inhibition and confusion stemmed in part from sexual taboos rooted in familial morality and religion. But these women had come to reject much of their parents' moral-religious outlook and were forming lives very different from those of their parents. I believe the barriers in their relationships with men derived in large part from their internal Anti-Traditional Figure's anxiety about getting embroiled in a Traditional Marriage Enterprise. They were especially afraid of pregnancy and of getting emotionally entangled with a man—conditions that they expected would lead to a failure to develop an independent self, and would lead to a life of domestic subjugation.

✑ JESSICA HALL

The four years at the firm (age 21–25) were absolutely devastating socially. Gradually I began to blossom a little and become more interesting to men. I dated but was not popular. At 22 I got my first real boyfriend. He was tall, exceedingly handsome, and worked in marketing. Very cafe society. He thought I was wonderful. We went to plays and drove about in his Mustang. He dressed in the latest mode and did the latest things. He had this exquisitely furnished apartment; it was fantastic.

That romance ended when he invited me to visit his parents' place in Boston, and I said no. His parents were away, and I just didn't want to go—I didn't even know why. I figured out two years later that he wanted me to go to bed with him! I only knew about kissing and necking, and a lot of boyfriends bit the dust for that reason. I didn't know what they were looking for. Until I was 26 years old I had no idea; it did not occur to me. I was scared to death about sex because I was afraid of getting pregnant. I had a terror of withering away like my mother and aunts, yet it seemed inevitable. Well, I didn't wither away, but I didn't have much fun either. After stopping with that first boyfriend at 23 I did some casual dating but nothing serious for several years. My leisure life had mainly to do with the ballet and museums and the NYC art world.

Love/Marriage/Family in the Second Phase

As the second phase of the Entry Life Structure began, sixteen career women (twelve businesswomen and four academics) were single-never-married. During the second phase nine young women married for the first time; and seven, all in the businesswomen sample, remained single-never-married.

The second phase was the career women's favorite time for starting a family: twelve career women, five businesswomen and seven academics, had their first child in it. Although the faculty members typically married much earlier, both groups most often had their first child at age 27 to 29. The pregnancy and birth were marker events of great magnitude: they filled the previously unfilled family component of the Entry Life Structure and brought this period to its end. The subsequent process of forming a family—and moving toward a new life structure containing both family and career—was part of the Age 30 Transition for these women. For the career women generally, the internal Anti-Traditional Figure had been predominant in the first phase, during which there were no new marriages and no first children. The internal Traditional Homemaker Figure began to assert herself in the Age 25 Shift. She could not tolerate the prospect of getting so involved with a career that her maternal prospects would be destroyed. Most single women got more interested in matrimony and motherhood, and most married-childless women began thinking more seriously about starting a family. (Conversely, the two who married and started a family in the Early Adult Transition, and who spent the first phase largely as homemakers, got more involved in career during the second phase.)

*   *   *

Let us now look more closely at the evolution of individual lives during the second phase of the Entry Life Structure. While focusing on love/marriage/family, I will also demonstrate the interweaving of this component with others, especially occupation.

The Businesswomen

At the start of the Age 25 Shift, twelve businesswomen were single-never-married and three were married without children. Most of the single women had previously been emotionally guarded and anti-matrimonial in their relationships with men. Marriage now had a much higher priority in their lives. They were less interested in casual dating and in men who were poor matrimonial prospects. Instead, they wanted a serious, marriage-oriented relationship based upon mutual respect and equality. At 25 or 26 almost all of the single businesswomen had their first romantic relationship of some duration, affection, and potential commitment, and it increased their emotional/sexual freedom with men. The path was often rocky and the outcome uncertain, but this relationship had from its onset a matrimonial potential that they had not formerly been ready to allow. In most cases the relationship ended, and the young women recognized that they were probably not ready to marry. Seven businesswomen remained single throughout the Entry Life Structure.

ᴥ   MELISSA HOWARD

At 25 I lived with Blaine for several months. What appealed to me was that his friends liked me, and we were acceptable as a couple. For the first time I learned to sleep in close proximity to someone; he always wanted to sleep holding on to me. For a few weeks I felt I couldn't breathe; it was awful. But after he left I missed it and had trouble sleeping alone. He was enamored with me and got too serious too fast. On the fourth date he was saying what kind of kids we'd have. He said, "Of course you'd have to give up your job." And I said, "Oh, and why is that?!" He wanted me to play the traditional wife role, and that I was not prepared to do. No way. For the first time I had somebody devoted to me whom I could enjoy and fool around with. But he wasn't my ideal dream; he didn't quite fit the picture. Then he suddenly got transferred to another country. That was the closest I ever came to getting married. I felt quite bereft for a few weeks, and then gradually it got to be spring. Actually, I missed him for a year or two but the point is, we were going to come to a conflict of wills, and I was not ready to go his way, so . . .

◆§ PAM KENNEY

For a few years after college I dated a fair amount but not one main person, mostly guys on Wall Street. I met Mark when I was almost 25, and we went together for two years. It was a big romance. He was 30, a really "older" man. We enjoyed things like bridge and small dinner parties. I was attracted to him because he was somewhat of a churchgoer like me, fairly ambitious, a hard worker, conservative, very smart. We didn't particularly talk about anything, but we got along really well.

After about a year we were very serious, and for six months we discussed getting married. That was a real emotional upheaval—were we or weren't we? Then all of a sudden, without saying anything, he got engaged to another girl and was transferred to London! I was pretty hurt at the time, but with hindsight I can see that it would have been a disaster. It would have been a *disaster*. I was very immature at that age. I think I was having a good time in NYC: the living arrangements were fine; I was earning my own living and wasn't ready to settle down and give up my independence. I was used to spending my money the way I liked, seeing people I liked, traveling some. I don't remember that we particularly talked about it, but it was understood that if you're 25 and get married, you're going to work another year or so and have a family and live in the suburbs. I wasn't ready to do that, and he really was. I knew that's what it meant to get married: being a housewife and staying home and taking care of the children. That just wasn't interesting to me at all. I don't know whether that was part of the breakup, but now I think it was there even if neither of us realized it.

Certainly I wasn't thinking about a career. It was sort of floating around in my mind, but I didn't mention it. I'm sure Mark would not have accepted having a career wife; nobody really did then. He was very definitely the kind of person who would take care of you, the way my father had. He would have been a really super husband and father. Home and children meant a lot to him. That's part of what attracted me to him. But I think maybe that also kind of scared me off. He was just too traditional, confining, for my life. That was never ever articulated at the time. We never talked about sex; it was simply understood that we would not sleep together until we got married. The sexual interest wasn't strong; I would say medium. I'm not a very demonstrative person and I don't remember that he was. I think if I had suggested such a thing, he would have been horrified—you don't do that with the woman you'll marry!

When Mark left a lot of other things kind of fell apart. I was getting tired of my job, which wasn't going anywhere. So I quit, not knowing what to do next. Then I went home for a few months, and my parents suggested that I go to graduate school. But I didn't want that either; I had no serious thoughts about a career.

When I returned to NYC I was still at loose ends and did temporary work for two months. Finally I got an administrative assistant job on Wall Street. I thought, "Aha, I'm going down to Wall Street, like those guys I've known." It sounded glamorous and fun, though I actually knew nothing about the companies or the work. It turned out there was no glamour and little fun. I worked in the back office as an assistant—a dead-end job. Actually it was okay for about two years. I wasn't really that serious about where it was leading; I was just enjoying life at the moment.

At 28 I started getting tired of living that way. I realized in a vague way that I had no future there. If I continued to work as an assistant, I would have no opportunity to move up or make more money or do more interesting things. I'd be stuck. My chances of getting married didn't seem too good, so I'd probably have to work. Besides, I enjoy working and prefer to have a job in any case, but I wasn't willing to sit behind a desk and type for the next thirty or forty years. I began to think that another field would offer more in terms of a career: opportunities to get out of secretarial work, move around, do different things. But I didn't make a change until a year later, at 29.

The Age 25 Shift led to a strengthening of the Anti-Traditional Figure within Pam Kenney. She made a greater investment of self in work and entered the financial world of the men she so admired, but she was not ready to start a career. The job she took was primarily secretarial yet she remained for two years, "enjoying life at the moment" and not being serious about advancement. Despite the stirrings of change Pam maintained the fragmented Entry Life Structure in which neither marriage nor work was a central component.

At 28 Pam first began seriously to question the Entry Life Structure and to enter her Age 30 Transition. She realized again—and more deeply—that working as an assistant would not provide the kind of future she wanted. She understood for the first time that work would probably be a permanent part of her life. She could no longer take it for granted that she would ever marry, even though marriage was still a goal. She still hoped to marry and form a modified Traditional Marriage Enterprise in which her husband would be the primary provisioner, and she would have a job. If she could not find an appropriate husband, however, occupation would be central in her life, and it became imperative to seek more interesting work with greater potential for advancement. At 29 Pam made the leap and got a staff position in a major corporation—her first overt step toward a new life. The Age 30 Transition began a year earlier, however, when she went through the preparatory inner changes.

Five businesswomen married in the second phase at 27 or 28, and two of the young women had a child as the period ended. In most cases, this was the young woman's first serious matrimonial relationship; it began within, or emerged directly out of, the Age 25 Shift. The young woman felt that it was now "time for matrimony" and that waiting longer might result in being permanently single. She did not idealize her husband as a remarkable or special person; his chief virtues were that he was part of her world and that he supported (or did not object to) her holding a job. Most of these young women had moderate or severe doubts about their potential for becoming a good wife and mother. They also had doubts, at the time of marriage or soon thereafter, about their husbands.

Finally, the three businesswomen who had married in the Early Adult Transition became mothers in the second phase. In the second phase they established a modified Traditional Marriage Enterprise, working full-time, limiting their ambitions, and taking primary responsibility for family. Their efforts to create a more equal balance of family and occupation began in the Age 30 Transition.

⤳ EMMA BEECHWOOD

Emma Beechwood married in the Early Adult Transition. Her husband was in the service, and she found a job in a bank. In the first phase of her Entry Life Structure she made a series of residential changes based upon her husband's work. Each move involved a considerable change in job, home base, and social life. The only constant was a very limited marital relationship and much time for work. Emma was, it appeared, a compliant, hardworking wife who followed where her husband led. The marriage was often rocky in the first phase: "Those first few years were terrible for me. Half the time my husband was gone, and when he was home he was very unhappy." She did, however, find an initial niche for herself in the corporate work world. Her Age 25 Shift started first in her work and then in her life generally:

> When I was almost 25 my husband was stationed in the South, so I moved there from NYC. My bank had just opened an operation in the South, and the head of it was looking for a jack-of-all-trades assistant who could type, take shorthand, and do some backup research on macroeconomic modeling [laughs]. Getting that job was one of the lucky breaks of the world for me. Most people would need five or six years of experience before they could do it. It was extremely challenging.
>
> After a few months my boss got fired and was not replaced, and I inherited everything he had been doing. I did the job but didn't quite know what I was doing. I felt completely overwhelmed. I was really scrambling, although in retrospect I see how valuable it was for my development. In my earlier jobs I was just marking time. That job was really interesting and fun and was a heck of a lot better than being a school-

teacher someplace. It started me toward a career, though I didn't think of it that way at the time. I was just working until my husband got more settled and we could start a family.

Then my husband unexpectedly got discharged from the military and decided that we were going back to New York City. My boss wanted me to stay and offered a very major raise, but I said no. It was very difficult leaving a job that I loved, where I could move up. I loved it in the South, but my husband hated it. It was just a mess—the worst time in our relationship I can remember. I was unhappy about leaving, but I knew it wouldn't work the other way either.

My company transferred me back to their New York office. When we first came here [age 25], we *did* start the life we were supposed to start three years earlier when we married. For the first time we got an apartment and bought furniture and started doing all those housekeeping things that get you established as a young married couple.

The move to New York was not very good for my career. The Southern office was small and unstructured; though I often felt way over my depth, I had great freedom. The New York office had more potential opportunities but was heavily supervised. Even after a year there I wasn't given a chance to do things I was capable of doing. I worked with two men, and we got along very well, but the woman we worked for was a terrible supervisor. She spent most of her time second-guessing the three of us. We spent a lot of time figuring out how to protect ourselves from her onslaughts. She was very temperamental; you could tell what time of the month it was. That was the most difficult working relationship I have ever had. It was hard for the men but worse for me. I really think it was a woman-woman problem. I was a rousing 26-year-old and had my own opinions of the world. She was about 40 and found it difficult to supervise a young woman with any opinions of her own. I still remember some big arguments—insofar as one was allowed to argue with her—about recommendations for investments. I just felt stifled.

When I was 27 a former colleague offered me a job on his staff at another company. It was a big adventure, a chance to go out on my own and to work with someone whose approach I liked. I wasn't thinking about a long-term career so the risk of failure didn't particularly bother me. It would be fun and interesting, so why not? I worked very hard at that job. We got to the point where my husband was also working hard; earlier I had often worked harder than he did. He worked three or four nights a week and weekends, and that was fine because I did the same thing and traveled a great deal.

Soon after starting the new job, I called a conference one night with my husband, and we decided it was time to start thinking about having kids. There hadn't been a sense of enough stability before that. Also, I was afraid I'd have a girl—and very afraid my husband wouldn't like a girl. He would make comments whenever our friends had girls. He obviously thought that it was bad to have a girl and good to have a boy; a lot of men seem to feel that way; I don't know why. But I very much wanted a child. After several months we decided—or *I* decided, not that he ever said it—that he was game to have a child even if it was a girl.

I got pregnant at 28 and had a little girl just after turning 29. In the pregnancy I made another big decision: after becoming a mother, I would keep working full-time for as long as I felt like it. I remember telling myself, "Well, if you change your mind you can always decide to stay home"—though I didn't really expect to. Work and motherhood were closely connected for me in two ways. First, the people at work really wanted me to come back after having the baby. I was a key member of the organization and part of a closely knit team. It was clear to me that of all the people in the department, I was the one that the boss most liked and had confidence in. It was extremely important to him that I continue. When the baby was due I packed up my files, took them home, went to the doctor, and had the baby that night. My boss wanted me to call clients from the hospital room, but I insisted on waiting until after I got home. Second, work was important for financial reasons. If my salary was lower, it would have been very difficult to work after the baby was born. But in fact I was making enough money so that it was very attractive to keep working. If you work full-time you want a private housekeeper, and that's very expensive. Also, we figured that my income was the second income that takes the brunt of the tax bite, even though I earned more than my husband. If you include taxes, other deductions, and the cost of the housekeeper, I earned only 60 percent of my salary. Fortunately, I have always ended up net ahead by working.

For Emma Beechwood the second phase was a time of increasing satis-faction and progress in her work. In her marriage she made uneven progress toward greater equality. It took her until 27 to propose having a child and to deal, even if only obliquely, with her husband's antipathy toward girls. In getting pregnant she was filling the unfilled family component of the Entry Life Structure and ensuring that her engagement in occupation would not get so strong as to jeopardize her responsibility for family.

A crucial change occurred at 28, during the pregnancy, when Emma made a clear decision to be both a mother and a full-time professional worker (although she was not yet ready to see herself as having a long-term career). This was a first step in terminating the Entry Life Structure and marked the start of her Age 30 Transition. It had become essential to continue full-time work after having a child. Unable to justify this choice on the grounds of her own needs and self-fulfillment, she rationalized it on external grounds: she was really needed by her occupational family (boss, work team, and organi-zation); and she was earning enough so that she could afford to work without burdening her domestic family.

ELLEN NAGY

The marriage worked very well on most levels for quite a long time and provided a backdrop within which I could grow. I needed to have the security of saying, "Look, I'm a normal woman because I'm married." But more than that I needed a person who was always gonna be there, whom I could count on, my haven. I needed that on an emotional level, and I got it. The marriage was not about intimacy or passionate love, and I started thinking fairly consciously in these terms in my twenties. I started traveling. I could venture out—literally, geographically, sexually, emotionally, or in job-related ways—knowing that I could always go home. Marriage provided the emotional stability that I needed in order to take some risks. I need one hand on the guide rope while the other hand reaches out for the next ledge. Starting at about 25 I had some brief nonintimate affairs; they enabled me to do more with my femininity/sexuality while remaining in the marriage.

As I got more into my work I needed less from my husband, but he remained supportive during those early years. When I started traveling I would cook and stock up the freezer with food, but gradually I started feeling less responsible for our home life, and my husband took on more and more of the domestic tasks. He was pretty uncomplaining about it, and this allowed me to get more involved in my work.

My husband graduated from medical school when I was 25, and we moved to Connecticut to be near his work. I looked for a job in the area, but my heart wasn't in it. We were both commuting but in different directions, and that was very symbolic. My increasing involvement in international travel led to a very different work life than his. When we had lived in New York we had rarely been alone with each other—he was always working late, and I was always taking courses at night—so we each had a full-time life with lots of other people and not together. When we moved out of the city we didn't have children and didn't know anyone in the new town. We were both involved in demanding jobs, were both tired, and evolving in different directions. Looking back on this time I can see that my husband and I were becoming isolated from each other, but I did not acknowledge this until several years later. I still thought that his career was the primary one and that he would be the primary wage earner who would always support the family.

My career progress accelerated through my work on the international team, and my expertise broadened to more general corporate business problems. During this time, my supervisor Lou and I formed a close working relationship in which he encouraged me to venture into new areas of work. Through his sponsorship I became a project leader, and with this increased responsibility came a growing sense of my own competence.

At 27 my husband and I decided to have a child; we just couldn't put it off any longer. I certainly didn't think about stopping work—ostensibly for financial reasons, but really I couldn't imagine being home on a full-time basis. We were under constant pressure to have kids from friends, business associates, family. The plan was that we would have three children, and I would work part-time.

The Faculty Members

During the second phase of the Entry Life Structure the fifteen faculty members had a relatively high incidence of major marker events such as marriage, divorce, remarriage, and initial motherhood, and they went through significant change in both occupation and marital relationship. Seven young women had their first child between ages 25 and 28. Only two became mothers earlier and two later; the remaining four women were childless at the time of the study and unlikely for various reasons to have a child.

Four faculty members had their first marriage at age 25 to 28. Megan Bennett and Grace Tobin got serious about matrimony at 25 and began relationships that culminated in marriage at 28, and neither had a child within the Entry Life Structure. Eva Pitcher and Alice Abel married in the Age 25 Shift. Their husbands were fellow graduate students who supported their wives' occupational development and independence. Alice Abel and her husband agreed to defer parenthood and formed a mutually satisfying enterprise as a childless dual-working academic couple. Eva Pitcher had her first child at 27 and received her doctoral degree at 28; she continued working but gave first priority to homemaking. For all four faculty members, major changes in marriage, family, and occupation took place in the Age 30 Transition.

Eleven faculty members had married in the Early Adult Transition. Love/marriage/family posed great difficulties for all of these young women in the Entry Life Structure, and several had a rock bottom time. Only Florence Russo's marriage was intact and relatively stable at the time of the study. Four women divorced at age 23 to 27; in the second phase two of them started second marriages that were better than the first yet still problematic. Another six women divorced in later periods, usually in the Age 30 Transition—the most likely time for divorce in all three samples—but the marital problems were evident in the Entry Life Structure.

The early marrying faculty members initially expected that marriage would provide the basis for a fulfilling modified Traditional Marriage Enterprise. Her husband's academic career would, each woman assumed, give her a valued place in the academic world; he often encouraged her interest in graduate studies and appreciated her intellectual/academic qualities. It was not clear to either spouse, however, what kind of long-term career she would have and how she would combine career and family. In the first phase of the Entry Life Structure it became increasingly evident that the young woman's hopes for the marriage were extravagantly unrealistic. Her husband was heavily absorbed in his own career. The early sense of shared academic pursuits turned out to be largely illusory; they had different friends, different interests, and barely overlapping social/occupational worlds. In some cases his career progress was problematic, and she became the primary breadwinner by taking a job that hampered her career while supporting his. If she was a "faculty wife" without her own primary academic role, she had the humiliating experience of being a second-class citizen—an outsider loosely appended to the academic world and not really part of it.

The young woman was also much more subordinate than expected within the marriage. She did most of the domestic chores. If they had children, she took most or all of the homemaking and child-care responsibilities, and he usually had little involvement in household or children. In many cases, the husband's initial willingness to defer parenthood turned out to be an aversion to becoming a father: he preferred not to have children, or to have them only if she was ready to be primarily responsible for their care. The young couple's sexual engagement, often weak at the start, progressively declined. Some couples had an explicitly "open" marriage in the second phase. In other couples, one or both partners had extramarital relationships that later became known to the other.

Nine of the eleven early marriers had a first child by age 28. Within a few years of motherhood most women began to understand that they were living essentially as traditional homemakers in a Traditional Marriage Enterprise on the fringes of academe. To live differently, they would have to wage an all-out fight against the Traditional Homemaker Figure in themselves, in their husbands, and in the surrounding culture, and they would have to commit themselves to an occupation. Otherwise they would be trapped in exactly the kind of life structure they had tried so hard to avoid. They attempted various changes: improving the marriage, ending the marriage, taking a job, getting on a clearer occupational path.

Two early marriers, Stacey Lane and Holly Crane, became mothers in the Early Adult Transition, and focusing on the limitations in marriage and occupation was a major part of the Age 25 Shift for both. In the second phase of the Entry Life Structure they made a sustained effort to do more with occupation and to improve their badly flawed life structures.

ஃ HOLLY CRANE

Holly Crane married a faculty member and became a mother and homemaker at 21. She did not go to graduate school, but became a "faculty wife." Although her husband was a professor, she had virtually no academic-intellectual life.

At 25 she understood that she was essentially a housewife in a Traditional Marriage Enterprise with three children and a terrible marriage:

> By 23 I was overwhelmed, exhausted, and depressed. When my husband went off to work in the morning I'd think, "What am *I* going to do today?" The long stretch of the day was empty, and it was the same day after day after day. I became very sad, very depressed. I went to a doctor and was given antidepressants. They helped me sleep better but didn't touch the feeling that my life wasn't as it was supposed to be. My husband, Ralph, was distant emotionally and sexually, and he was not involved with the children. I learned later that he began having affairs at that time.
>
> At 25 I began a movement out of the home. First I got involved in politics. Then I took a job, which gave me the feeling that I was a good, competent worker. Ralph supported this move; the busier I was the less I needed from him. I was guilty about leaving the kids but learned that having outside work made me a happier, better mother. At 26 I took a graduate course and loved it. The next year, with the encouragement of the people I worked with, I became a full-time graduate student and did extremely well. I finally got a glimmer of hope that I could do something professionally. I became more dissatisfied with the marriage and had an affair. At 29 I completed my master's degree, took a full-time job, and began to work on the feeling that my life must change.

Six of the eleven early marriers had their first child in the second phase, at ages 25 to 28. In the Age 25 Shift none of them was committed to a long-term career. Each one assumed, however, that as a mother she would continue to work (perhaps at a slower pace), while her husband contributed to the homemaking and accommodated partially to her work schedule. By the end of the second phase, however, most of these young women realized that these hopes were unrealistic. Their husbands contributed too little, and the young women felt stuck with the homemaking. Their self-development required them to get more strongly involved in an occupation and to find a better balance of family and occupation. Four divorced in the Age 30 Transition, and Rachel Nash was getting divorced when interviewed at 43.

Finally, three early marriers did not become mothers in the Entry Life Structure (or later). None of these marriages endured for long: Amanda Burns and Brooke Thompson divorced at 26/27; Kristin West began a permanent separation at 34, and none remarried.

AMANDA BURNS

At 23, two years after graduation, Amanda Burns married her college boyfriend. She had just obtained her master's degree, he his MBA:

In college I wondered whom I would marry, but not whether I would marry. My husband and I were both interested in more education and having a career, each in our own way. He claimed to be very interested in my career, and then it turned out he wasn't. I was clear with him that I wanted a family, but I wasn't going to be just a housewife—forget that. I didn't see having kids as changing my life in any way, other than enhancing it. I figured that we'd get students or somebody to live in and help with the kids, and I'd still pursue my career. Eight months after the wedding I got pregnant; it wasn't planned, but it fit into my vision of the future, so I accepted it. Three months later the doctor advised me to abort for medical reasons and I did. I was very sad about it at the time, but as I look back maybe it was just as well.

When I was 25 my husband insisted that I give up work, start a family, and become a housewife! I said, "I was clear with you from the beginning about how I felt, and I'm not going to throw it all away because you say so, even if you are the husband." At that point his career wasn't going very well, and he felt terrible about that. To make it worse, I was quickly promoted. We got into horrible fights in which he would lay on me that "This is what I think, and this is what you'll do." And I'd answer, "But that's not the way I see it." When he couldn't change my mind, he'd lose his temper and hit me. He abused me several times and broke my arm once. Years later, when I read about battered women, I realized, "My God, I was one of those people!" He was always very sad about losing control, but he was very volatile and would just snap. I had known him since I was 20, and he had never acted that way before. I guess I just wasn't doing what the book said you should do. He kept telling me, "Look at your mother, look at my mother, they're both educated women who stayed at home raising the children, and this is the way it's done." When I said, "But that's not the way I'll do it," it just infuriated him. When I turned 26 things got so bad that I moved out for good, and we divorced a year later. By then I was in a doctoral program and committed to a full-time career. I was also in a lesbian love relationship but I didn't rule out heterosexual marriage and family in the future, although they were becoming more optional.

Ending the Entry Life Structure

As the period of the Entry Life Structure ended, all fifteen academics and only eight businesswomen had been married. Fourteen career women (five in business, nine in academe) were mothers. Motherhood was both a fulfillment and a dilemma for these young women. They had assumed earlier that, after starting a family, they would devote several years primarily to homemaking before resuming outside work. At age 28 or 29, however, each woman began to question this basic assumption. She had an initial identity and sense of occupational competence that she was not ready to give up even temporarily. The internal Anti-Traditional Figure urged her to make occupation central in her life. Combining family and occupation became a major life task of the Age 30 Transition for these women.

Sixteen career women had no children by age 28 or 29. The shape of the next life structure was often more ambiguous for these women than for the mothers. All of them wanted to maintain or expand their engagement in work, and most wanted a family as well.

The Entry Life Structure was a time of personal development and growing occupational commitment for most career women. They had been responsible workers for several years and had gained a sense of independence and competence, and they wanted to establish occupation as a major part of their lives. They became more intolerant of dull, demeaning, or unrewarding work and took greater initiative in seeking advancement within the current workplace or elsewhere. As the period ended, most of the women had taken at least a modest step forward.

The career women learned in the Entry Life Structure that a woman cannot exist in the public world on good enough terms without having a serious, full-time occupation. She cannot do it by an entry level job or by being an eternal graduate student. Her husband and his career cannot provide the basis on which she makes a place for herself in the work world. If she wishes not to live within a Traditional Marriage Enterprise, she has to make her own way occupationally and to be valued for who she is.

By their late twenties the career women were beginning to recognize the importance of work in their lives. How much she would invest—in self, time, and energy—in occupation remained to be seen. In the life structure she began to imagine, family was the central component and occupation was important but second in priority. In what sense could she have a career *and* family? How could she combine the two? The answers to these questions continued to evolve in every developmental period thereafter.

13 Age 30 Transition: Career Women

The Age 30 Transition is a mid-era shift from the Entry Life Structure to the Culminating Life Structure. Its nature and developmental tasks have been discussed in Chapters 2 and 7. For the career women this period began at 28 or 29 and ended at 33 or 34. It was a time of significant change, a major turning point in the life course. In each life there were several marker events of great importance. There were also important "nonevents": highly anticipated events (such as promotion, marriage, pregnancy) that did not occur, and their nonoccurrence had an impact on the woman's life. Broadening our perspective from single events, nonevents, and relationships to the process of living over these years, we find a transitional period in which the Entry Life Structure for early adulthood is being terminated and the Culminating Life Structure for early adulthood is getting under way. In every case the life structure that emerged in the early thirties was appreciably different from that of the twenties.

By the early twenties, as we have seen, all thirty career women had outlined a life plan for early adulthood: after college, the young woman would take a job or go to graduate school and become more competent and independent. By her middle to late twenties she would have the ability to start a family without getting trapped in a Traditional Marriage Enterprise. Until then, she would either defer matrimony (the course taken by most businesswomen), or she would marry a man who was ready to delay having children (the usual choice of the academic women).

What did the woman expect to do when she started a family, presumably in her middle to late twenties? She envisioned some form of modified Traditional Marriage Enterprise in which she would initially do little outside work and gradually return to full-time work as the children got more independent. Family would be the central component of her life structure and occupation would be a second priority. Her husband would be the primary provisioner; he would take her seriously as a person and respect her occupational interests, but would be minimally involved in domestic work. The early marriers typically tried to form a modified Traditional Marriage Enterprise of the childless dual-working couple. This enterprise enabled both partners to lead relatively independent lives organized chiefly around work. Only two women started a family before 25 within a Traditional Marriage Enterprise.

Major Life Changes during the Age 30 Transition

Occupation

During this period, all the career women went through major changes in job, workplace, income, and occupational path. They came to a new understanding of the work world: the structure of corporations and universities, the ladders (usually highly camouflaged) that exist within them, and the place and prospects of women on various ladders. Many career women went through a marked, often painful process as they became aware of the competitive struggles, the "politics" of organizational life, and the diverse obstacles to advancement for women. The work world was not as caring nor as rational as the young women had expected, and the career women's progress within it depended upon much more than their own ability and expertise. The career women had to reappraise their occupational aspirations and the relative value they placed on work, family, and other aspects of life.

As the Age 30 Transition ended, both samples of career women were very diverse in their occupational status and prospects for the future. A few women had established themselves on a well-defined career path in a corporation or university. Some were on a career path, but their situation and prospects were more limited or ambiguous. Others were graduate students or were just moving from entry-level jobs to the beginnings of a career path on a corporate or academic ladder, and their prospects were fair to poor. Finally, a few businesswomen were on the verge of leaving the corporate world. Knowing that a woman is completing her Age 30 Transition does not tell us where she is occupationally. It does tell us that she is moving to a new place in her occupational development and that occupation will have a different place in her life structure than it did earlier.

Marriage, Divorce, Staying Single

As the Age 30 Transition began, twenty-one career women—eight in business, thirteen in academe—were married. Of the nine currently single women, seven were never-married, two divorced. During this period nine women divorced—more than in any other period. Four of the divorces were by businesswomen and five by faculty. In most divorces, the chief initiator was the woman, but in every case both partners played a significant part in terminating the marriage. The marriages that continued were often problematic (several subsequently ended in divorce), but they were "good enough" for the woman in that they initially made possible a workable combination of marriage/family and occupation. The marriage always had a different character at the end of this period than at the start.

All seven women who were single-never-married at the start of this period were in business. They became more matrimony-minded than before, and three of them married in the Age 30 Transition, despite strong qualms about the choice of husband. Each of the other four had at least one extended relationship in which matrimony was a clear issue. When the relationship failed, each woman suffered great disappointment and went through a painful reappraisal of her options for the future.

Extramarital Affairs

Fifty percent of the married career women had extramarital affairs, usually beginning in the Age 30 Transition. Several couples had open marriages. Many career women had not been in love or passionately engaged with the men they married, and the couples often lived parallel, unconnected lives. As time went on, these women began to feel a loneliness in their marriage and missed a more intimate/sexual connection with a partner. About half of the extramarital relationships were casual and nonintimate in character. The other half were not casual; some women fell in love for the first time and had a passionate engagement in the extramarital relationship that had been missing in their marital relationship. Often the extramarital affair was part of the woman's efforts to live more independently and more on her own terms.

ANONYMOUS

I met Brad at work in my late twenties. The personal relationship started slowly and got more intense. Work was very much a part of our relationship, and it existed in the work world. I found myself staying later and later at work, talking with Brad, finding our relationship very special. We started falling in love and started an affair when I was 29. That was my first and most important love relationship outside of marriage. It was a storybook romance—very intense, almost out of control. I never felt this strongly toward anyone else, and yet there was much that kept us apart—he was married; I was married. I knew I had my own marriage and could not consider giving it up. He had married early, had kids and was not ready to get divorced. It was all very irrational, tragic, really, yet exciting and fun, too. He generated a great sexual awakening in me and all sorts of other feelings. It was sexually fulfilling but much more than that. It was wildly romantic, everything I'd always imagined since I was a little girl.

Overall, it was more pain than pleasure. It was extremely costly, and I was full of guilt. The affair was against all my values about marriage and fidelity. I felt it was a threat to my marriage, my morals, my life. But it has been worth all the pain. Nothing has given me such a feeling of myself as a woman. It was a doomed relationship from the start, and it ended by my early thirties. We're both still in love; we just don't know what to do about it.

Sexual relationships outside my marriage have given me a certain sense of independence. I need to be my own person, and ultimately if that costs me my marriage I guess I'll pay the price, but I hope it doesn't. My husband has never learned of any of my affairs. I've never understood why I've been willing to take such enormous risk for so little in terms of real satisfaction. I think it has a lot to do with the need to be independent. There's a strong part of me that does not like family life. It's suffocating. I will just not suffer this kind of living death. If the cost of that is great pain and suffering, I'll pay it. It's been a very bad compromise, but I've needed the extramarital relationships for my own development and to go on with my marriage and family life. It's like a plant that doesn't get enough water. To play my role within the family I need some nourishment from outside, and while I've gotten most of that from my career, it's not enough. I need other relationships, too. I have always gotten involved with men who do not threaten my marriage because they are not free. I don't like myself for having the extramarital relationships, but I've come to accept it much more than when I was younger. We're all just muddling through.

Motherhood

Fourteen career women—five in business and nine in academe—were mothers as they entered the Age 30 Transition. As we have seen, the majority of the mothers had their first child at age 27 to 29. For these women having a child was part of the culmination of the Entry Life Structure; the child's arrival filled a long-unfilled component of that life structure, initiated the process of forming a family enterprise, and shaped the onset of the woman's Age 30 Transition.

"Giving birth" is a concrete event occurring on a specific date. "Becoming a mother" is a complex process that ordinarily takes two or three or more years. It requires an even longer process to transform a couple into a family and to form a family enterprise. For the career women the process involved several phases: a time of wondering, usually with some conflict, about having a child; a time of decision to become pregnant; a sometimes extended period of trying to get pregnant; the pregnancy; a few years after childbirth when the three are working out, individually and collectively, what it means to be a mother, a father, a child, and a family. The duration of each phase was quite varied.

This process was extremely challenging for the career women. Initially the challenge was to become a mother and a new kind of wife in relation to a new husband/father. In addition, each woman was developing a different, often deeper relationship to occupation and moving toward a new life structure in which motherhood, marriage, occupation, and perhaps other things might coexist in a reasonably satisfactory balance.

As the Age 30 Transition began, the twelve new couples-with-infant were becoming a family and starting to build a family enterprise. The two women who had started a family by 25 came to feel now that their marriage enterprise was intolerably traditional, and they began to question and modify it. During the Age 30 Transition four women had a first child. Most of the eighteen women who became mothers by the end of the Age 30 Transition were increasing their involvement in occupation and beginning to develop more long-term career goals. This period was thus the developmental context in which career women were attempting, for the first time, to create a life structure containing both family and occupation as central components. Eight were businesswomen, ten faculty.

The Absence of Motherhood

If being a mother is important in the Age 30 Transition, so, too, is not being a mother. Twelve career women had no children by the end of this period. Most of these women wanted to have children but feared they would not succeed. Seven were businesswomen, and four of these women were single-never-married. A fifth, Amy York, divorced without children at 31; as her Age 30 Transition ended she was in a matrimonial relationship with strong plans for marriage and family. Finally, Julia Hart and Pam Kenney were married but deliberately childless as the period ended; they formed a Culminating Life Structure as married working women who expected not to have children.

Five faculty members had no children as the Age 30 Transition ended. Three of them were divorced; without renouncing motherhood altogether, they were forming a new life structure in which career was primary. Two were married. After several miscarriages in the Age 30 Transition, Megan Bennett began coming to terms with nonmotherhood; she decided to remain in a childless marriage and make career central in her life. At 33, her career well launched, Alice Abel began thinking more seriously about having a child but deferred pregnancy for several years.

Family of Origin

Various changes occurred in the woman's relationships to her family of origin, especially parents, in the Age 30 Transition. She occasionally got closer to parents or siblings, but most often there was a growing emotional distance. At the same time the daughter, now an adult offspring rather than a child, often became more responsible and parental toward her aging and increasingly needy parents. It is another of life's great paradoxes that, as we free ourselves more fully from our dependency upon parents and from our vulnerability to their (and our own) image of us as children, we are frequently caught in a role-reversal that is no less burdensome and no more based upon genuine mutuality.

Crisis and Psychotherapy

The term "crisis" is often used but rarely defined (see Chapter 2). It has many implicit meanings. In psychiatry it usually indicates an actual or impending "breakdown," an inability to maintain one's usual life pattern, a state of emergency requiring drastic intervention. In everyday language it often refers to a state of inner turmoil, confusion, neediness so severe that urgent help is required. In a more basic sense it means a *turning point*, a place in a sequence where the subject's condition is likely to alter for better or worse. It is a time of danger but also of opportunity.

I use the term in this last sense. A crisis in life structure development is a time when the further evolution of the life structure is in considerable jeopardy. The present structure is not working well, but the possibilities for improvement seem limited or nil. It is hard to move forward yet virtually impossible to go back or to stay put. A transitional period is likely to be a time of crisis because the flaws in the existing structure become more evident but the options for change are not yet at hand. The outcome may be a much better or a much worse structure.

Some 90 percent of the career women had a moderate to severe crisis in life structure development during the Age 30 Transition. The woman usually focused on a specific problem: whether to remain in a deadening job or take the risk of seeking something better; being stuck in a hurtful love relationship; being devastated by the end of a relationship; severe marital conflict; difficulties related to having a child or not having a child; problems in managing a job and a household. A crisis in life structure development, however, is not simply a problem in "coping with" or "adjusting to" a single stressful situation. It stems, rather, from the experience that one's *life* has somehow gone wrong. The basic question is, "How do I want to live, and how can I move in that direction?" A person's concerns about this question underlie, and give greater weight to, her distress about the more concrete problems of work or love/marriage/family.

✑ DEBRA ROSE

Age 29–35 was a very difficult time in my life. My husband was very ill with liver disease, and it wasn't clear that he would live. I was very unhappy with my work because I had not been promoted. My mother was dying. It was a terrible time for me, one of the worst in my life. I was very depressed.

We think in our late twenties, "Now I'm really adult." Then your life and your whole conception of life are shattered; you realize you had a false picture. That happened to me. I was just unhappy with my life. I really didn't want to go on with my life; the content wasn't more specific than that. I couldn't see any alternative to getting on with the life that I had chosen to live, but I just didn't want to lead that life. Everything seemed hopeless.

Half of the career sample had psychotherapy lasting from several months to several years in the Age 30 Transition—a higher number than in any other period. The incidence of psychotherapy was much higher among the businesswomen and the faculty members than among the homemakers. The difference was due in part to the fact that psychotherapy was more available and more valued in the social-professional world of the career women. It was not, in my opinion, a matter of mental illness. The career women who obtained psychotherapy were not more neurotic, nor in worse straits, than those who did not—or than the homemakers who did not.

The Age 30 Transition is a uniquely difficult period, especially for women. It is a shock to recognize that the Entry Life Structure has major flaws and will not suffice for the rest of one's life. It is distressing to discover, at around 30 (and again at several other ages), that one still has so much growing up to do. And it is never easy to imagine, explore, and pursue a new life quite different from that of the twenties. Psychotherapy was a source of help that some women could turn to. Other means were used as well: college and graduate courses, body fitness programs, encounter groups, assertiveness training, cultural pursuits, and many others that change with the times. These activities are usually intended to bring about specific improvements in knowledge, skills, aesthetic enjoyment, physical health. Many persons who engage in them have the private hope that the activity will also bring about an improvement in the overall quality and structure of their lives.

Are developmental crises necessary? If we learn better how to cope or adapt, can we not avoid crises altogether? To avoid all crises in life structure development, a person would have to traverse the Early Adult Transition without great turmoil, build a highly satisfactory Entry Life Structure, and then go through so little change in self and external circumstances that major transformation of the life structure was never needed. Unfortunately, most life structures are flawed to some degree. We must build every structure (especially the Entry Life Structure for each era) without being fully prepared to do so. Crisis is less likely if the existing structure seems to require little or no change, if considerable change can be made without great suffering, or if we remain in an unsatisfactory structure without acknowledging its hurtful qualities.

In every life I know about in some detail—through research, psychotherapy, published biography, serious fiction, personal relationships, self-exploration—the person has gone through at least one crisis in life structure development by age 65. From time to time along the life course it becomes necessary to make a significant change in life structure. The need for change in structure derives partly from changes in the self that must be lived out. It derives also from changes in external conditions such as depression, prosperity, war, cultural and institutional change, personal circumstances, our movement from one generation to another with increasing age. Certain forms of crisis accompany our active struggle to create a better life. Other forms occur when we maintain too long a life structure that, however satisfactory it may initially have been, becomes decreasingly viable in the world and suitable for the self.

In the Age 30 Transition, many of the career women, like the homemakers, often came to feel that they had gone through the twenties with minimal awareness of themselves, of their future lives, and of their relationships with significant persons and groups. They realized that they had often lived from day to day, doing what was expected, without any clear sense of making choices. It was not surprising to find this experience among the homemakers, who had generally devoted themselves to following the scenario given by family, class, and community. The career women, in contrast, had had a stronger subjective sense of making choices. During their twenties most women were genuinely independent in many ways—deferring marriage or family, learning to be competent in the work world, becoming more separate from (and in some cases directly opposing) the family of origin. Yet they, too, became aware in the Age 30 Transition that they had been remarkably naive in their personal relationships and work life. The internal Traditional Homemaker Figure had operated with much greater force than they had realized and had limited their search for a different path. This awareness was sometimes furthered by psychotherapy but occurred as well without therapy.

Ellen Nagy had a very difficult Age 30 Transition, a rock bottom time. Through great effort and developmental work in the Age 30 Transition she was able to attempt to create the basis for a more satisfactory Culminating Life Structure.

ELLEN NAGY

I was pregnant at 28 and very happy. I loved my job and planned to work part-time after the baby was born. I felt like a total woman. I worked intensely all day at my job and returned home to build a nest, cook, decorate my home. Inwardly I still felt insecure and at times overwhelmed with the home, the marriage, and the career.

Jennifer was born as I turned 29. It took me about two weeks after I recovered to realize that I wanted to go back to work—that I had to get out of the house. I didn't notice any maternal instincts, quite frankly [laughs]. It took me months if not years to entangle my heart with hers. I felt lousy on all counts. I just hated it. I had a terrible sense of being trapped and didn't know what to do. I really felt that I was the only woman who ever felt this way, that I was some sort of monster. I was awful to live with— profoundly depressed and convinced that I was losing my mind. I was terrified to see a psychiatrist because I was sure he would tell me to stay home with my child. This depressed period lasted two years. No one gave me any support. My mother wouldn't spend any time with my child to give me relief. She was never interested in being a grandmother. I got overt support and covert undermining from my husband. He was very connected with Jennifer and felt strong competitiveness toward me: "I can be a better father to Jennifer than you can be a mother." Two months after my daughter was born I went back on birth control pills and back on the job full time. I was commuting four hours a day and traveling internationally. I also took a graduate course because my skills were rusty—and it gave me another excuse not to go home.

I functioned well on the job. Work was the only arena in which I felt all right about myself—competent, respected, and in control. This was in sharp contrast to the relationships at home where I often felt inadequate and bewildered. As my husband grew more impatient with me, I moved more into my career. At 29 I was promoted to manager of a group of ten with line authority over projects. It was a quantum leap for me, into line management. The promotion gave me a fair amount of authority, responsibility, and voice. I enjoyed the challenge and felt that I was learning a great deal. This promotion moved me away from my mentor, Lou; he had to be left behind. It was difficult for him to have his protégée move out from under him and then surpass him. He had been important in the sense that he gave me a lot of responsibility. The fact that I was female had nothing to do with it, and that was wonderful. Lou and I didn't socialize outside of work, and I had no other mentors.

Other than my boss, most people at work were overtly negative. "Don't you feel bad not being home with your child?" People who had been supportive earlier became really competitive. I realized that they had written me off as a woman who would eventually go home and have kids. Now they had to deal with me as a person who might be competing for the same job.

Soon after Jennifer's birth I was put on a task force to see whether the company was using women appropriately in the workforce. That task force altered my life. I hadn't paid much attention as to why there weren't women around. I was ignoring the fact that much of the workforce was female; they just happened to be secretaries and file clerks! My younger sister was becoming a pretty radical feminist. I thought she was full of crap, but I wasn't on good terms with her at that time.

In diabolical form they put in charge of this task force a man who was the original sexist, along with two former secretaries. They decided to have one woman—me—who was educated and a professional. The task force started asking basic questions about what women can and can't do. It was not apparent who was the most sexist, the men or the women sitting around that table. That forced me into a very activist position, and I began reading and thinking. We asked why there weren't more women in professional positions. Then we started looking at the hiring and training efforts. There was a high level of overt sexism, a conviction that women could not do this or that. Stuff that I had ignored or buried, just as a survival kind of thing, came flooding in. We made our presentation to the executive committee. I said, "Women can do these things; *I'm* doing these things," but no one would listen. All my awareness turned to anger. The anger came from a completely new awareness of what was going on in the world.

Being on the task force was a mixed blessing. At work most people saw me as a person with ability, but many saw me also as an uppity female who was out to cause all kinds of problems, who didn't fall into line, who wasn't docile, who didn't know her place. I had a reputation of being a tough and radical feminist, although I was still at the conservative end of feminism. It hurt my career and helped it at the same time. I got the ultimate "compliment" from the president of the company: "That woman has balls."

Feminism was an issue in my life by 30. This was a time of great disconnection: trying to integrate family and work, turning 30, finding my whole sense of myself as a woman changed. My business self and my personal self were split. I was involved with the struggle of: Can I be a businesswoman and also an attractive female? I assumed that once you became a mother men didn't look at you like you're a sexual person. Men don't turn 30 and wonder whether they are still sexual people, whether their sex life is over. No man who is successful in his job is ever thought of as not masculine. All of this questioning and inner change was going on within the context of the birth control pills, the task force work and feminism becoming an issue in my life, being a mother for the first time, the problems in my marriage, and the extraordinary level of despair which came from my life circumstances.

At 31 I went off birth control pills to see if it would help my depression, and within two weeks I felt better. I think the physical part of the depression was caused by the pills, but part of the depression had to have come from being stumped about what I wanted to do with my life and being unable to face the implications. Finally I began to ask, "What am I going to do to make my life not be so bleak?"

The marriage started coming apart when I was 31. For a long time I hung all our problems on my commuting—the four hours daily were so tiring and took such a chunk out of my life. I had been committed to marriage as forever, even if it wasn't working. I hadn't thought I had a choice, but then I started to sort all that out. I started to enjoy mothering and to regret the commute. Carl refused to find a job in New York, and I began to realize I didn't want to work outside the mainstream or go back to a much more junior level. Carl and I didn't fight, but we didn't have much. We had no connection. By then we had no sexual intimacy, which was certainly my preference. I felt that nobody knew me or cared what was happening to me. I finally concluded that I wanted a different relationship with a man. I wanted to have a physical component and to be with someone whose basic interests and attitudes were compatible with mine, and I wanted more children.

I separated at 32 and divorced at 33. I initiated the divorce, and Carl ultimately agreed. The split-up was difficult in that we were caring of one another. I moved to an apartment in New York City with my daughter and got a full-time housekeeper. We agreed that Jennifer would live with her father summers. There's no blame on my ex-husband in any sense. Who could have envisioned the changes in our lives? He was moving along a course that was relatively predictable when we were 20. If anyone changed beyond what could have been envisioned, it was me. It's one thing for a woman to work part-time, have three children, and put her husband's career first. This was the woman Carl had married. It's another thing to turn into this woman who was more developed, more focused outside the home, and more cosmopolitan. For the first ten years of marriage he was the right person for me and I for him, and I still think very highly of him.

When Jennifer was born, my colleagues expected me to curtail my involvement in career and channel it into parenting. When I did not do so, they gradually began to view me with more respect, and at 32 I was promoted to a senior executive position. Through my work my stature and influence increased dramatically.

Friendship

Half of the career women reported having had friendships with other women of some intimacy and importance. The other women reported a wish for such friendship and a sense of deprivation in not having it in their lives. Beginning in the Age 30 Transition the issue of friendship became central for almost all of the career women.

≼   DEBRA ROSE

One of my best friends today is one of my roommates from college, Carol. Although we have rarely lived in the same city and her life is completely different from mine, my friendship with her has always been a very important relationship in my life. I feel she is the one person who accepts me completely as I am.

For Debra Rose, as for many of her fellow career women, one great value of a close friend was as someone with whom she could be honest and open about herself. When she was 29, she wrote a letter to Carol that crystallized this theme. She spoke of the agonizing "real wilderness" she found herself in—a "wilderness" typical of the Age 30 Transition—and of the "many lies and illusions" that she felt forced to live by. Yet her friend was "still there, still a part of my life."

Career Paths in the Age 30 Transition

How far had the career women gone occupationally as the Age 30 Transition ended? Since pathways in the business world are different from those in the academic world, I'll discuss the two groups in turn.

Business Sample Career Paths

Taking into account each woman's work situation at 33/34 as well as her prospects and plans, we can distinguish four levels of advancement within the business sample:

(1)   Two women were relative "stars" in terms of advancement, prospects, and income. Ellen Nagy was on a ladder leading to the upper reaches of an international firm. Debra Rose had just been promoted to a top position in a bank. At 33, both women had had mentorial relationships. They had advanced farther than most women in their fields and had good reason to believe that they were getting launched on extremely promising careers.

(2)   Four women were entering a well-defined career path, but their situation and prospects were less favorable than those in (1). As the Age 30 Transition ended, Julia Hart and Molly Berger recognized that they were not strong contenders in the bitterly competitive race for promotion. They continued to develop their professional skills but understood that the next career move would take them to a less prestigious firm and/or a different organizational ladder. Abby Murphy had a top staff position in a medium-size company. She had decided to leave the corporate "major league"— subjectively a relief in many ways to those who do so, but also a disappointment. Emma Beechwood had a staff position with good prospects for advancement to a higher staff level, but she was not on a ladder that led to the top of the management structure.

(3)   Six women were just moving from entry-level jobs to the beginnings of a career path on a managerial or professional ladder. Their prospects for further advancement were fair to poor. At 30 Michele Proto took her skills as computer programmer to a financial corporation where she hoped to advance from a technical to a managerial ladder, and at 33 she was not clear about her chances for promotion. Pam Kenney spent her Age 30 Transition as an administrative assistant. At 33 she was promoted and, for the first time, thought seriously about moving into management. The other four had corporate jobs as managers and a chance, albeit a small one, of advancing up the staff ladder.

(4)   Three women were on the verge of leaving the corporate-financial world. They had come to feel that the psychological costs of a corporate career far exceeded the benefits. While intending to continue with some form of outside employment, they now gave first priority to family. They needed a while longer to make this change, but the plan took shape as the Age 30 Transition was ending. Jessica Hall had her first child at 34 and began planning to replace her career with a more manageable small business of her own. Sally Wolford gave up her job, had a child, and became a homemaker with part-time outside work. Amy York began a matrimonial relationship at 33, with plans to marry, have a family, and quit her corporate work in a few years. This group constituted only 20 percent of the present sample of 35–45-year-old women currently working in the corporate world. It would constitute a much larger percentage of a

sample of younger women, many of whom leave full-time corporate employment during the Age 30 Transition.

Faculty Sample Career Paths

To provide a context for discussing levels of advancement among the faculty members, let me note briefly the usual steps in an academic career. The university structure is a maze of positions and ranks. The prefaculty steps include: attending graduate school, obtaining a Ph.D. degree, and often holding a temporary position such as postdoctoral fellow, lecturer, or instructor. The "tenure track" faculty positions are assistant professor, associate professor, and professor, in that order. Tenure (a permanent appointment that can be terminated only for extreme cause) is most often granted at the rank of associate professor, occasionally one step higher or lower. There are also a number of nontenure track positions such as lecturer, adjunct professor, visiting assistant professor, instructor; these appointments may be made for one or more years and are renewable, but they provide no career path and no assurance that one will be considered for a promotion and/or tenure track position.

In evaluating the occupational level and prospects of the academic women at the end of the Age 30 Transition, we can distinguish three levels corresponding roughly to (1), (2), and (3) among the businesswomen. There was no faculty counterpart of level (4).

(1)   Five women were in the middle of, or were just completing, an assistant professorship and had made a promising start in the academic career. Four of them earned the doctorate at age 26 to 29. Most then spent a few years as postdoctoral fellows or lecturers and at around 30 became assistant professors on the tenure track. A faculty member not on the tenure track— and there are many, a growing number being women—has a rather precarious hold in the college or university and limited chances of promotion. Getting on the tenure track is the first step in a difficult struggle for advancement. For every woman graduate student who gets to this point, there are many who drop out, go elsewhere, or get pushed out along the way. Men face similar difficulties, but to a lesser degree.

During the Age 30 Transition each faculty woman became aware that being a faculty member is tremendously different, in external situation as well as subjective experience, from being a graduate student. As a graduate student the woman was completing her professional training, gaining skills and competence, earning a modest livelihood, performing various adult roles, forming her own home base, perhaps being a wife and mother. Yet she did not have the full responsibilities of adulthood. She lived in a relatively benign, protective environment. Her academic requirements, though at times stressful, were manageable. In the woman's private experience, however, she often felt mostly like a student without a sense of where it was leading. She had little sense of life after the doctorate. Being a graduate student was real, but being a professor oneself was a shadowy future possibility. Despite considerable success, the woman was often not entirely ready to become a full professional.

As the Age 30 Transition ended the woman had a much stronger sense of self and career and had established herself as a promising young member of the faculty. At this point Rachel Nash and Alice Abel had just become associate professors. Amanda Burns, Helen Kaplan, and Grace Tobin were in the middle of their terms as assistant professors. Advancing to this level did not mean that the women's difficulties were over. It meant, rather, that they had mastered the initial problems and were now confronted with the challenges of the next career step.

(2)   Six women were just becoming assistant professors and getting on the first rung of the faculty ladder. All completed the doctorate (for one of them, the Master of Fine Arts) at age 28 to 31 and then spent several years in fellowships or temporary jobs. They became assistant professors as the Age 30 Transition was ending.

The slower progress of this group of women had its sources both in external circumstances and in the woman's inner relationship to her career. Florence Russo spent from 29 to 33 earning her MFA, raising a family, and teaching high school. At 33 she obtained her first full-time academic position as assistant professor in a nearby university. Brooke Thompson was an off-and-on graduate student during most of her twenties. She entered a doctoral program at 29, obtained her Ph.D. degree at 31, and started an academic career at 33 after two marginal years. The other women provide variations on these themes.

(3)   Four women did not enter a doctoral program until sometime in the Age 30 Transition. They obtained their doctorates from ages 37 to 41. Holly Crane had become a full-time mother/homemaker at 21 and got her master's degree at 29. Entering a doctoral program at 34, she committed herself for the first time to an academic career. During her twenties Kristin West taught high school and supported her husband's faltering efforts to become a novelist. In the Age 30 Transition her own artistic/intellectual aspirations began to flourish. As the period ended she obtained a master's degree and, in an act of great self-affirmation, entered a doctoral program. At the same time she ended her marriage and became a single childless woman attempting to make career central in her life. After getting her master's degree at 25, Erica Warren spent several years as mother, homemaker, and part-time job holder. She entered a doctoral program at 30, divorced at 32, and remarried the following year. Stacey Lane returned to graduate school at 28; she earned her master's degree at

31 and her doctorate at 37. As the Age 30 Transition ended she was seeking, with limited success, to combine family, outside job, and preparation for an academic career.

For these women, entering a doctoral program was part of an effort to make occupation more central in their lives. The decision to attend graduate school was a basic life choice, not simply an occupational choice. It reflected a growing sense of self and awareness of personal aspirations. The process of making and implementing this life change was shaped by the developmental tasks of the Age 30 Transition.

Motherhood in the Age 30 Transition

Eighteen career women became mothers before the end of the Age 30 Transition. These women had the opportunity to work toward a Culminating Life Structure combining family and occupation. To what extent did they do so? Twelve career women did not have children by the end of this period. How did these women deal with the nonrealization of their plans, and what kinds of life structures did they go on to build? For both groups, I'll examine the changing place of occupation as well as family in the life structure.

The Mothers: Attempting to Combine Occupation and Family

Of the 18 career women who had their first child by the end of the Age 30 Transition, only two started a family before age 25. They initially formed a modified Traditional Marriage Enterprise and then sought to combine family and occupation in the Age 30 Transition. Thirteen became mothers at age 25 to 29, in the second phase of the Entry Life Structure; their Age 30 Transition began during the pregnancy or within a few years thereafter. In every case, the onset of the Age 30 Transition led to a severe questioning of the initial modified Traditional Marriage Enterprise and an effort to balance family and occupation more equally in the life structure. Three women had their first child late in the Age 30 Transition. Toward the end of the period most of the eighteen mothers made a firm decision to combine family and full-time occupation. Some women made the decision after being home with an infant for a while and finding full-time motherhood too limiting. Others, like Emma Beechwood, made the decision during the pregnancy. Every mother came to a new view of herself and the meaning of occupation. Work had become essential to her sense of self, and she wanted to have a significant place in the occupational world for the rest of her life.

Some women experienced a growing sense of career. They were forming an occupational identity and long-term goals based on cumulative accomplishment. Other women did not form, or considered and then rejected, the idea of a career with long-term goals. They wanted to make a contribution and be appropriately rewarded by it, but they expected to have a succession of jobs, each presenting itself as an unpredicted outcome of the previous one, without active planning or strategy on their part. The women had come to recognize that the organizational world was a highly competitive arena in which most others were engaged in bitter rivalries, and that women generally fared poorly in that game. They themselves chose not to "play politics" nor to seek highly ambitious goals but to take the best available options.

At the same time, each mother wanted a family and was prepared to accept primary responsibility for the homemaking and child care functions. She "managed" the home by hiring and supervising help, by devoting much of her evening and weekend time to domestic work, and by dealing herself with the recurrent emergencies of household and child care. The husband had to deal with unexpected demands. His new role in family life was not what he had envisaged. His wife was less available than he had imagined to children, to household, and to him personally. She needed his domestic labor, moral support, and involvement with children—not in large amounts, but to a degree that he sometimes found uncongenial or in violation of his own attitudes and values. Every couple had to work out a new marriage enterprise based in part upon a modified marital relationship and sense of self. This task was never simple or without difficulty.

A word about the husbands and their part in the career women's process of change. They had accepted their wives' occupational interests and limited involvement in domesticity, but they were by no means egalitarian feminists. Even in the initial phase of marriage as a childless dual-working couple, his career had been seen by both as the primary one, and she was responsible for most of the domestic work. Both partners preferred to give and to receive a good deal of emotional and social space; usually neither wanted an intense or entangling relationship. Many couples lived parallel, unconnected lives.

In many cases the husband's career progress was uncertain or troubled during the wife's twenties. By the end of her Age 30 Transition, the wife's earnings and prospects equaled or exceeded the husband's in about half of the business sample and a third of the faculty sample. When the first child arrived, the husband was accustomed to living on a dual income and had an interest in maintaining it. Although the couple shared the provisioning function, they had an agreement that he was the primary provisioner: his income covered the standard living expenses, whereas her "net income," after deducting expenses attributed to her working, was a kind of a bonus to be used for taxes, extra household costs, and savings. The couple went through all sorts of gyrations to downplay the woman's own career success and to make the husband feel more successful. Once the family began, some of the husbands gave more time to homemaking—but not much more. Each man did a limited amount and kind of domestic work. Anything beyond that limit, however, the husband often experienced as a threat to his career, his personal rights, and his masculinity.

In every couple, considerable effort was required by both partners to resolve the tensions and to create a new marriage enterprise. Divorces were obtained in the Age 30 Transition by three of the eight business mothers and by four of the ten faculty mothers—roughly 40 percent of all the career mothers, a larger percentage of divorce than in any other period.

During the Age 30 Transition, many career women realized that they wanted love/marriage/family *and* career to be co-central components of their next life structures. They started forming the combined Dream of the Successful Career Woman in a Neo-Traditional Marriage Enterprise. In this enterprise, the husband would be the primary provisioner, and his career would have first priority. At the same time, both spouses would recognize the legitimacy and importance of the wife's career. The woman assumed that she would continue to take major responsibility for the homemaking and child care, delegating some chores to paid household help and doing the rest herself. Under the current historical conditions, it was the best available compromise the women could find between the internal Traditional Homemaker Figure and the internal Anti-Traditional Figure. The faculty members were more successful than the businesswomen at transforming their modified Traditional Marriage Enterprises into more Neo-Traditional Marriage Enterprises or choosing second husbands who were more interested in Neo-Traditional Marriage Enterprises.

✍ EMMA BEECHWOOD

Emma Beechwood ended this period with two children, an intact first marriage, a newly structured marriage enterprise, and a new career path. In Chapter 12 we followed her course through the Entry Life Structure, culminating with her pregnancy at 28 and her unexpected decision to continue working full-time after the baby arrived. The story continues with her motherhood at 29:

> Jamie turned out to be an ideal child—cute as a button, very smart, very easy to deal with. I don't remember having a postpartum depression. I was very happy, very pleased with being a mother and having this lovely child. Despite his earlier negative attitudes about girls, my husband liked and

enjoyed Jamie, but he wasn't that actively involved in her care, and he pretty well left the entire thing to me. Our basic rule was and is: I'm responsible for the children; my working is secondary and not my main contribution. Even after my daughter was born, we ran our family finances on the theory that we lived off his income, whereas we saved and invested my income. If for some reason I stayed home it would not be a problem, since my husband supported the family. Until the pregnancy I had expected to follow the same course as my mother: work for several years after college, start a family in my late twenties, spend five or ten years raising kids, and then go back to work, but no career.

The odd thing is that although Russ sees me as responsible for the home, he also wants me to work. He didn't push me to work, but he made it clear that he was more than happy for me to continue working. He has always viewed his mother as lazy because all she ever did was stay home. For him, being a housewife in the suburbs is a real rip-off.

So I got a full-time housekeeper and went back to work when the baby was born. It wouldn't have worked at all if I had stayed home. Russ has always worked late a few nights a week and on weekends. I would have gone berserk very quickly, being home all day with a child. I'm perfectly happy to spend time with the children on the weekends when my husband is at the office or at the gym. When Jamie was born I cut down to a forty-hour workweek, at the office from 9 to 5, being a good mother and spending time with my daughter. But that was very hard on me. I felt fine as a mother but terrible about my work—very inadequate, like I wasn't working enough or doing it right, sort of postpartum work blues. After three months I went back to my usual schedule, leaving earlier for work and getting home around 7:00 p.m.

Wall Street had been in turmoil for five years. I got promoted and found that most titles don't mean a bloody thing; my title was a substitute for a real promotion and pay raise. I knew that Wall Street and I were not going to make it for the long term, and I began, slowly, to consider other jobs with more career potential.

When Jamie was about 6 months old, my husband and I decided to have another child, so I got pregnant again. A few months later I had a miscarriage. That was pretty sad, a trauma. I decided that was it with my job. I was not going to fool around taking week-long swings around the country and endangering a pregnancy.

Turning 30, I got an excellent job with a small financial company. I worked 9 to 5, had very little travel and more time with my child, which was ideal. There wasn't the tension and turmoil of Wall Street. Six months later there was another economic downturn, and they fired 25 percent of the staff, including me. Getting fired triggered the decision I had been contemplating for some months: to make a major career change and work in the safe, sane world of the corporation. I wanted a more stable work environment that would give me time for raising a family, and I wanted a place in which I could have a career—be able to change jobs periodically and have a sense of advancement. I hadn't been looking for either of those before.

At that point I got a job here, a major corporation, and it turned out to be a great decision. I learned later that I was hired as part of an affirmative action program for women. They wanted a woman from an Ivy League school who had a liberal arts background and some experience in the financial community. I more than met those requirements; after seven years on the Street, I was very competent and experienced.

There were lots of problems at the company but also real opportunities for a competent staff person to advance. There were very few junior women and almost no senior women. It is still extremely difficult for women here; that is not explicit policy, but it's how the world operates. So far I've done well—four promotions in seven years. Whenever I got bored with a job, I was offered another one.

Around this time I became concerned that I hadn't gotten pregnant again, and I really wanted more children, so the doctor gave me mild fertility drugs. Several months later I got pregnant. I had figured that the second child would be a snap. It would be a boy, and we'd have a nice family, and I'd go right back to work because that's easy, right? I worked until the day before childbirth. But I had a C-section! It was physically a killer, and recovery and taking care of an infant and a toddler was overwhelming through the first year for my husband and myself, even with our good housekeeper. I went back to work part-time three weeks after childbirth and full-time soon after that.

Another thing made that first year (age 32–33) really tough: I was promoted to manager. Just before the baby was born, my boss was promoted up a step, and I was promoted to his job. I had never known what my next job would be and have never plotted out my career in the sense of setting long-term goals. I just figured that as long as I'm performing well one job will lead to another.

Between the job and the kids, it was almost too much. My husband and I got married way before women's liberation. We have what I would call a traditional relationship where he works and I'm responsible for the house and children, although I work too. We've always had a housekeeper to do the household chores, but the child care is my responsibility, and my husband's help is an extra. I cook the dinners and wash the dishes. My husband occasionally cooks a fancy dinner. After the baby was born, my husband suddenly had to do a lot more. At night he would often get up and feed the baby. We were physically wiped out, just struggling to survive, for months after the baby was born. I remember going away to a management meeting and thinking it was fantastic. You could have breakfast peacefully and just deal with the day without changing diapers and cleaning up messes.

This was one of the hardest times for our marriage, though not the only one. I felt like I was working very hard, and I felt Russ didn't appreciate me. He may have felt the same way—that he was doing double duty, having a job and doing a lot with the kids, and I didn't appreciate him. Part of it was that I was more successful in terms of salary and advancement. We didn't discuss it, but I was becoming more aware that it bothered him. I tried not to mention my income, or getting a raise, but the tension was there.

When I was 33 the turmoil subsided a good deal. My son was a year old, and things were easier at home. My job was also much more in control. My boss was slated for a promotion and prepared me as his successor, and just before turning 34 I got the promotion. I didn't start out with any great career aspirations and still don't have them. I have never pushed for a salary increase or promotion; they just came. I think you do better if you're not pushy. It was somewhat haphazard that I got where I have. I have a good chance of getting into the corporate structure before long, but I don't dwell on that; others will make those decisions for me.

As the Age 30 Transition ended, Emma Beechwood was forming a Culminating Life Structure in which family and career were co-central components. For her, this life structure was flawed in some respects yet well worth its considerable costs. Her occupation was highly affirming and apparently led, in its meandering way, to an interesting future. She felt committed to her family and hopeful for its future as well. At the same time, there was evidence of discontent. The marital relationship gave her little personally and contained frictions that might in time become harder to tolerate. Likewise, she had done well thus far in her career without having to set long-term goals, to exercise a high level of authority, and to get engaged in competitive struggles for advancement. As she moved up the organizational ladder and into successive developmental periods, the questions of ambition, authority, and competition would probably have to be confronted more directly.

✑ ABBY MURPHY

I met Andrew at 25, just as I decided it was time to get married. I liked him, and he had the right credentials—good family, professional, getting an MBA, similar backgrounds and interests. We got married as I turned 27, and it was very nice. We went out to dinner a lot, met people, had companionship. I got home at 8 p.m. after a long commute, and he'd be sitting there reading the paper. Then I'd cook dinner and clean up and do everything, and that was fine with both of us. At the time I thought, "I really enjoy being married." What I had in mind was, "We will have a happy marriage and everybody will know that, and Thou Shalt Ignore Any Problems." I was busy putting up and keeping up this image. Looking back, I realize that I didn't know what a close relationship was; I didn't have one with my parents or see one between them or anyone else. My main idea was to be the perfect wife, which meant taking care of everything and everyone, including my husband.

A year after we married, Andrew wanted to have a baby. I had mixed feelings about it, and I was trying and not trying to get pregnant, but I got pregnant at 30. During the pregnancy I felt confused and isolated. I didn't want someone else dependent on me. I hated the idea that I had no control over what was happening to my body and that I was dependent on others for help. I felt ugly and fat. The combination of job, home, and pregnancy was just too much. Andrew wouldn't talk about it, and I couldn't talk to anyone else. For a while I even considered abortion.

Finally, I decided to keep working full-time. I would have this perfect child who would be wonderful and dressed in little pink dresses from Saks, and I would be the perfect mother—the opposite of my own mother and of myself as a child. I had never allowed myself to *feel* things. When I got so upset during the pregnancy, I couldn't understand where these feelings were coming from inside of me. I lost my self-control and got a little more introspective, but it took me several more years to begin to know myself somewhat better.

My dissatisfaction with Andrew began to surface during the pregnancy. One day I was weeding the garden and asked him to help me. "I don't do yard work," he says. I was furious! After that we got a yard service, but it was clear that he still wanted *me* to do it. That was the beginning of the end. I traveled for six months during the pregnancy—left on Monday, got home Friday night—but I still took responsibility for arranging Andrew's meals for the week, all the housekeeping chores, everything. At work, my boss gave me a hard time because I was pregnant, but I was determined to stay to the end, and I worked until the last day.

My daughter Mary was born when I was 31. It was an incredibly happy surprise! I felt immediate closeness and a great rush of feeling that I hadn't expected. I wanted to have more children. She loved to be cuddled, and I loved to cuddle her. I wanted a lot for Mary, and at the same time I started wanting more for myself. I would see the pressure Andrew put on her to fit a certain mold. I didn't want that for her, and I became less comfortable with the mold I had always accepted for myself—the good little girl who becomes a good housewife. Andrew liked the Abby he had first known: superefficient, uncomplaining, taking care of him and everything else. And as I learned later in my therapy, I had chosen a man who was weak so I could be the strong one, rather than weak like my mother. He couldn't enjoy Mary and resented my having fun with her. But we never fought because I never stood up for myself.

We had a live-in nurse during the week and a cleaning lady, but I was in charge of the whole shebang. Andrew was very critical of my performance as a mother and gave me no help. I remember once the baby started crying while I was taking a shower, and Andrew brought her to the shower door and insisted that I take care of her; he just couldn't! Early in the marriage we had a good, active sex life, but it gradually diminished, and after Mary's birth there were long stretches when we had no sex. I think we both contributed to that. I learned in therapy that I regarded sex as my giving to the man, not as receiving for myself, and after a while I didn't feel much like giving to Andrew. I also came to understand that the important thing to me was the emotional contact; the sex was secondary.

During Mary's first year I got more and more depressed. It wasn't her; she was the only good part of my life. But my job wasn't satisfying and neither was my marriage. It wasn't one thing—my *life* as a whole just wasn't working. In spite of my newfound resolution to work full time, I felt guilty for not staying home and taking better care of everything—the baby, Andrew, the household. I thought of Andrew as a good father even though his only responsibility was taking out the trash. I felt overwhelmed: "If the wind blows from the wrong direction, this whole house of cards will come tumbling down." Then I began to realize that I deserved more than I was getting. Instead of believing that I should do everything, I was bothered by all the demands people made on me.

Unfortunately, my job was awful, too. From 30 to 33 I had a position as manager at an international corporation. The job provided good experience, but the company was very impersonal, regimented. I didn't feel challenged or part of a working team. It was a staff role, and I need to be involved in the decision making. But they figured that women can't make decisions, so they put them in staff jobs and use that as evidence that women can't make decisions! I monitored men who didn't want anyone monitoring them, especially a woman. I was the only woman and the youngest manager in the department. When I'd talk to a project manager, he'd typically pat me on the head and send me away. I felt totally ineffective though I did better than most; all the other managers had ulcers and were counting the days to retirement. I was learning a lot and knew the job would look good on my résumé. It didn't matter that I hated the job, since I didn't seriously consider whether I enjoyed my work and what it gave me personally. Your own self-growth is not a relevant topic in the corporate world. Men see business as a game, with no room for feelings or intuition. A big part of my trouble was not understanding the game plan. I was set up in a no-win situation, and I wasn't good at the politics, manipulating people to do things for me. I just couldn't survive there.

At 33 I was going nuts about my job and knew that I had to make a change. I went to an intensive six-day personal growth workshop for managers, and it had a tremendous impact on my life. A few months later I took a new job with a big insurance company, another bad decision. I chalk it up by saying that my life was so bad I had to make it impossible before I could get myself out. My biggest problem was the marriage, but

I wanted to believe that the marriage would work if I just had a good enough job. I still think that, with a good enough job, I would have tolerated the bad marriage—that's how I was then. But the new job was *horrible*. I worked for a vice president and had a fancy title—bullshit! I did liaison work between companies within the corporation. I had to solve their problems without any authority of my own. I worked with men who were part of the Old Boys' Network, and there was no way they were going to let *me* in. They were looking for a scapegoat, someone who had the responsibility for creating an order they didn't want and who could then be blamed for its failure.

At 34, after six months in the new job, I got into intensive psychotherapy and soon decided to leave the marriage and the job, in that order. The best thing in my life was my relationship with my daughter, Mary. I couldn't stand to see her so sad and alone and lost, drifting aimlessly. I was beginning to focus on those feelings in myself, and it drove me crazy to see them in her. For the first time, I realized that what you need to give a child is not just food and clothing. It's listening to them, talking, cuddling, commiserating with them. My husband couldn't give her those things and neither could I for a while. In giving her what I hadn't received, I was giving to myself as well. The first few years I had offered her very little, partly because my own feelings were so blocked and partly because I was being drained by all the demands on me, especially from her father.

I felt that I was in a life-or-death struggle. I could have killed myself, not by actual suicide but by becoming alcoholic, being nothing, helpless, out of contact, childlike, dull, like my mother. And that would have been all right with Andrew—his mother was like that, too.

I left the marriage at 34. The amazing thing is that I stayed as long as I did. I believed that as long as I had a husband I was safe. Not that he'd meet any needs of mine—I wasn't aware that I had specific needs or that I had a right to have them—but just that I was safe. As long as my marriage looked like the fairy-tale marriage, it must be so; I had no right to be unhappy. It's like my parents' saying they loved me, and I believed it even though I felt so alone and unloved.

Andrew and I quickly got caught up in this horrible custody fight and court battle. That was my initiation rite, and I won every step of the way. We split our assets 50-50. I wanted no money from him for myself, just half of the expenses for child care and my daughter's education. I went back several times to try to come to a better understanding, but we have never forgiven each other. He sat and cried and said I'd ruined everything. He said, "I did a terrible thing by marrying you. I wanted someone who'd take care of me."

Andrew always said he supported my career, but he really didn't. He certainly wanted the money I made; together we earned a great deal. At the end of the marriage he admitted that he had always felt bad because

I consistently earned more money and was more competent. He felt that there was no room for him, that he was useless in the relationship. That was true in a lot of ways, and it got much worse after my daughter was born. I felt she deserved more, and I wanted to spend more time with her. It was like taking care of *two* babies, but she had a right to be a baby and my husband didn't. He wanted me to take care of everything and be home more, but it was essential for me to work because that was the only place I got recognition and stimulation from other adults.

Just before leaving, I phoned my parents and said, "I'm going to divorce Andrew. If you can't give me your support, don't call me anymore." I was feeling very fragile at that point. I waited for them to call, but they never did. I finally phoned them three months ago — over three years later. There is not much between us now. After I left the marriage I started a whole new life, and a year later I got a much better job.

As her Age 30 Transition ended at 34, Abby Murphy terminated her marriage, began seeking a new job, and started a new life structure as a divorced working mother. The central components of this structure were motherhood and career. Ending the marriage was a "life-or-death" struggle. To remain in it would be a living death like her mother's life. To terminate it gave Abby the possibility of living with greater engagement and vitality, more on her own terms. She hoped in time to marry again, but this was a question for the future.

✑   STACEY LANE

I got a fellowship for financial support. It was a validation and huge moral boost. It meant that somebody else thought I could do this, too. It was three years of courses, one or two a semester. The commuting and going back to school took a huge physical cost, but it was worth it because I wanted my own identity. I finished my courses at 32 and began a six-year project for my Ph.D. I wrote my dissertation a chapter a summer. During all those years I had part time jobs as instructor, lecturer, not getting paid very much for a great deal of work. It was a long, slow process, but I loved it, and I learned I was a good teacher.

✑   ERICA WARREN

In my late twenties I got involved in political activities and began to meet women who were in the Women's Movement. Then I began to see that it was a systemic problem, that other women were going through the things I was, and it wasn't just my personal problem. I wanted my husband to share in taking care of the child, but he was very resistant. His attitude was "I don't want to take the responsibility, and we can't afford baby-sitters, so you give up your outside activities — especially those women who are agitating and subverting my wife when she is supposed to be home taking care of the house and baby." At 28 I got a teaching job as instructor for one year in order to pay for child care. The chairman told me if I'd been a man I'd be paid $3,000 a year more! It was just an incredible amount of work for little pay. I started thinking I'd like to do some serious work, and I began questioning my marriage. I really liked teaching, and I was encouraged to go back for my Ph.D. I was a graduate student from 30 to 37; it was a great reclaiming of a course and self I had left behind so many years earlier. I enjoyed the combination of school and motherhood, and I felt better about myself as a person.

My husband and I hadn't resolved the business of who was going to do housework and child care, and I was still doing it all. There were incredible time pressures involved in trying to maintain all of these activities at once. My husband expected me to be able to manage the child care and the house on the one hand and going to graduate school on the other. But graduate school was an incredible amount of work and a lot of pressure. I just couldn't handle it all, and I wanted support from him. His reaction was, "If you can't handle it, quit graduate school." We had recurring battles which got louder and more unpleasant as time went on. If he did baby-sit I'd come home and he'd be sitting in front of the TV watching football with my daughter in the house all day, and nothing had been done about getting supper ready.

I felt there was no resolution. The conflict had been resolved each time by me accommodating and repressing my own needs. I began seeing lots of other women divorcing, but I just didn't see how I as a woman could pull that off. I just didn't have the strength or the financial independence. But then I thought, "I guess I *can* do it, too." By that time I didn't love my husband anymore. Our sexual relationship had deteriorated, and the last months we slept in separate rooms.

I met George when I was 30. He was a faculty member. We became friends, and we were also attracted to each other right away.

My husband and I separated when I was 32. The separation was orderly and rational and painful and poignant. I had an incredibly awful post-separation trauma. I lived in a collective situation, and I immediately began a relationship with George.

RACHEL NASH

I became a part-time lecturer at this college at 27 and had my second child, Paul, at 28. I loved the combination of work and family. I very much liked the students and trying to get their minds to stretch. It was only when I had been here for a while that I got a sense of what I wanted with my work in a positive sense.

Cynthia was an associate professor in my department, twenty years older than me. She was very encouraging and supportive, and we became good friends. She was a marvelous role model of a woman with a career and children. Gradually I got more separate from her and defined myself in a different way, but she certainly had an important early influence on me.

I was given a full-time two-year appointment as lecturer when I was 28. I felt, "Now I have a seriousness of my own; I'm not just a faculty wife." I got much more involved in my field. I hadn't done any research since my thesis, and I began to ask myself research questions and felt my thesis subject was sterile and didn't lead anywhere for me.

Gina was a researcher here, and we started working together. It was the first collaborative relationship I had had. She really introduced me to my field, but she was very difficult to work with. Gradually I moved away from her approach, but the main thing is that she opened the subject to me, and she encouraged me right down the line.

By the time my son was born my husband Bill's psychological difficulties had set in, and I think he was less enthusiastic about the baby than I was, more aloof. He has always treated Paul from a distance except to get angry at him. Paul has built up this absolute hate for him. Bill has a tremendous need for control, and for a long time I just accepted that. Mainly, at that time I thought of him as being helpful, allowing me to have the kind of life I wanted. Had he not been so helpful I could never have done what I have. We didn't have any domestic help, and he would be home in the morning when I was at work, and then I'd be home in the afternoons. He did a lot around the house, too. I thought our problems were due to the strains because we were running a circus for a while with the two small children and both of us on tenure tracks. Since Bill was having his emotional ups and downs, it seemed essential for me to do well and get tenure so that if he completely fell apart one of us would have a stable job to keep things going. By my early thirties we had a complete reversal of roles.

I was on such a limited time schedule because of the children. I was here from 10 to 2. I taught at 10 and 11 and then saw students, then I had to leave. My schedule was very, very, very tight. I would be sitting in my office trying to do all my work, and in would walk one of these men. He'd sit there and talk about how he wasn't being rewarded properly at the college. I was sitting there, and my time was ticking away. I'd get so mad! I thought they were just idiots. Here I am with this time constraint, and they're taking up my time. I had my office changed to the third floor.

By 30 I knew I didn't want to be part-time anything, because then I could be pulled out at any time by the demands of my children. I felt that I had to have an identity they could recognize apart from them, an identity that would be taken seriously as well as any other commitment, like my husband's work. I was still haunted by that image of women frittering away their time. I really wanted to build, not a career, but some sort of separate identity of my own outside the family. At 31 I got a three-year appointment as an assistant professor, so I knew I was going to be here awhile.

I don't think it ever dawned on me that having a career and family wouldn't work. I didn't see a conflict between being a mother and working because I felt being a mother didn't really have much substance to it. Many afternoons as a child I'd come home from school, and my mother would be at a neighbor's playing bridge until 4:00. I couldn't see how that was better for me than having a mother who did interesting work. The claim that my mother stayed home and took care of the children just didn't ring true to me. She probably did keep a cleaner house, but I don't see that that matters very much unless it becomes a health problem [laughs].

Work and motherhood worked out for me; marriage and self suffered. Work and children were mine in a way that the marriage wasn't. With Bill I always felt that somehow I wasn't quite up to what he wanted or doing what he wanted. I often felt I wasn't being authentically me. There was always a feeling that something would set him off when I least expected it. Gradually Bill came to want a sort of perfection in me. I didn't have that, and he began trying to force it on me. He'd get violently upset and physically abusive if everything did not work his way. And for reasons I don't understand I just accepted that pattern, and in some ways felt it was my fault. I had this feeling that I owed my husband everything for enabling me to have the kind of life I wanted. I just suppressed all my anger and tried to avoid conflict. The cost of that didn't register for a long time. I was trying to be the person he wanted and wasn't being authentically myself. And I was distressed to discover over time that despite my efforts to avoid conflict, Bill was a very, very unhappy person. I started seeing these things in Bill in my early thirties, but it has taken me until now to get more clear.

Work gradually became a very big part of my life. But for a long time I had to operate on two completely different levels. One level was at school, where I could be myself, and the other level was at home, where I did everything possible to avoid conflicts at all times. Bill ran the house totally, starting with financial. I never saw a penny. He did the shopping and the cooking and even chose the clothes I wore. He was controlling every aspect of our life.

Career Women Who Had No Children as the Age 30 Transition Ended

I turn now to the twelve career women—seven businesswomen and five faculty—who were not mothers by the end of the Age 30 Transition. Six were married for much or all of this period and six were single (never-married or divorced). A common theme in this group is that the women did not realize their earlier aim of becoming mothers by the late twenties. Three decided that it was preferable, or at least acceptable, not to have children. For the other nine, however, life in the Age 30 Transition was permeated by the concern with motherhood and the growing probability that it was not to be. Not having children was a great disappointment that colored the women's occupational involvement, love relationships, and sense of self. Each woman had to come to terms with the likely reality that motherhood would remain an unfilled component of her life.

What alternative life structures might there be, and how could one explore the possibilities? Occupation became the leading candidate for central component of the next life structure. By the end of the Age 30 Transition, most of these women were devoting themselves more fully than before to occupation and thinking more seriously about having a long-term career, though family continued to be a hoped-for central unfilled component. Within this common framework, the twelve women were extremely varied with regard to love relationships, marriage, occupational advancement, and hopes/plans for the future. Let us now look at some individual lives in more detail. For descriptive purposes I'll divide them into two subgroups, the single and the married.

Single Career Women without Children

Six of the twelve childless women were single (never-married or divorced) throughout the Age 30 Transition. All of the women had at least one significant love relationship in this period and all were interested in having a stable partner. With regard to love/marriage/family, perhaps the most important difference among the women was this: Four women gave first priority to occupation; they wanted to have a stable love relationship (with or without marriage), but preferred to postpone or rule out family. Two wanted above all to get married and have a family, even if this meant limiting their involvement in occupation.

The women who put occupation first wanted a stable romantic-domestic partnership, though not necessarily legal marriage or motherhood. Amanda Burns and Brooke Thompson were faculty members who had divorced at age 26 or 27 and did not subsequently remarry.

⋞ऽ   AMANDA BURNS

As we saw in Chapter 12, Amanda Burns's abusive husband insisted that she become primarily a traditional homemaker, in opposition to her own desire for a combination of family and career. She divorced at 27 and completed her Ph.D. degree at 29. During the Age 30 Transition Amanda expanded greatly in occupational identity and expertise. At 33 she launched a career that led subsequently to a senior academic position, and she had established a lesbian personal life. She was moving toward a Culminating Life Structure in which she was an achieving career woman and a partner in a lesbian relationship without children. She regretted the lack of children and did not rule out the possibility of having them in the future in a homosexual or heterosexual relationship. For the present, however, family had a lower priority in a life built around occupation and personal/social interests.

✑ TRISHA WALL

At 28 Trisha Wall was a single dating businesswoman. She wanted to be financially independent but had no occupational path and no sense of an occupational future. As her Age 30 Transition ended at 34, she had established a stable nonlegal marriage with Nat and was laying the groundwork for a managerial career.

> We met when I was 29 and Nat was 45. He had divorced in his thirties and was a mature and worldly man—extremely attractive, wealthy, cultured, exciting. We were chemically attracted to each other and spent a lot of time together, a wonderful new affair-type thing. I was a young in-transit character, naive, just beginning to learn about the world that he was so much a part of. It turned out that Nat was in transit, too. During the previous five years he had gotten divorced, left his career, and gone through a period of floundering. He was a loner and very elusive. He was doing the New York dating scene, dating the broad spectrum of available women that men have here.
>
> When I was 32 we started spending weekends and a few nights a week together. I got more committed to staying with Nat and building a more solid relationship. I was just about totally focused on him, and that was satisfying to both of us. I was the naive novice in awe of this fabulous man and willing to live pretty much on his terms. I was simply having a good time, with no thoughts about the future.
>
> Luckily, at 32 I got a job at a major firm. I had a staff of twenty-five, and I transformed a small, mediocre unit into an excellent, well-run department. It brought me to the beginnings of a managerial career. By 33, however, I had figured out the job and was again in a maintenance-type situation. In the next year the job was unexciting, but I didn't care that much, since Nat and I were deciding to live together.

Two single childless women tried without success to marry and give first priority to family. For Molly Berger and Michele Proto, family became an increasingly central, unfilled component of the life structure, and its absence cast a growing shadow on their lives in the Age 30 Transition. Despite this pattern's low incidence here, it merits our attention. For one thing, it probably occurs more often in the larger population than in this sample. For another, these women articulated wishes and experiences that were probably true of other childless women (married as well as single) who were less aware of them or less candid in voicing them. Some women who made a considered choice not to have children probably had at times the same feelings described by these two women.

Michele Proto and Molly Berger actively sought matrimony during this period and had a relationship in which marriage was the vainly desired outcome. Both went through a major crisis in which the key issue was: How will I live if I don't have a marriage and family? Is it possible to have a satisfying life as a permanently single childless working woman?

As the Age 30 Transition ended, these women gave occupation a more central place in the Culminating Life Structure. At the same time, love/marriage/family remained a central unfilled or partially filled component, and the women maintained a cautious hopefulness that it was not too late, that marriage and family might yet happen.

While focusing on occupation as a source of satisfaction and self-esteem, these women often found it difficult to invest the self fully in career. Their involvement in work during the Age 30 Transition was complicated by the severe disappointments in their love lives. The internal Traditional Homemaker Figure had bursts of self-righteous indignation: "I told you so! You were so devoted to independence and work that you have lost everything important—marriage, family, a 'normal' life." Even the internal Anti-Traditional Figure was aggrieved: "I urged you to become more self-reliant so you wouldn't get entrapped in domesticity, but you have really gone too far. Marriage and family are important as well."

The women's disappointment had external sources as well. In the traditional cultural meanings of gender, it is a profound failure for a woman not to become a wife and mother. A "spinster" is discriminated against, subtly and not so subtly, in work organizations, in informal community life, and in social circles composed chiefly of married couples. She is subject to harsh images of the cold ruthless competitor, the needy woman in search of matrimony, the pathetic woman leading an emotionally empty life. During the Age 30 Transition women are especially vulnerable to these images and to the assaults on their self-esteem.

∽ MOLLY BERGER

At 25 I was still living at home and dating Art, a surgeon. He was for all intents and purposes the perfect husband, but he was totally boring. My relationship with him involved no communication; it was like my mother being married to my father. My father tried to reassure me by saying that if I married Art and got bored, I could occupy myself by becoming president of the Ladies' Medical Auxiliary! It took me until my thirties to recognize the possibility that I might be able to get married and *not* be like my mother—though at 39 I'm still not entirely convinced.

At 26, after stewing for a year, I started graduate school and got my master's degree a year later. During that year I met Don and had my first sexual relationship. He thought I was wasting my life. That's one of my life themes: I get involved with men who are smart and nutty and help me do more in the world. Those five years living with my parents were like doing time in prison. It was stifling. I often think that I had to spend the next ten years in the city, working hard and traveling all over and being unstable, just to get away from my mother's life.

After getting my MA at 27 I moved to New York City. I worked in corporate finance. I was just one step above the typing pool, whereas most of the professionals with MBAs came in as managers. I had no idea of where it might lead or what I wanted, and I certainly could not picture myself in my present career. After a few months I noticed that there were women assistant managers, and I decided I wanted to do that, so I got myself assigned to a project.

As I turned 28 I worked on a project, and the next four years were the most exciting time in my life. The key person in that story was Ben. He became my mentor and lover and helped me in a million ways. We were the same age, but he was farther along in his career and destined to go much farther. People who work together so closely often share more of their lives than people who are married. The downside for the woman is that you never know whether you're getting ahead because of your relationship or your ability. The worst accusation of all is "She slept her way to the top."

Ben was brilliant, charismatic, tremendously involved in his work but difficult personally. I learned everything from him. It was fantastic to travel all over the world with him and do innovative work and have this secret love relationship, but it was rotten, too. We both dated other people. I did that in order to keep the secret, and he claimed the same thing, but after six months I realized that he enjoyed having a lot of girlfriends. I wasn't special to him, and he had no intention of getting married! I was intensely involved in the work with him, but for me getting married was important also. I was dating a lawyer from my hometown who wanted to marry me. He was a nice guy and everything I did *not* want, but I considered marrying him. Ben's comment was, "What do you want to do, marry him and become a baby factory?"

I was promoted to assistant manager at 29, after doing the work for six months without title or salary. That started the most exciting work time I've ever had—working with the smartest people; I absolutely loved the whole thing. By 30 I was in the middle of all the action. I was also the only woman assistant manager in my group. I had to raise hell to get to go to the meetings with clients. If you're the only woman, people don't expect a lot; you just sit there and listen. But I got to see all these guys in action. They were all stars, just terrific. The other women stayed in the office and never went to meetings with the clients. In a report on affirmative action that year, the company said that women managers would perhaps be acceptable in government, but certainly never in industry! There were only three women assistant managers out of one hundred in the company at that time, and I figured I should be thrilled just to be allowed to participate as I did.

By 30 my career was my top priority, and at 31 I felt I deserved a promotion to manager. I felt educationally disadvantaged for not having an MBA, but I also thought I was smart and deserving of the opportunity. My boss told me to talk with everyone on my team and learn my developmental needs. The men gave me some important but painful criticism. One told me to stop acting like a little girl, and he was right. Despite making progress in many ways, I was still playing dumb and deferring to men, as I had all my life. They insisted that I had to grow up if I wanted to advance. They were trying to be helpful, but in some ways it was very intimidating. For the first time I felt inferior to the guys: I was not older, I was not smarter, I didn't have their education and experience, I didn't have any of these reasons to act equal to or smarter than them. There were also the tough organizational realities. The company was a very hierarchical organization where it was hard to rise higher, especially for a woman. Often I was in deep despair and thought I'd never get promoted.

At 32 I finally got promoted to manager. It was a huge success but a mixed blessing. For two years I had dedicated all of my energies to getting promoted and having the possibility of a long-term career. I was also so wrapped up with my feelings about Ben I didn't have one other ounce of feeling. I knew that we would never marry, yet I still channeled all my feelings there.

Several months before I got the promotion my group broke up. I started working in another group, but it never had the same meaning and excitement for me as the earlier group. And, at the same time, I split up with Ben. I was 31. For the first six months of our relationship I thought we'd get married. Then I caught on about the other women. He was always dating other women—always, always, always. It got to be just awful. He was dating other women, living with other women, going on trips with other women. I mean, honestly, they were like live-in maids, ironing and washing his clothes! And he was always seeing me, too. I couldn't tell who had the worst deal, them or me. At 31 I told him I couldn't stand the situation any longer, and we stopped dating, but the feelings continued. At 32 I began dating Matt. I didn't want to marry him, and I dated other men as well, but Matt helped me get past Ben. With my changed work situation and breaking up with Ben, it was like a double divorce. The impact of both changes didn't register all at once, but over the next few years I had to re-evaluate my whole life and plans: Where do I go from here?

I'll talk about the work first. At 32 I got promoted and finally got to be a real person, according to that organization. But then I was on the bottom again, the most junior one at my level. I continued having the long hours and the travel and the pressure, but not the fun I'd had with Ben and the earlier group. The worst thing was having one's life completely wrapped up in work and having no personal life. I knew that I would never make the next level; there were only a few women at my level. Only about 5 or 10 percent of all people at my level would be promoted, and no woman had yet been promoted. By 33 I had a new idea of where I was going with my work life. I wasn't running on the standard game plan, aiming for promotion. Instead, I was building a portfolio that would help me get a job elsewhere. I planned to leave in two or three years; meanwhile, I continued full-time work and got more involved in my personal life.

The second big change was my final break-up with Ben. At 34 I met him on a project, and he asked me, "How would you like to have my children?" He was looking for someone to handle that job for him—to have his kids! I knew it was ridiculous, but I said I'd see him again if he'd stop seeing the woman he was living with. He said he would, and then I discovered he hadn't. So I learned again that I couldn't trust him. It's amazing how many times I had to relearn that. He was forever manipulating people, but I lent myself to it.

As her Age 30 Transition ended, Molly Berger could not build the kind of Culminating Life Structure she wanted most. Like many others in this situation, she formed a tentative structure with the hope of improving it soon. Her new occupational goal was to obtain a senior managerial position in another field. Toward this end she decided to remain a few years longer at the same company and improve her credentials. Likewise, she gave up the relationship with Ben. She thus moved toward a Culminating Life Structure as a single dating woman, devoted first of all to career, with love/marriage/family as a central unfilled component. She hoped soon to marry, make family central, and have a rewarding though less demanding career. The years from 33 to 36 thus had a very provisional quality. The start of the Culminating Life Structure at 33 was reflected, however, in a growing sense of urgency and the need to make key choices around which a new structure could be built.

Married Career Women without Children

Six women were married and childless during all or part of the Age 30 Transition. Three were in business and three in academe. For most married women, a crucial factor in deferring motherhood was the feeling that their marriages were too fragile to sustain a family. Amy York, a businesswoman, and Megan Bennett, a faculty member, provide variations on this theme.

✒ AMY YORK

Amy York started her first matrimonial relationship at 25, married at 27, and divorced after four years of a disastrous, emotionally abusive marriage. Most of Amy's Age 30 Transition was devoted to getting her marriage and occupation in order; her interest in motherhood did not emerge until the very end of the period.

> It was a shock that someone actually wanted to marry me. Having no confidence that I would get anyone else, I said, "Oh, well, I'll give it a try." I never thought I wanted children. My husband wanted someone who was bright, attractive, and independent, which I was. He also wanted someone he could criticize and push around, and I was more of that than I had understood. Nothing I did was right. Within a few months he lost his job, and I was supporting us financially! I started feeling totally trapped and getting panic attacks.
>
> At 28 I went to work as a programmer in a consulting firm, the best job I had ever had. I realized that the marriage was bad and that I had to move toward a different life. The firm's tuition payment plan allowed me to attend night school for an MBA. I continued for four years because it gave me some hope for the future, even though the classes were boring and I had no specific goals. Mainly, school was a refuge from my bad marriage—everything was a refuge from my bad marriage. I was miserable but couldn't imagine leaving my husband. Our friends thought we had a wonderful marriage, and I couldn't talk openly with them. My parents put up with Steve. They didn't really approve of him, but we weren't close, and I rarely saw them.
>
> At 30 I was getting more involved in my work and interested in advancing beyond being a little programmer. I told my boss I wanted to become an associate, the first MBA professional-level job. They made me corporate analyst, a new intermediate position created mainly for women which entailed more research but little contact with customers. As the work got better, the marriage reached an all-time low. Steve was screwing all my girlfriends, and they were telling me! The contrast between me in the marriage and me at work was overwhelming.
>
> At 31 I was promoted to associate and onto a ladder toward partner. I left the marriage. For the next two years my life was horrible. I worked 70 hours a week, traveled a lot, but that's about all I did. I had no friends for a while and no personal life. It was a low, low time.
>
> For years I had put most of my energy into my fantasy life, watching an internal TV in which an imaginary hero did all the things I secretly wanted. I made a tremendously important decision: to give up my vicar-

ious fantasy world and start remaking my life. I said to myself, "Okay, kid, you're really on your own now. If you don't like something about yourself, work on it. From now on I'll have *real* memories, I'll have reality inside my head." I started going through my whole psyche and sorting everything out. It was a slow process, and I spent several months by myself. Then I came out of my shell and started a relationship with Patrick. I wanted to put 100 percent of myself into the relationship, to be an equal contributing partner for the first time, but whenever I tried to get closer, Patrick ran.

Meanwhile, I started to get disillusioned at work. The traveling was horrible, and you were treated like a piece of garbage. You're an associate, which equals a chair, and that's how they treat you—as if you have no feelings and no personal life. I remember coming home on a plane and thinking about the kind of person I'd have to turn myself into so they would find me acceptable for partner—which no woman had ever done at that company. I just said, "No, to hell with this. It wouldn't leave anything else in my life." But it took a while to make the change.

At 33 things were going so badly that I got into therapy. I started the first session of therapy sobbing, "Help me! Please help me! What is going to become of me?" A few months later I had the strength to stop seeing Patrick.

I also changed my mind about having kids. I realized that I hadn't wanted kids until then because I felt I didn't have much to offer a child. Now, for the first time, I wanted a family, descendants, something stable that would go with me into the future and beyond me. When you strip everything else away, that's the only thing we're here for, really. I wanted to find a mate, and I wanted to have kids. I wanted something real. At that point I met Kirk. A week later I asked him to marry me, and he said yes. We have been living together in our little cocoon for the last three years in a good, healthy relationship, and we plan to marry next spring and have babies.

As I started with Kirk at 33 I also switched into a new work group at my company. I loved it! We worked together as a real team and had a chance to do something significant. Unfortunately, the group wasn't given the support needed to survive. A year later the group just fell apart—a total failure. I received a poor bonus and got slapped down for working in this off-beat group. Essentially they told me, "Get back into the mainstream, or leave."

So I tried the mainstream again but couldn't stand it; it meant going back into the pressure cooker. The decision to leave had been perking for a few years but one incident set it off: One Sunday I got a hysterical phone call from a partner above me. Why had one of the lackeys not sent out a memo? I got up from the dinner table. My stomach was in knots. I went to the office and got the job done, but I was completely fed up. I'd just had too many years of it. The next day I asked for a transfer.

Now, turning 36, my work future is uncertain. I may stay at this company or move to another company. I also might restore houses with Kirk or open a little bookstore. I don't buy this whole career thing to the exclusion of the rest of my life. Making money is okay, but it's not the meaning of my existence.

I'll marry and start a family in a year or so—gotta get the babies in before I'm 40. I've come to understand in the last few years that it's great to enjoy all aspects of civilization, but don't forget what we're here for. We are physical creatures. We shit and make love, we sneeze, we throw up, we die eventually. It's all part of the process, and so is having kids.

MEGAN BENNETT

At 27 I was a graduate student, dating a professor. I felt that Robert was a wonderful person to have an affair with, but it was a surprise when he wanted to marry me. I felt that if I didn't marry him I'd probably never marry, since the work side of me was so important by then. At the same time, I had very conventional ideas about becoming a wife and mother who would work and support her husband's career but not have a career of her own. In short, I had powerful interests in both career and family, without any sense of how to combine them. Fortunately, my husband had a sense of mission about my career just as I did about his. He wanted a coworker and partner, not a traditional wife.

We got married when I was 28. I got a part-time job as an instructor. For the first three years I invested very little in my job; all our joint energies went into Robert's work. He was having a terrible time with his career, and he went through an alcoholic period.

Our biggest problem was trying to have a family. I desperately wanted children, but I could not carry a baby to term. It was just overwhelming to have miscarriages, and after the second I got quite depressed. Then Robert had a catastrophic heart attack that kept him hospitalized for several months.

At 33 I decided that I would not have a family. The physicians told me that getting pregnant was almost impossible for medical reasons. Robert's illness absolutely forced me to become much more independent. I realized that I was not looking at my life in the right way. I had a devoted husband and a fascinating career and an interesting life—yet I was in a state of recurring grief about not having children. So I became more active professionally and put more of myself into my career.

I had a really consciousness-raising experience of gender. I discovered that the women faculty were paid several thousand dollars a year less than the men, though we were doing more teaching and research!

My work was very exciting, and I had a wonderful relationship with a woman colleague. We taught a course together, wrote some papers, and had a great friendship. She was a big stimulus to the work I did in my early thirties. Then she got a professorship at another university and left.

By 34 I had a tenure-track appointment, and my career was blossoming. I really enjoyed my work and was coming to be in control of my professional life, and I was entering the national scene in my research field. My career was becoming the main thing in my life.

Meanwhile, Robert was recovering, but his work was problematic, and he didn't get any joy out of the work. After five or six years of marriage things were to some extent reversed between us. He didn't expect a lot more from his career while mine was going well and promising more, even though its future trajectory was not clear. I had a very satisfying career, a good marriage, and no children. Now, ten years later, I still regret not having a family, but I have found partial substitutes and have largely come to terms with the loss.

Ending the Age 30 Transition

For the career women, as for the homemakers, the Age 30 Transition was a critical period in adult development. Virtually all of the women experienced much personal growth and development as they made significant changes in their relationships to occupation, love/marriage/family, life goals, and self. Those who made great external changes (in marriage, serious love relationship, education, job, family, place of residence) usually went through considerable questioning and turmoil. Even when no dramatic overt changes were made in a relationship, there were subtle changes in its nature and meaning for the woman. It is difficult to form a relatively satisfactory Culminating Life Structure without undergoing some difficulty in the Age 30 Transition.

In college, most of the career women had expected to be married and have a family within a modified Traditional Marriage Enterprise by their middle to late twenties. While attempting to develop some degree of financial independence and competence, they took it for granted that family would be central in their future lives, occupation peripheral. They had earlier assumed that a woman could have a family or a long-term career, but not both. In the Age 30 Transition this assumption was changed. Many of the career women's Anti-Traditional Dream evolved into a dual Anti-Traditional Dream of the Successful Career Woman within a Neo-Traditional Marriage Enterprise. Most of the eighteen mothers made the firm decision that career and family would be co-central components of the life structure they were starting to build. The twelve who did not have children made a greater commitment to occupation and saw it as central in their future lives. For most of them, family was a major unfilled component that they hoped in time to fill. Whatever their circumstances and preferences, all of the career women began to build a Culminating Life Structure at age 33/34.

14 Culminating Life Structure for Early Adulthood: Career Women

The Culminating Life Structure of Early Adulthood originates when the tasks of forming a life structure become more imperative than the explorations marking the Age 30 Transition. In the career sample it began at 33 or 34 and ended at 40 or 41. This structure was strikingly different, in its external aspects as well as its subjective meanings, from the Entry Life Structure of the twenties. At the same time, it was in some respects similar to and continuous with the previous structure. In comparing the two, and in examining the formation of the second structure, we must attempt to discern the forms of stability, the forms of change, and the qualitative differences between them. For most career women it was a time of great difficulty but also one of great personal growth and development.

Like the period of the Entry Life Structure, this period evolves through two distinct phases (see Chapters 6, 8, 12). The first phase is devoted to establishing and stabilizing a new life structure. It typically lasts two or three years and ends at 35 or 36. In the second phase, Becoming One's Own Woman, the primary task is to enhance one's life within the existing life structure and to realize the major goals and aspirations of early adulthood. A woman wants to become more independent, to speak more fully with her own voice, to be affirmed by others for the accomplishments and personal qualities most important to her. This phase lasts until about 40, when a woman enters the Mid-life Transition, and the life structure itself comes into question. Since the two phases were discussed in detail in Chapter 8 in relation to the homemakers, I will review them only briefly here.

The First Phase: Establishing a New Life Structure

This phase was not easy for most career women. Toward the end of the Age 30 Transition each woman had made at least a few major life changes such as embarking on a new job or occupational path, getting married or divorced, starting a family, beginning or ending a serious matrimonial relationship. Some women had not yet made an overt change but had set themselves new goals that they planned to act upon over the next several years. These women began the Culminating Life Structure with an "intended structure" that could not immediately be established. They needed a few years to make the key choices, to form the central relationships, and to integrate the components into a new life structure—or, failing this, to settle for something else.

The first phase was often a time of unwelcome instability and uncertainty just when a stable structure was urgently needed. Most of the unmarried childless women were eager to marry and start a family, but they were not in a matrimonial relationship or were in a relationship of ambiguous prospects. Most of the married childless women were not sure whether to have a child in a problematic marriage. The currently married mothers were desperately trying to manage a Neo-Traditional Marriage Enterprise and full-time career, as well as trying not to be too subordinate in family or workplace. The eight mothers who had recently divorced spent the first phase recovering from the desired yet disruptive change and exploring new ways of living as single working mothers.

There were corresponding difficulties in the domain of *occupation*. Some women had recently entered a career path leading to the upper reaches of the corporate or academic world. They were trying to find their way in exciting but rather alien territory. Others wanted a long-term career but knew that they would have to move to a less prestigious corporate or academic setting. The impending career shift cast its shadow on all their current involvements.

Several businesswomen decided at the start of this period that they would soon devote themselves primarily to family, perhaps leaving the corporate world altogether and working at things they enjoyed. They spent the first phase half-in and half-out of their current jobs, unable either to depart or to be much involved in the work world. Subjectively, they experienced this phase as a transitional time, and from a purely occupational point of view it was. In the context of life structure development, however, it was part of the Culminating Life Structure since the primary developmental task was to form a new life structure. The sense of urgency was especially acute because these women were living in an incomplete or provisional structure just when it felt so important to be establishing a new and satisfactory one.

By age 35 or 36 the first phase was completed, and the career women had established a Culminating Life Structure that would last until the end of this period. In some cases the new life structure amply realized their hopes; in others it was seriously flawed. Without exception, however, it was significantly different from the Entry Life Structure of their twenties.

The Second Phase: Becoming One's Own Woman

The first task of this phase is to maintain the life structure. If the life structure is highly unsatisfactory in certain respects, the woman may feel strongly impelled to make major changes in a central component. To do so is, in effect, to "break out" of the existing structure. The wish for change is countered, however, by a powerful conservative tendency that operates to maintain life structural stability. During this phase it is hard to change the life structure or to pursue aims outside its boundaries. An attempt to break out is sometimes made in the late thirties (see *The Seasons of a Man's Life*) but it usually leads to compromise or accommodation within the existing life structure rather than to a basic modification of the life structure. Many career women found themselves stuck in a highly flawed Culminating Life Structure: they could find no effective way to either improve their lives within it nor to break out and form a new life structure.

The second task of this phase is to enhance one's life within the life structure. A woman needs to attain the satisfactions and accomplishments available within the life structure and to start Becoming One's Own Woman (see Chapter 8). The Culminating Life Structure is the vehicle for concluding the era of early adulthood—for realizing the key aspirations of one's youth and laying a foundation for the impending era of middle adulthood. An unsatisfactory Culminating Life Structure does not allow us sufficiently to live out crucial aspects of the youthful self or to accomplish essential goals of early adulthood. Conversely, a relatively satisfactory Culminating Life Structure gives us a fighting chance of fulfilling our primary hopes and dreams.

All of the career women experienced some measure of success as well as disappointment with regard to both occupation and love/marriage/family. From the start of this period, most career women looked to *both* occupation and love/marriage/family as vital sources of satisfaction and self-esteem. They sought a great deal in the work world: to make a significant contribution, to earn advancement, recognition, and income consistent with their performance, to be taken seriously as a professional and a person. Likewise for love/marriage/family: If married, each woman wanted to be appreciated for her marital-maternal efforts, and, even more, to be valued for herself and not merely for her performance of domestic duties. If unmarried, she wanted a marriage or enduring love relationship on more equal terms. Most of the childless women wanted to be a mother within a mutually nurturing family.

By the end of this period, many married career women began to realize that their Neo-Traditional Marriage Enterprises were too hard on them. They were working full-time at demanding jobs, sharing the provisioning role with their husbands as coprovisioners, and they were also almost totally responsible for the "second shift" (the apt term is Arlie Hochschild's) of child care and domestic responsibilities. Whether married or single, many career women in the phase of Becoming One's Own Woman began to envision an *Egalitarian Marriage Enterprise* in which both partners would share provisioning *and* domestic rights and responsibilities on more equal terms. Several of the businesswomen and about half of the faculty women were able in the Culminating Life Structure or the Mid-life Transition to transform their Neo-Traditional Marriage Enterprises into Egalitarian Marriage Enterprises or to build Egalitarian Marriage Enterprises in a remarriage.

Occupation

In their twenties, the career women assumed that the work world was a meritocracy operating on terms of gender equality and rationality: benevolent authority would watch over women as well as men and promote those who deserved it. During the Age 30 Transition the women had become less naive about the work world. The businesswomen, for example, came to understand that a corporation could fill its entry-level positions with an endless supply of bright young women from excellent colleges. The entry jobs led nowhere. A worker could continue only by being promoted to the first rung of a managerial or technical ladder, and these positions were restricted largely to men. By their thirties most women who had held entry jobs dropped out (to seek a more congenial workplace, or, more often, to start a family), were pushed out, or both. The terminology was different but the reality similar for the faculty members.

The women studied here were among the small number of women who advanced beyond the entry level. During the Age 30 Transition they established a foothold, however precarious, at the bottom of a higher ladder. From this new vantage point they gained more perspective on the scene below and an initial sense of the terrain above. They realized that pursuing a career in their thirties would be extremely demanding and would severely constrain their relationships to family, friends, and self. Their chances for appreciable advancement were mostly uncertain or low. The corporation/university was not a quasi-family in which people worked and played together and cared for each other. It had a strongly hierarchical structure. A significant job change involved a new place in the hierarchy—a place higher or lower on the existing ladder or on a different ladder.

In the Age 30 Transition and throughout their thirties, the career women learned that competition was built into the pyramidal structure of the organization. Each level contained perhaps 10 to 20 percent as many people as the one below, and the percentage decreased as one moved up the ladder. At every point, many people were competing for one opening. Those who were not promoted might remain in the same position for a while or make a lateral move. Before long, however, they would be terminated or would quit, unable to tolerate the boredom or humiliation. The striving to perform well and to advance in one's field may stem from many specific motives—excellence, power, recognition, money, love, approval. Whatever their motives, however, people in their thirties must "succeed"—must do better than most of their peers—or they will have to move elsewhere and perhaps endanger their careers.

Each woman discovered that people were promoted not simply for their ability and the quality of their work. There was also an organizational game called "politics." People got ahead in part by playing this game well—manipulating others, practicing one-upmanship, forming alliances, and doing in competitors. In the woman's mind it was a man's game, something that many men engaged in as a matter of course. It was a game that she, like many other women (and many men), felt unwilling or unable to play. The woman rejected the game and believed that "the main thing is performing the work well, and I want to be evaluated and rewarded on that basis." At the same time she wondered how much her discomfort with the game was based on naiveté and the exclusion of women from the informal male sociability where so much "politicking" occurred. She began to realize that job performance, personal relationships, and social networks were inextricably interwoven in the life of the organization. Women were at a strong disadvantage in this world: they were badly outnumbered; men excluded them from many activities and relationships in which important decisions were made; and the women often had difficulty "playing the game" on men's terms.

The woman realized, too, that women and men were often on different ladders. A small number of budding stars were chosen and placed on a "fast track" (which is also a long-term career track leading far upward) by their early thirties—and with rare exceptions they were men. Not all of the initial stars would advance far, but very few others had much of a chance. The great majority of men would not move beyond the middle levels, and few women would go that far. Women were entering the corporate/academic world in larger numbers than ever before but the organizational gender splitting was still strong. Women worked largely in segregated female enclaves or as "tokens" in predominantly male groups, perhaps as staff to the top professors or executives, but they rarely had a place high in the power structure. When a high-level position formerly held by a man was given to a woman, there was often a reduction in salary and authority and an increase in responsibilities. This state of affairs was not created by a few sexist men in a particular corporation or university. It was (and is) a widespread phenomenon based upon the gender splitting in organizations, in individuals (women as well as men), and in society as a whole.

The issue of authority is crucial here. An authority is a source who has an influence on others and contributes to the management and understanding of an enterprise. There are many kinds of authority. A position of line authority confers the legitimate right to initiate and make decisions in an organization. Even when authority is handled in a relatively collaborative way, there is a point at which, failing consensus, the individual or subgroup with line authority must make a decision binding on the group. A position of expert authority may be held by a person who is seen as having special knowledge or understanding (such as a scientist or outside consultant). She has no authority to make a decision, but her views on the pros and cons of various options are given heavy weight by the decision makers. Many kinds of authority can be exercised in many different ways.

In the business world it is clear that higher rank generally involves greater line authority or, in the case of staff, more direct influence on those who exercise greater line authority. In academe faculty members are formally regarded as colleagues who work together on largely individualistic, equal terms. But the university also has a strongly corporate or bureaucratic character. An academic department is an organized division of the larger university organization. A private university is, in legal terms, a corporation. Faculty members are in principle equal, but some are more equal than others. It makes a huge difference whether one is a "junior" or a "senior" faculty member and on or off the "tenure track." Every department has a head and other managerial positions that to some degree control the teaching, research, administrative, and other activities of individual faculty members. Committees make crucial decisions regarding hiring, promotion, and the allocation of funds, persons, and other resources to various departmental ventures. Faculty members who have greater rank, research funds, and administrative authority exert greater influence on policy generally. Women at every level are often at a disadvantage in this entire process.

The basic reality is this: organizations tend to exclude women from positions of line authority. Most of the career women found it difficult to gain a sense of their own inner authority and to acknowledge (even to themselves) that they wanted such positions. They tended to equate authority with authoritarianism—the unilateral, exploitive use of power. This way of exercising authority is widespread in work organizations and a source of many problems. Improvement will come not from the elimination of organizational structure and authority but from the development of a wiser, more collaborative use of authority.

For many women, inner conflicts about authority compounded the powerful external obstacles to their advancement. At the same time, the developmental process of Becoming One's Own Woman made it increasingly important for women in their late thirties to speak with their own voice and to be affirmed through appropriate promotion and recognition. It gave a special urgency to their career struggles and reduced their tolerance of subordination and discrimination.

The cultures of corporations and universities abound with powerful though often shadowy imagery of women. To get ahead, a woman should be competent yet still "feminine." The word "yet" says it all; there is an assumption that femininity is fundamentally antithetical to competence, and thus to the exercise of authority. This assumption springs from the basic gender splitting. The qualities considered feminine are, by and large, those of the traditional homemaker: the charming little girl, the devoted wife and mother, the helpmate to a male hero but never a hero in her own right. The traditional homemaker may also be an extremely competent worker, providing care and service to others, furthering the man's career, being a program "coordinator" (a title often given predominantly to women for a work role that involves much responsibility without commensurate authority). But it seemed to many career women that a woman must tread softly when she attempts to be competent in the ways of the masculine/provisioner: head of the enterprise, policy maker, fierce competitor, inspiring leader, hero. Many career women believed that to succeed, a woman should be reasonably assertive but not too demanding or ambitious, caring yet not overly maternal, businesslike yet not cold.

Career Paths in the Culminating Life Structure

By age 40 or 41, all of the career women were at a turning point in their lives. The turning point marked the end of the Culminating Life Structure and the onset of the Mid-life Transition. Some women were getting divorced or remarried, or going through major changes in a love relationship. Others had teenage offspring and were coming to a new phase of their motherhood. Some were starting to think and feel in new ways about love relationships and marriage. Since career was so important to them all, it is perhaps not surprising that the most dramatic changes were in occupation.

I'll divide the sample into three broad groups on the basis of occupational achievement and indicate the kinds of change that were going on at this time.

High Achievement. Six women had very successful careers and a highly affirming Culminating Event. Ellen Nagy was promoted to a senior position at a major corporation, an event that fulfilled her youthful aspirations and brought her to the beginnings of senior membership in her world. Debra Rose was promoted to a regional directorship. Amanda Burns, Megan Bennett, Alice Abel, and Helen Kaplan became full professors and were gaining international recognition for their work.

Moderate Achievement. Seven women were making substantial career progress, but their situation and prospects were somewhat less bright than those above. When interviewed at 37 to 40, three of them had middle-management staff positions without line authority in large corporations. They were in fields such as human resources and corporate communications, largely staffed by women. Each had the possibility and the hope of rising higher but knew that the odds were not great. The outcome of their late thirties enterprise was not yet clear. Eva Pitcher had just been denied tenure and was moving to another university where she was offered a tenured professorship. She was dealing with mixed feelings of success and failure and reappraising her academic aims. At 40 Hillary Lewin and Rachel Nash had been tenured professors for several years but had been minimally involved in scholarly work. They now felt a need for greater intellectual achievement and began actively to pursue their research interests.

Low or Ambiguous Achievement. Seventeen women were making limited career progress. Nine of these were *businesswomen.* Michele Proto and Pam Kenney had corporate administrative positions offering some security but limited possibilities for advancement. Abby Murphy left the NYC corporate world in her mid-thirties and at 40 was a manager for a medium-size company. Kim Price moved to a large financial institution in hopes of improving both her income and her social contribution. When interviewed at 39, Melissa Howard was about to be demoted from a low-level management position. She knew that her corporate career was in shambles but was giving herself another year or two before seeking other options. Amy York, Sally Wolford, Jessica Hall, and Lisa Rourke left their corporate careers in the middle to late thirties in order to give family a higher priority and, in time, to pursue more limited occupational goals. We will see in the next chapter how life evolved in the Mid-life Transition for the businesswomen who were over 40 at the time of interviewing.

Of the eight faculty members in the low-achievement group, Kristin West and Holly Crane were late bloomers who first became assistant professors at

41 and 40, respectively. For each, this appointment was the Culminating Event of early adulthood. It was highly affirming to be identified as a promising scholar. It was also disconcerting to discover that most assistant professors were ten years younger and most of one's age peers were males of higher rank. These women had perhaps five years to prove themselves. The other six faculty members were 36 to 40 when interviewed and nearing the end of their appointments as assistant professors. Florence Russo at 39 had just received the devastating news that she had been denied tenure. Four others were approaching the "up or out" time when they would either be given tenure or terminated. Each had received a clear message that her chances for tenure were minimal. The women understood, too, that it would be almost impossible to obtain a tenured professorship at an institution comparable in standing to their present one. A difficult time to Become One's Own Woman! In considering new options, each woman had to think not only about the acceptability of various "lesser" institutions but also about becoming a low-level educational administrator or even moving entirely out of academe.

Mentoring and Intergenerational Relations

Virtually all of the academic women enjoyed their work in the academic world, first as students, then as researchers and teachers. They enjoyed teaching and their interaction with undergraduate and graduate students, especially with young women. Many of the faculty women provided much-needed role models to the upcoming generation of undergraduate women and men.

As they turned 40, the career women began to be seen, and to see themselves, as entering a relatively "senior" generation in contrast to the generation of "junior" women colleagues in their late twenties and early thirties. Due to previous gender discrimination, the current senior generation of women was much smaller than the junior and contained very few women over age 45. When they themselves were younger, our subjects had had little mentoring from other women or men. Now, many of them had an interest in being helpful to their younger female colleagues; the possibility of mentoring younger men was rarely mentioned. The generation of younger women (roughly age 25 to 35) looked to their seniors for mentorial relationships. However, despite the interest and potential benefit on both sides, very little mentoring occurred. There was a good deal of generational splitting in each group: the relationship between the two generations was conflictful or blocked rather than constructively engaged.

The younger career women generally experienced the older as unhelpful and in some basic sense irrelevant. The older women's knowledge and skills often seemed obsolete, rooted in an outmoded historical period. The senior women seemed too preoccupied with their own careers to take a mentorial interest in younger, potentially rivalrous women. The younger women found it hard to value or identify with an older woman who was not a wife or mother; the image of the Single Career Woman (see Chapter 3) operated powerfully. In addition, most of the senior women were in positions of limited rank and authority. The juniors usually accepted the current view that gender discrimination was minimal: women could now do and become anything they wanted; the only barriers to success were women's own lack of ability or motivation. Accordingly, the junior women generally blamed the seniors for not advancing farther and considered them irrelevant to their own aspirations.

The senior women were often disappointed in the younger, who seemed not to appreciate the struggles they had gone through to establish an initial beachhead for women in these male-dominated worlds. They felt that the young women looked primarily to the men above them for support and sponsorship. The men in turn seemed more interested in younger women, for reasons that sometimes seemed to have more to do with sexuality than with mentoring.

There was some truth and some distortion on both sides. Corrosive generational conflict exists in every historical period, among men as well as women. However, it was particularly unfortunate among these women, since it divided them at a time when they most needed each other. Many in the senior generation lost an opportunity for leadership, for mentorship, and for the satisfactions accruing from both. The junior generation lost the potential benefits of being mentored and of receiving the wisdom of its pioneering elders.

Of course, the relationship between these two generations, though crucially important for the well-being of society, is inherently problematic. Along with a convergence of interest, there is always going to be a fundamental conflict of interest between the senior generation, rooted in its own historical origins, and the upcoming junior generation eager to succeed it and to place its own stamp on history.

But the generational conflict experienced here also has sources in the socio-cultural conditions of the time. These women were part of the first and second generations attempting in some numbers to ascend the professional hierarchy of corporations and universities. To the extent that they succeeded, the traditional character of the organizations would be irrevocably changed. The change was supported by federal affirmative action laws and by a small number of male executives. However, it was resisted by a new conservative political regime, by many individuals, and by the inertia of organizational structures. One way that organizations resist the advancement of subordinate groups is to foster divisions within their ranks. The splitting of these two generations of women was strongly facilitated by organizational pressures opposing "feminism," and supporting the illusory view that gender barriers were so minimal that women need not worry about discrimination.

Finally, generational splitting has inner psychological sources within the personalities of individual women. The psychological sources vary in kind and degree. One general theme, however, is the conflict between the internal Traditional Homemaker Figure and the internal Anti-Traditional Figure. The Traditional Homemaker Figure feels uneasy and alien in the male work world. She regards men as the primary carriers of authority, power, and knowledge. In her view, the woman properly contributes by being "relational"—taking care of the personal needs of others, being a coordinator rather than an authority, assisting the men. She is put off by achieving, "pushy" women and by unauthoritative, "weak" men. She wants to perform well but is anxious about rising too high in the organization. Even the more "liberated" career woman has an internal Traditional Homemaker Figure who complicates her career strivings and her relationships with female and male coworkers. The Traditional Homemaker Figure tends to be maternal rather than mentorial with younger women.

The internal Anti-Traditional Figure plays her part as well. At best, she supports a woman's efforts to Become One's Own Woman and to foster the development of younger women. When this figure is sharply split off from all that is traditionally feminine, however, she may inhibit the mentoring function. She may insist, for example, on remaining a rational, impersonal, task-oriented worker who keeps all feelings out of her on-the-job relationships lest she be seen as an "emotional female" unable to do a man's work. It is hard to care for younger adults in a mentorial way if one is afraid of being seen as too maternal. Neither internal figure was entirely dominant in any career woman; integrating or balancing the two was a significant issue for all.

✺ EVA PITCHER

I had been a graduate student from 22 to 28. I liked graduate school and had a good reputation without being picked out as one of the stars. I'd married a graduate student at 25 and had my children at 27 and 31.

I came here at 32 on a non-tenure-track three-year lectureship. At 33 I became assistant professor, and at 36 I became an associate professor. That was an important promotion in the sense that it would make it a lot easier to leave here with that rank. I never thought my chances of getting tenure here were too good—they never are for associate professors—but I couldn't help thinking there might be a possibility. But two years ago at 38 I was denied tenure. Since I'm leaving I've just sort of said to hell with the school; I'm not going to be a good citizen when they're not going to keep me around.

I've done quite a bit of advising of students—purely academic relation-ships. It does take a lot of time, but I get a lot of satisfaction working closely with somebody on their project. I'm trying to get them to think on their own. My department has mostly male students, though I've worked with three or four women students, but nothing personal because I do think in dealing with students it's important to keep some distance. I'm not interested in becoming a sort of mother figure for these students. I have a feeling that if I showed more feeling that they would see me as being more maternal, and that is something I don't want.

My husband has always been very supportive of my career. We have each been offered and accepted full professorships elsewhere, although he would prefer to stay here. It's a good marriage. Since we're both academics we can really talk to each other about our work. He's very good with the children and plays with them and is very loving and in-terested in them. He's not a housework kind of person, though. Part of our marriage is that I in fact have given more time to home things than he has, and I've sort of accepted the fact that that's not going to be equal. I would rather it be equal. It really is a compromise that I have to make. He contributes at home, but not as much as I do. I go home earlier than he, and he works Saturdays and I stay home. Neither of us has had much time for anything more than work and family—you just sort of have to pare down your life. I have never had many friends, mostly just acquaintances. The children are getting older and more in-dependent now, which frees up some time.

I find a lot of satisfaction through motherhood and work, but it basically means I don't have time for other things. I'm very pleased that I've been able to combine kids and having a serious career, but it means compromise. I don't think anyone should think it's simple to combine work and family. If you want to have two big serious things in your life you've just got to be willing to tell people that you just can't do other things.

FLORENCE RUSSO

I'm 39 now. I became an assistant professor here at 33. I teach three art classes. Some students are talented, but at this school you get students who aren't talented, who couldn't make it into a better college, and they're not that motivated.

The higher achievers will give you the feedback that you need to keep excited about your teaching, and as long as you have a few good students it's worth it. I feel through my students I'm working and getting better, and I see a potential in them and can help them evolve as artists, and it's very rewarding. I've had one or two special students in the past five years, and this year I had one female student I did a lot with. She was very motivated, and she drained me. She got me thinking about things when she'd ask questions I didn't know the answers to, and then I'd try to find the answers. So I keep learning through my students, too.

My husband, James, and I are very close. We have two children, and I really enjoy the children and being a mother. My husband and I both teach, and we have a very important relationship in order to do what we're doing. To have the two children, for me to teach, for him to teach, for both of us to have projects, it's very difficult. My husband and I have a mutual understanding that if we're going to do two careers we have to do it together. He's *not* helping me; we're working together. The house really only gets cleaned when we have company. What we really need is a housekeeper, but we can't afford one. I'm balancing being a teacher, an artist, a mother, wife, and sometimes I feel very negligent in one or more areas. My life is a constant struggle in order to balance out all my energies. It's a constant conflict.

An important part of my life during the past few years is a project I've been working on for which I thought I'd be recognized. It was by some, but not where it really meant something in terms of promotion. The project was to begin a collection of women artists who are nationally and internationally known in my area. The collection carried the hope that I would get a tenured position here. It was a three-year project that was central to my life and carried a lot of hopes; it's comparable to writing a book in other fields.

I came to do the project when I had a majority of women students and felt there weren't enough role models for women artists. I think I'm supporting women by doing this project. Many women artists have been ignored; the textbook in art history is four inches thick and does not mention one woman.

I got up the collection and wrote the catalog, and we had a lovely opening. It was well received, and I think it has brought some attention to the college. I hope the collection will just keep growing and growing. I feel the pieces I have chosen as curator are strong and beautiful and will be strong statements when I'm gone. The collection will be something the college will always have even though it may not always have me.

This year I was recommended for promotion and tenure by the Promotions Committee but did not get it. I'm very, very frustrated and angry and bitter and feel very, very sad about this whole thing because there's nothing I can do about it. So in spite of all I've done if I don't get promoted next year I will have to find another job!

I've been feeling more and more competent in this position, and I'm angry that I didn't get that promotion, especially since I feel discriminated against because I'm a woman. I've been working toward this promotion for five years, and I deserve it. I have done things in five years that men on the staff who have been here forever have not done.

It's important to me to be affirmed in what I've been working so hard toward. I feel a lack of motivation and am very unhappy. I feel depressed and angry, and I cry a lot. I can't do any more than what I'm doing; I don't have any more time in my life to do more. I keep thinking where can I go?

What are my options? I can't think of any. The college is like bloodsuckers: they use assistant professors for seven years and then let them go and start out with fresh blood from newly graduated students.

Love/Marriage/Family

At the end of the Culminating Life Structure, twelve of the thirty career women were in their first marriage and five were in their second marriage. Nine were currently divorced. Four were single-never-married. No career woman had a first marriage in this period. Five remarried. Three got divorced.

Twenty career women were mothers as the Culminating Life Structure ended. Nine mothers were businesswomen (seven currently married, two divorced), and eleven were academics (seven currently married, four divorced). Of the ten women without children, six were in business, four in academe.

Only three career women had a first child in this period, as compared to seventeen in previous periods, chiefly the Entry Life Structure and the Age 30 Transition. This finding is consistent with survey and census data indicating that a very small percentage of women have a first child after age 34. The number has increased somewhat in the past decade, but it is still well under 10 percent of the population of mothers.

It is of interest also to look at mother's age when she had her last child. Of the women who started a family before age 34, no businesswoman and only four academics had an additional child after that. In other words, women who become mothers before the end of the Age 30 Transition (as the great majority do) generally have their last child by age 34. This finding holds for the homemakers as well. Little attention has been paid to mother's age at last child. Further study will show, I believe, that roughly 90 percent of all women who become mothers by 34 have no more children after that. In the past, before adequate birth control became available, childbearing often continued into the late thirties and forties. The change has important consequences for women's lives and development. It contributes to the historical process by which women increasingly participate in the labor force and look to occupation as a significant component of the life structure, especially in the years beyond the early thirties.

Family of Origin

During the Culminating Life Structure the career women became increasingly remote from the family of origin, which was usually rather fragmented, geographically dispersed, and lacking in integrative ties. In some cases a parent had become ill and was cared for out of loyalty or guilt. The physical and psychological distance from parents and siblings was generally not unwelcome, but it raised nagging questions about personal roots, about the continuity of generations and the evolution of familial ties over the course of adulthood.

Let us turn now from the single components to the evolution of the life structure in this period. Three broad types of Culminating Life Structures were built and maintained. I'll discuss each structure, showing how it evolved over the course of this period and giving individual variations on the main themes.

Life Structure A. Occupation and Family Co-Central

Seventeen career women formed a Culminating Life Structure in which both occupation and family were central components. Many of these women carried the dual Anti-Traditional Dreams of the Successful Career Woman and the Neo-Traditional Marriage Enterprise. This group included six businesswomen and eleven faculty members. Ten of these women were in a first or second marriage for much or all of this period. Most of them used the first phase of the Culminating Life Structure to crystallize a structure in which they took chief responsibility for family within a Neo-Traditional Marriage Enterprise while pursuing a more than full-time career.

The remaining seven women were divorced for much or all of this period. They were committed to both career and motherhood, and marriage was an unfilled component of the life structure. Although interested in remarrying, they were cautious in their relationships with men. To be minimally eligible as a partner, a man had to accord the women the right to equality, independence, and a career within an Egalitarian Marriage Enterprise.

All seventeen women in Group A built a Culminating Life Structure combining family and full-time career. In the process, they enriched their own lives as well as the lives of other persons and institutions. Motherhood enhanced their sense of fulfillment as women and their sense of legitimacy as career professionals. The career gave them the independence and the sense of a competent self that they believed they could not have had as full-time homemakers. But there were also serious problems. The internal Traditional Homemaker Figure and the internal Anti-Traditional Figure coexisted in an uneasy truce that exacted a considerable psychological toll on each woman. Even with housekeepers and other assistance, many of the women carried virtually all of the domestic responsibility. At the same time, they often spent fifty or sixty or more hours a week on their careers, and many women did a fair amount of job-related travel. Despite their best efforts, career and family were often antithetical rather than convergent.

By their late thirties most of these career women came to understand the illusory nature of the image of Superwoman, who could "do it all" with grace and flair. Their self-image was more that of the Juggler, who kept many spheres in the air without dropping any or losing a step in the perpetual forward motion. While continually seeking balance, most women found it impossible to give anything like equal priority to the various components of the life structure. In general, occupation was by far the first priority, with motherhood second, marriage a poor third, leisure and friendship a rare luxury, and, with all the external tasks to be done, almost no time for the self.

The women's lives were usually hectic, at times chaotic and exhausting. Nevertheless, most women considered their lives to be relatively satisfactory and worth the effort. They believed to attempt less would be worse, and many of the women they knew were struggling with similar or greater problems. It would get better in time, they hoped, as the children grew older and the career stabilized.

Marriage and love relationships were problematic in a different way (though not necessarily in a greater degree) for the women who combined motherhood and career than they were for the others. In the relationship with husband or lover the women wanted to be valued as women and as persons, and to have a balance of closeness and separateness, strength and dependency, rational competence and feeling. These wishes of the woman were often contested by the internal Traditional Homemaker Figure (who warned her of the dangers of seeking too much occupationally and losing the feminine) and by the internal Anti-Traditional Figure (who feared that any compromise would lead to subordination and loss of the self). There were also conflicting images and feelings in the husband and others.

In some respects most of the husbands held nontraditional views regarding marriage and supported their wives' occupational strivings. Like most other men and women, however, they were by no means free of internal gender splitting. Each husband had a traditional masculine self-image that kept him from sharing equally in the domestic responsibilities and made him uneasy about being less "successful" than his wife.

By the start of the Culminating Life Structure, many husbands were earning less than their wives and doing less well occupationally. This was especially true of the businesswomen's husbands; most of them were in business or business-related professions, where the prospects for men appeared to be better. The husband was distressed by his limited advancement in contrast with his wife's relative success. Emma Beechwood has given us an example of the disparity and of the couple's collusive effort to mask it during the Age 30 Transition (see Chapter 13). This theme took on greater significance in the Culminating Life Structure as Emma worked on Becoming One's Own Woman, he on Becoming One's Own Man. She had the marital task of supporting his career and tolerating his relative failure, without being deterred from pursuing and enjoying her own career. He in turn had the task of supporting and enjoying her career, without becoming too resentful of her success and too deprecating of himself. No easy matter! Given the many potential sources of discord, a couple did well to have only moderate problems in the Culminating Life Structure.

The same issues and themes were prominent in the Group A women's occupational endeavors. Four of the seventeen were high achievers. Ellen Nagy, for example, was promoted at 40 to a high managerial position of a national corporation—an unusually high rank for a woman though not at the top of the corporate structure.

✌ ELLEN NAGY

After my divorce at age 33 I knew I wanted a relationship, but I also knew that it really might not happen. I started dating, but I was very scared and wary. It was a difficult time. I had grown up without any living-alone experience, and I knew that I was highly dependent on men and needy of men. One reason I'd never contemplated divorce earlier was that I was terrified of being alone without a man. It was such a paradox: I was involved in the Women's Movement, very career-oriented and capable, but my feeling was that to be without a man was a fate worse than death. I really tried to build out of myself, and finally I came to the point where I just said, "Yes, I am a woman who is much happier living with a man." So it became a choice, and that was an important thing for me to learn at about 35.

I met my present husband, Roger, and it was an instantaneous love-at-first-sight chemistry. He was separated. By his late thirties he was a very successful businessman. We had a difficult, stormy relationship the first two years. We would back off then get back together again.

Despite the turmoil in my life during those years, my relationship with my daughter, Jennifer, became steadily better. Day after day after day my time and appreciation of that child and reward from her has been wonderful and increasing. I am able to deal with her far better than most everything else in my life. She's an interesting, thoughtful person. My pleasure around mothering grew, and I marveled at that—it was like an extraordinary blossoming flower. I have regretted that I couldn't have another child, but Roger is totally opposed to having one. I told him that I had completely accepted it, but it's very difficult.

When I was 35 Roger and I decided to live together. Roger quit his corporate job and went into business for himself for the next five years. It did not work out for him, and it was an extremely difficult time. Recently, he came to terms with the fact that he needs to do something else.

At 34 I was promoted at a large international company. I started to realize that, whether I wanted it or not, I was a symbol of success for other women: I had worked for over ten years, I had a managerial position, I had been married, and I had a child.

After a year or two in my position, I began to feel a growing concern about the future. I began to ask, "What's next? Where can I go from here?" The logical next step on the career ladder wasn't available to me at that company, and I wasn't sure many women would ever be in the top positions of any international corporation. I wanted to expand my horizons and test the entrepreneur part of me, so I got interested in Wall Street.

At 36, I joined a leading firm. It was a major career shift. It was a completely different field of work from what I had been doing for fifteen years where I was more comfortable than I had realized. I was hired into middle management. My otherwise all-male group was dominated by one man who didn't want me there, and my being a woman was absolutely critical. Being competent was not an issue. It was an awful situation, and I knew I had no future there. They told me they were not ready to promote a woman, "especially not *you*," because I was too assertive.

Age 36 to 38 was an extremely difficult period for me. A lot was going on in my life. Roger and I had a very close, emotionally competitive relationship. We needed to be together, but we needed to be separate, too. Life was unpredictable, and both of us had heavy career demands. I felt that his commitment to me was tenuous—that any day he would be offered a good position elsewhere and would leave me. And I had so much trouble with my career that it posed a significant strain on our relationship. After a terrible fight, Roger announced that he was moving out. I told him that leaving was not an option, that we had to stay together. After that argument we got more committed and married when I was 38. We stopped keeping our assets separate and made provisions for each other in our wills.

My firm decided that I should leave. That was fine because it had been apparent to me that it was not going to work, and I had already been looking for another job. Small- and medium-size companies are still unlikely to hire a woman for any senior role. Larger corporations are under more pressure and are hiring women in low-level jobs in management. I went to a medium-size corporation in a senior management position. I didn't yet have the credentials to be in a very large company, but this was fine. I have a forty-person staff.

It is interesting to be working at the very top of a corporation. I am not in one of the top positions, but I'm working very closely with the two or three people who are running the corporation. My job is very frustrating, unpredictable, and risky. It's difficult to have any level of continuing satisfaction because I have a lot of derived power but no direct power. I'm turning 40 and will have been here two years next month. I'm the highest-ranking woman in the company.

My personal interest in being involved in this research project is that I'm very much at a time in my life where I feel I need to take stock and think about which way to go now. I feel as if some kind of choice is coming. I'm not sure if it's going to be next week or next month, but it's coming. Where I am now, today, is that I am a full-time, married, committed executive and a mother, married to a man who is certainly a feminist; he just automatically deals with the stuff about our two careers and sharing domestic work. This little family of three was not an automatic family at all, and it has just started to work as a family.

My daughter, Jennifer, is growing. I know she has to separate, and I hope I will have the ability to let go and let her be where she has to be. It's like counting the grains of sand in the hourglass between now and the time when she turns 18 and goes away to college, because I know that's it. I hope we'll be friends and will see one another, but she will not be living with me after that. I feel as if every day is precious.

Turning 40 has absolutely been a big deal. I don't think I have dealt much with it, but I know it's going to grow. In some ways I feel my age, I like my age, and I like where I am in my life. I don't have a great wish to be some other age, but I associate 40 with someone who is ideally grown up. I associate it with a time by which one should be on a direction one is comfortable with and not contemplating a whole new change of direction, but that is not me. So maybe I'll grow up when I turn 50 [laughs].

In time I could get one or two more promotions, but as I look ahead I'm not sure that making it is a route to real satisfaction. I look at where I am now, and where I thought I would be at 40, and I realize that I have less of a sense of where I want to be now than I did at 30 or 35. When you're younger you're pursuing things more single-mindedly. Now I start to look at far more and focus on broader options. There are many things that I never had time for, and now I'm starting to let them in and enjoy them.

I've moved beyond my earlier goals, which were very low. I have always looked at the organization in terms of what could I reasonably aspire to. In recent years I have said, "Forget all about what I would like to do; I don't have any chance of getting there because I am a woman." Now we have whole crops of young women coming out of business school, law school, medical school, planning their careers from age 22, if not earlier. But there is increased conflict about family. Everything is in a state of change, and the young women are getting a lot of conflicting messages. Now there is a reversal. If there are four people competing for the next step you might get it because you're a woman and the company needs one woman in a visible place. Years ago they would tell you directly that you didn't have a chance of getting the job because you're a woman, and in some ways it's easier to deal with that open discrimination. They're hiding it much more now. But women can do any job as well as men. Sure we're different, but when it comes to work there is no difference. For women, being successful is not at all reinforced. If you're lucky people will say, "Gee, you're one of the few successful women executives who is also feminine." Translation: "Successful women executives are not feminine."

I want to do this job for a while, and I want to be successful at less cost to myself. That's part of the challenge now. I'd like to be in an environment with people with ideas. Important parts of me are not getting lived out. I don't always want to be climbing the next step on the corporate ladder. There's always a next step. I watch the 60-year-olds putting in their last energies trying to move up, and it's so foolish. Not only are you bankrupt when you're all used up, but you haven't had a whole lot of pleasure while you were doing it. Corporate executives are so clearly trapped because they're making so much money, and it's hard to give that up. I've been in this world twenty years, and I don't see much of the enjoyment part. I get enthusiastic about the things I'm doing, and I like being challenged, but I'm not always enjoying it a whole lot.

I'd like to do this for a while, but then I'd like to do something else. I have awful unfinished business in the form of having another child; I just can't seem to get that one dealt with except by default. Never have I wished to be a full-time mother, but the best part of my life has been the process of watching my child grow.

I have also been musing about the role of close women friends in my life. One of the things I do not like about this lifestyle is that it's hard to develop, maintain, expand friendships with anybody, and it's virtually impossible to do that with men. My life is so busy I just don't see my friends.

My family has always been a weight, never a joy, an obligation to be taken care of and not a source of support. My father had cancer recently, and my mother has been in a depressed state for ten years. I'm seeing my parents every three or four weeks and talking to them on the phone at least once every couple of days because of their health. My sister and I have an okay relationship. She has had a lot of problems and was just one more person in the family for me to take care of. We don't see each other much. I am there for her if she needs me, but I would never turn to her.

A final interview with Ellen occurred two months later, after she had accepted a major promotion in her company.

I've been promoted, and I love it, but I am working very long hours and not sleeping well. I have a lot of tension and pressure. I get up at 5 a.m. because I can't sleep, get into the office around 8 a.m., work late, go home, have dinner, and work until I go to sleep. I know that has to change. I love this job, but it is taking every ounce of ability and energy to get on top of it.

I came home from a trip the other night at 10 p.m., exhausted, with a splitting headache, hadn't eaten. When I walked in, my daughter Jennifer sat me down to help with her homework! I wanted to help, but it's very difficult. Roger just got a job that he is extremely happy with. Now we are both in highly taxing jobs that we love, and we're both traveling a lot most of the week. We have some difficult juggling to do. There's an awful lot of strain with each other because so much of our energy is caught up in our jobs right now.

When I look at my next stage I just don't know what that will be. I felt like I was in the middle of a mid-life crisis when we first began these interviews three or four months ago. But with the great fortune of getting a job I love at the level of responsibility I'm going to be having now, I don't feel concerned about where I am going next. I like my life the way it is now and would like it to continue like this. I like the combination of mothering and wifing and the job I'm in. I like the way that works. I like the balance in my life. I do have some regrets, though. I wish that I had had another child, although I know there's absolutely no way I could have done that. At some point I'll look for the next step, which I hope will be some kind of intellectual challenge, not necessarily in a corporate hierarchy. I'm clearly getting to the point at which the number of further steps on the pyramid, here or anywhere else, are few. I feel freed up from having to figure out what I want next.

It's a funny switch. You measure yourself by very external things for a long time, and then a switch takes place. You recognize that you're going to judge yourself and your happiness and your fulfillment by *internal* feelings, not by where you are on any ladder. It's the inner goal that I'm running against now. I don't have to prove to anybody except myself that I can do it.

I have a very odd sense of having always been the person out of step or marching to a different drummer. Except that somehow the music changed, the marching changed. I continued to march on the same path, and all of a sudden the world changed, and that path became the mainstream. Things that I did first and was widely attacked for are now widely reinforced. Many women are doing it all now as a matter of course.

Five of the women in Life Structure A were *moderate achievers*. Emma Beechwood, for example, had recently been promoted at 37 to director of a department, a position at the top of a staff ladder in a field that was relatively open to women. Although nothing was assured, she now anticipated further promotion, with the continuing support of her male sponsors. Hillary Lewin was full professor at a school she found intellectually and personally barren.

She also did part-time research at a nearby university; this work enriched her professional life but left her marginal between the two worlds.

Finally, eight of the women in Life Structure A were *low or ambiguous achievers*. For example, Jessica Hall had felt stuck in a position of considerable responsibility and limited authority and salary. At 39 she finally made the decision to leave the corporate world, to see what it was like to spend time with her 5-year-old daughter, and to explore the possibilities of opening her own small business. During her thirties Kim Price had reached a middle-management position but saw no chance for promotion or for significant contribution in her field. At 40, with a mixture of hope and trepidation, she moved to a large corporation. Holly Crane obtained her doctorate at 38, spent two years as a postdoctoral fellow, and at 40 became an assistant professor. She knew that, given her late start, she was at a disadvantage in the battle for tenure. Five other faculty members, among them Stacey Lane and Erica Warren, had been assistant professors for several years when interviewed at age 36 to 40. All of these women understood that they had poor prospects of obtaining tenure at their current institution or another comparable one. They were forced to consider the possibility of taking a faculty position at an institution not to their liking, of moving into low-level academic administration (not a preferred option), or of moving out of academe altogether. These five women constitute almost half of the eleven faculty members in Group A.

✎ STACEY LANE

At 31 I got my master's degree and began work on my doctorate. For the next six years my life was divided into so many parts—writing the dissertation, part-time teaching jobs in local colleges, and raising my three kids. At 37 I got the Ph.D. degree, and a year later took a three-year terminal assistant professorship here. My whole life has developed more by chance than by choice. At the time, this appointment seemed the best option even though it had no tenure-track possibilities. I don't regret taking it, although I don't know where it will lead. At 40 I'm in the terminal year—like a terminal disease.

My life for the past five years and my prospects for the future have been very much influenced by the end of my marriage at 35. Actually, the marriage came apart very slowly over a long period of time. There was a kind of separation going on throughout our marriage. We were each pursuing separate things and not making time for us. We were friends and intellectual companions, which was always very satisfying. We are still close friends. But Tyler seemed increasingly remote and had increasingly long periods of depression and wasn't able to seek professional help. I couldn't deal with his remoteness, and it began to bother me. I wasn't part of his private world, and I was very lonely in the marriage. My connection with the kids helped me feel an emotional bond and intimacy that filled the gap in the marriage. Tyler and I didn't have a satisfying sexual relationship, either. The emotional attachment seemed missing. We couldn't take and give to each other. I looked down the road five years, and I could see that it was likely that we'd be divorced, so why keep trying? I initiated the divorce.

I've made only two real choices in my life. The first was to go for my Ph.D., and the second was to leave my husband. The divorce was very civil and very sad. Explaining to the kids was hard. Tyler and I are still friends, and the kids spend weekends with him, so they have adapted very well. It came out that both of us had had brief sexual encounters, but nothing that special. I think the divorce was a good decision. One has some regrets, either being married or not married. I was very lonely while married, and I'm still lonely most of the time. There's not much of either love or leisure in my life now.

I haven't had an important love relationship since the separation, nothing that might grow into a permanent relationship, though that's what I'd like ideally. Two years ago I went out with a younger graduate student, but he got scared off and left me [tearful]. He was kinder and more attentive, more playful than anyone else I've known. It was a more passionate relationship that made me feel attractive and sexually viable. I didn't expect that we'd get married or anything, but it was so nice while it lasted. Why couldn't it go on longer?

The really big decision facing me now is what to do about work next year, and that ties in with family as well. My children are firmly rooted in this community, as I am, and they have close ties with their father. I am intrigued by the idea of moving to the South, where I grew up, but I can't try that for at least five years when all the kids will be in college. What I'd like most for now is to continue teaching here and living in this community with my family as it is, but that's not possible. If I could get another academic position around here, I would take it. I would even take two part-time jobs that could be put together, but I don't think any such option will become available.

This means that my career may have to be sidetracked for a while. I may decide to stay here and take a nonacademic job for a few years, but if I drop out of academia now, I'm not sure I can go back later. I don't know what I look like as a candidate for an academic job in comparison with recent Ph.D. graduates, who are younger and less expensive. I might apply for a fellowship next year to write a book on my dissertation, but I don't know whether I could get a fellowship, and my ambitions to publish the dissertation have eroded, along with my confidence that I'm up to the task. Giving up the whole career doesn't have any reality for me; it's just an unformed idea that I can hardly think about. I imagine I would be qualified for various positions, but I don't know what it would mean to abandon the very structured framework of academia that I have always lived within.

I realize that my entire adult life has been one of *accommodation* — first to husband, then to family, then to the needs of various departments. I've always gone from pillar to post. My sense of a professional plan has lacked force and continuity, and my career has been a fragmented affair. I was entirely a student and part of the student world right up until I got divorced, then all of a sudden I had to grow up. I am most secure and satisfied in my role as a mother, and I count this as my first responsibility and joy. I think that women's experience is more a day at a time, not looking ahead. I find teaching very rewarding but lack confirmation of myself as a scholar. In some ways the prospect of seeking a nonacademic job is a relief. I am a survivor. My academic future seems bleak, even if I had mobility and heart for the task. It's hard to imagine what my life will be like a year from now. I may be making Dunkin' Donuts.

ERICA WARREN

I divorced at 32. I am 38 and relatively happy now. Aside from the job pressures, I like my life and enjoy my colleagues very much. I'm very happy in my second marriage. We have a much more satisfying, equal relationship than I had with my first husband. My relationship with George is a much more egalitarian kind of relationship. It's not a perfect relationship, but generally our view is that we have equal responsibilities and rights, and we share the housework and child care pretty much fifty-fifty.

It's weird. In my school if a *man* takes a leave of absence to do child care it's applauded and admired, but if a woman does it she's seen as taking time away from her career and is seen as less serious about her career than a man. It's a very weird twist history has taken.

It's a central pressure for me to balance my family life with my career. There's something in the back of my head that says it's not worth it: having a career and kids and doing it all and living like this. Why do I have to keep trying to do it all? I'm 38 years old, and I feel like I should have a clearer vision of where I'm going in the next few years with my career. The next couple of years I'll be up or out, and I know what I have to do to get tenure. I'm at a choice point where I have to decide whether or not I want to put a large part of myself into my occupation. There's a part of me that says it's not worth it; I don't want to live my life like this anymore. But how else would I live? I don't know what other options there would be for me. I really love my work, and I have no other work experience as an adult other than teaching at colleges. I got my Ph.D. and became an assistant professor here at age 37. I love teaching and the interaction with students, and I'm an excellent teacher. I've begun to find research topics in my field that have importance to me.

My question for the next two years is this: Should I opt for family and have a child with my second husband or go for tenure? I've always had a major conflict over whether I wanted a job or a career, and taking time to raise children has probably cost me a career. Maybe if I worked hard enough and ran fast enough I might catch up. I've had a continual juggling act to balance my family life with my career, and after all these years I'm exhausted. There's a voice in me that says it's just not worth it anymore. Why do I have to keep trying to have it all? I think Superwoman is dead; she died of exhaustion.

Life Structure B. Family Central, Occupation a Peripheral or Unfilled Component

In this structure, family became for the first time central while occupation lost its formerly central place. It is exemplified by three women, all in business, all low or ambiguous achievers. No faculty members formed this structure, although, as we have just seen, several faculty women were having occupational difficulties in their late thirties and were not sure that an academic career could remain central after 40. Three businesswomen, Amy York, Lisa Rourke, and Sally Wolford became increasingly disenchanted with the corporate-financial world during the Age 30 Transition and the first phase of the Culminating Life Structure. Lisa Rourke and Sally Wolford had their first child during this time, when the idea of family acquired more immediate reality and emotional urgency than before. It was important to be a mother, though not a permanent full-time homemaker within a Traditional Marriage Enterprise. Starting a family did not mean that the woman gave up entirely on outside work and lived "merely" a domestic life—her internal Anti-Traditional Figure was too strong for that. But by 35 the woman did give up the aim of having a long-term corporate career and making occupation central in her life. Instead, she built a Culminating Life Structure around a modified Traditional Marriage Enterprise, giving first priority to family and planning to pursue some kind of outside work as domestic conditions permitted.

The women opting for this kind of Culminating Life Structure were making two heavy bets, with odds that were hard to judge. First, they were betting that family would be suitable for the self and viable in the world as the central component of the life structure. This meant that they would enjoy motherhood and at least a moderate load of domestic responsibility, that the marriage would be sufficiently durable, that her husband would be a good enough provider, father, and marital partner.

Second, they were betting that they could make a good-enough life structure with occupation as an unfilled or peripheral component. While giving up a career path that had turned sour, they assumed that it would be possible in time to have some kind of meaningful work. Even if occupation had little or no place in the Culminating Life Structure, it would become more central in the future as family came to provide fewer demands and satisfactions. One of the great hazards, of course, was that occupation had already become essential to these women's self-esteem and to the character of their relationships with persons and institutions. How would they go about Becoming One's Own Woman in the late thirties—achieving youthful goals, being affirmed, gaining a stronger sense of inner authority and competence, becoming a more senior member of their world—without occupation as a major vehicle? Could this developmental work be done primarily through motherhood and family life for these women?

⤤ SALLY WOLFORD

Sally Wolford married at 28 but did not attempt pregnancy for four years, devoting herself instead to work, independence, and leisure. At 32 she decided to start a family. The decision to get pregnant was triggered by her old timetable ("Thirty is as long as one can wait to start a family"), and by the recognition that her career was at an impasse. She had worked for almost ten years at a large firm, and she had not been promoted, despite recurrent promises. She was beginning finally to understand that she was in a dead-end job. For three years Sally tried without success to get pregnant. Hovering on the brink of motherhood, she could not bring herself to quit the stagnant job and seek new work. When she finally got pregnant at 35, she was more than ready to leave the corporate world for a while.

Life Structure C. Occupation Central, Motherhood an Unfilled Component

Ten career women—six in business, four in academe—had no children, and occupation was the central component of their Culminating Life Structure. Two women were high achievers, three moderate achievers, and five low or ambiguous achievers. Three were married throughout this period, three were single-divorced, and four were single-never-married. Life Structure C is of special importance. It comprises a third of the present sample but closer to 50 percent of women in professional careers, especially in the corporate-financial world. It is important symbolically as well: childlessness has traditionally been regarded as the bitter fate of excessively ambitious women. Many have argued, on just these grounds, that career is inimical to family and that a woman who wants a good family life should not involve herself in a demanding career. Others, at the opposite extreme, have maintained that women should have both career and family and, with modest support and ingenuity, can readily do so.

My findings suggest that the situation is more complex than either of these views recognizes, and that we need a deeper examination of women's (and men's) lives before drawing conclusions. Two thirds of the career women in this study *did* have children, and most of these combined family with full-time career. The mothers who had a career were at least as ambitious, successful, and satisfied with their lives as the childless career women. And, what is especially striking, the women without children were generally similar to the mothers in their feelings and expectations about motherhood. Both groups had entered adulthood with an interest in developing some occupational skills, but they expected to marry in due course and to give higher priority to family than to outside work. The women who became mothers were surprised to discover in the Age 30 Transition that they were ready to commit themselves to a full-time, long-term career along with family. Most of the nonmothers had a corresponding but more distressing surprise: for various reasons they would not have a family in the foreseeable future, perhaps not ever.

Only two of the women who remained childless throughout the Culminating Life Structure took the position that they would never, under any conditions, become a mother—that they simply did not want to have a child. The other childless women continued actively to hope that they would do so when conditions changed: the married women, when their marriage or other conditions improved; the single women, when they married. Some women came to understand that the chances for motherhood were minimal or zero in the Culminating Life Structure they formed. They accepted the loss with varying mixtures of anger, regret, resignation, despair, sadness, and relief. The desire to have children existed in almost all the women studied. Many also had the desire *not* to have children—not to be stuck with the entire burden of child-rearing and homemaking, not to be largely excluded from the public occupational world. Each woman had to deal with her multiple feelings on both sides of this dilemma, and with the cross-pressures emanating from loved ones, institutions, and the culture at large. As we have seen, some mothers in Life Structures A and B did not have the inner readiness or the external conditions they required for motherhood until the thirties. Likewise, a few of the ten women in Life Structure C may bear or adopt a child in the future, if their external conditions and inner readiness make it more feasible.

Let us look now at some individual variations among the childless women. Julia Hart and Pam Kenney had initially planned to marry soon after college and become homemakers with outside jobs. After marrying in the Age 30 Transition, they found their marriages so shaky that they put off starting families. In the first phase of the Culminating Life Structure these women made a conscious decision to focus on career and delay motherhood for the indefinite future. At the same time they experienced the absence of motherhood as a personal loss and a reminder of an inadequate marriage. Marriage gave them the benefits of a shared domicile, the legitimacy of being married rather than single (a real asset in the corporate world), and a base upon which to lead an independent life. But the partners spent little time together and had a limited personal relationship. Neither woman had a child when interviewed at 39 and 43, respectively.

✅ JULIA HART

After earning her MBA at 29, Julia Hart went to work for a large firm. She enjoyed her work and carried the Anti-Traditional Dream of the Successful Career Woman. She wanted a long-term managerial career and tried to get on a career path in her early thirties. At 34 she understood that her chances for being promoted were slim at best, especially since she was a woman and a late starter. Julia had not received the early mentoring which might have taught her something about corporate ladders and how they operate, and from 34 to 36 she explored other job possibilities. She then took a staff position at a major international corporation, hoping to make her way into line management and the corporate structure. The next three years were spent in a series of planning and troubleshooting assignments. These jobs, though of great importance to the company and to Julia's personal growth and development, did not form a career path leading into the upper reaches of management. When interviewed at 39, she was in the exquisitely ambiguous position of having made significant contributions to corporate growth yet also of having no clear basis for advancement. Julia's Culminating Life Structure was thus a decidedly mixed blessing. The career, though rewarding in many ways, was disappointing in the present and uncertain for the future. Her marriage, likewise, was satisfying in many ways, yet also limited. Ready neither to have a child nor to renounce motherhood totally, she was biding her time.

✅ BROOKE THOMPSON

Brooke Thompson had divorced at 26 after a stormy three-year marriage. When interviewed at 37 she was single and childless and had put together a satisfying life for herself, although her future was unclear. She had recently started a serious "commuting" relationship with a man who lived on the West Coast. She was coming to the end of her current appointment as assistant professor and knew that she would probably not be promoted.

> I came here at 33. Women friends have become increasingly important to me. At 34 I began a relationship with Jerry, an academic who is five

years younger than me. He is incredibly positive and playful. We've had a three-year commuting relationship. It's a wonderful relationship at this stage of my life because when we're together it's 100 percent on, and when we're apart I just concentrate on my work. We've both been married and divorced and have sort of an anti-marriage stance. I'm pretty sure I don't want children. As I get clearer about the family issue I get freer. I think for me and many women the family is not a good place to be.

I don't earn much money, but in a lot of ways this job seems almost too good to be true. It's a wonderful free situation. We're all young and really interested in what we do, and we work hard, and it's a good work situation. My courses are very successful, and I feel I have come into my own as a teacher. I'm hopeful about tenure, but I haven't published a great deal. I'm 37 now and want to publish my first book to establish myself in my field.

So many of my female students say, "We're going to have it all—career and family." First of all, that's a hard life. But who says that's "having it all"? It suggests that work and family are the only things in life, and you won't be happy without them. It's being built in as the expectation. It doesn't give a woman room to say, "I just want one of those things or something entirely different that will make *my* life meaningful." To "have it all," not only are you going to have to educate yourself to get a career, you're going to have to think about setting up a different kind of marriage and family life where you find a partner who will participate equally with you in the domestic work. It shouldn't be up to the woman to have to manage all these things alone somehow.

⋙ MEGAN BENNETT

Megan Bennett was a high achiever. Pregnancy followed by miscarriage was perhaps the dominant event of Megan Bennett's life during the Age 30 Transition. As her Culminating Life Structure began, she gave up trying to have a child and dedicated herself to an academic career. She made her own career primary and, with her husband's agreement, rearranged the marital relationship so that it contained her as the star and him as a supporting player. The recognition of her husband's limitations and the decision not to have children were great blows to her but also provided the beginning of a process of liberation: she became freer to pursue her own course and to have ambitions in her own right. During the Culminating Life Structure Megan became more her own woman and embarked upon a distinguished academic career. Her Culminating Event at 40 was her appointment as full professor and director of an academic research lab. Her childlessness was thus embedded, as both cause and effect, within her entire process of living.

✑ AMANDA BURNS

I came to this school at 38. I have a faculty position and do some minor teaching, but I'm basically an administrator. I have worked for some fantastic people and have had good mentors. I have also worked for people I don't have respect for, and I know I don't want to work for someone like that again. How you are enabled to work depends so much on your relationship with those who are in superior positions to you. I have a good working relationship with my boss here. I have had nothing but solid support from him and have been able to build and do what I think is important. I have grown through the process of my various jobs to the point where I believe I am a good administrator. I like my work here. I feel I am building an exciting department. I've always been reasonably successful, and the politics are great fun for me. I know what I need to do in order to play the game well. I know you have to have a power base and support from your superiors and an idea of the playing board. I'm very intrigued by what I'm doing here; there is an intellectual integrity and ability behind an administrator's ability to handle and deal with a system and the people within the system.

I have chosen a lesbian personal lifestyle. I think the difference in relationships with women is that there is more saneness in terms of understanding the emotional components of where you come from, and there is much more equality, and there isn't a set definition of roles in the relationship. In my marriage I got into a very competitive, angry thing, and that has not happened in my relationships with women. I made the choice to make the ongoing emotional connection be with women, though in my friendships I have close relationships with men. But I don't choose to live with men. There is a comfort and a naturalness and rapport with women that's just easily better for me.

I have had relationships with women since I was 26, after my divorce. I've loved each of these women, and I have a special love connection to each person even after the sexual relationship has ended. I think you outgrow people, be they men or women.

The woman I live with now is a very intelligent, sensitive, very caring person, very deep and very introspective and compassionate and understanding. She has a great capacity for sharing. I'm a very action-oriented, outer-oriented kind of person, and Linda provides a balance that is helpful for me. She is a close friend. There is not an expectation that we should always be together.

I have never thought of these relationships as marriages, although I think of each relationship as permanent at the time. It's another kind of relationship. It's a commitment between two people, but I would never want to emulate society's form of marriage. I don't want or need that extra baggage that has to do with roles and power. You can make a commitment between two people and live within the relationship when it's good for each of you, and you can end it without tearing each other apart, though endings are wrenching.

There is a lesbian community within the larger academic community here. People have always made innuendos; there has always been that speculation about me. If you're a lesbian and in certain kinds of positions then you're talked about. But you're talked about anyway if you're a single female at a certain level. I'm not public because I don't think it's ever in our lifetime going to be totally accepted, and I accept that.

There were four single-never-married women, all in the business world. By their early thirties each of these women had had at least one serious romantic-sexual relationship that ended without marriage.

In the first phase of the Culminating Life Structure, they felt acutely that they were in a hard place both matrimonially and occupationally. They came to the shocking realization that they might well not have a choice with regard to marriage and family—that the kind of man they wanted was extremely rare and probably already married. This meant that they would most likely have to work and support themselves until retirement. At the same time, they were becoming more realistic about their jobs and their career prospects. They could not imagine continuing in their present jobs for another thirty years. It became essential to get on an occupational path that would suffice for the long term: work that involved less competition, less overtime and travel, and more opportunity for a personal life. They were also becoming more aware of the limitations of the corporate world. It would not provide a quasi-familial supportive context. There was almost no room for women at the top of organizations and very little in the middle. The only way to have a minimally adequate life, it seemed, was to be part of a couple and family. Male colleagues were interested in romantic affairs as a supplement to, not a replacement for, their marriages. The social world was organized around couples. A single woman was a fifth wheel, and rarely included in the couples' network. To be single was to be relatively isolated.

By 35 or 36 the women established Culminating Life Structures as single, dating, marriage-oriented career women. The structure was based upon a deep compromise. They continued to seek matrimony while recognizing that it was becoming unlikely. They continued to pursue a corporate career, but they limited their aspirations, took gender-appropriate paths, and made more time for their personal-social lives. Occupation, the central component of the life structure, was a source of both satisfaction and suffering, and love/marriage/family was an unfilled or partially filled component.

The struggle between the two internal figures continued. The inner voice of the Traditional Homemaker Figure became more vociferous, more bitter: "You wouldn't listen to me! You wanted to be independent and able to take care of yourself, to be free of entangling relationships. You didn't want the kind of life that most women are glad to have. Well, you have lived that way and where has it gotten you? You are approaching 40 with no husband, no children, and an uncertain career. I told you so." The internal Traditional Homemaker Figure thus invoked the negative image of the Single Career Woman (see Chapter 3) and the ultimate personal disaster of being alone. At the same time, the internal Anti-Traditional Figure tried to make the best of this life: "Whatever its limitations, my work sustains my independence and my development. I would rather be single than caught in a deadening marriage like so many women I know."

The inner warfare between the two figures evolved through the second phase of the Culminating Life Structure. Sometimes one voice was stronger, sometimes the other, depending upon mood and circumstances. Improvement in work situation or a love relationship led to greater hopefulness and self-esteem, decline to growing despair. Some of the childless women went through a crisis in this period—a feeling that the life structure was intolerably bleak and pointless, yet unchangeable. Most of the single childless women had serious questions about the present and misgivings about the future: "I have worked so hard to have a fuller life, how did I get into this position? What are my possibilities for the future?"

In this condition it is often difficult not to get depressed and full of self-recriminations: "I was too critical of men, too naive about gender discrimination, too insistent upon my rights, not sufficiently feminine." The accusations from within received much implicit support from without. The oppressive image of the Single Career Woman is reflected upon a woman from parents, friends, coworkers, the mass media, and the texture of everyday social life. Very few single childless women in the Culminating Life Structure had come to terms with being childless. They could do so only by going through a painful developmental process of dealing with the loss and of gaining a new perspective on the possibilities of meaningful life in middle adulthood, and this process extended beyond 40.

Not having a child is a painful experience for many women in their thirties. By age 30, women who earlier had no special desire for motherhood often start having maternal wishes. According to a popular saying, "She hears the biological clock ticking." But the clock is not solely biological; it is psychological and social as well. Biologically, the woman has at least another ten or fifteen years to have a child. In the psycho-social timetable of the life cycle, however, a childless woman who wants a family but is not married in her thirties is in grave danger of remaining childless. A woman's anxiety about the loss of motherhood is likely to peak in the late thirties, in the phase of Becoming One's Own Woman.

The wish to be a mother involves much more than the wish for one's own offspring. Motherhood enables a woman to live within a family, giving care to others and being taken care of in ways important to her. It is often part of the foundation of her sense of self and of being in the world. Having a child guarantees nothing, but not having a child is experienced by many women as a loss with potentially catastrophic consequences. She often has the sense of an inner emptiness. One version of this theme is given by Michele Proto in Chapter 15. Here is another from a single-divorced woman approaching 40:

KRISTIN WEST

> When I graduated from college the choices seemed limitless. I wanted a chance to live independently for a few years but assumed I'd still have the option to have children. But somehow by making that one choice so many years ago I've come down a path that year by year has led me farther and farther away from motherhood. I turned 25, then 30, then 35, and the choices began to disappear. Now there's a strong probability that I'll *never* have a child. Not to have a child, ever—how is that possible? All women have children, that's just part of life, isn't it? How did this happen to me? I like my work and think I've developed as a person in ways I couldn't have if I'd had children in my early twenties. But the cost of not having children seems too great. What will it be like to be 45, 50, 60 without a child of my own? Will I come to mourn the loss of my unborn children? All I have in my life now is my work. What will happen when I don't have work *or* children—when there's nothing, a complete void in my life? It terrifies and saddens me. Being childless now feels like an all-encompassing black hole.

TRISHA WALL

At 33 Trisha Wall established a domicile and a stable quasi-marital relationship. The couple was still together when she was interviewed at 40. Both partners valued the relationship, and both had mixed feelings about marrying and having children. He was still hesitant about remarrying. Trisha was afraid that matrimony might limit her own independence and activate latent problems between them. She still vividly relived her experience as a daughter, precociously playing the traditional homemaker/mother with her siblings and her long-suffering widowed father—a martyr who lost all pleasure in life. "No more caregiving, no more total responsibility for others!" was her motto in home, work, and life. This self-restriction protected Trisha from becoming a traditional homemaker but also severely limited the investment of her self in her life. The fear of becoming overly responsible for a dependent husband led her to prefer a marital relationship in which neither partner made strong demands on the other. The fear of excessive maternal and wifely responsibilities kept her from having children. In her late thirties she had a relatively satisfying staff position, but she had little sense of a long-term career direction.

When I was 33 Dean and I moved in together, and we've been living together ever since. We feel like a couple and are accepted as a couple by our friends and relatives. He was ready to live together but not to marry because he has a lot of hurts and hang-ups from his first marriage. Actually, both of us are ambivalent about marriage. I have always seen some value in our getting married—building something together and not being such independent characters, yet I am also afraid of queering the deal.

Dean also had mixed feelings about having a child. He says that a child would really upset his life—but then sometimes he thinks he'd like to have a son. I'm clearer about that: I don't want to have children. I told him that there are lots of women in New York who would like to have his son; he should have it with one of them. If I had a child I would feel responsible, but I would also be resentful over giving time that I could have for myself. I occasionally feel like that with Dean when he gets too needy. That powerful feeling goes back to my childhood; my widowed father was devoted to his children and never had any life of his own. I picked up my attitudes about not wanting kids from him.

At 34 I got more serious about my career, although work has never been an all-consuming interest. You know, people say, "What are your goals, what direction are you going in?" I have to tell you, I have simply gone where the best job was at the time and done the best I could. When it seemed appropriate to leave, I found the best job I could go on to. At 32 I started to realize how tough it was, how poor most of the jobs were, and how many barriers there were for a woman in my field. I got fired from one job because I refused to spend the weekend with a client!

I had some really bad bosses and no good ones. When I left a job it was because I had no more challenges and was bored. A good boss would have transferred me. Until recently, my bosses were intent on climbing themselves; they had no conception of nurturing people and giving them room to grow, especially a woman. There was always a privileged inner circle of young fair-haired sons who were allowed to advance.

I got serious about advancement at 34 and looked for another position in the same company, but mostly I got discouraging remarks from people who saw no place for a female. At 35 I got a great job at an international corporation as director of a department. Since then my career has taken off; I am now one of the top thirty in the company, and I earn over 60 percent of our household income. Lots of things have happened over the past several years, but the big change began at 34, when Dean and I got more committed and started living together. That's also when I started becoming more aware professionally. Instead of being totally focused on Dean, I had a shared focus: him *and* work.

Ending the Culminating Life Structure

For most career women, the Culminating Life Structure was a time of great difficulty but also great personal growth and development. Almost all had found a place for themselves in an occupational world and were making their way, although the life structures they built were often very difficult. Many of the married career women with children began to realize that their Neo-Traditional Marriage Enterprises were too hard on them. They were working full-time at demanding jobs, sharing the provisioning roles with their husbands, and were at the same time almost entirely responsible for the "second shift" of domestic responsibilities and child care. Whether married or single, many career women in the phase of Becoming One's Own Woman began to envision an Egalitarian Marriage Enterprise in which both partners would share provisioning *and* domestic rights and responsibilities on more equal terms. Several of the businesswomen and about half of the faculty women were able in the Culminating Life Structure or the Mid-life Transition to transform their Neo-Traditional Marriage Enterprises into an Egalitarian Marriage Enterprise or to build an Egalitarian Marriage Enterprise in a remarriage.

By age 40 or 41 virtually all of the career women, whatever their circumstances, were entering a time of inner questioning of love/marriage/family and work that would continue in the next period of the Mid-life Transition.

15 Mid-life Transition: Career Women

The career women began the Mid-life Transition at age 40 or 41 and ended it at 45 or 46. In this cross-era transitional period the career women were considering major life choices that would provide a basis for a new life structure in a new era. About half of the thirty career women were under 40 when interviewed and still in the Culminating Life Structure. A few, at 40 or 41, were on the threshold of the new period but not far enough along to tell us much about it. I consider here the thirteen career women who were age 42 to 45 years old and well into the Mid-life Transition. Seven of these women were faculty members, six were businesswomen.

By the late thirties, many career women carried the individual Dream of the Successful Career Woman, which was held by the Anti-Traditional Figure, who co-existed in every career woman with the opposing internal Traditional Homemaker Figure. There were wide variations among the career women in the relative strength of the internal figures and in the women's ways of compromising or reducing the conflict between them. During their thirties some women devoted themselves primarily to the pursuit of their Anti-Traditional Dream, while others placed severe restrictions upon one aspect or another—limiting their career aspirations or their involvement in love/marriage/family. Their ways of dealing with the conflict evolved over early adulthood.

The individual Dream of the Successful Career Woman was embedded in a corresponding cultural myth. A myth is a culturally transmitted story that dramatizes a certain kind of life. It often portrays a hero struggling against great obstacles in quest of a noble goal. The contemporary myth of the Successful Career Woman is one of the few in which the hero is a woman. Every myth contains elements of reality, yet it always goes beyond reality to depict ultimate possibilities and dangers in human life. A myth invites the individual and the wider culture to accept (as well as oppose) the heroic struggle. Cultural myths provide a matrix from which individual Dreams may grow. Pursuing a mythic scenario always has both constructive and destructive consequences for the would-be hero and for others in her life.

The myth of the Successful Career Woman was not the private creation of a few unusual women, though each career woman gave it her own individual stamp. It was part of a historical process in American society that produced a "breakthrough generation" of career-oriented women. A small but significant minority of women first took more than entry-level positions in corporate, academic, and other institutions that had traditionally been the province of men. A seemingly powerful current of cultural change generated the impression that history was on the side of the career woman. If she could just persevere in the face of last-minute individual and institutional resistance, she would win the battle and give future generations of women the freedom to pursue the careers of their choice.

The myth of the Successful Career Woman portrayed a heroic woman who could realize "the incredible joy of having it all"—career, marriage, family, leisure, everything. It would not be easy, but in time all the pieces would fall into place. In this scenario the occupational world was becoming open enough and fair enough to admit women relatively freely into its upper-level, professional-managerial ranks. If a woman worked hard enough, and gave a superior performance, she would "make it" by around age 40 and live happily ever after. If she failed, according to the myth, it would be her own fault—a sign of her deficiencies of competence, character, or ability to compete successfully with men. Her self-esteem was tied inextricably to her career success or failure. Success would validate her as a person and provide a stamp of approval from the world she valued most; failure, no matter how it came about, would be clear evidence that she herself had failed.

There were similar contradictions in the career women's marriage and family life. Most of the husbands "permitted" or even encouraged their wives to engage in full-time careers and did not insist on functioning as traditional heads of household. Total family income was often great enough so that much of the domestic work could be delegated to paid help. At the same time, there was a widespread marital agreement, often implicit, that the husband might "help" her in certain ways with domestic chores but the wife was primarily responsible for household and child care.

The wives suffered this imbalance with various mixtures of acquiescence, resentment, and inner conflict. The internal Anti-Traditional Figure urged the woman to insist upon a more equitable division of labor. After all, she shared the provisioning with her husband, contributing 40 to 60 percent or more of the family income. Being under less pressure to earn a living, he presumably had more time to share the domestic duties with her. A fuller sharing would make them true partners in provisioning as well as homemaking. But the internal Traditional Homemaker Figure felt lucky that the husband didn't demand more domestically from her and guilty that she did not offer more, especially with the children. The end result was that the woman lived on a treadmill, endlessly running to meet the requirements of a demanding career and needy family. It was almost impossible to get beyond these two top priorities and to be engaged as well in marriage, intimate relationships, friendships, leisure, and the self. The career women endured these problems largely in the hope that as the children got older and their careers advanced, their lives would become more stable and satisfying.

Major Changes in the Mid-life Transition

During their thirties the career women had substantial evidence that the work world was only slightly more open than earlier and that gender discrimination was still prevalent. Nevertheless, most of the women sustained the myth of the Successful Career Woman. They continued to believe that the success of "having it all" would be theirs if they worked hard enough and that they themselves would be to blame if they failed.

By the early forties, however, the career women's lives came into question. The questioning came about partly because of the disparity between the myth-Dream and the reality, and partly through the developmental changes of the Mid-life Transition, which led each woman to reappraise and modify the Culminating Life Structure.

What were the women's situations with regard to career, love/marriage, and motherhood as this period began? Only two of the thirteen women "had it all"—full-time career, marriage, and motherhood. Both went through major changes in all three components during this period, and one woman was terminating her marriage when interviewed at 43. Eleven women (roughly 85 percent) had only one or two of the three components. Two career women left a full-time career for motherhood in their thirties and became primarily homemakers in a Traditional Marriage Enterprise with prospects for a limited career in the future. Two had a career and a marriage but no children. Four were single-divorced mothers with careers; earlier they had had it all, but keeping it all was not possible. Two of the four single-divorced mothers remarried at 45, forming a new marriage/family markedly different from the previous one. Finally, three had a career but neither marriage nor children (two were single-divorced, one single-never-married). The incidence of these patterns of career/marriage/motherhood cannot be generalized from so small a sample to a larger population. Whatever its frequency of occurrence, however, each pattern deserves further study.

In the Mid-life Transition the career women had a dilemma comparable to that of the homemakers: Each woman recognized that her efforts to combine love/marriage, motherhood, and full-time career had not given her as much satisfaction as she had hoped and that she would have to find a new basis for living in middle adulthood. The woman began more seriously to examine the reality and the illusion in her imagery of the Successful Career Woman. It became evident that she was not, despite the mass media hype and her own private wish, a Superwoman who could accomplish anything she set her mind to. She was, it turned out, more of a Juggler who managed to keep several spheres moving at the same time, but who had a very restricted life and little connection to her self and her inner spheres. She learned, too, to reconsider what it meant to "have" a career, a marriage, a family. One may have a career but be so driven by the work and the stresses of work life that the personal meaning and value of work are lost. Her own experience helped her understand that many men "have" both career and marriage/family but are enslaved by an externally successful career and are minimal participants in marriage and family.

During this period the career women went through significant changes in the nature and meaning of their careers, their love/marital relationships, and their motherhood (for those without children, new ways of being maternal or of coming to terms with not being a mother). Changes often occurred within a particular component of the life structure. For example: the prelude to or aftermath of divorce, severe marital tensions that were resolved or contained without divorce, the end of a serious love relationship, problems with offspring, her own illness, the illness or death of loved ones. In every case, however, the specific event raised (and/or was brought on by) deeper and broader questions about herself and her life. Faced with marital problems she asked not simply, "How can I fix them?" but, "What do I truly want with this man—or someone else? What place shall I give love/marriage in my life?" Experiencing dissatisfactions at work, she asked, "Do I want a different job of the same kind, or is it important to make a more basic change in career?" The central question was "What do I now want for my self?"

Almost every woman went through a moderate or severe developmental crisis—for some, truly a rock bottom time—in this period. A severe developmental crisis occurred when a woman felt that much of her existing life was coming to an end, that a drastic restructuring was necessary, and that she lacked the basis for making a new start. In a moderate crisis a woman felt the need for more limited changes and was more hopeful that they could be brought about, though it was still not entirely clear where she was going and whether she could get there from here. Six of the thirteen women—four in academe and two in business—obtained brief or extended psychotherapy during the Mid-life Transition. As I have noted in earlier chapters, those who sought psychotherapy were not noticeably more neurotic than those who did not. For those who received psychotherapy, the main aim was not the treatment of specific symptoms but an exploration of personal life issues and a modification of life structure. Those who did not seek psychotherapy often found other ways to explore the nature of their difficulties and the possibilities for a new life.

Let us now examine the evolution of key components of the life structure, notably career, motherhood, and marriage. To provide a context for looking at the evolution of these women's careers in the early forties, I'll first consider the evolution of careers for women and men generally.

Career Development of Women and Men in the Mid-life Transition

In early adulthood most men, and an increasing number of women, try to establish themselves within the occupational world. Our occupational success strongly influences our income and self-esteem, our place in society, and the material and social advantages we can provide for our children. Our involvement in occupation has both internal and external sources. We have diverse inner motives for pursuing occupational advancement—to gain fame, fortune, power, or achievement, to take care of our families, to contribute to human welfare, to fulfill or defy parental expectations—but most young adults are to some degree caught up emotionally in the process. We are also under strong external pressures to perform at increasingly higher levels and to advance up an externally defined ladder. The well-being of society requires that the generations in early adulthood work productively and provide not only for themselves but also for those in childhood and late adulthood. The world presents all sorts of rewards, enticements, and demands that lead us to seek "success" and to avoid "failure," as it defines both of these. Success in every field is equated with superior intelligence, motivation, character, and self-esteem, failure with inferiority in these respects. Every work organization and occupation offers a plethora of concrete markers by which we can gauge our career progress, such as promotions and salary increases.

In the Mid-life Transition we come to a crucial turning point. We are concluding our youthful strivings and, at the same time, beginning to form a life appropriate to the new era of middle adulthood. We are moving from junior to senior generation, but we know little about what it means to be a senior member and about the opportunities and dangers that await us. Things are more complicated and more ambiguous than before. External markers of our competence and progress are less available and less useful. Promotions are much less common and are often disappointing in comparison with the larger ones we had hoped for. It means less to earn a little more money, to publish another book or article like the previous ones, to be given another minor award. We need ten or fifteen years of living in middle adulthood to get a better sense of what the world offers and what we want—just as we did in early adulthood.

In short, during the Mid-life Transition we take the first step in a process of career change that will continue throughout middle adulthood. The basic change is not simply in the work we do. Above all, it is in our relationship with occupation. We experience work and career from a more private, personal perspective. It becomes less important to ask, "How successful am I in the eyes of the world?" and more important to ask, "What do I give to and receive from my work? How satisfying is my relationship with work?"

There is no simple way to determine, for oneself or for someone else, how satisfying a person's relationship with work actually is. It cannot be measured adequately by a standard test or survey technique. The following are some of the ways in which a satisfying relationship may be experienced: I feel excited and challenged in the process of working; work is often difficult, stressful, even painful, but it captures an inner spark and is rarely boring. I take critical pleasure in the products of my work (be they books, well-educated students, manufactured goods, a financially sound business). I am evolving as a worker, going beyond the technical skills acquired earlier and developing my own particular understanding, style, perspective. I have a sense of creativity in the work; though perhaps not as unique or remarkable as I had once hoped, it does bear the stamp of my individuality. The work is important to me: it reflects my self in ways that other work would not.

The greater emphasis upon my own self-fulfillment and satisfaction does not mean that I become indifferent to others. I enjoy being a member of my work world—my own enterprise, my own organization, the various persons, groups, and institutions that the work connects me to. I want to make a significant contribution in the form of a legacy to something outside myself—to my family, to my clients, students, colleagues, to art or science, etc. I want to be more mentorial, generative, caring, loving, responsible. I enjoy personal relationships more deeply. I want to receive more as well, but in a qualitatively different way: I want others to appreciate my work, to affirm me as its author, to care for me as a person, and to give me a reasonably valued place as a senior member of my world. Even when I succeed in these aims, I have not entirely outgrown my youthful vanity, pettiness, egocentrism, excesses of modesty and conceit. But the balance is slowly shifting. In short, I come to a new balance of engagement in and separateness from the world. I am more in the world yet also more separate, more free of its immediate demands, more ready to pursue my own goals even if others ignore or oppose what is so important to me.

To what extent do people in middle adulthood have a satisfying relationship with their work? We do not know, and we are probably not yet ready to find out. To do so, we will have to go beyond simple surveys of "job satisfaction" and "adjustment," and explore the individual's relationship to work more fully. My own tentative view is based upon my research, organizational consultation, observations, relationships with other individuals and myself, and readings of research, biographies, novels, plays, poems.

In my opinion, perhaps 10 to 20 percent of persons in middle adulthood have a moderately or highly satisfying relationship with their work. Another 20 to 30 percent receive limited psychological income from their work but have no major grievances, largely because it provides sufficient material income, comfort, and minor gratifications—and they do not ask for more. The largest group, roughly 50 percent, find that their work, even if it is to some extent rewarding, is in many respects demeaning, empty, damaging to the self. There are women and men in all three groups but women are found disproportionately more often in the third than in the first.

The basic dissatisfactions may be expressed in diverse ways: alcoholism and drug abuse, depression, accident proneness, absenteeism, burn-out, marginal work performance, early retirement, derivative problems in marriage and family, the search for youthful forms of excitement no longer appropriate in middle age, the inability to find more authentic sources of satisfaction in work or elsewhere. When we lose our inner-psychological connection to our work but are unable for various reasons to make a change, we may continue on the job but retire psychologically. I call this phenomenon "psychological retirement." Our job performance is minimally adequate, we do most of what is required, but we are not engaged in the work. In the extreme form, our relationship to the work is dead—and continuing it is to some extent a death of the self. Psychological retirement is not good for the person, the work organization, or the public who suffer from our products and services. It is also becoming more common. Witness the growing concern with "plateauing," with improving the motivation and performance of middle-aged employees at all levels, with "golden parachutes" and less golden incentives for early retirement. Virtually every work organization would like to decrease the number and improve the effectiveness of its employees, especially the middle-aged members at its middle and top levels—and no organization knows how to do it humanely. To learn how, we will have to overcome our vast ignorance of life and development in middle adulthood. We must also learn how to create organizations that are both productive and foster the adult development of their members.

One reason for the low level of satisfaction is that work organizations generally have a pyramidal structure, with far fewer persons at the middle than bottom levels, and even fewer at the top. For every 100 people at a given level, only 40, or 20, or 5 openings exist at the next. It is simply not possible for everyone to advance continuously, whatever their competence. The selection process is especially sharp at around age 40, when many who were formerly considered promising young women and men are fired, given "lateral" moves, move elsewhere, or are given positions that permit little or no further advancement.

The major job/career changes occurring at around age 40 bring us to the end of our early adult careers and to the beginning of a new career path. Where that path will lead is a mystery to the person embarking upon it. Almost no guidance is available from the popular culture or the social sciences, which have generally ignored the topic of career development in middle adulthood.

What is the further career evolution of persons who do not receive the desired promotion by 40 or 45? They may take various routes. Some become "a bigger fish in a smaller pond" by obtaining a higher position in an organization less prestigious than the one they were in. This is a comedown within the value system of that occupational world, although it may in the long run lead to a more satisfying career for the individual. Other people shift to a career path slightly or markedly different from the previous one; for example, from a brokerage firm to manufacturing, from faculty to educational administration, from a corporation to one's own small consulting firm—directions that were often considered and sometimes taken by the career women in this study. Still others continue in the same organization in a position that pays as well or slightly better than the previous one but leads nowhere. These people may receive small advances in salary or title but are essentially stuck in a mid-level slot, with nowhere to go.

What about those who advance as they had hoped, who move to the senior positions they sought in universities, or corporations, in government or small business or the arts? The consequences of relative success at mid-life are as diverse and unpredictable as those of relative failure. The advancement brings not just a new job, but a new kind of work and a new place in the occupational-social world of middle adulthood. We have moved from the top rung of one ladder to the bottom rung of a new ladder. It is surprising and often distressing to discover that, despite our previous accomplishments, we are novice members of this new generation and world, just as in our twenties we were novice members of the early adult world.

When the new work is sufficiently exciting, and the situation sufficiently supporting, we may become creatively engaged and continue to grow in the work over the course of middle adulthood. Under less favorable conditions we may perform adequately, and gain adequate rewards, but have a minimally satisfying relationship with our work. In the worst case the work is progressively deadening; we give little to it and receive little from it. Many of those who reach a comparatively high level of advancement by their forties are at a considerably lower level of external success, and especially of inner satisfaction, by their mid-fifties. Many middle-aged persons who hold middle- to high-level positions in work organizations would rather be employed elsewhere but believe, rightly or wrongly, that they have no better alternative. The higher one's position the fewer the attractive alternatives and the greater the potential fall.

Career Development of the Businesswomen and Faculty Members

As noted earlier, the subjects of this chapter are the thirteen career women who were 42 to 45 years old when interviewed. Four of them had achieved positions of senior rank and some prominence in the corporate or academic world and were beginning to learn about the benefits and costs of great success. Two women were tenured professors but had not yet done much scholarly work; during the Mid-life Transition they struggled with conflicts about achievement, ambition, and the place of occupation in their lives. Five women were at middle or junior levels but working hard to advance further up the occupational ladder. Finally, Sally Wolford and Lisa Rourke had in their thirties turned away from the corporate career and given first priority to family; they were now working part-time and reconsidering their career plans.

In their late thirties, many women who still had full-time corporate or academic employment felt that they were weathering the storms of the late thirties and gaining a foothold as more senior members of the work world. They had found, or had hopes of soon finding, an opening through the "glass ceiling" (the term was coined by A. Morrison) that prevented so many others from advancing further at that age. It seemed not unrealistic to believe that they were now on a career ladder leading to the upper echelons of their occupational system.

In the early forties, however, almost every woman went through a major reappraisal of her career and made significant changes in career as well as in other components of her life structure. The reappraisal was more soul-rending than in any previous period and dealt with the entire grounding of her adult life. She began to question the myth of the Successful Career Woman as it applied to herself and to women generally. She recognized that the term "glass ceiling" was a misnomer. A glass ceiling is a strong though invisible barrier to upward advancement. A few women get through it; most do not. Those who fail must seek an alternative and less desired path. How is it for the exceptional few who pass through? The term implicitly encourages the wishful assumption that the worst is over: "Once you become a tenured professor (or executive vice president) you'll be home free and able to do what you really want." In actuality, those who get through one barrier/ceiling generally find that the problems at the next level are greater, and the benefits less, than they had imagined or been told about in advance. There were multiple ceilings, not just one; and no matter what level we reach, we are never "home free." Again, these problems exist for men as well; they are just more acute for women. The woman realized, too, that the advancement at around 40 often got her to the top rung of the ladder she had been climbing—and placed her on the bottom rung of a new ladder. And, as she began quickly to learn, the possibilities for further ascent were limited indeed. The basic problems were similar in the corporate and academic worlds, but the concrete conditions differed.

The businesswomen were usually in the middle of the corporate hierarchy, several levels from the top. A woman might have a staff position that, though fairly high in the corporate structure, had no line authority. A position one or two levels above hers might have responsibility for a wide range of functions, and might be on a ladder leading upwards, but there was no way to get from her position to that one. She was, in short, at or near the top of a ladder from which no further advance was possible. In some cases a woman was promoted to a higher position and was given the same title and almost the same salary as the previous male incumbent. She then learned that the range of responsibilities had been narrowed and the level of authority reduced, and that her immediate boss—the man she reported to—was lower in the structure than her predecessor's boss. These restrictions were more than petty inconveniences or blows to inappropriate pride. They were implicit yet clear evidence that the woman was hitting a new and even less permeable ceiling in the corporation, and that gender was an important obstacle to promotion.

Of the six businesswomen in the Mid-life Transition, only Debra Rose had reached a high level in the corporate world. Michele Proto and Kim Price were at a middle level and unlikely to go much higher. Pam Kenney was still in the lower ranks of management and not sure whether it was feasible—or desirable—to remain in that world. Sally Wolford and Lisa Rourke had in their thirties become mothers/homemakers with part-time work and were now reappraising their career plans.

The faculty members were on a hierarchy containing two separate ladders. The "tenure track" had just three rungs: assistant professor, associate professor, and full professor. The other ladder had no formal name but consisted of adjunctive or marginal positions such as instructor, research associate, lecturer, adjunct professor. People in these positions generally had short-term contracts with no assurance of continued employment, though some of them hoped eventually to be appointed on the tenure track and thus to be in the running for a permanent appointment. Their compensation was generally much less than that of comparable tenure-track positions. The goal of junior faculty was to get on the tenure track and in due course become a full professor with tenure. The top rank is normally reached by about 40— rarely before 35 or after 45.

Two faculty members had obtained their doctorates at around 40; they were now assistant professors struggling to gain advancement and tenure within the next few years. The other five faculty members were full professors when interviewed. They had already gained an initial foothold in the senior world and learned a little about the opportunities and pitfalls it presented. Now at the top of the academic ladder, they were no longer working for a promotion in formal rank. This did not mean, however, that they simply went on doing what they had been doing. There was a further evolution in their teaching and scholarly work, their administrative activities, their participation in department, institution, discipline, and other related organizations. Being a professor involved a complex set of obligations, pressures, rewards, possibilities for satisfying or stultifying work. It was possible to gain additional recognition, to contribute in significant new ways, to gain a greater sense of achievement and meaning, to feel more fulfilled as a person. It was also possible to stagnate in an endless routine, to become a petty tyrant who exploited or neglected students rather than fostering their development, to do work of little value to self or others. Most faculty members had sparse counsel in finding their way during their thirties; they had even less after 40, though they needed it more.

The sexist obstacles and stresses were generally stronger in the senior ranks than below. In most departments the senior women constituted a small minority of the faculty. As tokens, they were at a disadvantage in the competitive struggles for space, students, grants, departmental and institutional resources. They were plagued by constraining, destructive images of women—tyrant, caring but powerless mother, uncaring mother, woman who sleeps her way to the top and uses sex to mask incompetence. They were likely to experience resentment from male colleagues and, often, from younger female colleagues who found them (rightly or wrongly) disappointing as mentor, exemplar, sponsor, or role model.

The various glass ceilings are thus only part of the problem. The basic problem for work organizations generally is the sexism: the negative images of women in careers (images given in the culture and held by women as well as men) and the alien character of the woman within the higher levels of the work institution. The sexism is reflected in every aspect of organizational life—in hiring, working together, training, supervising, promoting, creating career paths.

Here are two examples of career evolution during the Mid-life Transition.

DEBRA ROSE

At 40 I was promoted to regional director. The promotion meant having to move with my husband and family to Boston.

The job was a tremendous success. It was a marvelous, beautiful, satisfying fulfillment of a youthful dream. It wasn't just that it was such a great career success. It wasn't just that it was a significant accomplishment in and of itself. I did it very well. It challenged me intellectually and made full use of my talents. So much of the work I'd done and do is not worthwhile from anybody's point of view other than that I make a lot of money for the company. On a personal level it was so much of what I'd always wanted that I'd never had before and may never have again. It was a fulfillment personally; I have never felt so good about myself before or since. I was living exactly the way I wanted for about the only time in my life. I gave it everything I had, and I did very well. I was fairly conscious politically about thinking about strategy and how to maximize my influence and get across what I wanted to do.

At the end of two years Wallace demanded that we return to New York. I'd been so happy in Boston, and I had to give it up! Wallace had gotten an interesting job in Boston and really could have stayed but just refused for reasons that are not clear to me. He had nothing worthwhile to come back to, not a very good job nor a very good institution. He spoke then of retiring in eight years, and now he says he'll retire in two because there is so little in it for him. I think he just resented our move because I had all the attention, all the glory. It was such a dramatic illustration of the different paths our careers had taken; I was more successful than he was.

I'd been so happy! I did what I wanted for *myself*, and my family came second—my mother, my children, my husband. I just put all of my energies and efforts into my work, and Wallace didn't like that, either. He and the kids returned to New York. I said I wasn't ready to go back and stayed and went to New York on weekends. I stayed another six months, taking an apartment and living very independently. But then I gave up and went home.

It was also a time of great crisis. I had everything I ever really wanted in life, and then I had to face up to the harsh realization that I still was not emotionally satisfied, and I had a need for something that I couldn't get out of either family *or* my career. Even in that context of apparent total fulfillment I was still dissatisfied. I was unhappy and lonely in some ways, and in other ways I was very happy to be on my own, having my own apartment, kind of a new life in a way. I think if the children had been older I would have stayed on, and that might have been the end of the marriage; I had a very clear sense of going back for the children.

I returned to my company in New York at age 43. This was a good place for me before my promotion, but I should not have come back here. The company does not accord me the status I have earned. I have a high-sounding title, but I am actually very peripheral in the company and I have no power here and no allies.

My primary dissatisfaction in my life now is my job, and I ought to look for a change in my job situation. I am very ambitious, and so much of my present frustration in my life really has to do with the feeling now of getting nowhere with my career. I'm very unhappy with my work, but I stay because of the money. It enables my family to live a certain lifestyle that I'm not really prepared to give up, especially with my children about to go to college. I feel trapped in my job economically. We're all in some kind of game down here on Wall Street, and nobody tells you what the rules are; you don't even know if you're winning or losing, and you don't even know what it means to win. I don't quite know where I'm going from here. I am young to be at this senior level, and I'm not sure where I can go from here. I'm 44 and trapped in a kind of success. I'm not prepared to stay where I am for another two years if I can help it. I may have to but I don't want to.

Throughout my whole career and even now I was the only woman or one of a very few women in the job I was in. It just affects my development and my psychological development in all sorts of important and unimportant ways. When you're younger and you're discriminated against you keep wondering, "Maybe it's me, maybe I'm really inadequate." Now it just infuriates me. I'm finding it very difficult to find a position at my level, and I think discrimination is the reason. I'm just sick after twenty years of fighting discrimination against women. I think I'm much more aware of discrimination than I was when I was younger because when I was younger I never wanted to blame it for any failure to advance. I think as I have progressed in my profession and been very successful by any objective standard I am much more willing and ready to face up to discrimination when I come against it, and I'm sick of it. There are some situations where being a woman has helped me, but I'm still a woman in a man's field.

I have a lot of dissatisfactions in my marriage, but I've never been persuaded that there were better alternatives available to me. I am not interested in living alone. I have never thought that any other man would make me any happier than my husband, and that's the bottom line. Wallace and I have always been good friends; he could have been my brother, really. He is a very good father and has been very involved in the children's lives. After 25 years he is still in love with me, and I love him very deeply, but passion has always been missing in our relationship.

⊷§   MEGAN BENNETT

At 39, Megan Bennett became director of an academic science laboratory. Now, at 45, she had an international reputation. She was married and had no children. She was also at a turning point in her life—feeling the need to make a change but not yet ready to do so.

> I was a professor at another university before coming here six years ago. I have done some teaching and writing, but I knew at the start that the job was a more than full-time administrative responsibility. It was a huge career change. I made it because I knew I could do the job well. I had a timetable of five years. Then I would get back to all the research projects I had been involved in with graduate students and faculty colleagues. But I understood that returning would be very difficult, perhaps impossible—a fantasy that might never become a reality.
>
> I perform the job very well, but the first few years were difficult. The job has been a forcing ground for growth. My professional life here has been enormously interesting because of the demands it makes on the intellect and, at the same time, on one's emotional range. It has consumed all my energies, but I find my work fascinating. I have no leisure life except in the six weeks we take off every summer. I feel intensely the need for solitary time, but my current circumstances do not allow it. I continue to teach a little and to enjoy the relationships to students. I work very hard at creating opportunities for women; that is probably the most gratifying part of my job.
>
> For the past two or three years I've been at something of an impasse. I feel on the verge of a change. Just exactly what it will be I couldn't tell you. I don't yet understand in what direction to move or what to do with myself. I have become a more and more public person with very little private life. It's such a comedy—everybody sees me as such a successful person. I have a great feeling of accomplishment, but I realize that I am somewhat trapped by my success. I need a job that is at least as responsible, and important to me, as my present one. I am not likely to make a radical departure from the work and life I now have, but I increasingly doubt that such roles make sense for either men *or* women.

⊷§   HILLARY LEWIN

Hillary Lewin received her doctorate at a private university whose graduates ordinarily obtain faculty positions at similar, research-oriented institutions. Now 44 and a tenured professor, she has been very successful in a "minor league" of much lower academic standing than that of her professional origins.

In the past few years I've seen more clearly that I've always had a major conflict over whether I wanted a job or a career. It's an unresolvable conflict for me: part of me wants each, and I never integrate them; I just juggle them. A lot of me doesn't want achievement, which is what a career is about.

In academia you can fiddle around and take a little job at a place like this school, without trying for more. I came here at 30 and became a tenured professor at 37. I came to work here after my divorce, not for a career but for a financial base that would give me time to raise my son. I thought I'd stay until he was in school and then take a more challenging job. But good academic jobs weren't so available then, and I wasn't really sure I wanted one. Yet I felt badly about myself, about the lack of accomplishment, which for me meant recognition. I wanted to establish myself as a mature professional. My professorship here is a very, very easy job that pays the rent and buys the food. You teach the same thing over and over. The total time required is not great, but it's really boring. The students are nice but after a while you get so bored you do it automatically, and they don't even realize you're functioning like a robot. There is a pervasive aura of going nowhere among the faculty here. No piece of work ever reaches conclusion. Faculty committees keep meeting without accomplishing anything, until they die a natural death. There is a sense of stagnation. Most of the faculty feel stuck and depressed.

At 38 I bumped into Richard, the head of a lab at a better school. He asked me what I was doing with my career, and I told him. He said, "You were a graduate student with great promise; where did you go wrong? Don't you want to be famous? Let's meet and talk about research." So we met, and he decided to take me on part-time for a year. That marked a sharp professional change. It worked quite well, and I'm still with him. It made me feel good about myself.

Hillary Lewin's self-questioning and then starting a research project with Richard were, in my view, reflections of the developmental phase of Becoming One's Own Woman in her late thirties. At 40 a further change occurred: she decided to get a fellowship at Richard's lab and explore the possibilities for a career change. The fellowship was the Culminating Event of her early adulthood and launched her into the Mid-life Transition:

At 40 I got very depressed. I was a professor here, but that was only a job and not a career. Being part-time at Richard's lab made me wonder, "If I were full-time there, could I function?" I had to put myself to the test. So with Richard's support I got a fellowship for people midway in their careers, took a sabbatical, and worked full-time at Richard's lab. I worked terribly hard, and it was a good year after it was over. I felt more part of that school through the experience and decided that, "Yes, within reason I could be there full-time." Yet I also felt more grateful to my school because no one ever asked what you were producing.

That fellowship year gave me a beginning, but I knew that I could never make up for the career hiatus I took to be a mother—which I do not regret. In some ways I was like a new Ph.D., even though I had had my Ph.D. forever and could not be seen as a new Ph.D. and wouldn't want to be. There was the feeling that if you worked hard enough you could catch up, but also the feeling that at 40 your life is half over and you can't postpone everything for your career—there is a lot more to life than that. So I didn't form this really big goal that I'm really going to be somebody professionally. I'm reasonably happy with a rather middling level of accomplishment. I don't see myself as going anywhere special, though I might have if I'd started earlier.

When the fellowship ended three years ago I went back to my school and worked one-quarter time at Richard's lab. The idea of my switching full-time to Richard's lab came up several times, but I don't have the credentials to become even an associate professor there. So being at my school gives me a base and makes me an inexpensive staff person at Richard's lab.

Richard is a kind of mentor, especially by making opportunities available. We also have a sexual relationship, once a week or so. He is married but expects such sexual relationships with many of his female graduate students and junior colleagues.

What I really want in my life is more leisure. I would like a long-term intimate relationship with a man, but I have issues around intimacy. I relate much better with people if I have more leisure, but with the teaching, the research, and motherhood, I have no free time. I've recently made a resolution to give leisure a higher priority in my life. My best way of obtaining leisure so far is to go to Europe for a month or so alone. Going alone is really taking off—it's a very open, different kind of life. Last year in Spain I met a very pleasant guy from Paris. Not that it was going to exist beyond the vacation, but it really was very pleasant. What I learned is: I had leisure and then I met him. I want more of that in my life. Since my divorce I have had a few relationships that lasted a year or more, but nothing that led to marriage. I have several women friends with whom I used to be quite intimate. Although we are still connected, we have grown apart and don't talk the way we formerly did. I have friendly work relationships with some people at Richard's school, but they are as busy as I am. Intimacy with men and women is something I'd like to be available for; I just don't know where it will come from.

The Evolution of Family in Middle Adulthood

A couple becomes a family when they have offspring. Our offspring are initially children, then adults. In referring to them forever as "children," we in effect deny them the right to grow up within the family. Each offspring/

parent continues until death to have a relationship with our actual parent/ offspring in the external world, and with the internal parent/offspring we have constructed in our own psyches. What do young adults want from their middle-aged parents, and what do the parents want from them? In more cases than we like publicly to admit, there is very little interchange, except for occasional visits, telephone calls, and gifts. To have more than this, we must transform the previous relationship into one that is more mutual and less burdened by the earlier images of protective, authoritative, sometimes hurtful parents and growing, needy child.

Our cultural ideal is to establish a symmetrical relationship in which the parent regards the offspring as an adult friend, not a child, and the offspring regards the parent as a person in a more equal sense, not as an omnipotent dispenser of rewards, punishments, guidance and high or low self-esteem. The move toward greater equality is essential but necessarily incomplete. In the minds of both parent and adult offspring, the parent remains to some extent the parent in the earlier sense: "I am still her parent; she is still my child." We cannot entirely forget or undo the past, even if at times we'd like to. But middle adulthood gives parents an opportunity to re-evaluate the past and use it differently. We can start to acknowledge the hurtful things we did to our offspring. We can begin to forgive ourselves, while also recognizing our responsibility for what happened. At the same time we can begin to forgive our offspring for ignoring our wise counsel, violating our values, choosing the wrong occupation, spouse, religious or political outlook, misreading our altruism as control, and feeling no gratitude for all the sacrifices we made for them. The relationship must to some extent be ambivalent, since it engages the inner conflicts of both parties and the irreconcilable differences between us. It can be highly satisfying, however, when it draws upon many aspects of the child and adult selves in both of us.

A word here about our evolving relationships in middle adulthood to our aging parents. As we pass 40 our parents are ordinarily in their sixties or early seventies. Over the next twenty years we are at the height of our earning power, independence, and maturity, while they are becoming more dependent in some respects, and in the process of decline. Very little has been written about this relationship as it is lived and experienced by both parties.

When our parents die, whatever our age, we become orphans. Becoming an orphan in middle adulthood has a different meaning and impact than in other eras. When our parents die something in us dies, while other things in us can now emerge and live more fully. At their death we often realize how little we knew them and how much more we'd like to know. We realize, too, how many grievances there were on both sides, how many conflicts have been left unresolved. We might have given each other more love and understanding had we been able to confront the differences and to find a mode of reconciliation. In any case, when the external parents depart we are left with internal parental figures who have diverse feelings toward us: love, pride, gratitude, disappointment, resentment, indifference, concern, to name but a few. It is part of our development in middle adulthood, before and after their death, to work on the relationship with the external parent as well as the internal figure of parent in order to enhance its loving, creative aspects and to limit the destructive ones.

The Evolution of Motherhood in the Mid-life Transition

Of the thirteen career women in the Mid-life Transition, eight were mothers. Six mothers took responsibility for both a family and a demanding full-time career during their thirties. The other two mothers, after starting a family in their thirties, had devoted themselves primarily to homemaking, working a little and intending to resume some sort of business career when their children needed them less. How did their lives evolve in the Mid-life Transition?

Let's look first at the two businesswomen who put their careers on hold in the thirties, living within a Traditional Marriage Enterprise and doing little or no outside work for several years. In the early forties they began moving toward a modified Traditional Marriage Enterprise in which they began working more regularly and considering the possibilities for a further career in the financial world. At the time of the interviewing their future occupational course was not clear. It was clear, however, that they had neither the opportunity nor the desire to pick up where they had left off. What they wanted, and what was available to them, in both family and career, were different in the Mid-life Transition than in the previous period. The corporate world did not look kindly upon a woman in her forties who had taken time out, who was "more a mother than a professional." The woman herself entered a new phase in the struggle between the internal Traditional Homemaker Figure and the internal Anti-Traditional Figure. A good deal of exploration was needed to generate new options.

⋙ SALLY WOLFORD

Sally Wolford got pregnant at 35 after trying to conceive for over two years. She had worked for a Wall Street firm, but she had not been promoted to a professional position. Now 44, she had two children and a husband, and she worked out of their home.

I left the corporate race at 36, when my first child was born. I had worked in the same firm for thirteen years without getting recognition, title, or salary. There have been many blocks to my career development. If I let myself, I could work up a lot of resentment.

I don't think there's any way to know before you have children how fulfilling it is. When my son was born it was a wonderful feeling! No work I ever did was that perfect. But it was very boring to spend all that time with small children—their attention spans weren't very long. I wish there were courses on how to be a good mother. It is also very isolating being an older mother. The thing that gets to me is that it's so *confining*. It will still be a while before the light at the end of the tunnel, when I can leave them alone.

My husband is very devoted to the children, but I try to protect him from the family problems because I like having a husband who is the breadwinner, the leader—a certain father image. My father was always the leader of our family and my mother was a totally nonworking type. Besides, my husband is very busy. He will help with the children in a pinch, but basically I am responsible for the family and the apartment. I'm the chauffeur, cook, and personnel director in charge of getting all the help we need.

When I turned 40 I couldn't think past today, I was just coping with two small children. But I *had* to do something else, so I started my own firm and worked when I could.

At this point I'm trying to combine the best of both worlds. Predominantly I feel I'm a mother, and that's the first thing in my life. I also want to have a career and to be respected in that world, but it's very hard. My frustration rose to such a level that I'm overeating again after losing twenty pounds last spring. I'm trying to be a working mother *and* a nonworking mother at the same time, and I'm going out of my mind! I'd like to be seen as a professional and not lose status in the financial world, but they don't consider me professional. And the nonworking mothers don't fully accept me either. No one is quite sure where I belong.

I'm so busy and hectic that I can't cope—I don't have one second to spare in my life! Until 3:00 I work at my business. Then the children come home from school, and I become a full-time mother. I'm trying desperately to keep up with my business, but it's like a hobby now because family is still the main thing. I thought that as the kids got older it would get easier, but I spend so much time driving the children back and forth bringing them to activities. If you work full-time then presumably you're earning enough to hire somebody who can take over. But I'd feel guilty if I hired somebody else to raise my children.

I've tried to raise my daughter as a unisex child. I have encouraged her in every way to fit into a world where she will be expected to have a career. Recently I asked her what she wants to be, a doctor or lawyer or anything she would like. She said, "I want to be a mommy." My son I want to be a natural boy. Women are in a very difficult position. I hope my son and daughter will have a choice whether the woman wants to work, or has to work for financial reasons, or feels that she *must* have a career to be successful. I hope some mothers will be interested in staying home.

I hope to gradually have more time to develop my career. I won't have a big career in the earlier sense, but I'll keep busy doing various things that interest me.

The other six mothers had made family and a full-time career the cocentral components of the Culminating Life Structure. Two women were in the corporate world, four in academe. Their current marital situations were quite diverse. Debra Rose was in an intact first marriage throughout this period. Rachel Nash began a separation from her second husband at 43. Kim Price, Helen Kaplan, Hillary Lewin, and Holly Crane were single-divorced heads of household; Kim Price and Helen Kaplan remarried at 45. All six women had careers of moderate to high achievement, and all went through major changes in the nature of their motherhood, love/marriage, and professional career. They have much to teach us about life in the forties for women who try to combine motherhood and an achieving full-time career.

For most of these women the emptying of the nest began in the Mid-life Transition but did not end there. Each of them had at least one child in high school or college. The child's move toward adulthood gave the mother a strong signal that the terms of her motherhood were changing: her offspring, though still of crucial importance, would not play a central part in her future life. In the earlier Superwoman image of her thirties she had hoped, and at times believed, that she could have a demanding career without stinting in her maternal responsibilities. She had borne the reproaches of others who warned that her "selfish" involvement in career jeopardized her children's well-being. More privately, she had often reproached herself for being insufficiently maternal, for using work in part to escape from the physical and emotional demands of the home and children.

Reappraising and modifying her relationships with offspring were major developmental tasks of the woman's Mid-life Transition. During this period each woman came to terms, more fully than before, with the paradoxes in the life of mother with full-time career. She formed a more balanced view of her motherhood, avoiding the extremes of guilty self-accusation and defensive self-justification. She could more readily acknowledge that she had not been an ideal mother, that in some respects she had been insufficiently caring and protective of her children. Still, she had done the best she could, given her own multiple, partially contradictory needs as well as the contradictory external conditions that made it so difficult to combine family and career. She believed that living primarily as a homemaker would have been much harder on her and much more hurtful to her children. Having a career had in some ways limited her time and involvement with the children, but it had also enriched their relationship. She was more able to appreciate, and to partic- ipate in, the child's (especially the daughter's) development of competence, self-reliance, and occupational interests. She was more of a link between the child and the public world of education, work, and adult life.

In addition to reappraising their past relationships, some of the career women were also in the process of modifying their current relationships with offspring who were now moving into adulthood. The transition was in some respects easier for the career women than for most of the homemakers. Motherhood had been a less pervasive aspect of their lives. They were less prone to the resentful feeling that they had sacrificed themselves to moth- erhood, only to be abandoned by ungrateful offspring. They were more a part of, or connected to, the adult world that their offspring were entering. They had a stronger sense of their adolescent and young adult offspring as separate, independent selves who needed to go their own way yet might still have a significant relationship with them. They understood, too, that the relation- ship would change and that a new and better relationship would have to be earned by both parties. In comparison to most of the homemakers, the career women referred to their offspring more often by name and had a more differentiated sense of each one as a self with distinctive interests, values, talents, problems. The career women also spoke more often of what they were learning from their offspring and of ways in which a daughter's or son's development was affecting them. The relationship often became more mu- tual and less encumbered by old "parent-child" emotional ties.

At the same time, the career women began to invest themselves less in motherhood and to give it a less central place in their lives. Like the home- makers, but in their own idiom, the career women experienced the dimin- ishing of maternal responsibilities as both a loss and a liberation. The gradual shifting of this component from the center to the periphery of their lives stimulated and supported their efforts to reappraise and change the life structure as a whole. The change in life structure also involved a growing individuation of the self. They were more free to ask, "Now that I have less inner sense of obligation and guilt, and less external demand to be a certain kind of mother, what do I want to receive from and give to my offspring? What kinds of new relationships will I seek with them?"

⋖§   HILLARY LEWIN

My best relationship is probably with my 17-year-old son, David, who will be going off to college next year. He is a nice person: sensitive and even-tempered and considerate. His life is going well. He has a job and plays sports and has good relationships with friends. I feel he's making good choices around work and leisure. He has a seriousness and idealism that I remember having once myself. I now perceive him as a grown-up person with whom I share a home.

Having an older teenage son, you become very aware of what he sees missing in you. I think he is fairly accurate in his criticism of me: he feels that my life is too narrow, that I'm locked too much into my work. Part of my view of myself comes from him. He forms a mirror, but a slightly disturbing mirror, as I'm beginning to realize. The relationship between single parent and only child is closer but also more complicated. If there were another child, or a husband, we wouldn't focus so much on each other. His leaving will open up another space in my life, and I feel that already. I felt after the divorce that there was only me for him, and he was my first priority. With his growing up I have increasing freedom, but also a sense of loss. Now I need to look for more loving adult relationships and a more balanced life.

Five of the thirteen career women had no children as the Mid-life Transition began, and none of them became mothers during this period. The incidence of childlessness is much higher among women in these kinds of careers than in the general population, where it is about 10 percent. Larger studies of career women, especially in the corporate world, find similar or higher rates of childlessness. A few of the younger childless women in this study had hopes of starting a family, and some may subsequently have done so, but the incidence of having a first child after 40 is very low, despite media reports of a considerable increase.

Three childless women were in academe, two in business. Megan Bennett and Pam Kenney were currently married, Kristin West and Amanda Burns single-divorced, and Michele Proto single-never-married. In their twenties all five women had expected to have a family. In their thirties they recognized that, for a variety of reasons, motherhood was impossible or highly unlikely. By 40 most of them had largely (but not entirely) come to terms with the sense of loss. Several formed quasi-parental relationships with the children of friends or relatives. From time to time, however, various incidents evoked a continuing sense of sadness and/or resentment over their loss of motherhood. Perhaps the strongest grievance was that they had sacrificed motherhood for a career that, as they now realized, would not provide the satisfactions they had hoped for.

The Evolution of Marriage in Middle Adulthood

In middle adulthood raising a family is no longer a primary task of the marriage enterprise. What then is the point of marriage in middle adulthood, and how can it be made more valuable for both spouses? One possibility is to make the marriage itself a central part of the spouses' lives, enriching the relationship and sharing mutually enjoyable activities. This option is extremely gratifying when it goes well, but is fraught with difficulties and often brings limited benefits. Improving the marriage is not simply a matter of spending more time together; being together can be grating as well as pleasing. The present relationship is bound to be colored by disappointments, angers, voiced and silent grievances from the past.

The fundamental issue is that the marital relationship must be restructured. Both partners must come to know each other in new ways, to connect to new aspects of the other's self, and to get beyond some of the basic limitations and incompatibilities of the relationship in early adulthood. In some cases the spouses change in different directions, so that her newly emerging identity, wishes, and values are different from, and perhaps antithetical to, his. The couple may not have enough common ground on which to build a satisfactory new marriage. Under these conditions some persons divorce. Others—a much larger number—remain in a tolerable yet psychologically constricted marriage, seeking greater satisfaction and self-fulfillment in other contexts such as work, leisure, friendships, extramarital relationships, political or religious interests. Not infrequently, the psychological connection between the spouses is so tenuous that we have a condition of psychological divorce: the spouses remain married and share a domicile, but each gives and receives a bare minimum. The durability of a marriage is not a criterion of its quality or its value to the spouses and family. A great deal has been written on courtship, marriage, and divorce in early adulthood. Much less is known about these matters in middle adulthood, yet the problems here are more severe and the need for understanding even greater.

Love and Marriage in the Mid-life Transition

As the Mid-life Transition began, six of the thirteen career women were married. They began to reappraise the marital relationship and to ask: "What is the nature of this marriage? What aspects of it would I like to modify or eliminate? I am now at a turning point—where do I go from here?"

Most of the married career women wanted more love and equality in their lives, and many women wanted to transform their Neo-Traditional Marriage Enterprises into Egalitarian Marriage Enterprises. The predominant theme (with many variations) in their view of a good marriage was this: Marriage should be based on a relationship of mutuality in love, passion, intimacy, play, and work. We should have an equal partnership with regard to provisioning, household management, and decisions affecting both partners. We should be strongly engaged with each other but also separate and independent when our interests diverge. My main grievances in the marriage stem from a deficiency of some or all of these qualities.

None of these women's marriages had come close to this ideal at the time of the interviewing. Five women experienced moderate to severe marital problems. Rachel Nash decided to end her marriage and began a legal separation. Four others continued in the marriage but attempted to transform its character. They found it difficult to consider divorce but saw it as an ultimate option.

❧   ANONYMOUS

My husband has had bouts of serious physical illness throughout our marriage. For the past several years he has been well about a third of the time and ill two thirds. I make sure we have an ordered, quiet, private life. It has been very painful for me. Since I am accustomed to bringing change for the good into other people's lives, it is a great sadness to be unable to alter the course of an illness for the person I am closest to. And there is a lot missing from the relationship—sexuality, companionship, being mutually involved and in touch, and I miss being taken care of. It's pretty much a one-way sharing: when somebody is so ill, you can't dump more on them by asking them to be more involved with you. I think I work so hard partly in order to protect myself from feeling all that I miss, and to gain other satisfactions.

I have not gotten involved in any other relationship. For a while I assumed that my husband would get better soon—he would overcome the illness once he tried hard enough. Recently I have become aware of another and probably stronger reason: he is completely dependent on me and could not tolerate my having another relationship, which would force him to acknowledge that he is seriously ill. I work hard instead of having an affair, and he tolerates my long work hours for that reason. If I had an affair it would shatter his illusion that he is a great husband.

Two years ago I decided that, if I could figure out the time, I would have an affair. The decision was triggered by my husband's hospitalization. The doctors were brutally frank with me: my husband would be recurrently ill, so I had better organize my life on that basis. This incident helped me to focus on things that I had half-known for several years, but I wasn't ready earlier to recognize and face my predicament.

I haven't yet had an affair, although I get lots of offers. I still don't know how to live with my husband and, at the same time, live more for myself. I have the kind of job where I can't be with him, but through it he receives the intellectual stimulation and the personal care from others that he couldn't otherwise have. In any case, my own needs remain: I want an intense sexual relationship, I want to be taken care of in a loving way, and I want to live more for myself.

❧ ANONYMOUS

My children really don't consider the possibility that my husband and I might pack it in in terms of the marriage. They very strongly believe that we have a stable, permanent marriage and family situation, although that is not really true. It's such a fraud, really. I feel trapped in my marriage. I feel very trapped in my family situation in terms of breaking out of what is unsatisfactory in my life and having a more satisfactory situation. Personally I want more. It's no use to me to fulfill my ambitions and find myself alone. I want to share my life with somebody in a female/male relationship.

I am very depressed. I would like to figure out how I can improve my life, but I don't really see much hope for myself, and some days I feel total despair. My life is a mess. I can't leave my marriage, but I'm unhappy with it.

In some ways I have much less hope for my future than I had when I was younger. I used to have a greater belief that things would work out. I feel very discouraged now, and I'm not at all confident that things *will* work out. I think there is a certain kind of lonely desperation at the center of my life.

The seven *single* women, like the married, wanted a more egalitarian love relationship or marriage involving mutuality, love, passion, play, intimacy, and separateness. Those women who had been divorced regarded their earlier marriages as prime examples of what they did *not* want in a marriage enterprise, in a husband, and in themselves. Most of them came to feel in the Mid-life Transition that they had had an illusion of marital equality when in fact they had been relatively subordinate and had paid an enormous price for the partial freedom to pursue a career. Some recognized that in their own eagerness for independence, they had not been ready to engage in an intense personal relationship. Some experienced a growth of the self which led to greater intimacy, sexuality, passion, and possibilities of living.

In this period the single women sought new kinds of love relationships, a more meaningful but less driven relationship to work, and a fuller enjoyment of leisure. When interviewed, some women felt that they were making significant progress in these respects; others were still early in the struggle. None had yet gone as far as they wished in modifying the self and the life. Most hoped for matrimony in the long run but were still guarded about getting married. They preferred to have a sexual-romantic relationship for a time, in order to increase the likelihood that the relationship could bear the burdens of legal marriage. They saw marriage in middle adulthood as less necessary, and as serving different functions for both partners, than in early adulthood. The Egalitarian Marriage Enterprise they had in mind was built primarily around a satisfying marital partnership rather than raising children.

Six of the seven single women had one or more serious love relationships during the Mid-life Transition. Michele Proto was single-never-married and in the fifth year of a relationship far better than any previous one. Helen Kaplan and Kim Price were single-divorced mothers: both had a long-term relationship and remarried at 45 as the Entry Life Structure for Middle Adulthood got under way. Hillary Lewin, Holly Crane, and Amanda Burns were seeking new and richer relationships in their lives. Kristin West at 43 was going through a rock bottom time: she was in the aftermath of a painful divorce, without a sustaining love relationship, experiencing the fatigue and anxiety of a recurrent undiagnosed illness, and in the initial phase of a late-starting academic career. In her words, "It takes all my strength to meet my heavy work schedule; there is no room left for love or play. I accept that, but it is depressing."

The Evolution of the Life Structure in the Mid-life Transition

The vignettes above focus chiefly upon a single component of the life structure, while giving evidence that no component exists in isolation. Here are some vignettes that show more fully how various components are interwoven within the life structure.

❧   PAM KENNEY

I married Craig at 31. I think I finally decided if I was going to get married I had better get married. I knew he drank a lot before I married him, but I probably thought he would stop drinking and we'd be a nice little model couple. Craig's work really got messed up. When I was 33 he quit his job and decided to set up his own business. His business really turned into nothing, and he was drinking a lot. He really hasn't gotten back into earning money since then. At first I was really upset but then I decided not to let it have a big impact on my life. A few years after we married I decided not to have children with him. I started traveling on vacations a lot without him and developed a cool, detached attitude toward him. It seems to me he has a good deal with me as his wife; I support him. He has all the benefits: higher living standard, an apartment, and he can drink all he wants. What could be better? But I really hate the feeling that I'm just being used.

At 37 I got more ambitious and moved from a staff position into a middle-management position. I got interested in working long-term and wanted something solid where I could earn more money. I've devoted a great deal of time to my career, and I am re-evaluating that now, at 43.

I was recently promoted. My responsibilities remained the same with higher pay, although I know I am still underpaid by about 30 percent. The next step is not possible for me. I might take a lateral move or perhaps move out of the city within the next few years and into some other kind of work. I look forward to retirement in another twenty years. I like my job well enough. If I stay here I think I could just take it easy. I could probably qualify for a new title when I'm 57 or 58. I'd probably take early retirement as soon as I could and then do something else.

⋙ MICHELE PROTO

At 43 Michele Proto was a mid-level manager in a large corporation where she had worked since her early thirties. She was single-never-married and had no children. The central components of her life were her career and her love relationship with Harry, a colleague four years older. The interviewing occurred at a time of considerable turmoil, when the two components of career and love/marriage/family were totally interpenetrated and in conflict. Also, her father had a terminal illness, and her mother was in poor health. In her late thirties, when the theme of Becoming One's Own Woman predominated, the stage was set for the Mid-life Transition:

A lot of changes began when I was 37. Harry was my boss, though we were not personally involved at that point. He was promoted four months before the deadline for a big project, and I was afraid that the senior manager would put a new person in over me. I thought, "I'll be damned if he puts a man in there, and I'll be killing myself, and then this guy walks off with the credit, and if it fails I'll get the blame. If there is credit or blame to be taken *I'll* take both because I'd get the blame anyway." So I asked Harry to recommend me. I said, "Nobody in this company can do a better job on this than me; if you think you're pulling in somebody off the street that I'll have to train, forget it." He hemmed and hawed but finally agreed, and I got the job. I literally killed myself on that project. I worked every single night and weekend for four months, and the project was ready on schedule. That was a big feather in my cap — it really put me on the map at the company. I was out to prove myself, maybe to the senior manager, maybe to the world. At the end I went out and bought myself a mink coat. It was like, "Goddam it, I deserve *something!*"

Soon after that Harry took me out to dinner. I thought he was a tremendous guy, but I wasn't in love with him at that point. I just liked him and could always talk to him. Also, I was desperately hurt from a relationship that had recently ended, and I was very, very lonely. Harry was unhappily married and had three kids. He and I often worked late and then had dinner together, and sometimes we traveled on projects. Soon we began an affair, a wonderful relationship that remained totally secret.

Two major changes occurred around 40 and 41, one in Michele Proto's relationship with Harry, the other in her career. These were, I believe, the joint Culminating Events of early adulthood, and they ushered in her Mid-life Transition.

After I turned 40 the relationship with Harry became so good it was hard to bear. I didn't want it to be a secret, part-time thing, and I felt terribly guilty toward his wife and kids. At 41 I told him that the illicit relationship was too much for me, and I wanted to end it. I never once said, "Get a divorce." I didn't want the responsibility for his ending the marriage, but I couldn't continue on those terms. A few months later he separated from his wife and then divorced. We have been very happy together the past two years, and it has changed my life.

The other big change at about 40 was a promotion that I really fought for. At that time I had a staff of about twenty-five. My boss hired Luke, a newcomer, for another job at my level. Three months later my boss was promoted and reorganized the department. He put Luke in charge, over me! That was simply unacceptable. I got my résumé together and started looking for another job. My boss took me to lunch and said, "I really don't think you're that career-oriented." I said, "How can you say that? I've been here a long time." But he insisted that I wasn't ready for it. Frankly, I had mixed feelings about the whole thing. I was already making good money. I thought, "Do I really want all this responsibility?" By the same token I was a little bothered—a lot bothered—that this johnny-come-lately should get the job. It was made clear that my boss was taking a chance on a man but wouldn't take a chance on me. Here I had done well by him, yet he'd rather take a chance on an unknown male. Luke soon resigned because he couldn't do the job, and my boss called me: "I'd like to tell you how much you've developed in three weeks." So that's how I got my biggest promotion—the few I've gotten since were just titles and small salary increases. For a few months I didn't know whether I was coming or going. I had a whole new area that I didn't know anything about, and a staff of over sixty. I have been the highest-ranking woman in the company for the past six years, and the only woman ever to reach this level. I was never a career planner. I never said, "This is the direction I'm going in, and that is where I want to be." Things just sort of happened.

Another tremendous upheaval is just beginning: my boss just announced that he is leaving. Harry and I are the two candidates for his job—a senior slot, really up there. My boss's leaving is devastating for a multitude of reasons. He was the best boss I ever had; mostly they've been terrible. He brings out the best in me. His leaving causes great conflict between Harry and me. I want our relationship to last, but I'm afraid this will kill it. Here I finally establish the best relationship I ever had with a man; what if he becomes my boss? I have this fear of marriage as controlling.

Investments are the key to our company. The new position has responsibility for both development and investments. Harry has had investments experience, but I haven't because they wouldn't let me do it—another Catch-22 for a woman. My boss was grooming me to be his replacement, though he also told me it would be very hard to do it without investments experience. Actually, I'm not even sure I want the job. It's a pressure cooker and really is too difficult for me. I don't want to kill myself anymore, and I earn enough so I don't care about a little more money. I've asked around about another job in the company, but there's nothing. Still, there's a little jealousy and resentment that Harry would take my boss's job instead of me. Whether he gets the job or I do, our personal relationship will be jeopardized, and that is the worst thing of all. We already carry too much of our work home. We're just beginning to come out of hiding with our relationship. I'm sure a lot of people know about us, not that we run around holding hands or anything.

In the next interview Michele Proto reported a new turn of events:

My boss has announced that he is not leaving. What a relief! He will probably be promoted within six months, and the situation will rear its ugly head again. By that time Harry will probably be promoted, so the scenario in which I work for him has died down. But the incident stirred up so much in me! It brought to the foreground all my feelings about the woman's situation—feelings of having been deprived, and anger that I was not being chosen to replace my boss because I am a woman.

Harry thought I was overreacting, which angered me more. He felt that I couldn't handle the promotion, and in six months I'd want out of it. He is generally understanding, but he doesn't understand about the inequities for women in this world. You've got to experience it to understand it. I was very vocal with him about not wanting to work for him. He said, "Maybe this job is more important to you than our relationship," and I was starting to feel guilty. Then I thought that men are allowed to put work first but women feel guilty about it.

As a result of all this turmoil, I realize how important Harry is to me. I think we both realize how much the relationship means to both of us. He is the most important part of my life, more important than the job. I could never find another man I'm this compatible with. He's a very fine person—very kind, very generous. If I have a relationship with a man it has to be on *equal* terms; that's the key to it. Harry is probably the only man I could ever marry because he is so patient, and he makes absolutely no demands. He's a sweetheart of a man. He's not perfect, I'm not perfect, but we're good for each other. In the next five years I would like to be married to him.

Harry and I have talked a lot about this job situation. I say maybe I should start looking for another job; maybe we both should. But basically, neither of us wants to change. Harry will get a promotion of some kind soon, which I hope he does—he deserves it. But I want a promotion, too. Because, damn it, I have twenty-three years invested in my career, and I've sacrificed a lot more. I mean he at least has children, and I have sacrificed family. The only thing I regret about not marrying is not having children. Men can have *both* work and family. It's more difficult for working women. We don't know how you put together a professional career and a personal life—love *and* family. It's a Catch-22: men intellectually want a woman who is their equal, who has been out in the world, who they can discuss things with. Emotionally they want a housewife who says, "Here's your dinner, honey. Did you have a good day at the office?" It's really hitting me at this point: I have no marriage and no children, and it's a terrible sacrifice and conflict. I'm close to my brother's kids, and I spend a lot of time with them in the summer. Still, it's not the same. A career woman who has a husband and children at home certainly has her struggles, but it's taken too much more of a personal toll on me. I'm not enjoying life, and I really feel that.

The past few months have been very hard. My father is 82 and has been in a nursing home for four years and is now dying. Last year when I was promoted he gave me some sign of recognition for the first time in my life—just when he was on his deathbed! It almost doesn't matter anymore. For a good part of my life I was trying to get my father to recognize me. I finally got respect from men and recognition on the job. As I began to gain self-confidence I put aside my need for my father's recognition. He came from a poor immigrant family and didn't finish high school. He couldn't get into the corporate world like I did, but he had more smarts than most of the high-level people I deal with. He has built a very successful company; I'm sure I'll never be as successful as my father. In the past year, for the first time, I made an effort to tell my father that I loved him and that he was a good father.

My mother had a very hard life, and my father was not an easy man to live with. He could be very generous, but he was also controlling. He didn't spend a lot of time with his wife or his children. I feel sorry for my mother. She never encouraged us to enjoy ourselves, and she can't enjoy herself either. I was always dependent on my mother. Even at 30 I still looked to her for approval in anything I did. It took me until my mid-thirties to break my dependence on my mother and begin to emerge—if one ever gets over it completely. She still gets to me, but not the way she used to. Now she depends a lot on me. I have taken her on a few special vacation trips in the last four years, and she really loved them. We're very close. When I say close, I don't mean we were ever bosom buddies. Maybe close is the wrong word because it implies that we're pals, and we're not pals. She often misses the point of what I tell her and gets argumentative, but I don't argue with her. I just say I love her.

My sister leans on me a lot. She is always phoning to tell me the details of all her problems. I usually listen, but sometimes I lose my patience. Whatever I do for her I'm doing for my parents. I'd do anything for her because she's my sister, but she is a very annoying person. I can honestly say that I love her and feel sorry for her, but I don't like her very much.

My oldest brother is the one I am closest to. He gave me more guidance and had much more emotional presence than my parents. He has a nice wife, but nothing that girl does can please my mother.

The biggest question now is what to do about my job and my career. I don't have to make a decision right away, but I need time to sort things out and get clearer about what I want. If I'm offered my boss's job I'll take it—you don't have a choice. If a man got the job he'd get the new title immediately, but I wouldn't because I'm a woman and I'd be on trial. I had my present job for two years before getting the title. I don't want to be shortchanged out of what I think I'm due. Actually, I'd be very happy to go on working another five years for my boss. If I take this job now, it'll kill me. In most of my jobs I've been promoted before I got the job under enough control so that I could relax. I am emotionally drained by the pressure, the long hours, the deadlines. There's 25 percent of me that would never turn down an opportunity for advancement. But 75 percent of me says, "My God, am I going to be killing myself for the rest of my life?" I'm tired.

Do I enjoy my work? Yes and no. The grind gets to me, but at times I realize that I like it. But now I'm beginning to examine the toll the work takes, and it's tremendous. I want to start to slow down. I would take a lateral move and work 9 to 5 and have a more normal life, but I don't think that's feasible, and I don't want to take a demotion.

I don't think I'm different from many men in the same boat: I work hard, I get certain rewards, I am a kind of success. But what defines success? I wish I had a feeling that what I do is important. My work is geared toward making a lot of rich people richer. There is not one social benefit in anything I do, not one redeeming thing. Let's face it, there are no redeeming factors. What the hell am I doing this for? My tombstone will read: "She delivered projects on schedule."

✎ꝰ KIM PRICE

At 40 Kim Price began two major life changes, apparently quite separate yet psychologically interrelated. She left a career of over a decade to start afresh in the corporate world; and, after being divorced for a few years, she entered a serious love relationship very different in character from her previous ones.

Indeed, starting the new job/career and the new love relationship were the twin Culminating Events of her early adulthood. Her life story in the Mid-life Transition centers largely around the evolution of these two relation-ships. When interviewed at 45, she had come to a new place in both. Although she had performed well and received several promotions, she un-derstood that her possibilities for further advancement up the corporate ladder were very limited. She was reappraising the personal and social value of her work and considering options for change. Her love relationship had grown over the previous five years, and she remarried as the interviewing began.

> In my thirties I was very much into my career. I thought I was Super-woman: I could do anything. My first husband regarded me as special; he supported my career and didn't ask me to do much of the domestic stuff. I was ambitious, worked sixty to seventy hours a week, and always had work on my mind. But by 38 I was getting disillusioned with the work. The head of my unit left, and I didn't get promoted, though I was really next in line. So I asked for another assignment. I was given a position with a lot of responsibility but no authority, and it didn't lead anywhere. I felt that the company didn't really have me in mind—no way. If you weren't political with the higher-ups you had to struggle for everything you had, and you were treated like a stepchild. The work had no meaning. I was bored and really hated it.
>
> At 40 I decided, "There must be something better, and I'm going to try for it." I was also aware of the discrimination against people over 40; if I got older, the opportunities would be more limited. I interviewed at quite a few places before deciding to come here, an international corporation.
>
> In five years I have received a few promotions and raised the status and independence of my department. I have a sense of accomplishment. I received a bonus for last year's performance, and that was exciting; bo-nuses on the staff side are unusual. There is no other black woman at my level in the company, and only a few others in this industry. I need to strengthen my management skills, especially the delegation of authority, and I've been working on that with an in-house consultant. My standards are very high, for myself and others. I want to be a tough but fair manager. My staff know I love them, but I can be abrasive. Delegating more will improve staff morale and productivity and will also reduce the stress on me.
>
> I'm starting to think about where do I go from here? There is not much room for movement and no position I want in this organizational struc-ture. I don't want to be a line manager, and a lateral move would be detrimental to my career. I'd like a higher-level job, but that isn't likely. I don't think I'll ever get to a very high level; I'm too low at this age, and they're not ready for a female or a black. A woman heading a personnel

department is all right because it's almost like teaching or nursing— female nurturing—and not where the profit-making is. I'm not interested in personnel or the finance part of the corporation. You have to be out there at night, and travel, and you don't have much control over your life. Women in that position talk about being single and overseas alone. Earlier it would have been perfect for me; now I want a fuller life.

My desire to write is strong and it gets clearer and clearer every year. But writing is difficult for me. I'd much rather tell people my ideas and have them implement them. I know I'm going to write; I just don't know what or how or when. Now I give twenty-five lectures a year at universities and public groups, and I belong to several groups of women in business. Some of these women believe that women bring special characteristics to business and will change the character of corporations. I think that that's not necessarily so: some women, like some men, are out for power and achievement and not necessarily to change the world or make it a more humane place.

I'd like to be on the board of a noncorporate organization, or a non-profit, or even a corporation, but women have not been accepted in policy-making positions. You have to establish credibility, and being a black woman makes it doubly hard.

Probably the best next step for me, if it were feasible, is to start my own small business. I'd be connected to the corporate world but not directly within it. I'm just beginning to look into that. Lots of women have tried it, but I don't know how it has worked for them.

So where am I now? At this point the job is okay because I have enough challenges, but a year or two from now it might be quite different. I might feel bored and stuck and ready for another move. It's as though a big change is just around the corner, but I haven't quite come to the corner. I am more comfortable with myself, and I have more control of my environment. I have finally come to feel that I can do things, that I have a lot to offer. I was always a workaholic, which was partly an escape from the rest of my life. I used to come to work at 7 a.m. and work late. Now I'm trying to sleep later, leave earlier, and delegate more. I feel more relaxed, less anxious and driven. Above all I want to improve my life.

Kim Price's evolving relationship to career is interwoven with her relationship to love/marriage and to self:

I met Scott at 38, around the time of my divorce. It was almost two years before I realized that I was in love with him; at first I was just enjoying being with him. There was a chemistry, but I didn't feel that he was taking it very seriously, and I wasn't ready to be that serious either. At 40 I realized that I was in love with him, he divorced, and we moved in together. For the first time, I felt I had to live with someone for a few years before I could know we could be together permanently. But even then the relationship was tremendously important for me, a turning point in my life. It was a liberating and romantic relationship for the first time in my life. He did all the things I never went through because I was so much with the career. He released something in me. He helped me feel that I had something of *myself* to offer, in a personal relationship and in my work, and that gave me the inner strength to make the big career change. In my previous relationships the man had always been there for me, whereas with Scott we were there for each other. I was sensitive to his needs more than I ever had been before. He had me cooking! I got excited about making a meal for him. My mother was shocked [laughs]. We enjoyed music, dancing, sports, sex.

I'm an aggressive person in my work, but I was never aggressive in sex with any other man. I'd always say, "You come to me." With Scott I'll initiate sex; I'm demonstrative in terms of hugging and kissing and I can be aggressive and feel comfortable with it. I understand now that sex isn't just physical; it is a relationship that is connected to the way the two people fit into each other's life. I've always felt that I had to be in control of everything or I was in danger. In this relationship I've had no control and it is okay. I can just be myself. There is a mutuality in our feelings for each other; we can be together without saying a word. He is part of me as a person, blending in with my needs and interests in a totality of things. I never had that experience before, and it is a time in my life, finally, when I am ready for that.

The strengths in our personal relationship are very important because so many things in the world are pulling us apart. He is about my age and has kids from a previous marriage. The problems with his kids are still a source of dissension in his life and between us.

Another source of tension between us is career. Traditionally people of like occupations and lifestyles are together. In the black community you don't have that luxury. You consider yourself a professional if you have a job in government or a union; it gets a little fuzzy because of the limited opportunities. I am more ambitious than Scott and more involved in my career, and I have more income and professional status. He has worked for twenty years and is now stuck in a secure job that he hates. His personality keeps him from pursuing other careers that he might be interested in, even though he has a lot of talent.

My aggressiveness and professionalism complicate my relationship with him and with other men I've been close to, and we have gotten into some violent arguments about that. I try to convince him: "This is what you should tackle, or you should focus on this, for these reasons, and here's what gets in the way." Then he says, "Look, you're not my boss, don't give me an analysis of the situation." I'm finally learning how to just listen; if he wants to hear something I'll give it to him as opposed to overwhelming him with what I feel I know. Around the work things I have to watch what I say, whereas in the touch and feel closeness we seem to communicate understanding, which I get so little of in the everyday world. I help him move toward a new career, and he helps me calm down and enjoy myself more.

Money is also a bone of contention between us. I make more money, and it bothers Scott. If he earned more money I would be freer to start my own business and do more writing. I'd like that, but I haven't quite gotten over that feeling of having my own income, being in control, not depending on someone else. I now manage our finances. He'd like me to turn the bills over to him, but I'm not ready.

For a while we had problems about my son Taylor. Taylor was rebellious and lax on his homework, and we were in a constant battle. I got upset because Scott didn't take enough interest in Taylor; he had a more traditional parenting style and felt I didn't discipline Taylor enough. A few years ago I realized that, with my son at home, Scott and I couldn't work out our relationship. I sent Taylor to a private high school, for his sake as well as ours. I don't have many problems with him. I feel closer to him now than earlier; we didn't relate at all until he was about 14, but each year has gotten better. I feel good because he's doing well and feels good about himself, and we can talk on a person-to-person basis. I can see him developing. I like his personality and his independence; he has his own life. He goes to his grandmother for the maternal stuff, always has.

I worry about my mother, too, She went to the hospital recently with a bad heart condition and almost died. I was shocked that she's getting older and might die. She's always been there.

So I have some problems, but the good things far outweigh them. My big concern is to enrich my personal life. Before 40 I concentrated totally on career and wasn't home much. I always worried about the next occupational step—the main thing was to keep moving ahead. What is important now is the *meaning* of what I'm doing. I have a strong sense of home life—being comfortable, enjoying a home, and enjoying a partner in the home. I'd like to entertain more, especially people from work so that work and home are not so split apart. I want more leisure—vacations, travel, time with Scott, and time for my self. That's a change! [Interviewer: It brings a bright smile to your face.] Yes, it's really exciting. The main thing I want for the future is the feeling of being free to explore things—new ideas, writing, career possibilities, relationships, pampering myself, exercise, taking care of the inner self instead of having all the stress all the time. Freeing my self.

HOLLY CRANE

In my mid-thirties my life was not going well. My husband and I were very distant. He was always at work, and the kids were very much into their own lives, and I was in graduate school. My husband was never involved with the kids at all; he was always busy with his work. We both realized how bad the marriage was. He began to talk about it, and I began to express my dissatisfactions. He told me he'd been having affairs all along.

I felt this emptiness in the marriage. I wanted a close relationship, and I wanted help with the house and the children, and he saw me as too demanding. I was very depressed. We went into marital therapy.

I had an affair, which was very good for me. The man was married, so it was safe. He was very good for me sexually. He was the first person I really enjoyed sex with; I had a playmate in him. The affair showed me how poverty stricken my marriage was.

By the time I was 38 the kids were growing and leaving, and my marriage was crumbling. We separated at 39 and divorced at 40. I became an assistant professor here at 40 as well.

My sexual system went to sleep after the separation. I wasn't attracted to anyone, no masturbation, nothing. It's like a faucet got turned off. Then all of a sudden it got turned on through a one-night stand. It was just pure sex, and it was wonderful. It was like my whole body just came alive. I began to date and have brief sexual relationships. I learned that you don't have to be in love with someone to have good sex.

I connected right away with the academic community here and began to make close friendships with women. I got involved in my work, too. I was so happy. I couldn't believe you could get paid for doing work you were so happy with. When I looked back on my life and marriage I was appalled.

At 41 I had a one-year affair with a graduate student. He was just a cute little kid of 23 when I met him at 41. I wanted a lover, and I was really feeling the need for more sex in my life. I was clear that I didn't want a live-in lover or anything that would lead to marriage. I was clear with him from the start that this was just a lovely interlude for both of us. Sexually it was a wonderful relationship. I think he hoped I would be his mentor. In fact, I was quite embarrassed by him intellectually; I couldn't take him places in the academic community. When the relationship ended I felt a great loss. I had a major depression and mourned the loss of him.

At 42 I met a man five years younger. We're very much in love but he's married with a baby. He is everything I want in a man: gentle, caring, a playmate with similar intellectual interests. We are sexually and politically compatible.

My work is very important to me, and I have a good reputation. I would like to leave this world with some things known that weren't known before I came.

I want love and work in my life now.

RACHEL NASH

The three principal things in my life now are my children, my work, and my marriage, and the kinds of investments they require are changing. The kids are getting older. Work seems more exciting. For the first time I'm coming into my own intellectually. There are also a lot of changes in my marriage, which I think is ending. It's very painful but probably can't be helped.

I became a full professor here at 38. Since then I have increasingly concentrated on my research and curricular matters. I spend twenty hours a week teaching, twenty-plus hours a week on research. I came back from sabbatical at 40 much more geared up to work, much more purposeful and clearer than I had ever been before, and since then I have had real collaborations with people in my field in this country and internationally. I was recently honored by being asked to chair an international meeting.

At this point I do and don't have a sense of having had a career. I can't imagine not doing what I'm doing, and I'm certainly willing to sacrifice a lot to do it, but I'm not thinking in terms of where I will be in ten years or where I was ten years ago. I don't think in those terms; I just think in terms of what I want to understand and accomplish intellectually. I love being a full professor here, and I can't imagine going anywhere else. I'm certainly not going into administration. I just assume that I will be here for another twenty-five years, very happily churning away. I just want to make sure I can do the work I really want to do and continue to grow intellectually.

Since I returned from sabbatical at 40 my husband has really changed for the worse. He was totally running the children's lives, yelling and being violent. He was dangerous. I felt that he had had a nervous breakdown. I realized that I had to make enormous structural changes in the marriage and in my life because it was really destructive for the children, and I had to be responsible for them. Bill became more and more violent. He was on antidepressants, but they didn't help. Nothing I tried helped him. I think now that the only thing that will help him is for us to separate so that he can be on his own and decide what he wants to do by himself.

When I look around my school I see that I'm one of the few women who have done work *and* family. Some students organized a conference and invited faculty women to come and talk about the choices they have made in their lives. They asked me to participate: "We want someone who is senior and has children, and you're the only one almost." I told them I couldn't participate.

My daughter told me that she felt she got very conflicting messages from growing up in our family—about the roles of men and women, because on the one hand here I was having my work and enjoying it and Bill encouraging me, and then on the other hand his dominating every aspect of our lives and being physically abusive to me. She felt this was such a conflicting set of messages that she was very confused and unsure of herself. It was very hard for me, but I finally came to understand what had to be done. I realized that I simply had to protect the children. I finally realized that my husband was mentally ill. The children and I became much closer and began talking. Before, I was busy with my work, and we just weren't talking.

I went to Bill's doctor. He felt that Bill had been a very disturbed person for a long time. We got Bill to go in and see him. That's when I realized what had happened to me and the kids. Earlier I thought I was the cause who deserved what I got. I finally saw myself as someone who had to be an adult and take responsibility for the children's welfare. That was the role I cast myself in from that time till this year, when things got much worse. I was still not asking myself, "What do I really want?" Now I realize I have to take responsibility for *myself*, too, if I am going to be here for the children. I had to stand up to my husband and not let him bully me.

I turned 40 and realized the way I acted as a faculty member had to be brought home. I had been strong at work for a long time; it's just that I hadn't done it at home. That's when I finally integrated the two lives, work and the personal.

I went to see my mother recently. Just as I was about to leave she started screaming at me. My first reaction, of course, was, "I can't explode. I have to control myself." Then I thought, "What the hell!" I exploded at her. I just gave it to her. For the first time in my life I really said what was on my mind. I told her about her abusiveness of me as a child. I don't think it hurt her to hear exactly what I had to say, and that was an amazing experience for me, too.

I began therapy two months ago. I had to ask myself what I really wanted from the marriage, whether I wanted to go on with it. My identity is all wrapped up in this marriage, and it may not be easy to separate. I felt confused, alone, paralyzed. I couldn't see any way out of it, but I just came to the conclusion that I had had it. I feel I just have to separate from the marriage or I won't be able to function. I'm on the verge of tears all the time and very sad. I feel strongly about the separation, though. I have this terrible need to be by myself. I want some peace and quiet. I want time to figure out why I entered into the marriage and stayed in that abusive situation without change. I also want time to be by myself. It's just agony; I'm emotionally finished. I am so worn that I cannot go on with the marriage. I need some relief, which I've never allowed myself to feel before.

I am getting clearer about why I quickly remarried at 23 and started a family right away. Being a full-time mother and housewife was a real threat to me, but being a full-time academic was also a threat. There was a whole positive side about why I wanted children, but there was also this other side of it. I realized what I was afraid of when I married Bill, why I ran to him. What I was really afraid of was the picture that my mother, and I guess society, painted of a single successful woman. I couldn't face it: the image of a successful single woman who goes home and cries at night because she has no family, nothing—the bitter pinnacle of success.

If I had remained single and pursued a career, I would have had to face that image, and I wanted to be sure that I escaped that image forever. Marriage, I knew from experience, wasn't enough to guarantee that. You have to have children. Then you will never have to be up there competing, succeeding, trying to carve out this kind of life that is so threatening to me.

Having children took me out of the running in a certain sense, though it has also led me back, now that the kids are grown. When you have kids, you have a certain handicap in your career, and it was a handicap I was more than happy to have. I really wanted the kids, and I also really wanted the handicap. Then anything I did was just pure extra in a sense. Any work I did was great, and I wasn't a threat to anybody, and I wasn't a threat to myself. There was the sense that having kids takes you out of the running in a way that I appreciated and wanted.

I really had a fear of success in terms of the consequences of success. The consequences would be total personal disaster. I had no way of imagining a woman having a personally satisfactory life and being successful. The kind of work that I'm doing here is successful at a certain level and very satisfying to me. I don't see any inherent conflict between that and having a family. But to be at a school like Harvard or Yale, that would be a whole different order of demands and would be much harder to manage with a family. I could not have accepted a position where the demands on me would have created a conflict in the family. Real success would require a different kind of marriage than the one I had, a marriage where you'd really be apart a lot of the time.

I might have chosen to go for that kind of success and not have a family. I chose instead to have a family—but it was an unconscious choice. In choosing to have children, I also chose to avoid a certain career path that I found very threatening. To put my career first would have meant not having a personal life. That was something I couldn't face because that image of a single successful woman is so terrifying to me. I just couldn't face it.

I had no image of a single successful woman who had really made career the center of her life. There was only this notion that she had to be coldhearted, she had to be grasping, she had to be cruel, she had to be embittered, frustrated, wishing she had done anything just to be sitting by the fireside knitting in the evening with her children. I never really met any woman who had made a different kind of choice and who really had a satisfactory life. The terrifying part was that on the way to becoming successful you have to go through such agony and sacrifice so much on a personal level—just to become the kind of person that was so appalling to me. [Interviewer: But I see you as successful. I can't believe you're sitting here as a full professor at this school, saying that you gave up success!]

Well, I haven't. But I still have to face the question of that other kind of success, *real* success. I will be free to work, now that my kids are older and pretty independent and I'll be separated from my husband. Next year I'll be on sabbatical. There is nothing now except myself to stop me from doing the work I want to do. It's a question of ability, but it's also a question of whether psychologically I'm up to it. I have always doubted whether I was psychologically strong enough to take the loneliness that I believed success would entail.

Ending the Mid-life Transition

The Mid-life Transition of the career women and the homemakers were similar in certain respects. They all went through the Mid-life Transition at the same ages, 40 or 41 to 45 or 46. During this period both groups made the cross-era shift from early to middle adulthood, and they all terminated the Culminating Life Structure of the outgoing era of early adulthood and formed the basis for the Entry Life Structure of the next era of middle adulthood. The shift in era and life structure was a wrenching one for almost all of the women.

There were also important differences between the homemakers and the career women. The homemakers had attempted in early adulthood to make family the central component of their life structures within the framework of a Traditional Marriage Enterprise. In the Mid-life Transition most of them recognized that their marriage enterprise had been a partial or massive failure and that, whatever its previous value, they wanted a different kind of marriage, family, and life structure in the next season.

The career women, in contrast, had attempted in early adulthood to pursue an Anti-Traditional Dream. Many carried a dual Anti-Traditional Dream of the Successful Career Woman and a Neo-Traditional Marriage Enterprise. They came to want to combine a full-time career with marriage/family in a satisfactory balance. More time actually went to career than to marriage/family, but all three components were central in their lives. The aim was not to be an employed housewife. It was, rather, to have a more equal marriage within a Neo-Traditional Marriage Enterprise, a satisfying motherhood, and a career that gave her a valued, nonsubordinate place in the occupational world and in society generally.

Through the developmental process of the Mid-life Transition, each career woman came to reappraise and modify her life. She came to understand more fully the sexism inherent in work organizations. In the Mid-life Transition the career women asked more strongly, "What do I want?" Their answer was often, "More passionate engagement and equality in love and work."

For all the career women, occupation would have a different place in the ensuing life structure than in the previous ones. Their great hope was that work would provide a stronger experience of creativity, satisfaction, and social contribution, that it would become more playful and loving rather than a matter of proving oneself in a highly competitive world. The great fear was that they would find no satisfactory place for themselves as valued members of a valued world—that they would be squeezed out altogether or get stuck in a position that offered little to the self and required little from it.

The career women studied here represent the first generation in American history in which a sizable minority of women chose an anti-traditional path. These women found new paths that brought them into the corporate/business and academic worlds on career paths. The career women juggled work and personal life, dealing with work institutions that gave mainly lip service to career advancement for women beyond middle levels, with the hope of making it better in time. Their personal growth and development were great as they struggled with the essential questions of who they were and what they wanted.

IV Conclusions

16 Concluding Thoughts: Adult Development, Gender, and Historical Change

The findings of this study support and amplify a view of the human life cycle as an overlapping sequence of eras: childhood (age 0–22), early adulthood (17–45), middle adulthood (40–65), late adulthood (60–85), and late late adulthood (80–?). For women as for men, the eras are separate seasons, each with its own distinctive character. Within each era, women and men go through the same sequence of periods in adult life structure development, and at the same ages.

In this study, our primary focus has been on the era of early adulthood, which begins with the Early Adult Transition, occurring between the ages of 17 and 22. It forms a boundary between the eras of childhood and early adulthood and is part of both. In the Early Adult Transition we create the basis for the Entry Life Structure (22–28). The Age 30 Transition (28–33) is a mid-era shift in which we move from the first structure to the Culminating Life Structure (33–40). In the Mid-life Transition (40–45) we terminate early adulthood, initiate middle adulthood, and start forming an Entry Life Structure for the new era. The Mid-life Transition is both the final period of early adulthood and the initial period of the next era. In middle adulthood we go through the same alternating sequence of structure building/maintaining and transitional periods.

This conception of life cycle, eras, and periods in life structure development provides a framework for the study of the human life course. We have found that the framework holds for human beings generally. One of its most important functions is to highlight variations between and within cultures, classes, historical epochs, genders, and individuals. It also helps us understand specific changes in biological, psychological, and social functioning, which do not follow a highly age-linked sequence in adulthood.

Imagine, for example, a study of the life structure development of a random sample of 43-year-old women and men from any large population. The study would show, I believe, that virtually all of these women and men are going through the Mid-life Transition—moving from the Culminating Life Structure of early adulthood to the Entry Life Structure of middle adulthood. At the same time, their lives will be diverse in many other ways: in the kind of Culminating Life Structure now being terminated, the kind of Entry Life Structure being formed, the character of the transition and the kind of satisfaction and suffering it entails. These people will also vary widely in occupation, education, marital/familial condition, moral functioning, cognitive skills, personality, external stress, bodily fitness and illness.

This perspective on the life cycle and adult development is like a navigational chart that gives latitude and longitude and certain features of the territory, without the geographical detail. It is not a blueprint for the concrete course of an individual life. We can better understand particular changes in one part of a person's life, however, if we examine them within the context of her or his current position in the pattern of life structure development.

This study has generated and utilized a gender perspective—a framework for understanding how women and men differ in life circumstances, life course, and ways of going through the developmental periods. The key concept is gender splitting: a rigid division between female and male, feminine and masculine, in all aspects of human life. Of particular importance is the splitting between the domestic sphere and the public occupational sphere; female homemaker and male provisioner within a Traditional Marriage Enterprise; women's work and men's work; feminine and masculine within the self. The splitting is encouraged by the existence of a patriarchal society in which women are generally subordinate to men, and the splitting helps to maintain that society.

Gender splitting has predominated, with many variations in degree and pattern, throughout the history of the human species. The evolution of society in the past few centuries has reduced the splitting. Humanity is now in the early phases of a transformation in the meanings of gender and the place of women and men in every society. The general direction of change is clear: the lives and personalities of women and men are becoming more similar. For most women, permanent full-time homemaking is less feasible and less desirable than in previous generations. New forms of marriage enterprises are emerging. Society requires more women to work outside the home, and women are playing a less subordinate part in the public occupational sphere.

The fifteen homemakers in this study tell us about the life sequences, dilemmas, and satisfactions of women who attempt to maintain the traditional pattern. Each of them had within herself a Traditional Homemaker Figure who wanted to live within a Traditional Marriage Enterprise. This figure originated in childhood, took her initial adult shape in the Adolescent

Life Structure and the Early Adult Transition, and evolved further in subsequent periods. Each woman also had an internal Anti-Traditional Figure—a self who wanted to be more independent, to be more a part of the public world, to exist on more equal terms with men. The internal Traditional Homemaker Figure was predominant during the twenties. In some women the internal Anti-Traditional Figure subsequently became stronger and exerted more influence on the evolving life structure. In others she played a minor part or remained rudimentary.

The career women, in contrast, attempted to modify the traditional pattern. A recurrent theme in their lives was the intense conflict between the internal Traditional Homemaker Figure and the internal Anti-Traditional Figure. The relative dominance of the two figures, and the ways of dealing with the conflict between them, varied from one woman to another and from one period to another.

The homemakers and the career women went through the same sequence of periods, but there were great differences between and within the two groups. In the Early Adult Transition they formed different inner scenarios for adult life. Over the course of early adulthood their life structures evolved differently and rarely in accord with their initial views. In the Mid-life Transition, as one era ended and a new one began, both groups were re-examining their past lives and trying to establish a new life structure more appropriate to middle adulthood. They had different resources and constraints, internal as well as external. For most, the road ahead seemed more an uncharted territory—or, worse, an unbridged abyss—than a well-lit path.

The difficulties of these women must be placed in social-historical context. We live in a time when the Traditional Marriage Enterprise, and the gender meanings, values, and social structures that support it, are undergoing major change. The homemakers' lives give evidence that the traditional pattern is difficult to sustain. Most women who tried to maintain this pattern formed life structures that were relatively unsatisfactory—not viable in the world, not suitable for the self. The few who were more or less contented paid a considerable price in restriction of self-development. The career women tried to anticipate the future: to reduce the gender splitting, to enter formerly "male" occupations, to work on equal terms with men, and to establish a family life in which homemaking and provisioning were more equally divided. Their lives attest to the pleasures and problems of innovation, of attempting to realize values not well supported by the current culture and institutions.

Every woman in both groups had her share of suffering and joy. At the worst, she was engaged in a bitter struggle for survival; at the best, in a struggle for greater meaning and self-fulfillment. Each life, seen empathically and in broad perspective, contributes to our understanding and evokes our admiration, respect, compassion, and sorrow.

But, a reader may ask, "Why does this study reveal so much hardship — anguish, stressful or traumatic experiences, difficulty in marriage, motherhood, occupation, personal relationships? Does the sample contain a disproportionately large number of women with serious problems?" I believe not. Great efforts were made in the sampling procedures to maximize demographic diversity and to minimize volunteer bias. These women fall within the broader population range with regard to their psychological problems and strengths, as well as their external stresses and supports. They comprise a diverse, though far from complete, cross-section of the American population. They vary widely along the spectrum from normal to abnormal, successful to unsuccessful, well to poorly adjusted, however these are measured. To put it most simply, they are garden-variety members of various worlds within our society. In every person's life there is an admixture of joy and sorrow, success and failure, self-fulfillment and self-defeat. Good biographers intuitively know this: every reasonably complete biography contains them all. The study of adult development requires no less.

It might be argued that we have placed more emphasis than we should on what went wrong in a given woman's life than on her satisfactions and accomplishments. Again, I believe that we have not. The mode of interviewing was not clinical, in the sense of providing psychotherapy for a troubled patient. It was, rather, biographical. My aim was to enable a woman to tell her life story in her own words, with attention to both external realities and subjective meanings, and these accounts are the result. I remain convinced that such an approach is more fruitful in the study of life-structure development than the standard research methods of laboratory experimentation, surveys, tests, and brief structured interviews. These methods give too narrow, too cross-sectional, and usually too bland a picture of the individual life. For a while, at least, more intensive interviewing and personal documents must be used to follow the evolution of life structure over a span of years.

These interviews were done in the early 1980s. It may be questioned whether social conditions have not changed markedly since then, in the direction of greater freedom for women to become and do what they want. It is true that many studies have examined changes in specific attitudes, behaviors, laws, and institutional practices over the past twenty or thirty years, but the findings are quite mixed.

In the mid-1990s, as compared with 1980, the conditions of life for women are better in some ways, worse in others. The great majority of women are still employed in low-paying, unskilled jobs and predominantly female occupations. The "feminization of poverty" continues. Far more women than men exist below the poverty line, receive no health insurance, and have no pension. Wives with outside jobs generally have almost total responsibility for the "second shift" of domestic labor. Working mothers are doing it all but not having it all. More women are entering certain professions, but they are still advancing at a slower pace than men and earning less, and hitting sexist barriers ("glass ceilings"). Ten percent of top executives in Fortune 500 companies are women. Fifteen percent of academics on tenure tracks are women. Women's earnings were formerly about 70 percent of men's in the same kind of job; it is still 70 percent in some fields and up to 75 to 85 percent in others, but the discrepancies in rank and pay continue.

When women comprise roughly 70 percent or more of a given occupation, it is identified as "women's work" and paid less. When they comprise 20 percent or less, the occupation is regarded as "men's work" and women in it tend to be seen as token or marginal members who have yet to prove themselves. Finally, when a formerly male occupation becomes roughly half female, there is a growing tendency for the occupation to be "feminized"— regarded as women's work, devalued, and rendered unattractive to men. The basic gender splitting thus makes it difficult for women to avoid occupational segregation and subordination.

The level and intensity of gender conflict have risen since 1980. We live in a state of gender warfare—often covert but with flare-ups of overt antagonism. Dramatic incidents occur more frequently. There are more accusations, lawsuits, and investigations. Harassment and discrimination take a greater variety of forms, gross as well as subtle. Unsettled, conflictful relationships between women and men are increasingly represented in plays, movies, novels, TV talk shows, the 1995 conservative Congress with its views on the family, children, and "women's issues." There is a growing public awareness that many women are abused, discriminated against, and hindered in their personal development. Efforts to bring about greater gender equality are opposed by institutional inertia and by the fear that the ongoing changes will tear apart the fabric of social life without creating a better alternative.

The conflict is not only between women and men. It exists also among women and among men. Our established customs, laws, and values are in question. What do we mean by "feminine" and "masculine"? What are the rights and responsibilities of each partner in a marriage? How should the partners divide the provisioning, domestic labor, and child care? How should we (women and men) divide our investments in occupation and family? What shall we do about the growing incidence of divorce, singlehood, and single-parent households? In a diverse, pluralistic society, there can be no single legitimate answer to any of these questions. Diversity makes life richer and more interesting, but we are still learning how to contain many diverse elements within a single tapestry. The current intensification of gender conflict is one aspect of the historical transition from patriarchy and the Traditional Marriage Enterprise to new and still hardly imaginable forms of individual and social life.

What about the future? The long-term evolution of human society is leading, I believe, toward a reduction in gender splitting, an increase in gender equality, and a fuller participation of women in all aspects of social life. During the past few centuries some remarkable advances have been made in legal rights, education, suffrage, control of reproduction, occupational choice and development. Whether we welcome or oppose this change—and most of us, men and women, do both—it will continue. Yet, paradoxically, the recurrent advances have brought new forms of restriction, subordination, and what Susan Faludi has called "backlash." It will probably take another century, not a few decades, to see how far the gender transformation will go and what various meanings may be ascribed to gender in various cultures, social institutions, and individual lives.

Early in its history the human species established various kinds of social order based upon the Traditional Marriage Enterprise and the sharp distinction between the feminine homemaker/wife/mother/caregiver and the masculine provisioner/husband/father/occupational achiever. This order served species survival but also had great limitations. Men were prohibited from engaging in pursuits identified as feminine and alienated from feminine aspects of the self. To an equal or greater extent, women were cut off from the masculine. Yet we now know that every man has some "feminine" interests, feelings, and talents, and every woman something of the "masculine." The taboo on being "opposite gender" made it difficult to develop and live out those aspects of the self. A high degree of self-sacrifice, often not evident to the person or others, was required of everyone. Men had to sacrifice the internal feminine in order to be highly independent, masterful, heroic. Women had to sacrifice the internal masculine in order to put the needs and feelings of others ahead of their own.

Communal survival—obtaining essential resources and guarding against serious threats—had to be the first priority under conditions of severe scarcity and danger. The development of the self was a luxury available (at best) only to members of the small elite groups who had responsibility for leadership and management of communal life. In the past few centuries, however, technological and social advances have brought more of humanity to a level of material advantage, safety, and education that makes possible, and indeed requires, the self-development of the population generally. Society now offers more to its individual members, but it also requires us to contribute more. This in turn requires that we become more knowledgeable, skilled, understanding, ethical, creative—in short, more developed as persons. We are concerned not only with survival but with the personal meaning of our lives.

Self-development is furthered by the value placed on individuality, on individual rights, desires, choices. The person must have some freedom to ask, "Who am I? What is important to me? How can I pursue my aims?" Individualism is restricted by externally given requirements (and an internalized sense of obligation) to live within a narrow, gender-based scenario of choices and relationships. But individuation is *not* rugged individualism, "selfishness" (in the sense of egocentrism or self-indulgence), or lack of concern for others. It involves a balancing of responsibility to and for others with responsibility to and for oneself. A woman cannot become very individuated when she lives primarily as a traditional homemaker and suppresses most of the "masculine" in her self. Likewise, a man's individuation is limited when he dedicates himself to living as a provisioner and suppresses the "feminine."

What are the potential consequences of a long-term reduction in gender splitting? As I imagine it, the lives of women and men will be more variegated and there will be fewer differences between us. The meanings of gender will be more inclusive, complex, and individualized. We will learn more about biologically given gender differences and take account of these in the socio-psychological construction of gender, while freeing ourselves from narrow, culture-bound images of feminine and masculine. Women and men will be freer to participate in both the domestic and public worlds. We will be less different in the ways we give and receive care, and in loving, working, achieving, competing, cooperating. Both genders will have a greater range of choice in building our life structures and in using transitional periods to change ourselves and our lives. We will derive greater meaning and satisfaction from every season of life.

Lest this view sound too utopian, let me add that such changes are a matter of degree. We can reduce but not eliminate our uniquely human proclivities for damaging the bodies and souls of others, for self-abnegation, self-aggrandizement, and self-deception, for regarding life from a primitive (rather than more developed) sense of good versus evil, for the irrationalities that have plagued us throughout our history. We can do better. We must do better. But we have a long way to go.

In Chapter 3 I quoted from an essay by Virginia Woolf, who has been both a subject and a mentor to me in this study of women. The essay, "Professions for Women," was based upon a talk she gave in 1931, at the age of 49, to an association of young professional women. She clearly identified herself as a middle-aged career woman speaking intimately to a younger generation of women who were embarking on careers in a seemingly more open world and carrying the hope of occupational freedom for women generally. Her audience was the historical counterpart of the younger women who may read this book, over sixty years and three or four generations later.

In the essay, Woolf described the Angel in the House—the Victorian version of the Traditional Homemaker Figure—and other obstacles to women's full participation in social life. After portraying her mortal combat with the Angel, Woolf concluded: "Killing the Angel in the House was part of the occupation of the woman writer." She then raised a further question:

> The Angel was dead; what then remained? You may say that what remained was a . . . young woman in a bedroom with an inkpot. In other words, now that she had rid herself of falsehood, that young woman had only to be herself. Ah, but what is "herself"? I mean, *what is a woman?* I assure you, I do not know. I do not believe that you know. I do not believe that anybody can know until she has expressed herself in all the arts and professions open to human skills. That indeed is one of the reasons why I have come here—out of respect for you, who are in process of showing us by your experiments what a woman is, who are in process of providing us, by your failures and successes, with that extremely important piece of information. . . . Even when the path is nominally open . . . there are many phantoms and obstacles . . . looming in her way. To discuss and define them is I think of great value and importance; for thus only can the labour be shared.
>
> . . . It is necessary also to discuss the ends and aims for which we are fighting, for which we are doing battle with these formidable obstacles. These aims cannot be taken for granted; they must be perpetually questioned and examined. . . . You have won rooms of your own in the house hitherto exclusively owned by men. You are able, though not without great labour and effort, to pay the rent. You are earning your 500 pounds a year. But this freedom is only a beginning; the room is your own, but it is still bare. It has to be furnished; it has to be decorated; it has to be shared. How are you going to furnish it, how are you going to decorate it? With whom are you going to share it, and upon what terms? These, I think, are questions of the utmost importance and interest. For the first time in history you are able to ask them; for the first time you are able to decide for yourselves what the answers should be.

These remarks have a curiously contemporary relevance and provide a fitting theme for the conclusion of this book. Woolf's questions still need to be asked, the answers still elude us, and the obstacles are many. A similar talk might be given today by a woman in middle adulthood to a group of younger women. It is perhaps a sign of progress that a man in late adulthood can now attempt to raise, study, and discuss similar questions in a different historical context.

This book is addressed to women of all ages, not solely early adulthood— and to men as well. I consider myself a feminist, but also an equalist. The struggle for gender equality is not for the benefit of women alone and cannot be won by women alone. Men must understand women better, and women men, if we are to understand ourselves. Both genders will gain from a greater appreciation of our common humanity and of the elemental gender differences—whatever they may turn out to be—that complicate and enrich our lives. All of us, men as well as women, must continue our experiments in living so that we can begin to conceive of hitherto unimagined possibilities.

It is a paradox of human existence that we are impelled to create noble ideals and to work for their realization, while acknowledging that the ideals may be unattainable and perhaps illusory. The ideas of gender equality and adult development are now in our cultural awareness and have been tentatively placed on our cultural agenda. They also evoke great anxiety and run counter to our traditional ways of thinking. Despite our individual and institutional reluctance to examine them more deeply, we must make the effort to find and smooth a path for the generations of daughters and sons who will come after us.

Selected Bibliography

Acker, J. "Hierarchies, Jobs and Bodies: A Theory of Gendered Organizations." *Gender and Society* 4 (June 1990): 139–58.

——, and D. R. Van-Houten. "Differential Recruitment and Control—The Sex Structure of Organizations." *Administrative Science Quarterly* 19 (1974): 152–63.

Alexander, Charles, and Ellen Langer, eds. *Higher Stages of Human Development.* New York: Oxford University Press, 1990.

American Council on Education, *Fact Book on Women in Higher Education,* 1990–1991, Tables 76, 78.

Arendell, Terry. *Divorce: Women and Children Last.* Berkeley: University of California Press, 1986.

Ariès, Philippe. *Centuries of Childhood.* New York: Basic Books, 1962.

Bell, Quentin. *Virginia Woolf: A Biography.* 2 vols. New York: Harcourt Brace Jovanovich, 1972.

Bem, S. L. *The Lenses of Gender: Transforming the Debate on Sexual Inequality.* New Haven: Yale University Press, 1993.

Berheid, C. "Women Still Stuck in Low-Level Jobs." *Women in Public Service Bulletin.* Center for Women in Government. Albany: State University of New York, Fall 1992.

Bernard, Jessie. *The Future of Marriage.* New York: World, 1972.

Bielby, W. T., and J. N. Baron. "A Woman's Place Is With Other Women: Sex Segregation in Organizations." In *Sex Segregation in the Workplace: Trends, Expectations, Remedies,* edited by B. Reskin. Washington, D.C.: National Academy Press, 1985.

Brady, Julie A. *An Economic History of Women in America.* New York: Schocken Books, 1982.

Bureau of Labor Statistics. *1990 Employment and Earnings.* Vol. 37.

Bureau of Labor Statistics. *1991 Employment and Earnings.* Vol. 38.

Campbell, Joseph, ed. *The Portable Jung.* New York: Viking, 1971.

Catalyst. *Catalyst's Study of Women in Corporate Management.* New York: Catalyst, 1990.

——. *On the Line: Women's Career Advancement.* New York: Catalyst, 1992.

Chodorow, Nancy. *The Reproduction of Mothering.* Berkeley: University of California Press, 1978.

Clausen, John A. "The Life Cycle of Individuals." In *Aging and Society,* vol. 3, edited by M. W. Riley, M. Johnson, and A. Foner. New York: Russell Sage, 1972.

Cole, J. R., and B. Singer. "A Theory of Limited Differences: Explaining the Productivity Puzzle in Science." In *The Outer Circle: Women in the Scientific Community,* edited by H. Zucker-man, J. R. Cole, and J. T. Bruer. New York: Norton, 1991.

Cott, Nancy F. *The Bonds of Womanhood.* New Haven: Yale University Press, 1977.

——. *The Grounding of Modern Feminism.* New Haven: Yale University Press, 1987.

Coverman, Shelley. "Gender, Domestic Labor Time, and Wage Inequality." *American Sociological Review* 48 (1983): 623–36.

de Beauvoir, Simone. *The Second Sex.* Edited and translated by H. M. Parshley. New York: Knopf, 1953.

Drazin, R., and E. Auster. "Wage Differences Between Men and Women: Performance Appraisal

Ratings vs. Salary Allocation as the Locus of Bias." *Human Resource Management* 26 (Summer 1987): 157–68.

Edel, Leon, Justin Kaplan, Doris Kearns, Theodore Rosengarten, Barbara W. Tuchman, and Geoffrey Wolff. *Telling Lives: The Biographer's Art*. Washington, D.C.: New Republic Books, 1979.

Erikson, Erik H., ed. *Adulthood*. New York: Norton, 1980.

——. *Childhood and Society*. New York: Norton, 1950.

——. *Gandhi's Truth*. New York: Norton, 1969.

——. *Young Man Luther*. New York: Norton, 1958.

Estes, Carol, and Anne Machung. "Berkeley Work-Family Project." Women's Center for Continuing Education. Berkeley: University of California, 1986.

Faludi, Susan. *Backlash*. New York: Crown, 1991.

Friedan, Betty. *The Feminine Mystique*. New York: Dell, 1963.

——. *The Second Stage*. New York: Summit, 1981.

Gersick, Connie J. G. "Revolutionary Change Theories: A Multilevel Exploration of the Punctuated Equilibrium Paradigm. *Academy of Management Review* 16, no. 1 (1991): 10–36.

Gilbert, Sandra M., and Susan Gubar. *The Madwoman in the Attic*. New Haven: Yale University Press, 1979.

——, eds. *The Norton Anthology of Literature by Women*. New York: Norton, 1985.

Gilligan, Carol. *In a Different Voice*. Cambridge, Mass.: Harvard University Press, 1982.

Gooden, Winston E. *The Adult Development of Black Men*. Ph.D. diss., Yale University, 1980.

Gould, Roger. *Transformations: Growth and Change in Adult Life*. New York: Simon & Schuster, 1978.

Gutmann, David. "The Cross-Cultural Perspective: Notes Toward a Comparative Psychology of Aging." In *Lifespan Developmental Psychology: Normative Life Crises*, edited by James E. Birren and K. Warner Schaie. New York: Academic Press, 1977.

Hareven, Tamara K., and Kathleen Adams, eds. *Aging and Life Course Transitions: An Interdisciplinary Perspective*. New York: Guilford, 1982.

Hennig, M., and A. Jardim. *The Managerial Woman*. Garden City, N.Y.: Doubleday, 1977.

Herbert, James I. "Adult Psychosocial Development: The Evolution of the Individual Life Structures of Black Male Entrepreneurs." Ph.D. diss., Yale University School of Management, 1985.

Hess, B. B., and M. M. Ferree, eds. *Analyzing Gender*. Newbury Park, Calif.: Sage, 1987.

Hochschild, Arlie. *The Second Shift: Working Parents and the Revolution at Home*. New York: Viking, 1989.

Holt, Jonathan. "An Adult Development Psychobiography of C. G. Jung." Senior thesis, Yale University School of Medicine, 1980.

Huber, Joan, and Glenna Spitze. *Sex Stratification, Children, Housework and Jobs*. New York: Academic Press, 1983.

Jung, Carl G. *Man and His Symbols*. New York: Doubleday, 1964.

Kaminer, Wendy. *A Fearful Freedom: Women's Flight from Equality*. Reading, Mass.: Addison-Wesley, 1990.

Kanter, Rosabeth Moss. *Men and Women of the Corporation*. New York: Basic Books. 1977.

Kaplan, Sheila, and Adrian Tinsley. "The Unfinished Agenda: Women in Higher Education Administration." *Academe* 75 (1989): 18–22.

Kellerman, Barbara L. "Willy Brandt: Portrait of the Leader as Young Politician." Ph.D. diss., Yale University, 1975.

Kram, Kathy E. *Mentoring at Work*. Glenview, Ill.: Scott, Foresman and Co., 1985.

Levine, Linda. "The Glass Ceiling: Access of Women and Minorities to Management Positions." Congressional Research Service, number 91-623E. Washington, D.C.: Library of Congress, 1991.

Levinson, Daniel J. "A Conception of Adult Development." *American Psychologist* 41 (1986): 3–14.

——. "Explorations in Biography." In *Further Explorations in Personality*, edited by Albert Rabin, Joel Aronoff, Andrew Barclay, and Robert Zucker. New York: Wiley, 1981.

——. "Middle Adulthood: The Least Explored Season of the Life Cycle." Unpublished lecture presented at the Smithsonian Institution, Nov. 1991.

——. *The Seasons of a Man's Life*. New York: Knopf, 1978.

——. "A Theory of Life Structure Development in Adulthood." In *Higher Stages of Human Development: Perspectives on Adult Growth*, edited by C. N. Alexander and J. Langer. New York: Oxford University Press, 1990.

——. "Toward a Conception of the Adult Life Course." In *Themes of Work and Love in Adulthood*, edited by N. Smelser and E. H. Erikson. Cambridge, Mass.: Harvard University Press, 1980.

——, and Winston Gooden. "The Life Cycle." In *Comprehensive Textbook of Psychiatry*, 4th ed., edited by H. I. Kaplan and B. J. Sadock. Baltimore: Williams and Wilkins, 1985.

Machung, Anne. "Talking Career, Thinking Job: Gender Differences in Career and Family Expectations of Berkeley Seniors." *Feminist Studies* 15 (Spring 1989): 35–58.

McNally, Jeffrey A. *The Adult Development of Career Army Officers*. New York: Praeger Publishers, 1991.

Mead, M. *Male and Female*. New York: New American Library, 1955.

Miller, Jean Baker. *Toward a New Psychology of Women*. Boston: Beacon Press, 1976.

Morrison, A. M., R. P. White, E. Van Velsor, and The Center for Creative Leadership. *Breaking the Glass Ceiling*. Reading, Mass.: Addison-Wesley, 1987.

Neugarten, Bernice L. "Adult Personality: Toward a Psychology of the Life Cycle." In *Middle Age and Aging*, edited by B. Neugarten. Chicago: University of Chicago Press, 1968.

Newton, P. M., and D. S. Newton. "Erik Erikson and His Psychobiographical Conception of the Life Cycle: From Psychoanalyst to Biographer and Social Clinician." In *Comprehensive Textbook of Psychiatry*, 6th ed., edited by H. Kaplan and B. Sadock. Baltimore: Williams and Wilkins, 1995.

Newton, Peter M. *Freud from Youthful Dream to Mid-Life Crisis*. New York: Guilford Press, 1995.

Ortega y Gasset, José. *Man and Crisis*. New York: Norton, 1958.

Pfeffer, Jeffrey, and Alison Davis-Blake. "The Effect of the Proportion of Women on Salaries: The Case of College Administrators." *Administrative Science Quarterly* 32 (1987): 1–24.

Piaget, Jean. *Structuralism*. New York: Basic Books, 1970.

Reskin, B., and H. Hartmann, eds. *Women's Work, Men's Work: Sex Segregation on the Job*. Washington, D.C.: National Academy Press, 1986.

Rhode, D. "Gender Equality and Employment Policy." In *The American Woman: 1990–91*, edited by S. Rix. New York: Norton, 1991.

Ries, P., and A. Stone, eds. *The American Woman: 1992–93*. New York: Norton, 1993.

Riley, Matilda W., et al. *Aging and Society*, 3 vols. New York: Russell Sage, 1972.

Rose, Phyllis. *Parallel Lives*. New York: Knopf, 1983.

——, ed., *The Norton Book of Women's Lives*. New York: Norton, 1994.

Rossi, Alice S., ed. *The Feminist Papers: From Adams to De Beauvoir*. New York: Columbia University Press, 1973.

——, ed. *Gender and the Life Course*. New York: Aldine, 1985.

Rubin, Lillian B. *Intimate Strangers*. New York: Harper & Row, 1983.

——. *Worlds of Pain: Life in the Working-Class Family*. New York: Basic Books, 1976.

Ruffin, Janice E. "An Exploratory Study of Adult Development in Black, Professional Women." Ph.D. diss., City University of New York, 1986.

Sartre, Jean-Paul. *Existential Psychoanalysis*. New York: Philosophical Library, 1953.

Scarf, Maggie. *Unfinished Business: Pressure Points in the Lives of Women*. New York: Doubleday, 1980.

Schreiber, C. T. *Changing Places: Men and Women in Transitional Occupations*. Cambridge, Mass.: MIT Press, 1979.

———, K. Price, and A. Morrison. "Workforce Diversity and the Glass Ceiling: Practices, Barriers, Possibilities." *Human Resource Planning* 17, no. 2 (1994): 12–17.

Scott, H. *Working Your Way to the Bottom: The Feminization of Poverty*. Boston: Pandora Press, 1984.

Shaevitz, Marjorie H. *The Superwoman Syndrome*. New York: Warner, 1984.

Smelser, Neil J., and Erik H. Erikson, eds. *Themes of Work and Love in Adulthood*. Cambridge, Mass.: Harvard University Press, 1980.

Steinem, Gloria. *Revolution from Within: A Book of Self Esteem*. Boston: Little, Brown, 1992.

Stewart, Wendy A. "The Formation of the Early Adult Life Structure in Women." Ph.D. diss., Teachers College, Columbia University, 1976.

Stroh, L. K., J. M. Brett, and A. H. Reilly. "All the Right Stuff: A Comparison of Female and Male Managers' Career Progression." *Journal of Applied Psychology* 77 (1992): 251–60.

Taylor, Susan. "Seven Lives: Women's Life Structure Evolution in Early Adulthood." Ph.D. diss., City University of New York, 1981.

———. "The 'Satisfactory-Enough' Life Structure: Some Preliminary Explorations." Paper presented at symposium "Levinson's Seasons," Yale University School of Medicine, New Haven, Conn., 1990.

Unger, Rhoda, and Janis Sanchez-Hucles, eds. *Psychology of Women Quarterly Special Issue on Gender and Culture* 17 (Dec. 1993): 4.

U.S. Department of Commerce, Bureau of the Census. 1987 *Statistical Abstract of the U.S.* Table 736. Washington, D.C., 1991.

U.S. Department of Labor. *Pipelines of Progress: A Status Report on the Glass Ceiling*. Washington, D.C., August 1992.

Vaillant, George. *Adaptation to Life*. New York: Little, Brown, 1977.

van Gennep, Arnold. *The Rites of Passage*. Chicago: University of Chicago Press, 1960 (first published in 1908).

Weitzman, Lenore, J. *The Divorce Revolution: The Unexpected Social and Economic Consequences for Women and Children in America*. New York: Free Press, 1985.

White, Robert W. *Lives in Progress*. New York: Dryden Press, 1952.

Williams, Christine. *Still a Man's World: Men Who Do "Women's Work."* Berkeley: University of California Press, 1995.

Winnicott, Donald W. *The Maturational Processes and the Facilitating Environment*. London: Hogarth, 1965.

Woolf, Virginia. "Professions for Women." In *The Death of the Moth and Other Essays*. New York: Harcourt Brace Jovanovich, 1942.

Index